Steve Fallon

Budapest

The Top Five

1 Art Nouveau Architecture
Admire the Zsolnay-tile decoration of the 1912 Elephant House (p72)

2 Thermal Baths
Soak in the atmospheric Gellért Thermal Baths (p136)

3 Statue Park
Explore the trash heap of socialist history (p62)

4 The Danube
Reflect on the past at the Shoes on the Danube memorial (p66)

5 Music, Music, Music
Classical or modern – make your selection (p130)

Published by Lonely Planet Publications Pty Ltd
ABN 36 005 607 983

Australia Head Office, Locked Bag 1, Footscray, Victoria 3011, ☎ 03 8379 8000, fax 03 8379 8111, talk2us@lonelyplanet.com.au

USA 150 Linden St, Oakland, CA 94607, ☎ 510 893 8555, toll free 800 275 8555, fax 510 893 8572, info@lonelyplanet.com

UK 72–82 Rosebery Ave, Clerkenwell, London, EC1R 4RW, ☎ 020 7841 9000, fax 020 7841 9001, go@lonelyplanet.co.uk

Printed through SNP SPrint Singapore Pte Ltd at KHL Printing Co Sdn Bhd Malaysia

Contents

The Author

Steve Fallon

Steve made his first visit to Budapest during the early 1980s with three things on his 'to do' list: (1) visit a thermal spa; (2) drink masses of Tokaj wine; and (3) buy some fruit for his friends in Poland whose children, born under the neofascist regime of General Wojciech Jaruzelski, had never seen (much less tasted) such 'exotics' as bananas. Having accomplished all three, he visited Budapest again and again, moving there in 1992, where he learned to love the Hungarian language, *pálinka* more than Tokaj and very hot thermal water – not necessarily in that order. Now based in London, Steve returns to Budapest regularly for a fix of all three. He has worked on every edition of *Budapest* and *Hungary*.

STEVE'S TOP BUDAPEST DAY

Let's just say for the sake of argument that I wake up late on my last day in Budapest, work accomplished and conscience (if not head) clear. I skip breakfast and head for the Gellért Baths (p136). After a therapeutic soak and a 15-minute tussle with a mountainous masseur, I hobble across Independence Bridge (p57), glancing up behind me at my best girlfriend, Lady Liberty (p57) holding a palm frond above her head atop Gellért Hill, and jump on tram 2, which runs along the river to Újlipótváros, Budapest's Upper East Side. There's no better place in town than the Móri Kisvendéglő (p114) for some post-party Hungarian soul food. From here it's just a hop, skip and a jump to Margaret Island (p62). I may stroll, I may cycle, I may kip in the sun, but I'm sticking to the beaten track, thank you very much – in this city of passion and pricey real estate, lovers seize every opportunity and, frankly, any bush will do. Afterwards, I need a fix of Art Nouveau/Secessionist architecture and the No 1 metro (the 'little underground') beckons. It's dorky being a trainspotter but, as the Dalai Lama once told me, 'You only live twice' (or did he say 'thrice'?). Sinuous curves, asymmetrical forms and other bizarre shapes now under my belt, I can think about the really important things – a slice of something sweet at Lukács coffee house (p126), or a sundowner at one of the terrace café-bars on Liszt Ferenc tér (p123). Dinner will be at the Múzeum (p117) next to the National Museum, still my favourite upmarket Hungarian eatery after all these years (1885 – the restaurant, of course – to be precise) and the rest of the evening hopefully debauched at one of the *kertek* (p129) – the 'gardens' (or any outdoor venues) that open at night in the warmer months.

PHOTOGRAPHER

Richard Nebesky

Born one snowy night in the grungy Prague suburb of Zizkov – one of the world's most photogenic cities – it was not long after Richard got out of his cot that his father, an avid photo enthusiast, gave him his first point-and-shoot unit. Ever since, the camera was by his side on wander treks, ski adventures, cycling trips and while researching Lonely Planet books around the globe. He has also worked for various magazines and travel guide book publishers, and had plenty of social photography projects.

Photographing Budapest in winter, with regular drizzle and grey skies, was a challenge. Just as well that this imperial city of the former Hungarian empire is full of such wonderfully photogenic structures.

LONELY PLANET AUTHORS

Why is our travel information the best in the world? It's simple: our authors are independent, dedicated travellers. They don't research using just the Internet or phone, and they don't take freebies in exchange for positive coverage. They travel widely, to all the popular spots and off the beaten track. They personally visit thousands of hotels, restaurants, cafés, bars, galleries, palaces, museums and more – and they take pride in getting all the details right, and telling it how it is. For more, see the authors section on **www.lonelyplanet.com**.

Introducing Budapest

More cosmopolitan than Prague, more romantic than Warsaw and more beautiful than both, Budapest straddles a gentle curve in the Danube, with the Buda Hills to the west and what is essentially the start of the Great Plain to the east. With parks brimming with attractions, museums filled with treasures, pleasure boats sailing up and down the scenic Danube Bend, Turkish-era thermal baths belching steam and a nightlife throbbing until dawn most nights, the Hungarian capital is one of the Continent's most delightful and fun cities.

And the human legacy is just as remarkable as Mother Nature's. Architecturally, Budapest is a gem, with a wealth of baroque, neoclassical, Eclectic and Art Nouveau (or Secessionist) buildings. Overall it has a *fin-de-siècle* feel to it, for it was then, during the industrial boom and the capital's 'golden age' in the late 19th century, that most of what you see today was built. In some places, particularly along the Nagykörút (Big Ring Road) and up broad Andrássy út to the sprawling Városliget (City Park), Budapest's sobriquet 'the Paris of Central Europe' is well deserved. Nearly every building has some interesting detail, from Art Nouveau glazed tiles and neoclassical bas-reliefs to bullet holes and shrapnel scorings left from WWII and the 1956 Uprising.

At times, Budapest's scars are not very well hidden. Over the years, industrial and automobile pollution has exacerbated the decay, but in recent years the rebuilding and renovations have been nothing short of astonishing. Indeed, some people think the city is tidying itself up a bit too quickly. When I first moved to the city in the early 1990s, a stylish local guidebook advised potential visitors to 'hurry up and come before Budapest turns into just another capital of just another nice social-democratic European country' (or words to that effect). 'As if', I remember thinking in those 'Wild East' days of rapid-fire change and disillusionment. 'Yeah, as if...'

It's true that in the process of reclaiming its well-deserved title of *világváros* (world-class city) over the past decade, Budapest has taken on all the baggage that such a process usually involves: faceless modern architecture, organised criminal activity, a mobile phone at the ear of every 'suit', an international fast-food outlet on every corner. Yet Budapest remains – and will always stay – Hungarian: exotic, sometimes inscrutable, often passionate, with its feet firmly planted in Europe but with a glance every now and then eastward to the spawning grounds of its people.

Budapest is fabulous, romantic and exciting at any time, but especially so just after dusk in spring and summer when Castle Hill is bathed in a warm yellow light. Stroll along the Duna korzó, the riverside embankment on the Pest side, or across any of the bridges past young couples embracing passionately. It's then that you'll feel the romance of a place that, despite all attempts – from both within and without – to destroy it, has never died.

LOWDOWN

Population 1.75 million

Percentage of Hungary's population living in Budapest 18%

Time zone Central European Time (GMT + one hour)

Three-star double 12,500Ft to 25,000Ft (€50 to €102)

Coffee in a café 200Ft to 380 Ft

Bus/metro ticket 170Ft

Metro stations 40 on three lines

Budapest's ranking in terms of size among EU cities sixth (London, Berlin, Madrid, Rome and Paris come first)

Percentage of Hungarian women who would forgive infidelity 66% (rest of Europe: 54%)

Suicide rate 60.1 per 100,000 people (UK 15.1, USA 21.7)

No-no Clinking glasses when drinking beer (it is said that's what the Habsburgs did after executing the Martyrs of Arad in 1849)

City Life

City Life

BUDAPEST TODAY

How fares Budapest as the capital of one of the 10 'accession' countries that joined the EU in 2004? Many people here will tell you that the question is irrelevant, that Hungary and its capital have not seen any changes at all. In some regards, that is true – Budapest today is what Budapest was yesterday and what Budapest will be tomorrow. In many other ways, the city has changed dramatically.

Unemployment and inflation are down, real income and tourism figures are up (OK, the most visible new arrivals are British lager louts with big mouths and thirsts but they spend money). *Fapados* ('wooden bench' – ie budget) airlines like SkyEurope, EasyJet and Wizzair have landed in Budapest and are now winging Mr and Mrs Kovács and their 1.3 kids to Corsica for a 10-day holiday. Budapest is being redeveloped – putting on a very bright new face in some parts – and property prices are booming. The once canyonlike gap between Hungary and wealthy Western European nations is rapidly closing, and people in Budapest are spending more money than ever on home-entertainment centres, mobile phones, travelling and even food. The world is one big oyster and all that is missing is the cocktail sauce, right?

Wrong. And why? Because Hungarians are *still* not happy. They were not happy under socialism – they were the ones who electrified the barbed-wire fence separating themselves from Austria in the first place – and they weren't happy four years later when a poll taken in mid-1993 found that a full 76% of them were 'very disappointed' with capitalism and their living standard. A full dozen years, at least one car, a couple of foreign trips and a fair few more hot meals later, a survey carried out by the public-policy think tank DEMOS Magyarország has found that the vast majority of Hungarians remain *elégedetlen* – something like 'not enoughed' but meaning 'dissatisfied' or 'disgruntled' – as ever. Only 36% – the lowest in the EU and less than half the EU average of 73% – said they were satisfied with their quality of life.

Enough is enough already, will the Magyar ever be happy? Probably not if history repeats itself; we know this all too well from their art, their music, their *honfibú* (p11), and that disgruntledness goes back centuries. But why? Well, anyone who has lived here for any length of time knows that it's part of the social fabric, it's in the blood.

HOT CONVERSATION TOPICS

- Gyurcsány vs Orbán – Socialist schoolmaster or arrogant neo-con?
- *Kertek* – Who is charging the most extortionate rent for this year's hottest (or, rather, coolest) 'gardens'?
- M4 – Is the last metro line just a figment of the collective imagination?
- Property prices – Who is buying up Budapest this month? The Spanish? The Irish?
- Reality shows – How far will the likes of the 'humiliating', the 'sadistic' *Benne leszek a tévében!* (I'm Gonna Be on TV!) and the trashy *Való Virány* (Real World) go?
- Road works – Won't Budapest look great when it's finished?
- Travel – Thailand for the beach or Kenya for the wildlife? Decisions, decisions...

CITY CALENDAR

Every season has its attractions – and its limitations – in Budapest. For details see p186. Countless festivals and events are held in and around Budapest each year. The following abbreviated list gives you a taste of what to expect, but get hold of the HNTO's annual brochure *Events Calendar* for a complete listing. To ensure that your trip does not coincide with a public holiday, when most *everything* will be shut up tight, see p189.

JANUARY

NEW YEAR'S DAY CONCERT

www.hungariakoncert.hu

This is an annual event usually held in Pesti Vigadó on 1 January to herald in the new year.

INTERNATIONAL CIRCUS FESTIVAL

www.maciva.hu

This biennial (2008, 2010 etc) event is held under the big top of the Municipal Great Circus in late January.

FEBRUARY

OPERA BALL

www.operabal.com

This very prestigious event is held annually at the Hungarian State Opera House.

MARCH

BUDAPEST SPRING FESTIVAL

www.festivalcity.hu

The capital's largest (200 events at 60 venues) and most important cultural festival takes place at venues throughout the city.

APRIL

NATIONAL DANCE HOUSE MEETING & FAIR

www.tanchaz.hu

Hungary's biggest *táncház* (p131) is held over two days at the Budapest Sportaréna.

MAY

BUDAPEST EARLY MUSIC FORUM

www.festivalcity.hu

A festival focusing on ancient music – classical music as it was played when first composed at the Ferenc Liszt Music Academy and at churches around Budapest.

JUNE

DANUBE FOLKLORE CARNIVAL

www.dunaart.hu

A pan-Hungarian international 10-day carnival of folk and world music and modern dance, held in Vörösmarty tér and on Margaret Island.

BRIDGE FESTIVAL

www.festivalcity.hu

Also known as the Budapest Fair, this day-long festival of music, dance and street theatre is held on the city's bridges and by the river.

FERENCVÁROS SUMMER FESTIVAL

www.festivalcity.hu

Local groups perform music and dance in the streets of Budapest's district IX from mid-June to mid-July.

BUDAPEST FAIR

www.festivalcity.hu

Citywide 'Budapesti Búcsú' of concerts and street theatre marking the departure of Soviet troops from Hungarian soil in 1991.

MUSEUM NIGHT

www.museum.hu/events

Two dozen museums across town throw open their doors at 6pm and don't close to the very wee hours.

AUGUST

FORMULA ONE HUNGARIAN GRAND PRIX

www.hungaroring.hu

Hungary's prime sporting event held in Mogyoród, 24km northeast of the capital.

Hungarian State Opera House (p71), Andrássy út

SZIGET MUSIC FESTIVAL

www.sziget.hu

Now one of the biggest and most popular music festivals in Europe, held on Budapest's Hajógyár Island. The island becomes a festival city complete with camping and service facilities.

CRAFTS CELEBRATION

www.nesz.hu

Prominent craftspeople from around Hungary set up kiosks and hold workshops in the Castle District over a three-day period. There's also folk dancing and music.

JEWISH SUMMER FESTIVAL

www.jewishfestival.hu

Showcases Jewish culture through exhibitions, gastronomy and a book and film week.

SEPTEMBER

BUDAPEST INTERNATIONAL WINE FAIR

www.winefestival.hu

Hungary's foremost winemakers introduce their wines to festival goers in the Castle District. Children's activities available.

TOP FIVE UNUSUAL EVENTS

- Budapest Fair (June)
- International Circus Festival (January)
- Museum Night (June)
- National Dance House Meeting & Fair (April)
- Sziget Music Festival (August)

OCTOBER

BUDAPEST INTERNATIONAL MARATHON

www.budapestmarathon.com

Eastern Europe's most celebrated foot race goes along the Danube, across its bridges, through Margaret Island to City Park.

BUDAPEST AUTUMN FESTIVAL

www.festivalcity.hu, http://bof.hu

Cultural events at venues throughout the city until early November.

DECEMBER

NEW YEAR'S GALA & BALL

www.viparts.hu

Gala dinner and ball held at the Hungarian State Opera House on 31 December.

CULTURE

IDENTITY

With some 1.75 million inhabitants, Budapest is home to almost a fifth of the national population. The overwhelming majority are Magyars, an Asiatic people of obscure origins who do not speak an Indo-European language and make up the vast majority of Hungary's 10.083 million people. The population density of Budapest is 3333 people per sq km against a national average of 109 per sq km.

No exact breakdown exists, but the ethnic make-up in the capital reflects the national one. According to the 2001 census just over 92% of the population is ethnically Magyar. Minorities include Germans (2.6%), Serbs and other South Slavs (2%), Slovaks (0.8%) and Romanians (0.7%). The number of Roma is officially put at 1.9% of the population (or 193,800 people), though in some sources the figure is twice as high.

Life expectancy is very low by European standards: just over 68 years for men and almost 77 for women. The nation also has one of Europe's lowest rates of natural population increase – 9.76 per 1000 people, with a population growth of -0.26%. Sadly, it also has one of the highest rates of suicide (see boxed text, opposite). Currently 57% of all Hungarian marriages end in divorce.

Hungary is a highly cultured and educated society with a literacy rate of over 99% among those 15 years and over. School is compulsory for 10 years until the age of 16. About 65% of the population have completed secondary-school and 10% are university graduates, a quarter of which are in engineering and economics.

There are currently 19 universities and the most prestigious ones are largely based in Budapest, including the Loránd Eötvös Science University (ELTE; www.elte.hu), which was founded in 1635 and moved to Budapest in 1777 from what is now Trnava (Hungarian: Nagyszombat) in Slovakia; the 200-year-old Semmelweis University of Medicine (SOTE; www.sote.hu); the Budapest Technical and Economic Sciences University (BME; www.bme.hu), established in 1782; and the Budapest University of Economic Sciences (known as 'Közgáz'; www.bke.hu). Budapest-based and English-language Central European University (CEU; www.ceu.hu), founded in 1991 by philanthropist George Soros, has gained an international reputation in just over a decade.

Throughout history, religion has often been a question of expediency here. Under King Stephen I, Catholicism won the battle for dominance over Orthodoxy and, while the majority of Hungarians were quite happily Protestant by the end of the 16th century, many donned a new mantle during the Catholic Counter-Reformation under the Habsburgs. During the Turkish occupation in the 16th and 17th centuries, thousands of Hungarians converted to Islam – though not always willingly.

As a result, Hungarians tend to have a more pragmatic approach to religion than most of their neighbours, and little of the bigotry. It has even been suggested that this generally sceptical view of matters of faith has led to Hungarians' high rate of success in science and mathematics (p12). You'll never see Christian churches in Budapest full, even on important holy days. The Jewish community in Budapest, on the other hand, has seen a great revitalisation in recent years though mostly due to the influx of Orthodox Jews.

Of those Hungarians declaring religious affiliation in the 2001 census, about 52% said they were Roman Catholic, 16% Reformed (Calvinist) Protestant and nearly 3% Evangelical (Lutheran) Protestant. There are also small Greek Catholic (2.5%) and Orthodox and other Christian (1%) congregations. Hungary's Jews (though not always religious) number about 80,000, down from a prewar population of nearly 10 times that through wartime executions, deportations and emigration, with almost 90% living in Budapest.

LIFESTYLE

In general Hungarians – and people from Budapest in particular – are not uninhibited like the extroverted Romanians or sentimental Slavs who laugh or cry at the drop of a hat (or drink). They are reserved, somewhat formal people. Forget the impassioned, devil-may-care, Gypsy-fiddling stereotype – it doesn't exist and probably never did. The national anthem calls Hungarians 'a people torn by fate' and the overall mood is one of *honfibú* (literally 'patriotic sorrow', but really a penchant for the blues with a sufficient amount of hope to keep most people going).

This mood certainly predates what Hungarians call '*az átkos 40 év*' (the accursed 40 years) of communism. To illustrate what she saw as the 'dark streak in the Hungarian temperament', the late US foreign correspondent Flora Lewis recounted a story in *Europe: A Tapestry of Nations* that was the talk of Europe in the early 1930s. 'It was said,' she wrote, 'that a song called "Gloomy Sunday" so deeply moved otherwise normal people [in Budapest] that whenever it was played, they would rush to commit suicide by jumping off a Danube bridge.' The song has been covered in English by many artists, including Billie Holiday, Sinéad O'Connor and Björk, and is the subject of German film director Rolf Schübel's eponymous romantic drama (p24).

Hungarians are almost always extremely polite in social interaction, and the language can be very courtly – even when doing business with the butcher or having your hair

A DUBIOUS DISTINCTION

Hungary has one of the world's highest suicide rates – 60.1 per 100,000 people in 2001, surpassed only by Russia and several other former Soviet republics. Psychologists are still out to lunch as to why Hungary should have such a high incidence. Some say that Hungarians' inclination to gloom leads to an ultimate act of despair (above). Others link it to a phenomenon not uncommon here in the late 19th century – as the Hungarian aristocracy withered away, the *kisnemesség* (minor nobility), some of whom were no better off than the local peasants, would do themselves in to 'save their name and honour'. As a result, suicide was – and is – not looked upon dishonourably as such, victims may be buried in hallowed ground and the euphemistic sentence used in the newspaper obituaries is: 'János Kádár/Erzsébet Szabó died suddenly and tragically.' About 60% of suicides are by hanging.

cut. The standard greeting for a man to a woman (or youngsters to their elders, regardless of the sex) is *Csókolom* ('I kiss it' – 'it' being the hand, of course). People of all ages – even close friends – shake hands profusely when meeting up.

But while all this gentility certainly oils the wheels that turn a sometimes difficult society, it can be used to keep 'outsiders' (foreigners and other Hungarians) at a distance. Perhaps as an extension of this desire to keep everything running as smoothly as possible, Hungarians are always extremely helpful in an emergency – be it an accident, a pick-pocketing or simply helping someone who's lost their way.

HEAD OF THE CLASS

Hungary's contributions to specialised education and the sciences have been far greater than its present size and population would suggest. A unique method of music education devised by the composer Zoltán Kodály (1882–1967) is widespread and the Pető Institute in Budapest has a very high success rate in teaching children with cerebral palsy to walk. Albert Szent-Györgyi (1893–1986) won the Nobel Prize for Medicine or Physiology in 1937 for his discovery of vitamin C; Georg von Békésy (1899–1972) won the same prize in 1961 for his research on the inner ear; and Eugene Paul Wigner (1902–95) received a Nobel Prize in 1963 for his research in nuclear physics.

Like Spaniards, Poles and many other people with a Catholic background, Hungarians celebrate *névnap* ('name days') rather than (or as well as) birthdays. Name days are usually the Catholic feast day of their patron saint, but less holy names have a date too. Most calendars in Hungary list them, and it's traditional for men to give women – colleagues, classmates and neighbours as well as spouses and family members – at least a single blossom.

The gay and (less so) lesbian communities are quite active in Budapest but keep a relatively low profile compared with Western European capitals. Both groups can enter into domestic partnerships in Hungary, but such arrangements carry very few legal rights. The government is considering introducing partnership legislation similar to that of the UK.

By and large Hungarians tend to meet their friends and entertain outside at cafés and restaurants. If you are invited to a Hungarian home, bring a bunch of flowers (available in profusion all year and very inexpensive) or a bottle of good local wine (see p30). You can talk about anything under the sun – from religion and politics to whether the Hungarian language really is more difficult than Japanese and Arabic – but money is a touchy subject. Traditionally, the discussion of wealth – or even wearing flashy jewellery and clothing – was considered to be gauche in Hungary. Do not expect (or ask for) a tour of the house or apartment; that is just not done here.

Although it's almost impossible to calculate (with the 'black economy' being so widespread and important), the average monthly salary in Hungary at the time of writing was 146,000/94,000Ft gross/net (or €599/386). The minimum wage is currently set at 57,000Ft (€224) per month but it will be raised to between 63,000Ft (€248) and 77,000Ft (€303), depending on educational achievement.

Hungarians as a whole are extremely fond of animals and Budapest has scores of *állatdíszhal bolt*, pet shops selling everything from puppies and hamsters to tropical fish. Budapesters are especially fond of dogs (you can't miss breeds indigenous to Hungary – the moplike *puli* herding dog, the sleek

WHERE THE FIRST COMES LAST

Following a practice unknown outside Asia, Hungarians reverse their names in all uses, and their 'last' name (or surname) always comes first. For example, John Smith is never János Kovács to Hungarians but Kovács János, while Elizabeth Taylor is Szabó Erzsébet and Francis Flour is Liszt Ferenc.

Most titles also follow the structure: Mr John Smith is Kovács János úr. Many women follow the practice of taking their husband's full name. If Elizabeth were married to John, she might be Kovács Jánosné (Mrs John Smith) or, increasingly popular with professional women, Kovácsné Szabó Erzsébet.

To avoid confusion, all Hungarian names in this guide are written in the usual Western manner – Christian name first – including the names of museums, theatres etc if they are translated into English. Budapest's Arany János Színház is the János Arany Theatre in English. Addresses are always written in Hungarian as they appear on street signs: Kossuth Lajos utca, Rákóczi Ferenc tér etc.

vizsla or the giant white *komondor* sheepdog) – and people of all ages go gaga over a particularly friendly or attractive one.

Hungarians let down their hair in warm weather, and you'll see more public displays of affection on the streets than perhaps anywhere else in the world. It's all very romantic, but beware: in the remoter corners of Budapest's parks and on Margaret Island you may stumble upon more passionate displays.

FASHION

In general, dress is very casual in Budapest – in summer, daringly brief, even by Continental European standards – and many people attend even the opera in denim. Men needn't bother bringing a necktie; it will be seldom – if ever – used.

Like everywhere, Budapest has its own fashion boutiques and home-grown designers. Keep an eye open for funky pieces from local talent Anikó Németh, high-fashion ready-to-wear and accessories from Paris-trained Tamás Náray, and Art Deco–inspired, very geometric designs from wunderkind Katti Zoób, whose spring/summer 2005 collection was showcased in the Magyar Magic – Hungary in Focus road show in the UK.

Judging from what's on offer in some of the used or 'second-generation' clothing shops such as Iguana (p149) and Ciánkáli (p148), the über-trend on the street is for retro (1950s to 70s) and fetishist (leather, military) foundation pieces and accessories. What the masses are going for is another matter. The high-street favourite (and very ordinary) Brussels-based C&A has launched three new stores in Budapest and Spanish fashion chain Zara, much beloved by the braces-and-bubblegum brigade, has opened a 2400-sq-metre outlet on V Váci utca.

SPORT

Hungarians enjoy attending sporting matches and watching them on TV as much as they do participating (p138). The most popular spectator sports (p139) are football and water polo, though motor racing, horse racing – both trotting and flat racing – and even *sakk* (competitive chess) have their fans.

Football is far and away the nation's favourite sport, and people still talk about the 'match of the century' at Wembley in 1953 when the Magic Magyars beat England six goals to three – the first time England lost a home match. There are a dozen premier league football teams in Hungary, with four of them based in the capital (p140), including the ever-popular Ferencváros.

In water polo, Hungary has dominated the European Championships (12 times) and Olympic Games (eight times) for decades so it's worthwhile catching a professional or amateur match of this exciting seven-a-side sport (if for no other reason than to watch a bunch of guys in skimpy bathing suits horsing around). For details see p140.

The Formula 1 Hungarian Grand Prix (p9), the sporting event of the year, takes place near Budapest in August.

MEDIA

As in most European capitals, printed news has strong political affiliations in Budapest. Almost all the major broadsheets have left or centre-left leanings, with the exception of the conservative *Magyar Nemzet* (Hungarian Nation).

TOP FIVE MEDIA WEBSITES

- Budapest Week Online (www.budapestweek.com) Especially good for arts and entertainment.
- Budapest Sun Online (www.budapestsun.com) Similar to Budapest Week Online but stronger on local news, interviews and features.
- Hungarian Quarterly (www.hungarianquarterly.com) Excerpts from the country's most scholarly journal in English.
- MTI (www.mti.hu) The government-funded Hungarian News Agency is an excellent source for up-to-date news and opinion.
- Pestiside (www.pestiside.hu) A positive favourite and useful in all respects, this website will have you culturally and politically fluent in Budapest-speak before you even arrive.

The most respected publications are the weekly news magazine *Heti Világgazdaság* (World Economy Weekly), known as HVG, and the former Communist Party mouthpiece *Népszabadság* (People's Freedom), the daily broadsheet that is now completely independent and has the highest paid circulation (198,000) of any newspaper. Hard on its heels is the Swiss-owned *Blikk*, a brash tabloid that focuses on sport, stars and sex – not necessarily in that order. Specialist publications include the weekly intellectual *Élet és Irodalom* (Life and Literature), the satirical biweekly *Hócipő* (Snowshoe) and the mass-circulation *Nemzeti Sport* (National Sport).

For information on Budapest's English-language print media see p191.

With the sale of the state-owned TV2, Magyar Televízió (MTV) controls only one channel (MTV-1), though there is a public terrestrial channel (M2) and a public satellite one (Duna TV), a second private terrestrial channel (RTL Klub) and some 20 private cable and satellite channels nationwide, broadcasting everything from game and talk shows to classic Hungarian films. Most midrange and top-end hotels and *pensions* in Budapest have satellite TV, though mainly in German.

The public Magyar Rádió (MR; Hungarian Radio) has three stations. They are named after Lajos Kossuth (jazz and news; 98.6AM), the most popular station in the country; Sándor Petőfi (1960s to 1980s music, news and sport; 94.8FM); and Béla Bartók (classical music and news; 105.3FM). Radio Budapest (www.english.radio.hu), the external arm of Hungarian Radio, broadcasts in English on 88.1FM and 91.9FM.

Juventus (89.5FM), a popular music station for youngsters, claims the second-highest audience in the country. Rádió 88 (95.4FM) plays the top music of the 1980s and 90s – just what students want. Danubius Rádió (98.3 and 103.3FM) is a mix of popular music and news.

LANGUAGE

The Hungarians like to boast that their language ranks with Japanese and Arabic as among the world's most difficult tongues to learn. All languages are hard for non-native speakers to master, but it is true: Hungarian is a bitch to learn to speak well. This should not put you off attempting a few words and phrases, however.

For assorted reasons – the compulsory study of Russian in all schools until the late 1980s being one of them – Hungarians are not polyglots and even when they do have a smattering of a foreign language, they lack experience and are generally hesitant to speak it. Attempt a few words in *magyarul* (Hungarian), and they will be impressed, take it as a compliment and be extremely encouraging.

QUIRKY LANGUAGE

Hungarian is full of what the French called *faux amis* – 'false friends' or misleading homophones that have the same sound but totally different meanings. Thus in Hungarian *test* is not a quiz but 'body', *fog* is 'tooth', *comb* is 'thigh' and *part* is 'shore'. *Fatál* – admittedly with an accent – just means 'wooden plate' and is a popular Budapest restaurant, and Apáthy is a less-than-enthusiastic family name. *Ifjúság*, pronounced (very roughly) 'if you shag', means 'youth'; *sajt* (pronounced somewhat like 'shite'), as in every visiting Briton's favourite *sajtburger*, means 'cheese'.

The best foreign language for getting around with here was always German; historical ties, geographical proximity and the fact that it was the preferred language of the literati until almost the 20th century have given it almost semi-official status. But with the advent of the Internet and the frequency of travel, most young people now have at least a smattering of English while older people speak German. If you are desperate to make yourself understood in English, look for someone under the age of 25.

For obvious reasons, Russian is best avoided; there seems to be almost a national paranoia about speaking it, and many people revel in how little they know 'despite all those years in class'. Italian is understood more and more in Hungary because of tourism. French and Spanish are virtually useless.

ECONOMY & COSTS

Two years after joining the EU, Hungary looks set to miss its target of abandoning the forint for the euro by 2010 as the government puts the upgrading of the country's highways and hospitals ahead of economic targets set by Brussels.

Prime Minister Ferenc Gyurcsány, who was re-elected in April 2006, bolstered his popularity by cutting taxes, increasing child support subsidies and pensions, and trying to bring the nation's as well as the city's overworked roads into the 21st century. All this spending by the government – more than 810,000 Hungarians, or 29% of the 2.8 million workforce are state employees – meant that Hungary was being run on borrowed money. The country would have to cut its budget deficit in half – to less than 3% of gross domestic product – to be eligible to adopt the euro as its currency. It would also have to slow down inflation, cut government debt, lower interest rates and keep the currency stable, according to EU rules.

Hungary's economy grew about 4.1% in 2005, the second-slowest rate after Poland among the eight Eastern European states that joined the EU in 2004. Still, the country's expansion outpaces growth rates in Western Europe as the Hungarian economy benefits from such exports as automobile engines made by Volkswagen AG's Audi unit and medicines made by Gedeon Richter Rt.

HOW MUCH?

Litre of petrol 265Ft to 273Ft

Litre of bottled water 150Ft

Korsó (0.5L) of Dreher beer in pub/café 350Ft to 600Ft

Souvenir T-shirt 1500Ft

Street snack (kolbász sausage) 250 FT

Cheap/good bottle of wine (75cL) in supermarket 600/2000Ft

Bed in private room from 4500Ft

Cup of coffee in café 200Ft to 380 Ft

Local English-language newspaper 395Ft to 590Ft

Dinner for two (with wine) at a good restaurant 15,000Ft

The country has attracted about $47 billion of the $192 billion foreign direct investment that flowed into the four biggest Eastern European economies since 1989, which is the highest per-capita level in postcommunist countries. Companies from places like South Korea are setting up shop in Hungary, which is set on becoming a world power in manufacturing consumer electronics.

Foreign companies pick Hungary for their factories because the workforce is considered flexible, skilled, highly educated and relatively inexpensive. Wages in Budapest are about 25% higher than the national average. The unemployment rate in the capital are around 3%, compared with 7.6% nationwide.

Budapest is no longer the bargain-basement destination for foreign travellers that it was even five years ago, but it is still cheaper by a third or even a half than most Western European countries. If you stay in private rooms, eat at medium-priced restaurants and travel on public transport, you should get by on €40 a day.

Travelling in more style and comfort – restaurant splurges with bottles of wine, a fairly active nightlife, small hotels/guesthouses with 'character' – will cost about twice as much. Those putting up at hostels or college dormitories, eating *burek* street food for lunch and at self-service restaurants for dinner could squeak by for as low as €25 a day.

For price ranges of accommodation in Budapest see p153 and for the average cost of restaurant meals see p92.

GOVERNMENT & POLITICS

National Government

Hungary's 1989 constitution provides for a parliamentary system of government. The unicameral assembly sits in the Parliament building and consists of 386 members (36 women at present, four of whom held ministerial portfolios within the government) chosen for four years in a complex, two-round system that balances direct ('first past the post') and proportional representation. Of the total, 176 MPs enter Parliament by individual constituency elections, 152 on the basis of 20 district lists and 58 on the basis of national lists. The prime minister is head of government. The head of state, the president, is elected by the house for five years.

For a party to win mandates in Parliament, it should obtain at least 5% of valid votes cast on regional party lists. In the most recent election (April 2006), only four parties were seated in the National Assembly: the ruling socialist MSZP (Hungarian Socialist Party) in coalition with the liberal SZDSZ (Alliance of Free Democrats) with 210 seats and the centre-rightist Fidesz-MPP (Alliance of Young Democrats-Hungarian Civic Party) together with the conservative MDF (Hungarian Democratic Forum) making up the opposition (176 seats). Other parties are the agrarian conservative FKgP (Independent Smallholders' Party) and the xenophobic and ultranationalist MIÉP (Hungarian Justice and Life Party).

Local Government

Budapest is governed by a *fővárosi önkormánzat* (municipal council), whose 66 members are elected to four-year terms and whose leader is the *főpolgármester* (lord mayor). The current mayor, SZDSZ liberal Gábor Demszky, handily won his fourth term in office in October 2002 after his party and its coalition partners, the MSZP socialists, received almost 60% of the popular vote. The next elections are due in October 2006.

Arts & Architecture

Arts & Architecture

The arts in Budapest have been both starved and nourished by the pivotal events in the nation's history. King Stephen's conversion to Catholicism brought Romanesque and Gothic art and architecture, while the Turkish occupation nipped most of Budapest's Renaissance in the bud. The Habsburgs opened the doors to baroque influences. The arts thrived under the Dual Monarchy, through truncation and even under fascism. The early days of communism brought socialist-realist art celebrating wheat sheaves and muscle-bound steelworkers to a less-than-impressed populace, but much money was spent on music and 'correct art' such as classical theatre.

While the artistic, cultural and literary hypertrophy of Budapest is indisputable, it would be foolish to ignore folk art when discussing urban (and urbane) fine arts here. The two have been inextricably linked for several centuries and have greatly influenced one another. The music of Béla Bartók and the ceramic sculptures of Margit Kovács are deeply rooted in traditional Hungarian culture. Even the architecture of the Secession (p20) incorporated many folk elements. The best place in Budapest to see this type of art is the Ethnography Museum (p64).

MUSIC & DANCE

Hungary has made many contributions to the world of classical music, but one person stands head and shoulders above the rest: Franz – or Ferenc – Liszt. Liszt (1811–86), who established the Academy of Music in Budapest and lived in a four-room 1st-floor apartment on VI Vörösmarty utca (p71) from 1881 until his death. Liszt liked to describe himself as 'part Gypsy', and some of his works, notably the 20 *Hungarian Rhapsodies,* do in fact echo the traditional music of the Rom.

Ferenc Erkel (1810–93), who taught at the Academy of Music from 1879 to 1886 and was the State Opera House's first musical director, is the father of Hungarian opera. Two of his works – the stirringly nationalistic *Bánk Bán,* based on József Katona's play of that name, and *László Hunyadi* – are standards at the State Opera House. Erkel also composed the music for the Hungarian national anthem, *Himnusz.*

Béla Bartók (1881–1945) and Zoltán Kodály (1882–1967), were both long-term residents of Budapest (their former residences are now museums; see p61 and p72), made the first systematic study of Hungarian folk music, travelling and recording throughout the Magyar linguistic region during 1906. Both integrated some of their findings into their own compositions – Bartók in *Bluebeard's Castle,* for example, and Kodály in his *Peacock Variations.*

Away from classical music, it is important to distinguish between 'Gypsy' music and Hungarian folk music. Gypsy music as it is known and heard in Hungarian restaurants from

TOP FIVE CDS

- *The Prisoner's Song* – Some say this is the best CD produced by Muzsikás with Marta Sebestyén and includes her song 'Szerelem, Szerelem' (Love, Love), made famous in the film *The English Patient* (Anthony Minghella, 1996).
- *Romano Trip: Gypsy Grooves from Eastern Europe* – This CD from the incomparable Romano Drom is where Roma folk meets world music, with an electronic twist.
- *Lechajem Rebbe* – This is the latest effort from the Budapest Klezmer Band, arguably the best ensemble anywhere playing traditional Jewish music.
- *Hungarian Astronaut* – Anima Sound System mixes Western beats with East European tonal flavours.
- *With the Gypsy Violin around the World: Sándor Déki Lakatos & His Gypsy Band* – No-one's Hungarian musical education is complete without this compilation, the epitome of saccharine *csárdás* music played in fancy hotel restaurants across Budapest.

Budapest to Boston is urban schmaltz and based on recruiting tunes called *verbunkos,* played during the Rákóczi independence wars. At least two fiddles, a bass and a cymbalom (a curious stringed instrument played with sticks) are *de rigueur*.

To confuse matters, real Roma – as opposed to Gypsy – music traditionally does not use instruments but is sung a cappella (though sometimes it is backed with percussion and even guitar). Two of the best-known modern Roma groups are Kalyi Jag (Black Fire), from northeastern Hungary and led by Gusztav Várga, and Romano Drom.

Hungarian folk musicians play violins, zithers, hurdy-gurdies, bagpipes and lutes on a five-tone diatonic scale. There are lots of different performers, but watch out for Muzsikás (with the inimitable Marta Sebestyén or on her own); Ghymes, a Hungarian folk band from Slovakia; the Hungarian group Vujicsics, which mixes elements of South Slav music; and the energetic fiddler Félix Lajkoa from the Magyar-speaking area of northern Serbia. Attending a *táncház* (literally 'dance house'; p131) is an excellent way to hear Hungarian folk music and even to learn to dance.

Traditional Yiddish music is not as well known as the Gypsy and Roma varieties but it is of similar origin, having once been closely associated with central European folk music. Until WWI, *klezmer* dance bands were led by the violin and cymbalom, but the influence of Yiddish theatre and the first wax recordings inspired a switch to the clarinet, which is the predominant instrument in this type of music today. *Klezmer* music is currently going through something of a renaissance in Budapest.

There are two ballet companies based in Budapest, though the best in the country is the Győr Ballet from Western Transdanubia. For modern dance, however, the capital is *the* centre (p134). Among the finest orchestral companies are the Budapest Festival Orchestra and the Hungarian Radio Symphony Orchestra, which uses the name Budapest Symphony Orchestra on certain domestic and all of its foreign recordings.

ARCHITECTURE

You won't find as much Romanesque and Gothic architecture in Budapest as you will in, say, Prague – the Mongols, Turks and Habsburgs destroyed most of it – but the Royal Palace incorporates many Gothic features and the sedile (niches with seats) in the Castle District, most notably on I Úri utca and I Országház utca, are pure Gothic. The chapels in the Inner Town Parish Church (p64) have some fine Gothic and Renaissance tabernacles, and you can't miss the Renaissance stonework – along with the Gothic wooden sculptures and panel paintings and late-Gothic triptychs – at the Hungarian National Gallery (p54).

Baroque architecture abounds in Budapest; you'll see examples of it everywhere. St Anne's Church (p58) on I Batthyány tér in Buda and the Óbuda Parish Church (Map pp226–7) on III Flórián tér are fine examples of ecclesiastical baroque while the Citadella (p56) on Gellért Hill in Buda and the municipal council office (Map p224) on V Városház utca in Pest are baroque in its civic or secular form.

While modern architecture in Budapest is almost completely forgettable – with the one notable exception of Imre Makovecz, who has developed his own 'organic' style using unusual materials like tree trunks and turf and whose work can be seen at the office building at VIII Szentkirályi utca 18 (Map p222) and the spectacular funerary chapel with its reverse vaulted ceiling at the Farkasréti Cemetery (Map p216) located in

Ferenc Liszt Academy of Music (p131), Erzsébetváros

UNCOVERING BUDAPEST'S ART NOUVEAU TREASURES

One of the joys of exploring the 'Queen of the Danube' is that you'll find elements of Art Nouveau and Secessionism in the oddest places; keep your eyes open and you'll spot bits and pieces everywhere.

Some people go out of their way for another glimpse of such 'hidden' favourites near City Park as the **Geology Institute** (Map pp218–19; XIV Stefánia út 14), designed by Lechner in 1899, and Sándor Baumgarten's **National Institute for the Blind** (Map pp218–19; XIV Ajtósi Dürer sor 39) dating from 1904, or the **Philanthia** (Map p224; V Váci utca 9), a flower shop with an exquisite Art Nouveau interior (Kálmán Albert Körössy; 1906) in the Inner Town.

Other buildings worth a detour are the former **Török Bank House** (Map p224; V Szervita tér 3), designed by Henrik Böhm and Ármin Hegedűs in 1906 and sporting a wonderful Secessionist mosaic by Róth in the upper gable called *Patrona Hungariae,* depicting Hungaria surrounded by great Hungarians of the past; Ármin Hegedűs' **primary school** (Map p222; VII Dob utca 85), built in the same year and with mosaics depicting contemporary children's games; and the delightful **City Park Calvinist church** (Map pp218–19; VII Városligeti fasor 7), a stunning example of late Art Nouveau architecture by Aladár Arkay (1913), with carved wooden gates, stained glass and ceramic tiles on the façade. **Bedő House** (Map p222; V Honvéd utca 3), an apartment block by Emil Vidor and completed in 1903, is one of the most intact Art Nouveau structures in the city. It contains some striking interior features and the exterior (ironwork gate, majolica flowers, faces) has been renovated.

The style was hardly restricted to public buildings in Budapest, and the affluent districts to the west of City Park are happy hunting grounds for some of the best examples of private residences built in the Art Nouveau/Secessionist style. The cream-coloured **Egger Villa** (Map pp218–19; VII Városligeti fasor 24), designed by Emil Vidor in 1902, is among the purest – and most extravagant – examples of Art Nouveau in the city. On the other side of the road, the green **Vidor Villa** (Map pp218–19; VII Városligeti fasor 33) with the curious turret was designed by Vidor for his father in 1905 and incorporates any number of European styles in vogue at the time, including French Art Nouveau and Japanese-style motifs. Other interesting buildings in this area are **Lédere Mansion** (Map p222; VI Bajza utca 42), a block with mosaics built by Zoltán Bálint and Lajos Jámbor in 1902, and **Sonnenberg Mansion** (Map pp218–19; VI Munkácsy Mihály utca 23). Designed by Albert Körössy in 1903, it is now the headquarters of the MDF political party.

district XII – that is not the case with the unique style of architecture that arrived in Budapest at the end of the 19th and the start of the 20th centuries.

Art Nouveau architecture and its Viennese variant, Secessionism, abound here, and examples can be seen throughout the city; it is Budapest's signature style. Its sinuous curves, flowing, asymmetrical forms, colourful Zsolnay tiles and other decorative elements stand out like beacons in a sea of refined and elegant baroque and mannered, geometric neoclassical buildings.

Art Nouveau was both an architectural style and an art form that flourished in Europe and the USA from about 1890 to 1910. It began in Britain as the Arts and Crafts Movement founded by William Morris (1834–96), which stressed the importance of manual processes over machines and attempted to create a new organic style in direct opposition to the imitative banalities spawned by the Industrial Revolution. It soon spread to Europe, where it took on distinctly local and/or national characteristics. In France it became known as Art Nouveau or Style 1900, in Germany as *Jugendstil* and in Italy as Stile Liberty.

In Vienna a group of artists called the Secessionists lent its name to the more geometric local style of Art Nouveau architecture: *Sezessionstil* (Hungarian: *Szecesszió*). In Budapest, the use of traditional façades with allegorical and historical figures and scenes, folk motifs and Zsolnay ceramics and other local materials led to an eclectic style. Though working within an Art Nouveau/Secessionist framework, this style emerged as something that was uniquely Hungarian.

Fashion and styles changed as whimsically and rapidly at the start of the 20th century as they do a century later, and by the end of the first decade Art Nouveau and its variations were considered limited, passé, even tacky. Fortunately for the good citizens of Budapest and us, the economic and political torpor of the prewar period and the 40-year 'big sleep' after WWII left many Art Nouveau/Secessionist buildings here beaten but standing – many more, in fact, than remain in such important Art Nouveau/*Jugendstil* centres as Paris, Brussels and Vienna.

The first Hungarian architect to look to Art Nouveau for inspiration was Frigyes Spiegel, with his exotic and symbolic ornamentation. At the northern end of VI Izabella utca at

No 94 is the restored Lindenbaum apartment block (Map p222), the first in Hungary to use Art Nouveau ornamentation – suns, stars, peacocks, shells and long-tressed nudes.

The master of the style, however, was Ödön Lechner (1845–1914), and his most ambitious work in Budapest is the Applied Arts Museum (p69). Purpose-built as a museum and completed in time for the millenary exhibition in 1896, it was faced and roofed in a variety of Zsolnay ceramic tiles, and its turrets, domes and ornamental figures lend it an 'Eastern' or 'Indian' feel. However, his crowning glory is the sumptuous former Royal Postal Savings Bank (Map p222) at V Hold utca 4, a Secessionist extravaganza of floral mosaics, folk motifs and ceramic figures just off Szabadság tér in Lipótváros and dating from 1901. The bull's head atop the central tower symbolises the nomadic past of the Magyars while the ceramic bees scurrying up the semi-pillars towards their hives represent organisation, industry and economy.

The Ferenc Liszt Academy of Music (p131), designed by Kálmán Giergl and Flóris Korb in 1907, is not so interesting for its exterior as for its decorative elements within. There's a dazzling Art Nouveau mosaic called *Art Is the Source of Life* by Aladár Kőrösfői Kriesch, a leader of the seminal Gödöllő Artists' Colony, and some fine stained glass by master craftsman Miksa Róth, whose home and workshop is now a museum (p69). Also note the grid of laurel leaves below the ceiling, which mimics the ironwork dome of the Secession Building (1897–1908) in Vienna, and the large sapphire-blue Zsolnay ball finials on the stair balusters.

Some buildings have got (or are getting) face-lifts and are being used for different purposes, including the gem-like Gresham Palace (Map p224) at V Roosevelt tér 5-6, designed by Zsigmond Quittner (1907) and now housing a five-star hotel (p159).

PAINTING & SCULPTURE

Distinctly Hungarian art didn't come into its own until the mid-19th century when Mihály Pollack, József Hild and Miklós Ybl began changing the face of Budapest. The romantic nationalist school of heroic paintings, best exemplified by Bertalan Székely (1835–1910), who painted much of the interior of Matthias Church (p55), and Gyula Benczúr (1844–1920), gratefully gave way to the realism of Mihály Munkácsy (1844–1900), who received a state funeral in Hősök tere. But the greatest painters from this period were Kosztka Tivadar Csontváry (1853–1919) and József Rippl-Rónai (1861–1927), both habitués of Café Japan (see boxed text, p126), whose works are on display at the Hungarian National Gallery (p54).

The 20th-century painter Victor Vasarely (1908–97), the so-called 'father of op art', has his own museum (p60) in Óbuda as does the contemporary sculptor Imre Varga (p60).

A turning point for modern art in Hungary came in 2005 when the Ludwig Museum of Contemporary Art (p70) moved from Castle Hill to its new (and purpose-built) premises in the Palace of Arts opposite the National Theatre on the Danube.

LITERATURE

Sándor Petőfi (1823–49), who led the Youth of March through the streets of Pest in 1848, is Hungary's most celebrated and accessible poet, and a line from his work *National Song* became the rallying cry for the 1848–49 War of Independence, in which Petőfi fought and died. A deeply philosophical play called *The Tragedy of Man* by his colleague, Imre Madách (1823–64), published a decade after Hungary's defeat in the War of Independence, is still considered to be the country's greatest classical drama. Madách did not participate in the war due to illness but was imprisoned in Pest for assisting Lajos Kossuth's secretary in 1852.

The defeat in 1849 led many writers to look to Romanticism for inspiration and solace: heroes, winners, and knights in shining armour became popular subjects. Petőfi's comrade-in-arms, János Arany (1817–82), whose name is synonymous with impeccable Hungarian and who edited two Pest literary journals in the 1860s, wrote epic poetry (including the *Toldi Trilogy*) and ballads.

Another friend of Petőfi, the prolific novelist Mór Jókai (1825–1904), who divided his time between his villa in XII Költő utca in Buda and his summer retreat at Balatonfüred on Lake

Balaton, wrote of heroism and honesty in such wonderful works as *The Man with the Golden Touch* and *Black Diamonds*. This 'Hungarian Dickens' still enjoys widespread popularity. Another perennial favourite, Kálmán Mikszáth (1847–1910), wrote satirical tales such as *The Good Palóc People* and *St Peter's Umbrella* in which he poked fun at the declining gentry. Apparently the former US president Theodore Roosevelt enjoyed the latter work so much that he insisted on visiting the ageing novelist in Budapest during a European tour in 1910.

Zsigmond Móricz (1879–1942), one of the cofounders of the influential literary magazine *Nyugat* (West; 1908) was a very different type of writer. His works, in the tradition of the French naturalist Émile Zola (1840–1902), examined the harsh reality of peasant life in late-19th-century Hungary. His contemporary, Mihály Babits (1883–1941), poet and the editor of *Nyugat*, made the rejuvenation of Hungarian literature his lifelong work.

Two other important names of this period are the poet and short-story writer Dezső Kosztolányi (1885–1936), who met his lifelong friend Babits at university in Pest, and the

RUBIK CUBES, BIROS, VITAMIN C & ZSA ZSA

It is not enough to be Hungarian – one must also have talent.

Slogan spotted in a Toronto employment office in the early 1960s

The contributions made by Hungarians in any number of fields – from films and toys to science and fine art – both at home and abroad have been enormous, especially when you consider the nation's size and relatively small population. The following is a list of people whom you may not have known were Hungarian or of Hungarian ancestry. Should you want the list expanded on, get a hold of *Eminent Hungarians* by Ray Keenoy, a 'light-hearted look' at the phenomenon, or check out www.webenetics.com/hungary/famous.htm.

Biro, Leslie (Bíró József László; 1899–1985) Inventor of the ballpoint pen, which he patented in 1938.

Brassaï (Halász Gyula; 1899–1984) Hungarian-born French poet, draftsman, sculptor and photographer, known for his dramatic photographs of Paris by night.

Capa, Robert (Friedmann Endre Ernő; 1913–54) One of the greatest war photographers and photojournalists of the 20th century.

Cukor, George (Cukor György; 1899–1983) Legendary American film producer/director (*The Philadelphia Story*, 1940).

Curtis, Tony (Bernard Schwartz; 1925–) Evergreen American actor (*Spartacus*, 1960).

Eszterhas, Joe (Eszterhás József; 1944–) American scriptwriter (*Basic Instinct*, 1989).

Gabor, Eva (1919–95) American actress chiefly remembered for her starring role as a New York city socialite making her comical life on a farm in the 1960s TV series *Green Acres;* younger sister of Zsa Zsa.

Gabor, Zsa Zsa (1917?-) Ageless-ish American starlet of grade BBB films and older sister of Eva.

Houdini, Harry (Weisz Erich; 1874–1926) American magician and celebrated escape artist.

Howard, Leslie (Steiner László; 1893–1943) Quintessential English actor most famous for his role in *Gone with the Wind* (1939).

Lauder, Estée (Josephine Esther Mentzer; 1908–2004) American fragrance and cosmetics baroness.

Liszt, Franz (Liszt Ferenc; 1811–86) Piano virtuoso and composer.

Lugosi, Béla (Blaskó Béla Ferenc Dezső; 1882–1956) The film world's only real Dracula – and minister of culture under the Béla Kun regime (p45).

Rubik, Ernő (1944–) Inventor of the hottest toy of the 1980 Christmas season – an infuriating plastic cube with 54 small squares that when twisted out of its original arrangement has 43 quintillion variations.

Soros, George (Soros György; 1930–) Billionaire financier and philanthropist.

Szent-Györgyi, Dr Albert (1893–1986) Nobel Prize-winning biochemist who discovered vitamin C.

Vasarely, Victor (Vásárhelyi Győző; 1908–97) Hungarian-born French painter of geometric abstractions and the 'father of op art'.

Wilder, Billy (Wilder Samuel; 1906–2002) American film director and producer (*Some Like It Hot*, 1959).

TOP FIVE BUDAPEST BOOKS

- *Under the Frog* (Tibor Fischer, 2001). Amusing account of the antics of two members of Hungary's elite national basketball team in Budapest from WWII through to the 1956 Uprising.
- *Homage to the Eighth District* (Giorgio and Nicola Pressburger, 1990) Poignant account of life in what was a Jewish working-class section of Budapest during and after WWII by twin brothers who emigrated to Italy in 1956.
- *Liquidation* (Imre Kertész, 2003) Set in Budapest in the aftermath of the fall of communism, *Liquidation* is the story of a book editor coping with the suicide of a friend.
- *Memoir of Hungary: 1944–1948* (Sándor Márai, 2001) Remembrances, including the war-time destruction of Budapest and the Red Army's arrival and occupation, of the celebrated playwright and author of *Embers*, performed in London during 2006, who fled Budapest in 1948 to escape communist persecution.
- *Prague* (Arthur Phillips, 2002) Cleverly titled debut novel – it takes place in Budapest and the title supposedly refers to the desire by many of the book's characters to live in the 'more' bohemian paradise of the Czech capital – by a young expat American that focuses on life in Budapest in the first years after the changes from a communist past.

novelist Gyula Krúdy (1878–1933), who lived in Óbuda and liked the bone marrow on toast as served at Kéhli (p96) so much that he included a description of it in his *The Adventures of Sinbad*.

Two 20th-century poets are unsurpassed in Hungarian letters. Endre Ady (1877–1919), who is sometimes described as the successor to Petőfi, was a reformer who ruthlessly attacked the complacency and materialism of Hungary at that time, provoking a storm of protest from right-wing nationalists. He died in his flat on V Veres Pálné utca in Pest at the age of 42. The work of the socialist poet Attila József (1905–1937), who was raised in the slums of Ferencváros, expressed the alienation felt by individuals in the modern age; *By the Danube* is brilliant even in English translation.

A recent 'rediscovery' is the late Sándor Márai (1900–89), whose crisp, spare style has single-handedly encouraged worldwide interest in Hungarian literature.

Among Hungary's most important contemporary writers are Imre Kertész (1929–), György Konrád (1933–), Péter Nádas (1942–), Péter Esterházy (1950–) and Magda Szabó (1917–), the most prominent female author writing in Hungary today. Konrád's *A Feast in the Garden* (1985) is an almost autobiographical account of the fate of the Jewish community in a small eastern Hungarian town. *A Book of Memoirs* by Nádas concerns the decline of communism in the style of Thomas Mann. In his *The End of a Family Story*, he uses a child narrator as a filter for the adult experience of 1950s communist Hungary. Esterházy's *Celestial Harmonies* (2000) is a partly autobiographical novel that paints a favourable portrait of the protagonist's father. His subsequent *Revised Edition* (2002) is based on documents revealing his father to have been a government informer during the communist regime. Whoops. Szabó's *The Door* (1987) is the compelling story of a woman writer and the symbiotic relationship she has with her housekeeper.

In 2002 novelist and Auschwitz survivor Kertész was awarded the Nobel Prize for Literature, the first time a Hungarian has ever gained that distinction. Of his eight novels, only three – *Fateless* (1975), *Kaddish for a Child Not Born* (1990) and *Liquidation* (2003) – have been translated into English.

CINEMA

The scarcity of government grants has limited the production of quality Hungarian films to less than 20 in recent years, but a handful of good (and even great) ones still get produced. For classics, look out for anything by the Oscar-winning István Szabó *(Sweet Emma, Dear Böbe, The Taste of Sunshine)*, Miklós Jancsó *(Outlaws)* and Péter Bacsó *(The Witness, Live Show)*.

Other favourites are *Simon Mágus*, the surrealistic epic tale of two magicians and a young woman in Paris directed by Ildikó Enyedi, and her more recent *Tender Interface*, which deals with the brain-drain from Hungary after WWII.

TOP FIVE BUDAPEST FILMS

- *Kontroll* (Inspection; Hungary, 2003) Hungarian-American director Nimród Antal's high-speed romantic thriller set almost entirely in the Budapest metro in which assorted outcasts, lovers and dreamers meet and interact.
- *Evita* (USA, 1996) You'd never know it, but that Buenos Aires cathedral in Alan Parker's opus is the Basilica of St Stephen, the grand, tree-lined boulevard is Andrássy út and the swarthy horse guards belong to the Hungarian cavalry.
- *Ein Lied von Liebe und Tod* (Gloomy Sunday; Germany/Hungary, 1999) German director Rolf Schübel's romantic drama set in a Budapest restaurant just before the Nazi invasion and revolving around the famously depressing tune 'Gloomy Sunday' (p11).
- *Amerikai Rapszódia* (American Rhapsody; Hungary, 2001) Film by Éva Gaŕrdos with Nastassja Kinski and a very young Scarlett Johansson, involving a Budapest couple's escape from communist Hungary and their daughter's later search for identity.
- *Napoléon* (France, 2002) Yves Simoneau's epic film about the French emperor's life starring Gérard Dépardieu, Isabella Rossellini and John Malkovich was filmed in Budapest and is the most expensive European production to date.

Péter Timár's *Csinibaba* is a satirical look at life – and film production quality – during the communist regime. *Zimmer Feri,* set on Lake Balaton, pits a young practical joker against a bunch of loud German tourists; the typo in the title is deliberate. Timár's *6:3* takes viewers back to 1953 to that glorious moment when Hungary defeated England in football (p140). Gábor Herendi's *Something America* is the comic tale of a filmmaking team trying to profit from an expatriate Hungarian who pretends to be a rich producer.

If you're looking for something really different, don't miss *Hukkle* by György Pálfi, a curious film in which dialogue has been replaced with a bizarre cacophony of hiccups, belches, buzzing and grunting. Classic, sinister David Lynch-like film or lad's movie? You decide.

Food & Drink

Food & Drink

A lot has been written about Hungarian food. Some of it has been true, an equal amount downright false, including our all-time favourite told to us by, of course, a Hungarian: 'The world has three essential cuisines – Chinese, French and Hungarian'. Even the 'truisms' of Hungarian cuisine beg qualification. It has had many outside influences but has changed relatively little over the centuries compared with many other styles of cooking. And while cooks here make great use of paprika, that spice's hottest variety (called *csípős*) is pretty tame stuff; a taco with salsa or chicken vindaloo from the corner takeaway will taste a lot more 'fiery' to you.

HISTORY

Budapest's reputation as a food capital of the world dates largely from the late 19th century and, bizarrely, to a certain degree from the chilly days of communism. During the heady period following the promulgation of the Dual Monarchy in 1867 and right up until WWII, food became a passion among well-to-do Budapesters, and writers and poets were generous in their praise of it. This was the 'gilded age' of the famous chef Károly Gundel and the confectioner József Dobos, and of Gypsy violinists such as Jancsi Rigo and Gyula Benczi, when nothing was too extravagant. The world took note and Hungarian restaurants sprouted up in cities across the world – including a 'Café Budapest' in Boston, Massachusetts – complete with their imported Gypsy bands and waiters who sounded like Bela Lugosi.

After WWII, Budapest's gastronomic reputation lived on – most notably because everything that was offered in the other capital cities of the region was so bad. Food here was, as one observer noted, 'a bright spot in a culinary black hole'. But most of the best chefs, including Gundel himself, had voted with their feet and left the country in the 1950s, and restaurants were put under state control. The reputation and the reality of food in Budapest had diverged.

CULTURE

Although still relatively inexpensive by European standards and served in huge portions, Hungarian food today remains heavy and, at times, can be unhealthy. Meat, sour cream and fat – usually pork – abound and, except in season, *saláta* (salad) means a plate of pickled vegetables. Things are changing, however, in the Hungarian capital with more vegetarian and international choices available (see p92).

ETIQUETTE

People in Budapest tend to meet their friends and entertain outside of their homes at cafés and restaurants. Drinking is an important part of social life in the capital of a country that has produced wine and fruit brandies for thousands of years. Consumption is high; only the Luxembourgeois and Irish drink more alcohol per capita in Europe than the Hungarians. Alcoholism in Hungary is not as visible to the outsider as it is, say, in Poland or Russia, but it's there nonetheless; official figures suggest that as much as 9% of the population are fully fledged alcoholics. There is little pressure for others (particularly women) to drink, however, so if you really don't want that glass of apricot brandy that your host has handed you, refuse politely.

It is said that Hungarians don't clink glasses when drinking beer because that's how the Habsburgs celebrated the defeat of Lajos Kossuth in the 1848–49 War of Independence (p43), but most Magyars say that's codswallop.

HOW BUDAPESTERS EAT

Hungarians are for the most part not big eaters of *reggeli* (breakfast), preferring a cup of tea or coffee with an unadorned bread roll at the kitchen table or on the way to work. As it is a meal at which most Magyars hardly excel, expect the worst of hotel breakfasts – ersatz coffee, weak tea, unsweetened lemon water for 'juice', tiny triangles of processed 'cheese' and stale bread. You may be pleasantly surprised, however.

Ebéd (lunch), eaten at around 1pm, was once the main meal of the day and might still consist of two or even three courses. *Vacsora* (dinner or supper) is less substantial when eaten at home, often just sliced meats, cheese and some pickled vegetables.

It's important to know the different styles of eateries to be found in Budapest. An *étterem* is a restaurant with a wide-ranging menu, sometimes including international dishes. A *vendéglő* or *kisvendéglő* is smaller and is supposed to serve inexpensive regional dishes or 'home cooking'. But the name has become 'cute' enough for a lot of large places to use it indiscriminately. An *étkezde* is something like a *vendéglő* but cheaper, smaller and often has counter seating. The term *csárda* originally signified a country inn with a rustic atmosphere, Gypsy music and hearty local dishes. Now any place that hangs up a couple of painted plates and strings a few strands of dry paprika on the wall is a *csárda*.

A *bisztró* is a much cheaper sit-down place that is often *önkiszolgáló* (self-service). A *büfé* is cheaper still with a very limited menu. Here you eat while standing at counters.

Hentesáru bolt (butcher shops) in Budapest sometimes have a *büfé* selling cooked *kolbász* (sausage), *wirsli* (frankfurters), *hurka* (blood sausage or liverwurst), roast chicken, bread and pickled vegetables. Point to what you want; the staff will weigh it all and hand you a slip of paper with the price. You usually pay at the *pénztár* (cashier) and hand the stamped receipt back to the staff for your food. You pay for everything here, including a slice of rye bread and a dollop of mustard for your *kolbász*.

Food stalls, known as a *Laci konyha* (Larry's kitchen) or *pecsenyesütő* (roast ovens) are often near markets or train stations. One of the more popular traditional snacks is *lángos*, deep-fried dough with various toppings (usually cheese and sour cream).

STAPLES & SPECIALITIES

BREAD & NOODLES

It is said that people here will 'eat bread with bread' and *kenyér* (leftover bread) has been used to thicken soups and stews since at least the reign of medieval king Matthias – or so contemporary reports would have us believe – and *kifli* (crescent rolls) gained popularity

Gulyás (goulash), Menza restaurant (p114), Terézváros

during the Turkish occupation. But, frankly, bread available commercially in Budapest is not as memorable as the flour-based *galuska* dumplings and the *tarhonya* (egg barley pasta) served with *pörkölt, paprikás* and *tokány* (see below) dishes.

SOUPS

Most Hungarian meals start with *leves* (soup). As a starter this is usually something relatively light like *gombaleves* (mushroom soup) or *húsgombócleves* (meat-filled dumplings in consommé), but more substantial varieties are beef *gulyásleves* (below) and *bableves,* a thick bean soup usually made with meat, which are sometimes eaten as a main course. Another favourite is *halászlé* (fisherman's soup), a rich soup of poached carp, fish stock, tomatoes, green peppers and paprika.

MEAT & FISH

People here eat an astonishing amount of meat, and 'meat-stuffed meat' is a dish commonly found on Budapest's menus. Pork, beef, veal and poultry are the meats most often encountered and they can be breaded and fried, baked, turned into some paprika-flavoured concoction or simmered in *lecsó,* a tasty mix of peppers, tomatoes and onions (and one of the few sauces here that does not include paprika). Goose livers and legs and turkey breasts – though not much else of either bird – make it on to most menus. A typical menu will have up to 10 pork and beef dishes, a couple of fish ones and usually only one poultry dish. Lamb and mutton are rarely eaten here.

Freshwater fish, such as the indigenous *fogas* (great pike-perch) and the smaller *süllő* from Lake Balaton, and *ponty* (carp) from the nation's rivers and streams, is plentiful but can be expensive in Budapest.

PAPRIKA

Many dishes are seasoned with paprika, a spice as Magyar as St Stephen's right hand (p64); indeed, not only is it used in cooking but it also appears on restaurant tables as a condiment beside the salt and pepper shakers. It's generally quite a mild spice and is used predominantly with sour cream or in *rántás,* a heavy roux of pork lard and flour added to cooked vegetables. *Töltött,* things stuffed with meat and/or rice, such as cabbage or peppers, are cooked in *rántás* as well as in tomato sauce or sour cream.

There are four major types of meat dishes that use paprika. The most famous is *gulyás* (or *gulyásleves*), a thick beef soup cooked with onions, cubed potatoes and paprika and usually eaten as a main course. *Pörkölt,* or 'stew', is closer to what foreigners call 'goulash'; the addition of sour cream, less paprika and white meat such as chicken makes the dish *paprikás. Tokány* is similar to *pörkölt* and *paprikás* except that the meat is not cubed but

TOP FIVE FOOD & WINE BOOKS

- *The Cuisine of Hungary* (George Lang, 1985) Celebrated restaurateur and *bon vivant* Lang offers a comprehensive history of Magyar cooking and examination of its regional differences. His subsequent autobiography, *Nobody Knows the Truffles I've Seen* (1998), is worth purchasing for the title alone.
- *Culinaria Hungary* (Aniko Gegely et al, 2000) This is a beautifully illustrated 320-page tome on all things involving Hungarian food, from soup to nuts and more, and is as prized for its recipes as the history and traditions it describes.
- *The Hungarian Cookbook* (Susan Derecskey, 1987) If you don't need pictures but you do need simple, easy-to-follow recipes for Hungarian comfort food, this practical book is for you.
- *Terra Benedicta: Tokaj and Beyond* (Gábor Rohály et al, 2004) This attractive tome is both a useful source book and a richly illustrated record of Hungarian wine, with regional, illustrative photographs and lots of detail on wineries.
- *The Wines of Hungary* (Alex Liddell, 2003) For a look not just at the wines themselves but the whole picture, this no-nonsense guide is ideal.

is cut into strips, black pepper is on equal footing with the paprika, and bacon, sausage or mushroom are added as flavouring agents.

VEGETABLES

A main course served in a restaurant usually comes with some sort of starch and a little garnish. Vegetables and salads must be ordered separately.

Fresh salad as it's usually known around the world is called *vitamin saláta* here and is generally available when lettuces are in season; almost everything else is *savanyúság* (literally 'sourness'), which can be anything from mildly sour-sweet cucumbers, pickled peppers and almost acid-tasting sauerkraut. It may seem an acquired taste, but such things actually go very well with heavy meat dishes.

Zöldség (boiled vegetables), when they are available, are *angolos zöldség* ('English-style'). The traditional way of preparing vegetables – real Hungarian 'comfort food' and enjoying a major comeback at 'retro-style' eateries across the city – is in *főzelék*, in which peas, green beans, lentils or marrow are fried or boiled and then mixed into a roux with milk and topped with a few slices of meat.

A MAGYAR MATCH MADE IN HEAVEN

The pairing of food with wine is as great an obsession here as it is in Paris. Everyone agrees that sweets like strudel go very well indeed with a glass of Tokaji Aszú, but what is less appreciated is the wonderful synergy that this wine enjoys with savoury foods like foie gras and cheeses such as Roquefort, Stilton and Gorgonzola. A bone-dry Olaszrizling from Badacsony is a superb complement to any fish dish, but especially the pike-perch indigenous to Lake Balaton. Villány Sauvignon Blanc is an excellent accompaniment to goat's cheese.

It would be a shame to 'waste' a big wine like a Vili Papa Cuvée on traditional but simple Hungarian dishes like *gulyás* or *pörkölt;* save it for a more complex or sophisticated meat dish. Try Kékfrankos or Szekszárd Kadarka with these simpler dishes. Cream-based dishes stand up well to late-harvest Furmint, and pork dishes are nice with new Furmint or Kékfrankos. Try Hárslevelű with poultry.

DESSERTS

Budapesters love sweets and consume them with gusto – though more intricate pastries such as *Dobos torta*, a layered chocolate and cream cake with a caramelised brown sugar top, and the wonderful *rétes* (strudel) filled with poppy seeds or cherry preserves, are usually consumed midafternoon in one of Budapest's ubiquitous *cukrászdák* (cake shops or pâtisseries). Desserts more commonly found on restaurant menus include *somlói galuska*, sponge cake with chocolate and whipped cream, and *Gundel palacsinta*, flambéed pancake with chocolate and nuts.

DRINKS

A *kávéháv* is literally a 'coffee house' – ie a café (see boxed text, p126) – and the best place to stop if you just want something hot or soft and cold. An *eszpresszó*, along with being a type of coffee, is essentially a coffee house too, but it usually also sells alcoholic drinks and light snacks. A *cukrászda* serves cakes, pastries and ice cream as well as hot and cold drinks.

To sample some local brew or vintage try visiting the *sörözők*, pubs with *csapolt sör* (draught beer) available on tap; *borozók*, establishments (usually dives) serving wine; and *pincék*, which can be either beer or wine cellars but are usually the latter and also called *bor pincék*.

NONALCOHOLIC DRINKS

Most international soft drink brands are available in Budapest, but *ásvány víz* (mineral water) seems to be the most popular libation for teetotallers in cafés, pubs and bars. Fruit juice is usually canned or boxed fruit 'drink' with lots of sugar added, though some us are addicted to the cherry variety.

Budapesters drink a tremendous amount of *kávé* (coffee) – as a *feketes* (single black), a *dupla* (double) or *tejes kávé* (with milk). Most cafés now serve some variation of cappuccino. Decaffeinated coffee is *koffeinmentes kávé*.

Black tea (tea; pronounced '*tay*-ah') is not as popular as coffee in Budapest; in fact, it can often be difficult to find 'English' tea in small grocery stores, though you'll always be able to choose from a wide range of herbal teas and fruit tisanes. People here never add milk to tea, preferring lemon, honey or even rum.

ALCOHOLIC DRINKS

Hungarians are big drinkers and enjoy a tipple at the drop of a hat (or a forint or a glass). Beer, especially lager, is extremely popular with the young, older folk drink homemade fruit-flavoured brandies and wine is drunk by everyone.

Beer

Hungary produces a number of its own beers for national distribution, and the most common ones are Dreher, Kőbányai and Arany Ászok, all brewed in or near Budapest. Bottled Austrian, German and Czech beers are readily available. Locally brewed and imported beer here is almost always lager, though occasionally you'll come across Dreher Barna, a 'brown' or stout.

At a pub, beer is served in a *pohár* (0.3L) or a *korsó* (0.4L or 0.5L). In an old-fashioned wine bar, the wine is ladled out by the *deci* (decilitre, 0.1L), but in more modern places it comes by the ill-defined *pohár* (glass).

Brandy & Liqueur

Pálinka is a strong (about 40% alcohol) brandy or *eau de vie* distilled from a variety of fruits but most commonly from apricots or plums. There are many different types and qualities, but among our favourites is *Óbarack*, the double-distilled 'Old Apricot', the kind made with *málna* (raspberry) and anything with *kóser* (kosher) on the label.

Hungarian liqueurs are usually unbearably sweet and artificial tasting, though Zwack (p70) is reliable. Zwack also produces Unicum, a bitter aperitif that has been around since 1790. Habsburg emperor Joseph II supposedly named it when he first tasted it, exclaiming 'Das ist ein Unikum!' (This is a unique drink!).

Pálinka, *Magyar Pálinka Ház (p149), Józsefváros*

Wine

Wine has been produced in Hungary for thousands of years, and it remains very important both economically and socially. You'll find it available by the glass or bottle everywhere in Budapest – at very basic wine bars, food stalls, restaurants, supermarkets and 24-hour grocery stores – usually at reasonable prices. If you're seriously into wine, visit the speciality wine shops on both sides of the Danube and reviewed in the Shopping chapter.

Before WWII Hungarian wine was much in demand throughout Europe, but with the advent of socialism and mass production, quality went down the drain. Most of what wasn't consumed at home went to the Soviet Union where, frankly, they were prepared to drink anything. Political and economic circumstances provided little incentive to upgrade antiquated standards of wine-making. All of that has changed over the past decade and

MENU READER

Restaurant menus are often translated into German and English, with mixed degrees of success. The following is a sample menu as it would appear in many restaurants in Budapest. It's far from complete, but it gives a good idea of what to expect. The main categories on a menu include those below; *készételek* are ready-made dishes that are just heated up while *frissensültek* are made to order. Other words you might encounter are *halételek* or *halak* (fish dishes), *szárnyasok* (poultry dishes), *édességek* (another word for 'dessert') and *sajtok* (cheeses).

Előételek (Starters)

hortobágyi palacsinta – meat-filled pancakes with paprika sauce
libamájpástétom – goose-liver pâté
rántott gombafejek – breaded, fried mushrooms

Levesek (Soups)

bableves – bean soup
csontleves – consommé
gombaleves – mushroom soup
húsgombócleves – meat-filled dumplings in consommé
jókai bableves – bean soup with meat
meggyleves – cold sour-cherry soup (in summer)
újházi tyúkhúsleves – chicken broth with noodles

Saláták (Salads)

cékla saláta – pickled beetroot salad
ecetes almapaprika – pickled peppers
paradicsom saláta – tomato salad
uborka saláta – sliced pickled-cucumber salad
vegyes saláta – mixed salad of pickles
vitamin saláta – seasonal mixed salad

Zöldség (Vegetables)

gomba – mushroom
káposzta – cabbage
karfiol – cauliflower
sárgarépa – carrot
spárga – asparagus
spenót – spinach
zöldbab – string (green) bean
zöldborsó – pea

Köretek (Side Dishes)

főzelék – Hungarian-style vegetables
galuska – dumplings
rizi-bizi – rice with peas
sült hasábburgonya – chips (French fries)

Készételek (Ready-Made Dishes)

csirke paprikás – paprika chicken
gulyás – beef goulash soup
halászlé – spicy fish soup
pörkölt – stew (many types)
töltött paprika/káposzta – stuffed peppers/cabbage

Frissensültek (Dishes Made to Order)

bécsiszelet – Wiener schnitzel
brassói aprópecsenye – braised pork Braşov-style
cigánypecsenye – roast pork Gypsy-style
csülök – smoked pork knuckle
fogas – Balaton pike-perch
rántott hátszínszelet – breaded, fried rump steak
rántott ponty – breaded, fried carp
rántott pulykamell – breaded, fried turkey breast
sertésborda – pork chop
sült csirkecomb – roast chicken thigh
sült libamáj – fried goose liver

Édességek (Desserts)

Dobos torta – multilayered 'Dobos' chocolate and cream cake with caramelised brown sugar top
Gundel palacsinta – 'Gundel' flambéed pancake with chocolate and nuts
rétes – strudel
somlói galuska – Somló-style sponge cake with chocolate and whipped cream

Gyümölcs (Fruit)

alma – apple
cseresznye – sweet cherry
(földi)eper – strawberry
körte – pear
málna – raspberry
meggy – sour (Morello) cherry
narancs – orange
őszibarack – peach
sárgabarack – apricot
szilva – plum
szőlő – grape

Cooking Methods

főtt or *főve* – boiled
főzelék – frying or boiling vegetables, then mixing into a roux with cream
füstölt – smoked
pirított – braised
rántva or *rántott* – breaded and fried
roston – grilled
sült or *sütve* – fried or roasted

a half. Small- to medium-sized family-owned wineries such as Tiffán, Bock, Szeremley, Thummerer and Szepsy are now producing very fine wines indeed.

When choosing a Hungarian wine, look for the words *minőségi bor* (quality wine) or *különleges minőségű bor* (premium quality wine), Hungary's version of the French quality regulation *appellation controlée*. Generally speaking, *évjárat* (vintage) has become important only recently so should not be much of a concern just yet.

The first word of the name on the label of a wine bottle indicates where the wine comes from while the second word is the grape variety (eg Villányi Kékfrankos) or the type or brand of wine (eg Tokaji Aszú, Szekszárdi Bikavér). Other important words that you'll see include: *édes* (sweet), *fehér* (white), *félédes* (semisweet), *félszáraz* (semidry or medium), *pezsgő* (sparkling), *száraz* (dry) and *vörös* (red).

Hungary now counts 22 distinct wine-growing areas in Transdanubia, the Balaton region, the Northern Uplands and on the Great Plain. They range in size from tiny Somló (essentially just one hill) in Western Transdanubia, to the vast vineyards of the Kunság on the Southern Plain, with its sandy soil nurturing more than a third of all the grapevines growing in the country.

Of course it's all a matter of taste, but the most distinctive red wines come from Villány and Szekszárd in Southern Transdanubia and the best whites are produced around Lake Balaton and in Somló. The reds from Eger and sweet whites from Tokaj are much better known abroad, however, and these two regions are the most dynamic when it comes to wine production.

CELEBRATING WITH FOOD

Traditional culture, particularly where it involves food, is not exactly thriving in Hungary, though a popular event for Budapesters with tenuous ties to the countryside is the *disznótor,* the slaughtering of a pig followed by an orgy of feasting and drinking. (The butchering, gratefully, is done somewhere out the back by an able-bodied peasant.) The celebration can even boast its own dish: *disznótoros káposzta,* which is stuffed cabbage served with freshly made sausages. Wine festivals, now mostly commercial events with rock bands and the like, occur during the harvest in September and October and are always a good excuse for getting sloshed (see p10).

It's traditional to eat *csirke paprikás* (paprika chicken) and *sajtos rétes* (strudel) at name-day feasts (see p12).

History

History

THE RECENT PAST

THE REPUBLIC OF HUNGARY REBORN

It may come as a surprise to some, but Budapest has only been the capital of the Republic of Hungary for just over a decade and a half – since 23 October 1989, the 33rd anniversary of the 1956 Uprising. For some four decades before this, it had been the chief city of the socialist People's Republic of Hungary.

At its party congress in February 1989, the ruling Hungarian Socialist Workers' Party – having seen the handwriting on the wall – changed its name to the Hungarian Socialist Party (MSZP) and later in the year 'generously' agreed to surrender its monopoly on power and to hold elections. Its new programme advocated not jailing dissidents or shooting people who attempted to flee across the border but social democracy and a free-market economy. Most voters saw them as evil, two-faced despots who had just changed their outfit; hollow promises were not enough to shake off the stigma of four decades of autocratic rule.

The 1990 election was instead won by the centrist Hungarian Democratic Forum (MDF), which advocated a gradual transition to capitalism and was led by a softly spoken former museum curator, Jozsef Antall. The social-democratic Alliance of Free Democrats (SZDSZ), which had called for much faster change, came in a distant second with 18% of the vote. As Gorbachev looked on, Hungary changed political systems as if it were clothing and the last Soviet troops left Hungarian soil in June 1991. Street names in Budapest such as Lenin körút and Marx tér ended up on the rubbish tip of history and monuments to 'glorious workers' and 'esteemed leaders' were packed off to a socialist-realist zoo called Statue Park (p62).

In coalition with two smaller parties – the Independent Smallholders (FKgP) and the Christian Democrats (KDNP) – the MDF provided Hungary with sound government during its painful transition to a full market economy. Those years saw Hungary's northern (Czechoslovakia) and southern (Yugoslavia) neighbours split along ethnic lines; Prime Minister Antall did little to improve Hungary's relations with Slovakia, Romania or Yugoslavia by claiming to be the 'emotional and spiritual' prime minister of the large Magyar minorities in those countries. It was also a relatively lawless period so fittingly described in Julian Rubenstein's *Ballad of the Whiskey Robber* (see p41).

Despite initial successes in curbing inflation and lowering interest rates, a host of economic problems slowed the pace of development, and the government's laissez-faire policies did not help. Like most people in the region, Hungarians had unrealistically expected a much faster improvement in their living standards.

In the May 1994 elections the MSZP, led by Gyula Horn, won an absolute majority in parliament. This in no way implied a return to the past, and Horn was quick to point out that it was in fact his party that had initiated the whole reform process in the first place. (As foreign minister in 1989, Horn had played a key role in opening the border with Austria; see p48) The following year, Árpád Göncz of the SZDSZ was elected for a second five-year term as president of the republic.

THE ROAD TO EUROPE

After its dire results in the 1994 elections, the Federation of Young Democrats (Fidesz) – which until 1993 limited membership to those aged under 35 in order to emphasise a past untainted by communism, privilege and corruption – moved to the right and added 'MPP'

TIMELINE

AD 895–96	1000
Nomadic Magyar tribes enter and settle in the Carpathian Basin	Stephen (István) is crowned 'Christian King' of Hungary on Christmas Day

(Hungarian Civic Party) to its name to attract the support of the burgeoning middle class. In the elections of 1998, during which it campaigned for closer integration with Europe, Fidesz-MPP won government by forming a coalition with the MDF and the agrarian and conservative FKgP. The party's youthful leader, Viktor Orbán, was named prime minister.

Despite the astonishing economic growth and other gains made by the coalition government, the electorate grew hostile to Fidesz-MPP's – and Orbán's – strongly nationalistic rhetoric and perceived arrogance. In April 2002 the largest turnout of voters in Hungarian history unseated the government in the country's most closely fought election ever and returned the MSZP, now allied with the SZDSZ, to power under Prime Minister Péter Medgyessy, a free-market advocate who had served as finance minister in the early Horn government. In August 2004, amid revelations that he had served as a counterintelligence officer in the late 1970s and early 1980s while working in the finance ministry, Medgyessy resigned, the first collapse of a government in Hungary's postcommunist history. Sports Minister Ferenc Gyurcsány of the MSZP was named in his place. In April 2006 the MSZP-SZDSZ coalition became the first government to win consecutive general elections since 1989.

Hungary joined NATO in 1999 and, with nine other 'accession' countries, was admitted into the EU in May 2004. In June 2005 parliament elected László Sólyom, a law professor and founding member of the MDF, as the third president of the republic to succeed Ferenc Mádl.

FROM THE BEGINNING

Budapest has been called 'the Janus-faced city' because it looks in opposing directions. It is at the same time one of the oldest and one of the youngest cities in Europe. The Romans settled here early in the 1st century AD and built what would eventually become one of their most thriving metropolises. At the other end of the spectrum, the story of modern Budapest only begins in 1873 when hilly, residential Buda and historic Óbuda on the western bank of the Danube (Duna) River merged with flat, industrial Pest on the eastern side to form what was at first called Pest-Buda. But, of course, a whole lot more happened here before then.

EARLY INHABITANTS

The Carpathian Basin, in which Hungary lies, has been populated for hundreds of thousands of years. Bone fragments found and exhibited at Vértesszőlős near Tata, some 70km northwest of Budapest, in the 1960s, and believed to be half a million years old, suggest that Palaeolithic humans were attracted to the area by its thermal springs and the abundance of mammoth, buffalo and reindeer. The capital may have been something of a slow starter, however; the earliest evidence of human settlement in the greater Budapest area is the remains of a Neanderthal hunting camp in the Érd Valley to the southwest. Complete with tools, cutters and scrapers, the camp is thought to date back 50,000 years.

During the Ice Age, temperatures in the area rarely exceeded 15°C even in the height of summer. During the Neolithic period (around 5000 BC), a warming of the climate forced much of the indigenous wildlife to migrate north. The domestication of animals and the first forms of agriculture appeared, as they did in much of Central Europe. The first permanent settlement in this area – on the Buda side near the Danube – dates from between 4600 and 3900 BC. Remains from this culture, including bone utensils, fishing nets and even a primitive loom, have been unearthed as far north as Békásmegyer and as far south as Nagytétény.

Indo-European tribes from the Balkans stormed the Carpathian Basin from the south in horse-drawn wheeled carts in about 2000 BC, bringing with them copper tools and weapons. After the introduction of more durable bronze, forts were built and a military elite

1222
King Andrew II signs the Golden Bull, according the nobility more rights and powers

1241–42
Mongols sweep across the country, killing some 100,000 people in Pest and Óbuda alone

Ruins of Roman military amphitheatre (p60), Óbuda

developed. The remains of several settlements dating from this time have been uncovered on Csepel Island in the Danube.

Over the next millennium, invaders from the west (Illyrians and Thracians) and the east (Scythians) brought iron, but the metal was not in common use until the Celts arrived in the area in about the 3rd century BC, settling at Békásmegyer and Óbuda, which they called Ak Ink (Ample Water), and erecting one of their signature *oppida* (palisaded settlements) on Gellért Hill. The Celts introduced glass and crafted some of the fine gold jewellery that can still be seen in the Hungarian National Museum (p69).

Around the beginning of the Christian era, the Romans conquered the area west of the Danube and established the province of Pannonia. Subsequent victories over the Celts extended their domination, and the province was divided into Pannonia Superior and Pannonia Inferior. The Romans brought writing, viticulture and stone architecture to the area, and at the end of the 1st century AD established Aquincum, a key military garrison and trading settlement along the Danube in today's Óbuda.

Aquincum (p59) became the administrative seat of Pannonia Inferior in AD 106 and a fully fledged colony in 194. A fortress was built at Contra Aquincum in what is now V Március 15 tér (Map p224) in Pest and the proconsul's palace on a secure island in the Danube (now Óbuda Island; Map pp226–7). Villages nearby, such as Vindonianus (Békásmegyer) and Vicus Basoretensis (Kiscell), were populated by Celts, who were not granted Roman citizenship.

THE GREAT MIGRATIONS

The first of the so-called Great Migrations of nomadic peoples from Asia reached the eastern outposts of the Roman Empire in Dacia (now Romania) late in the 2nd century AD. Within two centuries, the Romans were forced by the Huns, whose short-lived empire was established by Attila, to flee Aquincum and abandon the rest of Pannonia. Aquincum offered little protection to the civilian population; in the late 430s, the Huns razed it.

After the death of Attila in 453, Germanic tribes such as the Ostrogoths, Gepids and Longobards (or Lombards) occupied the region for the next century and a half until the Avars, a powerful Turkic people, gained control of the Carpathian Basin in the late 6th century. At first they settled on the Pest plains, but their chieftains soon established their main base at the northern end of Csepel Island.

The Avars were overcome by Charlemagne in 796 and the area around Budapest and the Danube Bend was incorporated into the Frankish empire. By that time, the Carpathian Basin was virtually unpopulated except for scattered groups of Turkic and Germanic tribes on the plains and Slavs in the northern hills.

THE MAGYARS & THE CONQUEST OF THE CARPATHIAN BASIN

The origin of the Magyars, as the Hungarians call themselves, is a complicated issue, not helped by the similarity (in English, at least) of the words 'Hun' and 'Hungary', which are *not* related. One thing is certain: Magyars belong to the Finno-Ugric group of peoples, who inhabited the forests somewhere between the middle Volga River and the Ural Mountains in western Siberia as early as 4000 BC.

1458–90

Medieval Hungary enjoys a golden age under the enlightened reign of King Matthias Corvinus

1514

Peasant uprising is crushed, with 70,00 people – including leader György Dózsa – killed

By about 2000 BC, population growth had forced the Finnish-Estonian branch to move west, ultimately reaching the Baltic Sea. The Ugrians moved from the southeastern slopes of the Urals into the valleys of the region, and switched from hunting and fishing to farming and raising livestock, especially horses. Their equestrian skills proved useful half a millennium later when more climatic changes brought drought, forcing them to move north onto the steppes.

On the grasslands, the Ugrians turned to nomadic herding. After 500 BC, by which time the use of iron had become commonplace among the tribes, a group moved west to the area of Bashkiria in Central Asia. Here they lived among Persians and Bulgars and began referring to themselves as Magyars (from the Finno-Ugric words *mon* – to speak – and *er* – man).

After several centuries, another group split away and moved south to the Don River under the control of the Turkic Khazars. Here they lived among different groups under a tribal alliance called *onogur*, or '10 peoples'. This is thought to be the origin of the word 'Hungary' in English and (more obviously) 'Ungarn' in German. The Magyars' last migration before the so-called *honfoglalás* (conquest) of the Carpathian Basin brought them to what modern Hungarians call the Etelköz, the region between the Dnieper and lower Danube Rivers north of the Black Sea.

Nomadic groups of Magyars probably reached the Carpathian Basin as early as the mid-9th century AD, acting as mercenaries for various armies. It is believed that while the men were away during one such campaign in about 889, a fierce people from the Asiatic steppe called the Pechenegs allied themselves with the Bulgars and attacked the Etelköz settlements. When they were attacked again in about 895, seven tribes under the leadership of Árpád – the *gyula* or chief military commander – struck out for the Carpathian Basin. They crossed the Verecke Pass in today's Ukraine sometime between 896 and 898.

Five of the seven tribes settled in the area that is now Budapest and the two principal leaders of the tribes made their bases here. Árpád established his seat on Csepel; according to the chronicler Anonymous, it was Árpád's overseer, a Turkic Cuman called Csepel, who gave his name to the island. Árpád's brother, Kurszán, the chief *táltos* (shaman), based himself in Óbuda. On Kurszán's death, Árpád took all power for himself and moved his seat to Óbuda; Buda and Pest were no more than small villages.

The Magyars had met almost no resistance in the Carpathian Basin. Being highly skilled at riding and shooting (a common Christian prayer during the Dark Ages was 'Save us, O Lord, from the arrows of the Hungarians'), they began plundering and pillaging in all directions, taking slaves and amassing booty. Their raids took them as far as Spain, northern Germany and southern Italy, but they were stopped at the Battle of Augsburg by the German king Otto I in 955.

BLAME IT ON THE BIRD

The ancient Magyars were strong believers in magic and celestial intervention, and the *táltos* (shaman) enjoyed an elevated position in their society. Certain animals – for example bears, stags and wolves – were totemic, and it was taboo to mention them directly by name. Thus the wolf was 'the long-tailed one' and the stag the 'large-antlered one'. In other cases the original Magyar for an animal deemed sacred was replaced with a foreign loan word: *medve* for 'bear' comes from the Slavic *medved*.

No other ancient totemic animal was more scared than the *turul*, a hawklike bird that supposedly impregnated Emese, the grandmother of Árpád. That legend can be viewed in many ways: as an attempt to foster a sense of common origin and group identity in the ethnically heterogeneous population of the time; as an effort to bestow a sacred origin on the House of Árpád and its rule; or just as a good story – not dissimilar from the one about the Virgin Mary begotten with child by the Holy Spirit anthropomorphised as a dove.

In the recent past, the fearsome-looking *turul* has been used as a symbol by the far right – much to the distress of average Hungarians, who simply look upon it as their heraldic 'eagle' or 'lion'.

1526

Hungary is defeated at the Battle of Mohács; the Turkish occupation lasting more than a century and a half begins

1541

Buda falls to the Ottomans; Hungary is partitioned and shared by the Turks, the Habsburgs and the Transylvanian princes

This and subsequent defeats – raids on Byzantium were ended in 970 – left the Magyar tribes in disarray, and they had to choose between their more powerful neighbours to form an alliance: Byzantium to the south and east or the Holy Roman Empire to the west. Individual Magyar chieftains began acting independently, but in 973 Prince Géza, Árpád's great-grandson, asked the Holy Roman emperor Otto II to send Catholic missionaries to Hungary. Géza was baptised in his capital city, Esztergom, 46km upriver from Budapest, as was his son Vajk, who took the Christian name Stephen (István). When Géza died, Stephen ruled as prince, but three years later was crowned 'Christian King' Stephen I, on Christmas Day in 1000, with a crown sent from Rome by Otto's erstwhile tutor, Pope Sylvester II. Hungary the kingdom and Hungary the nation had been born.

KING STEPHEN I & THE ÁRPÁD DYNASTY

Stephen ruthlessly set about consolidating royal authority by expropriating the land of the clan chieftains and establishing a system of *megyek* (counties) protected by *várok* (fortified castles). Much land was transferred to loyal (mostly Germanic) knights, and the crown began minting coins. Stephen did not find the area of Budapest suitable as a base; he made his seat at Székesfehérvár, 66km to the southwest. Esztergom remained the religious centre.

Shrewdly, Stephen sought the support of the Church and, to hasten the conversion of the populace, he ordered one in every 10 villages to build a church. He also established 10 episcopates throughout the land. Monasteries staffed by foreign scholars were set up around the country; in Óbuda it was the religious Chapter of Saint Peter. By the time of Stephen's death in 1038 (he was canonised less than 50 years later), Hungary was a nascent Christian nation. But pockets of rebellion remained; in 1046 a Venetian-born bishop named Gerard (Gellért in Hungarian), who had been brought to Hungary by Stephen himself, was hurled to his death from a Buda hilltop in a spiked barrel by pagan Magyars resisting conversion. Gellért Hill (Map p220) now bears the bishop's name.

The next two and a half centuries – the reign of the House of Árpád – would further test the new kingdom. The period was one of relentless struggles between rival pretenders to the throne, which weakened the young nation's defences against its more powerful neighbours. There was a brief hiatus under King Ladislas I (László; r 1077–95), who fended off attacks from Byzantium, and under his successor Koloman the Bookish (Könyves Kálmán), who encouraged literature, art and the writing of chronicles until his death in 1116.

Tension flared again when the Byzantine emperor made a grab for Hungary's provinces in Dalmatia and Croatia, which it had acquired by the early 12th century. He was stopped by Béla III (r 1172–96), who had a permanent residence built at Esztergom (by then an alternative royal seat to Székesfehérvár), but was headquartered at Óbuda. Béla's son Andrew II (András; r 1205–35), however, weakened the crown when he gave in to local barons' demands for more land in order to fund his crusades. This led to the Golden Bull, a kind of Magna Carta signed at Székesfehérvár in 1222, which limited some of the king's powers in favour of the nobility, recognised the 'Hungarian nation' and allowed for a diet, or assembly, of nobles to meet regularly in a meadow in Pest. It was during Andrew's reign that Óbuda grew from just a centrally located town to a royal and military seat.

When Béla IV (r 1235–70) tried to regain the estates that Andrew had forfeited, the barons were able to oppose him on equal terms. Fearing Mongol expansion and realising he could not count on local help, Béla looked to the west and brought in German and Slovak settlers. In March 1241 Béla amassed his troops at Óbuda and crossed over into Pest. But his efforts were in vain. The Mongols, who had raced through the country as easily as the Magyars had conquered the Carpathian Basin some 2½ centuries before, attacked from every direction. By the end of the final attack in January 1242, Pest and Óbuda had been burned to the ground and some 100,000 people killed.

To rebuild the nascent royal capital as quickly as possible after the Mongol retreat, Béla, known as the 'second founding father', again encouraged Germans and Saxons to settle

1686	1699
Austrian and Hungarian forces liberate Buda from the Turks with the help of the Polish army	Last Turks are driven from Hungarian soil by Eugene of Savoy

Kings and knights adorn the walls of the Basilica of St Stephen (p64), Lipótváros

here. He also ordered those still living in Pest and Óbuda to relocate to Castle Hill and build a fortified town there. Béla proclaimed Buda a municipality by royal charter in 1244 and bestowed civic rights on the citizens of Pest in 1255; another century would go by before Óbuda's citizens won the same rights. By the start of the 14th century, all three had begun to develop into major towns.

But Béla did not always play his cards right. In a bid to appease the lesser nobility, he handed over large tracts of land to the barons. This enhanced their position and bids for more independence even further. At the time of Béla's death in 1270, anarchy ruled. The Árpád line died out with the death of the heirless Andrew III in 1301.

MEDIEVAL BUDAPEST

The struggle for the Hungarian throne after the death of Andrew III involved several European dynasties, but it was Charles Robert (Károly Róbert) of the French House of Anjou who finally won out (with the pope's blessing) in 1307 and was crowned in Buda a year later. He didn't stay there long though; until his death in 1342, Charles Robert ruled from a palace he had built on the Danube at Visegrád, 42km to the northwest. Buda would not play a leading role in Hungarian history for another five decades, but after that it would never look back. In the meantime, Pest had started to develop as a town of wealthy and independent burghers; by 1406 it had its own royal charter and full independence from Buda.

Under Charles Robert's son and successor, Louis the Great (Nagy Lajos; r 1342–82), the kingdom returned to a policy of conquest. A brilliant military strategist, Louis acquired territory in the Balkans as far as Dalmatia and Romania and, through an alliance, as far north as Poland. But his successes were short-lived and the menace of the Ottoman Turks increased.

As Louis had no sons, one of his daughters, Mary (Mária), succeeded him. This was deemed to be unacceptable by the barons, who rose up against the 'petticoat throne'. Within a short time, Mary's husband, Sigismund (Zsigmond; r 1387–1437) of Luxembourg, was crowned king. Sigismund's long reign brought peace at home, and there was a great flowering of Gothic art and architecture. Sigismund enlarged the Royal Palace on Castle Hill, founded a university at Óbuda (1389), oversaw the construction of the first pontoon bridge over the Danube (until then the only way to cross the river was by ferry) and set national standards of measurement, including the 'Buda pound' (490g) for weight and the 'Buda *icce*'

1703–11	1848–49
Ferenc Rákóczi II fights and loses a war of independence against the Habsburgs	War of Independence; Lajos Batthyány and 13 of his generals are executed for their role

(about 0.85L) for liquids. But despite these advances and his enthronement as Holy Roman emperor in 1433, he was unable to stop the march of the Turks up through the Balkans.

A Transylvanian general born of a Wallachian (Romanian) soldier, János Hunyadi began his career at the court of Sigismund. When Vladislav I (Úlászló) of the Polish Jagiellon dynasty was killed fighting the Turks at Varna (now Bulgaria), Hunyadi was declared regent. His victory over the Turks at Belgrade (Hungarian: Nándorfehérvár) in 1456 checked the Ottoman advance into Hungary for 70 years and assured the coronation of his son Matthias (Mátyás), the greatest ruler of medieval Hungary.

Matthias, nicknamed 'the Raven' (Corvinus) from his coat of arms, ruled from 1458 to 1490. Wisely, he maintained a mercenary force of up to 10,000 soldiers through taxation of the nobility, and this 'Black Army' (one of the first standing armies in Europe) conquered Moravia, Bohemia and even parts of Austria. Not only did Matthias Corvinus make Hungary one of Central Europe's leading powers, but under his rule Buda enjoyed something of a golden age and for the first time became the true focus of the nation. His second wife, Beatrice, the daughter of the king of Naples, brought artisans from Italy who completely rebuilt, extended and fortified the Royal Palace; the beauty and sheer size of the residence astonished visitors, and its royal library of more than 2000 codices and incunabula became a major cultural and artistic centre of Renaissance Europe.

But while Matthias busied himself with centralising power for the crown in the capital, he ignored the growing Turkish threat. His successor Vladislav II (Úlászló; r 1490–1516) was unable to maintain even royal authority as the members of the diet, which met to approve royal decrees, squandered royal funds, sold off the royal library and expropriated land. In May 1514, what had begun as a crusade organised by the power-hungry archbishop of Esztergom, Tamás Bakócz, turned into an uprising against the landlords by peasants who rallied near Pest under their leader, György Dózsa.

The revolt was brutally repressed, some 70,000 peasants were tortured and executed, and Dózsa himself was fried alive on a red-hot iron throne. The retrograde Tripartitum Law that followed in 1522 codified the rights and privileges of the barons and nobles, reduced the peasants to perpetual serfdom and banned them from bearing arms. By the time Louis II (Lajos) took the throne in 1516 at the tender age of nine, he couldn't rely on either side.

THE BATTLE OF MOHÁCS & TURKISH OCCUPATION

The defeat of Louis' ragtag army by the Ottoman Turks at Mohács in 1526 is a watershed in Hungarian history. On the battlefield near this small town in Southern Transdanubia, some 195km south of Budapest, a relatively prosperous and independent Hungary died, sending the nation into a tailspin of partition, foreign domination and despair that in some respects can still be felt today.

It would be unfair to put all the blame on the weak and indecisive boy-king Louis or on his commander-in-chief Pál Tomori, the archbishop of Kalocsa. Bickering among the nobility and the brutal crackdown of the Dózsa uprising a dozen years earlier had severely weakened Hungary's military power, and there was virtually nothing left in the royal coffers. By 1526, Ottoman sultan Suleiman the Magnificent (r 1520–66) had taken much of the Balkans, including Belgrade, and was poised to march on Buda with a force of some 80,000 men.

Unable – or unwilling – to wait for reinforcements from Transylvania under the command of his rival John Szapolyai (Zápolyai János), Louis rushed from Buda with a motley army of 26,000 men of mixed nationalities to battle the Turks and was soundly thrashed in less than two hours. Along with bishops, nobles and an estimated 20,000 soldiers, the king himself was killed – crushed by his horse while trying to retreat across a stream.

The Turks then turned north, sacking and burning Buda before retreating. John Szapolyai, who had sat out the battle in the castle at Tokaj, was crowned king three months later but, despite grovelling before the Turks, he was never able to exploit the power he

1867	1896
Act of Compromise creates Dual Monarchy of Austria (the empire), based in Vienna, and Hungary (the kingdom), seat in Budapest	Millennium of the Magyar conquest of the Carpathian Basin is marked by a six-month exhibition in City Park

TOP FIVE HISTORY BOOKS

- *An Illustrated History of Budapest* (Géza Buzinkay, 1998) This large, illustrated and somewhat lightweight tome is an easy entry to the complicated history of the Hungarian capital.
- *Budapest 1900: A Historical Portrait of a City and Its Culture* (John Lukacs, 1990) This classic is an illustrated social history of the capital at the height of its *fin-de-siècle* glory.
- *The Siege of Budapest: 100 Days in WWII* (Kriztián Ungváry, 2005) Ungváry examines the battle to capture a major European capital often overlooked in favour of Warsaw or Berlin.
- *In the Name of the Working Class: The Inside Story of the Hungarian Revolution* (Sándor Kopásci, 1987) Though hard to find, this is a very readable account of the events leading to the 1956 Uprising revolution by Budapest's then chief of police, Sándor Kopásci, who was imprisoned, given amnesty in 1963 and emigrated to Canada in 1975.
- *Ballad of the Whiskey Robber* (Julian Rubinstein, 2005) A rollicking rollercoaster ride of a read, telling the almost unbelievable story of one Attila Ambrus, who takes up bank robbing when not playing professional ice hockey. It's a true-to-life portrait of what was (and we experienced) the 'Wild East' of Budapest in the early 1990s.

had so desperately sought. As would be the case as late as the mid-20th century, greed, self-interest and over-ambition had led Hungary to defeat itself.

After the Turks returned and occupied Buda in 1541, Hungary was divided into three parts. The central section, with Buda – Budun to the Turks – as the provincial seat, went to the Ottomans while parts of Transdanubia and what is now Slovakia were governed by the Austrian House of Habsburg and assisted by the Hungarian nobility based at Bratislava (Hungarian: Pozsony). The principality of Transylvania east of the Tisza River prospered as a vassal state of the Ottoman Empire. This division of the country would remain in place for almost a century and a half.

The Turkish occupation was marked by constant fighting among the three divisions: Catholic 'Royal Hungary' was pitted not only against the Muslim Turks but the Protestant Transylvanian princes as well. Although Habsburg Hungary enjoyed something of a cultural renaissance during this period, the Turkish-occupied part and Buda itself suffered greatly, with many people fleeing the town to Pest, where some churches remained. The Turks did little building in Buda apart from a few bathhouses, dervish monasteries and tombs and city walls; for the most part, they used existing civic buildings for administration and converted churches into mosques. Matthias Church (p55) on Castle Hill, for example, was hastily converted into the Büyük Cami, or 'Great Mosque', and the heart of the Royal Palace became a gunpowder store and magazine. In 1578 lightning struck and much of the Danube wing was reduced to rubble.

Turkish power began to wane in the 17th century, and with the help of the Polish army, some 45,000 Austrian and Hungarian forces advanced down both banks of the Danube from Štúrovo (Hungarian: Párkány), now in Slovakia, to liberate Buda in 1686. An imperial army under Eugene of Savoy wiped out the last Turkish army in Hungary at the Battle of Zenta (now Senta in Serbia) 11 years later. Peace was signed with the Turks at Karlowitz (Serbia) in 1699.

HABSBURG RULE

The expulsion of the Turks did not result in a free and independent Hungary. Buda and the rest of the country were under military occupation and governed from Bratislava, and the policies of the Catholic Habsburgs' Counter-Reformation and heavy taxation further alienated the nobility. In 1703 – the very year in which both Buda and Pest regained their privileges as royal free towns – the Transylvanian prince Ferenc Rákóczi II raised an army of *kuruc* (Hungarian mercenaries) against the Habsburgs. The war dragged on for eight years, during which time the rebels 'deposed' the Austrians as rulers of Hungary. But superior imperial forces and lack of funds forced the *kuruc* forces to negotiate a separate peace with

1918
Austria-Hungary loses WWI in November and the political system collapses; Hungary declares itself a republic

1920
Treaty of Trianon carves up much of central Europe, reducing historical Hungary by almost two-thirds

COUNT OF ALL KNOWLEDGE

The contributions that Count István Széchenyi made to Hungary were enormous and extremely varied. In his seminal 1830 work *Hitel* (meaning 'credit' and based on *hit*, or 'trust'), he advocated sweeping economic reforms and the abolition of serfdom (he himself had distributed the bulk of his property to landless peasants two years earlier). The Chain Bridge, the design of which Széchenyi helped push through parliament, was the first permanent link between Buda and Pest and for the first time everyone – nobles included – had to pay a toll.

Széchenyi was instrumental in straightening the serpentine Tisza River, which rescued half of Hungary's arable land from flooding and erosion, and his work made the Danube navigable as far as the Iron Gates in Romania. He arranged the financing for Hungary's first train lines from Budapest north and east to Vác and Szolnok and west to Bécsu (now Wiener Neustadt in Austria) and launched the first steam transport on the Danube and Lake Balaton. A lover of all things English, Széchenyi got the upper classes interested in horse racing with the express purpose of improving breeding stock for farming. A large financial contribution made by Széchenyi led to the establishment of the nation's prestigious Academy of Science.

Széchenyi joined the revolutionary government in 1848, but political squabbling and open conflict with Vienna caused him to lose control and he suffered a nervous breakdown. Despite a decade of convalescence in an asylum, Széchenyi never fully recovered and tragically he took his own life in 1860.

For all his accomplishments, Széchenyi's contemporary and fellow reformer, Lajos Kossuth, called him 'the greatest Hungarian'. This dynamic but troubled visionary retains that accolade to this day.

Vienna behind Rákóczi's back. The 1703–11 War of Independence had failed, but Rákóczi was the first leader to unite Hungarians against the Habsburgs.

Though the compromise had brought the fighting to an end, Hungary was now a mere province of the Habsburg empire. Its main cities – Buda, Pest and Óbuda – counted a total of just over 12,000 people. With the ascension of Maria Theresa to the throne in 1740, the Hungarian nobility pledged their 'lives and blood' to her at the diet in Bratislava in exchange for concessions. Thus began the period of enlightened absolutism that would continue under her son, the 'hatted king' (so-called as he was never crowned in Hungary) Joseph II, who ruled for a decade from 1780. By then the population of Buda and Pest had risen to almost 35,000 – a significant number, even in the sprawling Habsburg empire.

Under the reigns of Maria Theresa and Joseph, Hungary took great steps forward economically and culturally, though the first real moves towards integration with Austria had also begun. Buda effectively became the German-speaking town of Ofen and the city's first newspaper – in German, of course – was established in 1730. Funded by the grain and livestock trades, Pest began to develop outside the city walls. In 1749 the foundations for a new palace were laid in Buda, the university was moved from Nagyszombat (now Trnava in Slovakia) to Buda in 1777 and seven years later Joseph ordered the government to move from Bratislava to Buda, the nation's new administrative centre.

Joseph's attempts to modernise society by dissolving the all-powerful (and corrupt) monastic orders, abolishing serfdom and replacing 'neutral' Latin with German as the official language of state administration (1781–85) were opposed by the Hungarian nobility, and the king rescinded some of these reforms on his deathbed, but not the ones pertaining to freedom of religion and the serfs.

Dissenting voices could still be heard, and the ideals of the French Revolution of 1789 began to take root in certain intellectual circles in Budapest. In 1795 Ignác Martonovics, a former Franciscan priest, and six other prorepublican Jacobins were beheaded at Vérmező (Blood Meadow; Map p220) in Buda for plotting against the crown.

By 1800 Pest, with a population of about 30,000, was the nation's most important commercial centre while Buda, with 24,000 people, remained a royal garrison town and developed under the eye of the monarch. But 90% of the national population worked the land, and it was primarily through agriculture that modernisation would come to Hungary.

1941	1944
Hungary joins the Axis led by Germany and Italy against the Allies in WWII	Germany invades and occupies Hungary; most Hungarian Jews are deported to Nazi concentration camps

Liberalism and social reform found their greatest supporters among certain members of the aristocracy in Pest. A prime example was Count István Széchenyi (1791–1860), a true Renaissance man (see boxed text, opposite) who advocated the abolition of serfdom and returned much of his own land to the peasantry, proposed the first permanent link between Buda and Pest (Chain Bridge) and oversaw the regulation of the Danube as much for commerce and irrigation as for safety; the devastating Danube flood of 1838 had taken a heavy toll, with three-quarters of the homes in Pest washed away and some 150 people drowned.

The proponents of gradual reform were quickly superseded, however, by a more radical faction demanding more immediate action. The group included such men as Miklós Wesselényi, Ferenc Deák and the poet Ferenc Kölcsey, but the predominant figure was Lajos Kossuth (1802–94). It was this dynamic lawyer and journalist who would lead Hungary to its greatest ever confrontation with the Habsburgs.

THE 1848–49 WAR OF INDEPENDENCE

The Habsburg empire began to weaken as Hungarian nationalism increased early in the 19th century. The Hungarians, suspicious of Napoleon's policies, ignored appeals by France to revolt against Vienna, and certain reforms were introduced: the replacement of Latin, the official language of administration, with Hungarian; a law allowing serfs alternative means of discharging their feudal obligations of service; and increased Hungarian representation in the Council of State in Vienna.

The reforms carried out were too limited and far too late, however, and the diet became more defiant in its dealings with the crown. At the same time, the wave of revolution sweeping Europe spurred on the more radical faction. On 3 March 1848 Kossuth, who had been imprisoned by the Habsburgs at I Táncsics Mihály utca 9 (Map p220) on Castle Hill for three years (1837–40), made a fiery speech in parliament demanding an end to feudalism. On 15 March a group calling itself *Márciusi Ifjúság* (Youth of March) led by the poet Sándor Petőfi, who read out his poem *Nemzeti Dal* (National Song) on the steps of the Hungarian National Museum (p69), took to the streets of Pest with hastily printed copies of their Twelve Points to press for radical reforms and even revolution.

The frightened government in Vienna quickly approved plans for a new Hungarian ministry responsible to the diet, led by the liberal Lajos Batthyány and to include Deák, Kossuth and Széchenyi. The Habsburgs also reluctantly agreed to abolish serfdom and proclaim equality under the law. But the diet voted to raise a local army, testing Habsburg patience.

During September 1848, Habsburg forces under the governor of Croatia, Josip Jelačić, launched an attack on Hungary and Batthyány resigned from government. Pest and Buda fell to the Austrian army in the following spring, and the Hungarians hastily formed a national defence commission and moved the government seat from Pest to Debrecen, where Kossuth was elected leader. The parliament declared Hungary's full independence and the 'dethronement' of the Habsburgs for the second time.

The new Habsburg emperor, Franz Joseph (r 1848–1916), was not at all like his feeble-minded predecessor, Ferdinand V, and quickly took action. He sought the assistance of Russian tsar Nicholas I, who obliged with 200,000 troops. Support for the revolution was already crumbling, however, particularly in areas of mixed population where the Magyars were seen as oppressors. Weak and vastly outnumbered, the rebel troops were defeated by August 1849 and martial law was declared.

A series of brutal reprisals ensued. Summary executions of 'spies' (mostly simple army deserters) took place in the gardens of the National Museum. Batthyány was executed in Pest, 13 of his generals (the so-called Martyrs of Arad) were incarcerated and shot in Romania and Kossuth went into exile in Turkey. (Petőfi had been killed in battle.) Habsburg troops then went around the country systematically blowing up castles and fortifications lest they be used by resurgent rebels. What little of medieval Buda and Pest that had remained after the Turks and the 1703–11 War of Independence was now reduced to rubble.

1945

Budapest is liberated by the Soviet army in April, a month before full victory in Europe

1949

Communists are in full control; Hungary is declared a People's Republic

THE DUAL MONARCHY

Hungary was again merged into the Habsburg empire as a vanquished province and 'neo-absolutism' was the order of the day. Hungarian war prisoners were forced to build the Citadella (p56) atop Gellért Hill to 'defend' the city from further insurrection, but by the time it was ready in 1854 the political climate had changed and the fortress had become obsolete. Passive resistance among Hungarians and disastrous military defeats by Prussia in 1859 and 1866 pushed Franz Joseph to the negotiating table with liberal Hungarians under Deák's leadership.

The result was the Compromise of 1867 (Ausgleich in German, which actually means 'balance' or 'reconciliation'), which created the Dual Monarchy of Austria (the empire) and Hungary (the kingdom). It was a federated state of two parliaments and two capitals – Vienna and Budapest (the result of the union of Buda, Pest and Óbuda six years later). Only defence, foreign relations and customs were shared. Hungary was even allowed to raise a small army.

This 'Age of Dualism' would carry on until 1918 and spark an economic, cultural and intellectual rebirth in Budapest – a golden age the likes of which the city has never seen again. Trade and industry boomed, factories were established and the composers Franz (Ferenc) Liszt and Ferenc Erkel were making beautiful music. The middle class – dominated by Germans and Jews in Pest – burgeoned, and the capital entered into a frenzy of building.

Much of what you will see in Budapest today – from the grand boulevards and their Eclectic-style apartment blocks to the Parliament building, State Opera House and Palace of Art – was built at this time. The apex of this *belle époque* was the six-month exhibition in 1896 in City Park, celebrating the millennium of the Magyar conquest of the Carpathian Basin. A small replica of Vajdahunyad Castle in Transylvania, but with Gothic, Romanesque and baroque wings and additions to reflect architectural styles from all over the country, was built to house the exhibits (it now houses the Hungarian Agricultural Museum; p72). Around four million visitors from Hungary and abroad were transported to the fairground on Continental Europe's first underground railway (now the M1 or 'little yellow' line). By the turn of the 20th century the population of the 'new' capital jumped from about 280,000 at the time of the Compromise to 750,000, Europe's sixth-largest city.

Parliament building (p65), Lipótváros

But all was not well in the capital. The city-based working class had almost no rights – and the situation in the countryside was almost as dire as it had been in the Middle Ages. Minorities under Hungarian control – Czechs, Slovaks, Croats and Romanians – were under increased pressure to 'Magyarise' and viewed their new rulers as oppressors. Increasingly they worked to dismember the empire.

WWI & THE REPUBLIC OF COUNCILS

In July 1914, a month to the day after Archduke Franz Ferdinand, the heir to the Habsburg throne, was assassinated by a Bosnian Serb in Sarajevo, Austria-Hungary entered WWI allied with the German empire. The result of this action was disastrous, with heavy destruction and hundreds of thousands killed on the Russian and Italian fronts. At the Armistice in

1956	1958
Hungary is in revolution after riots in October; János Kádár is installed as leader	Imre Nagy and others are executed by the communist regime for their role in the uprising

November 1918, the fate of the Dual Monarchy (and Hungary as a multinational kingdom) was sealed.

A republic under the leadership of Count Mihály Károlyi was set up in Budapest immediately after the war, and the Habsburg monarchy was dethroned for the third and final time. But the fledgling republic would not last long. Widespread destitution, the occupation of Hungary by the Allies, and the success of the Bolshevik Revolution in Russia had radicalised much of the working class in Budapest.

In March 1919 a group of Hungarian communists under a former Transylvanian journalist called Béla Kun seized power. The so-called *Tanácsköztársaság* (Republic of Councils) set out to nationalise industry and private property and build a fairer society, but mass opposition to the regime unleashed a reign of 'red terror' in Budapest and around the country. In August Romanian troops occupied the capital, and Kun and his comrades (including Minister of Culture Béla Lugosi, later of *Dracula* fame) fled to Vienna. The Romanians camped out at Oktogon, taking whatever they wanted when they wanted it, and left the city in November – just ahead of Admiral Miklós Horthy, the hero of the Battle of Rijeka, mounted on a white stallion and leading 25,000 Hungarian troops into what he called the *bűnös város* (sinful city).

THE HORTHY YEARS & WWII

In the nation's first-ever election by secret ballot (March 1920), parliament chose a kingdom as the form of state and – lacking a king – elected as its 'regent' Horthy, who remained in that position until the penultimate year of WWII. The arrangement confused even US president Franklin D Roosevelt in the early days of the war. After being briefed by an aide on the government and leadership of Hungary, he reportedly said: 'Let me see if I understand you right. Hungary is a kingdom without a king run by a regent who's an admiral without a navy?'

Horthy embarked on a 'white terror' – every bit as brutal as the red one of Béla Kun – that attacked Jews, social democrats and communists for their roles in supporting the Republic of Councils. As the regime was consolidated, it showed itself to be extremely rightist and conservative, advocating the status quo and 'traditional values' – family, State and religion. Though the country had the remnants of a parliamentary system, Horthy was all-powerful, and very few reforms were enacted. On the contrary, the lot of the working class and the peasantry worsened.

One thing everyone agreed on was that the return of the territories lost through the Treaty of Trianon (see boxed text, p46) was essential for national development. Budapest was swollen with ethnic Hungarian refugees from Romania, Czechoslovakia and the newly formed Kingdom of Serbs, Croats and Slovenes, unemployment skyrocketed and the economy was at a standstill. Hungary obviously could not count on the victors – France, Britain and the USA – to help recoup its land; instead, it would have to seek help from the fascist governments of Germany and Italy.

Hungary's move to the right intensified throughout the 1930s, though it remained silent when WWII broke out in September 1939. Horthy hoped an alliance would not mean actually having to enter the war but, after recovering northern Transylvania and part of Croatia with Germany's help, he was forced to join the Axis in June 1941. The war was just as disastrous for Hungary as the 1914–18 one had been, and hundreds of thousands of Hungarian troops died while retreating from Stalingrad, where they'd been used as cannon fodder. Realising too late that his country was again on the losing side, Horthy began negotiating a separate peace with the Allies.

When Hitler caught wind of this in March 1944 he sent in his army, with Adolf Eichmann in command from the Buda Hills and the Wehrmacht billeted in the Astoria Hotel. Under pressure, Horthy installed Ferenc Szálasi, the leader of the pro-Nazi Arrow Cross Party, as prime minister in October and the regent was deported to Germany and later found exile in Portugal, where he died in 1957.

1968

Plans for a liberalised economy are introduced but rejected as too liberal by conservatives

1988

János Kádár is forced to retire in May after more than three decades in power

'NEM, NEM, SOHA!'

In June 1920, scarcely a year and a half after the Armistice was signed ending WWI, the victorious Allies drew up a postwar settlement under the Treaty of Trianon at Versailles, near Paris, that enlarged some countries, truncated others and created several 'successor states'. As one of the defeated enemy nations and with large numbers of minorities clamouring for independence within its borders, Hungary stood to lose more than most. And so it did. The nation was reduced to 40% of its historical size and, while it was now a largely homogeneous country, for millions of ethnic Hungarians in Romania, Yugoslavia and Czechoslovakia, the tables had been turned: they were now in the minority.

'Trianon' became the singularly most hated word in Hungary and *'Nem, Nem, Soha!'* (No, No, Never!) the rallying cry during the interwar years. The *diktátum* is often reviled today as if it were imposed on the nation yesterday. Many of the problems it created remained in place for decades, and it has coloured Hungary's relations with its neighbours for more than 80 years.

The Arrow Cross Party moved quickly to quash any opposition, and thousands of the country's liberal politicians and labour leaders were arrested. At the same time, its puppet government introduced anti-Jewish legislation similar to that in Germany, and Jews, who were relatively safe under Horthy, were rounded up into ghettos by Hungarian pro-Nazis. During the summer of 1944, less than a year – 10 months! – before the war ended, approximately 430,000 Hungarian Jewish men, women and children were deported to Auschwitz and other labour camps in just over eight weeks, where they either starved to death, succumbed to disease or were brutally murdered by the German fascists and their unsayable henchmen. Many of the Jews who did survive owed their lives to Raoul Wallenberg, a Budapest-based Swedish diplomat (p68) and the Swiss consul, Carl Lutz.

Budapest now became an international battleground for the first time since the Turkish occupation, and the bombs began falling everywhere – particularly around Castle Hill and, in Pest, in the northern and eastern districts of Angyalföld and Zugló, where there were munitions factories. The resistance movement drew support from many sides, including the communists, and by Christmas 1944 the Soviet army had surrounded Budapest. When the Germans and Hungarian Nazis rejected a settlement, the siege of the capital began. By the time the German war machine had surrendered in April 1945, three-quarters of the city's homes, historical buildings and churches had been severely damaged or destroyed. Some 20,000 Hungarian soldiers and 25,000 civilians of Budapest had been killed. As their goodbye gift, the vindictive Germans blew up Buda Castle and knocked out every bridge spanning the Danube.

THE PEOPLE'S REPUBLIC

When free parliamentary elections were held in November 1945, the Independent Smallholders' Party received 57% (or 245 seats) of the vote. But Soviet political officers, backed by the occupying Soviet army, forced three other parties – the Communists, Social Democrats and National Peasants – into a coalition. Limited democracy prevailed, and land-reform laws, sponsored by the Communist minister of agriculture, Imre Nagy, were enacted, wiping away the prewar feudal structure. Budapest experienced the worst hyperinflation the world has ever known at this time, with notes worth up to 10,000 trillion pengő issued before the forint was introduced. Still, Independence Bridge, the first of the spans over the Danube to be rebuilt, reopened in 1946.

Within a couple of years, the Communists were ready to take complete control. After a rigged election held under a complicated new electoral law in 1947, they declared their candidate, Mátyás Rákosi, victorious. The Social Democrats were forced to merge with the Communists into the Hungarian Socialist Workers' Party.

In 1948 Rákosi, a big fan of Stalin, began a process of nationalisation and unfeasibly fast industrialisation at the expense of agriculture. Peasants were forced into collective farms,

1989

Communist monopoly on power is relinquished; Imre Nagy is reburied in Budapest; Republic of Hungary is declared

1990

Hungarian Democratic Forum wins first free elections in 43 years; Árpád Göncz elected first president and Gábor Demszky as mayor of Budapest

and all produce had to be delivered to state warehouses. A network of spies and informers exposed 'class enemies' such as Cardinal József Mindszenty (see p67) to the secret police, the ÁVO (or ÁVH after 1949), who interrogated them at their headquarters at VI Andrássy út 60 (now the House of Terror; p71) in Pest and sent them to trial at the then Military Court of Justice on II Fő utca (Map pp218–19) in Buda. Some were executed; many more were sent into internal exile or condemned to labour camps like the notorious one at Recsk in the Mátra Hills to the east. It is estimated that at some stage during this period a quarter of the adult population of Budapest faced police or judicial proceedings.

Bitter feuding within the party began, and purges and Stalinesque show trials became the order of the day. László Rajk, the Communist minister of the interior (which also controlled the ÁVH), was arrested and later executed for 'Titoism'; his successor János Kádár was jailed and tortured. In August 1949, the nation was proclaimed the 'People's Republic of Hungary'. In the years that followed – among the darkest and bleakest in Budapest's history – apartment blocks, small businesses and retail outlets were expropriated by the state and new cultural and sports facilities, including Népstadion, or People's Stadium (now the Ferenc Puskás Stadium), were built.

After the death of Stalin in March 1953 and Khrushchev's denunciation of him three years later, Rákosi's tenure was up and the terror began to abate. Under pressure from within the party, Rákosi's successor, Ernő Gerő, rehabilitated Rajk posthumously and readmitted Nagy, who had been expelled from the party a year earlier for suggesting reforms. But Gerő was ultimately as much a hardliner as Rákosi had been and, by October 1956 during Rajk's reburial, murmured calls for a real reform of the system – 'Socialism with a human face' – could already be heard.

THE 1956 UPRISING

The nation's greatest tragedy – an event that for a while shook the world, rocked international communism and pitted Hungarian against Hungarian – began in Budapest on 23 October when some 50,000 university students assembled at II Bem József tér (Map pp218–19) in Buda, shouting anti-Soviet slogans and demanding that Nagy be named prime minister. That night a crowd pulled down and sawed into pieces the colossal statue of 'József Sztálin' on Dózsa György út on the edge of Városliget (City Park; Map pp218–19) and shots were fired by ÁVH agents on another group gathering outside the headquarters of Hungarian Radio (Map p222) on VIII Bródy Sándor utca in Pest. In the blink of an eye, Budapest was in revolution.

The next day Nagy formed a government while János Kádár was named president of the Central Committee of the Hungarian Workers' Party. For a short time it appeared that Nagy might be successful in transforming Hungary into a neutral, multiparty state. On 28 October the government offered an amnesty to all those involved in the violence and promised to abolish the ÁVH. On 31 October hundreds of political prisoners were released, and widespread reprisals against ÁVH agents began. The following day Nagy announced that Hungary would leave the Warsaw Pact and decree its neutrality.

At this, Soviet tanks and troops crossed into Hungary and within 72 hours began attacking Budapest and other centres. Kádár, who had slipped away ratlike from Budapest to join the Russian invaders, was installed as leader.

Fierce street fighting continued for several days – fighting was especially heavy in and around the Corvin Film Palace (p133), VIII József körút and the nearby Kilián army barracks opposite on IX Üllői út in Pest, and II Széna tér (Map pp218–19) in Buda – encouraged by Radio Free Europe broadcasts and disingenuous promises of support from the West, which was embroiled in the Suez Canal crisis at the time. When the fighting was over, 25,000 people were dead. Then the reprisals – the worst in the city's history – began. An estimated 20,000 people were arrested and 2000 – including Imre Nagy in 1958 and his associates – were executed. Another 250,000 refugees fled to Austria. The government lost what little

1991

Last Soviet troops leave Hungarian soil in June

1994

Socialists win general election and form a government for the first time since the changes of 1989

credibility it had and the city many of its most competent and talented citizens. As for the physical scars, just look around you in some of the older parts of Pest: the bullet holes and shrapnel damage on the exterior walls still cry out in silent fury.

HUNGARY UNDER KÁDÁR

The transformation of János Kádár from traitor and most hated man in the land to respected reformer is one of the most astonishing *tour de force* of the 20th century. No doubt it will keep historians busy well into the next.

After the revolt, the ruling party was reorganised as the Hungarian Socialist Workers' Party, and Kádár, now both party president and premier, launched a programme to liberalise the social and economic structure based on compromise. (His most quoted line was 'Whoever is not against us is with us' – a reversal of the Stalinist adage that stated 'Those not with us are against us'.) In 1968 he and the economist Rezső Nyers unveiled the New Economic Mechanism (NEM) to introduce elements of a market to the planned economy. But even this proved too daring for many party conservatives. Nyers was ousted and the NEM whittled back.

Kádár managed to survive that power struggle unscathed and went on to introduce greater consumerism and market socialism. By the mid-1970s Hungary was light years ahead of any other Soviet-bloc country in its standard of living, freedom of movement and opportunities to criticise (softly) the government. Budapesters may have had to wait seven years for a Lada car or 12 for a telephone, but most could at least enjoy access to a second house in the countryside and a decent material life. The 'Hungarian model' attracted much Western attention – and investment.

But things began to sour in the 1980s. The Kádár system of 'goulash socialism', which had seemed 'timeless and everlasting' as one Hungarian writer has put it, was incapable of dealing with such 'unsocialist' problems as unemployment, soaring inflation and the largest per-capita foreign debt in Eastern Europe. Kádár and the 'old guard' refused to hear talk about party reforms. In June 1987 Károly Grósz took over as premier, and in May 1988 Kádár was booted out of the party and forced to retire. He died the following year.

THE END OF AN ERA

A group of reformers – among them Nyers, Imre Pozsgay, Miklós Németh and Gyula Horn – took charge. Party conservatives at first put a lid on any real change by demanding a retreat from political liberalisation in exchange for their support of the new regime's economic policies. But the tide had turned and there was no stopping it.

Throughout the summer and autumn of 1988, new political parties were formed and old ones revived. In January 1989 Pozsgay, second-guessing what was to come as Mikhail Gorbachev kissed babies and launched his reforms in the Soviet Union, announced that the events of 1956 had been a 'popular insurrection' and not the 'counter-revolution' that the regime had always said it was. In June 1989 some 250,000 people attended ceremonies marking the reburial of Imre Nagy and other victims of 1956 in Budapest. Towards the end of the year the communists agreed to give up their monopoly on power, paving the way for free elections in spring 1990.

In July 1989, again at Pozsgay's instigation, Hungary began to demolish the electrified wire fence separating it from Austria. The move released a wave of East Germans holidaying in Hungary into the West and the opening attracted thousands more. The collapse of the communist regimes around the region was now unstoppable. What Hungarians call *az átkos 40 év*, 'the accursed 40 years' of sham, drudgery and broken dreams, had come to a withering, almost feeble, end.

1999	2004
Hungary becomes a fully fledged member of NATO	Hungary is admitted to the EU

Sights

Sights

Budapest spreads over 525 sq km. Its borders are Csepel Island in the Danube River to the south, the start of the Danube Bend to the north, the Buda Hills to the west and the start of the Great Plain to the east. With few exceptions (the Buda Hills, City Park and some excursions), however, the areas beyond the Nagykörút (literally the 'Big Ring Road') in Pest and west of Moszkva tér in Buda are residential or industrial and of little interest to visitors. It is a well laid-out city, so much so that it is difficult to get lost here. For more information see page p182.

If you look at a map of Budapest you'll see that two ring roads – Nagykörút and the semicircular Kiskörút (the 'Little Ring Road') – more or less link all of the most important bridges across the Danube and define central Pest. The Nagykörút consists of the contiguous Szent István körút, Teréz körút, Erzsébet körút, József körút and Ferenc körút. The Kiskörút comprises Károly körút, Múzeum körút and Vámház körút. Important boulevards such as Bajcsy-Zsilinszky út, leafy Andrássy út, Rákóczi út and Üllői út fan out from these ring roads, creating large squares and circles.

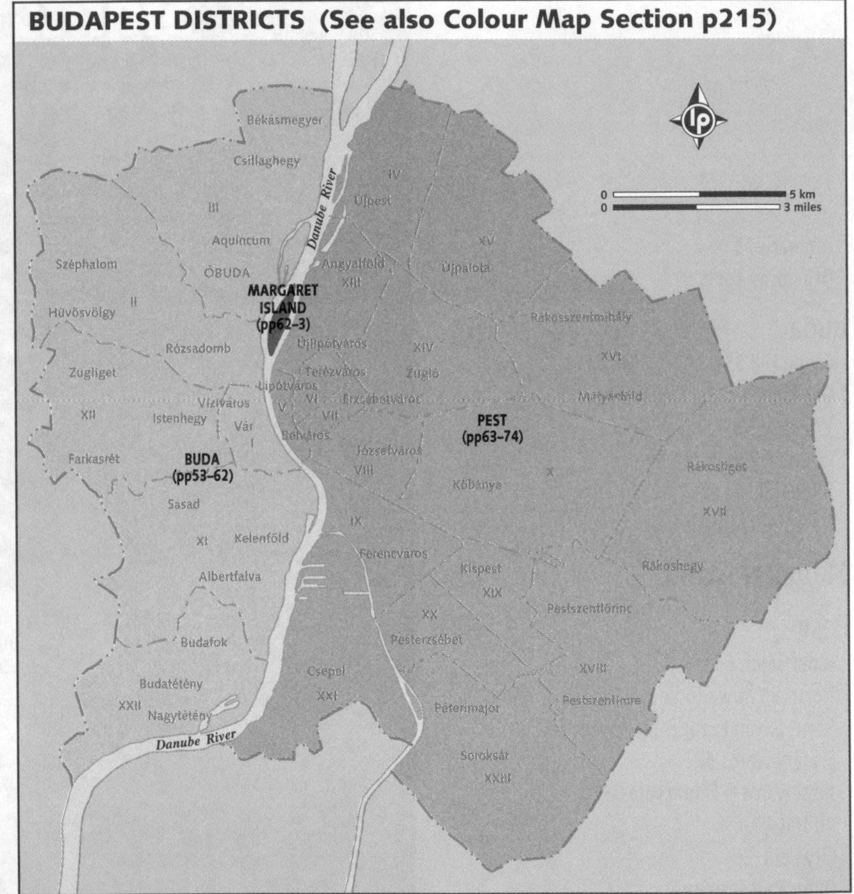

Buda, on the other hand, is dominated by Castle and Gellért Hills; the main square on this side is Moszkva tér. Important roads are Margit körút (the only part of either ring road to cross the river), Fő utca and Attila út on either side of Castle Hill, and Hegyalja út and Bartók Béla út running west and southwest.

Budapest is divided into 23 *kerület*, or districts, which usually also have traditional names such as Lipótváros (Leopold Town) in district XIII or Víziváros (Watertown) in district I. The Roman numeral appearing before each street address signifies the district.

ITINERARIES

If you want a general overview of Budapest before striking out on your own, take one of the tours described in this chapter (below). At least you'll be sure to see the highlights even on a very brief visit.

One Day

If you've just got one day in Budapest – what *were* you thinking? – spend most of it on **Castle Hill** (p53), taking in the views and the sights and visiting a museum or two. In the afternoon ride the **Sikló** (p53) down to Clark Ádám tér and, depending on the day of the week, make your way to the **Király** (p136) or the **Gellért Baths** (p136) for a relaxing soak. In the evening head for **Liszt Ferenc tér** for drinks and dinner at **Menza** (p114) and perhaps attend a performance at the **Ferenc Liszt Academy of Music** (p131).

Three Days

With another couple of days to look around the city, concentrate first on the two icons of Hungarian nationhood and the places that house them: the **Crown of St Stephen** (p65) in the **Parliament** (p65) and the saint-king's mortal remains in the **Basilica of St Stephen** (p64). Take a late-afternoon coffee (and cake) break at **Gerbeaud** (p125) in Vörösmarty tér and stop in at the **Hungarian State Opera House** (p71) before going clubbing. The next day, consider taking a **walking tour** (p76), such as the one up Andrássy út, stopping off and visiting whatever interests you along the way – be it the **House of Terror** (p71) or the **Museum of Fine Arts** (p71). The **Lukács** (p126) cake shop is conveniently located en route and you could take the waters at the **Széchenyi Baths** (p136) in City Park. **Robinson** (p119) or **Bagolyvár** (p119) are convenient places for an evening meal. Then take a well-watered tour of the city's best 'gardens' (p129).

One Week

If you have a full week in Budapest you could manage to see a good many of the sights listed in this chapter, including 'secondary' gems such as **Gül Baba's Tomb** (p58) and the **Ferenc Hopp Museum of East Asian Art** (p70), markets like the **Nagycsarnok** (p149) and **Ecseri Piac** (p150) and do a little shopping. You could also make trips to places further afield, such as **Statue Park** (p62), and take a ride up into the Buda Hills on the **Cog Railway** (p61) for a ramble. You might even leave Budapest for a couple of days' excursion to the Danube Bend, Lake Balaton or the Great Plain (for tours of these regions, see p169).

ORGANISED TOURS

Boat

LEGENDA Map p224

☎ 317 2203, 06 30 944 5216; www.legenda.hu; V Vigadó tér, pier 7; Ⓜ M1 Vörösmarty tér

This long-established operator has both day (3600Ft) and night (4200Ft) cruises on the Danube, with taped commentary in up to 30 languages. The night lights of the city rising to Buda Castle, Parliament, Gellért Hill and the Citadella make the evening trip far more attractive than the afternoon one. Check Legenda's website for the schedule.

MAHART PASSNAVE Map p224

☎ 484 4013, 318 1223; www.mahartpassnave.hu; V Belgrád rakpart; 🚊 2 or 2/a

This outfit offers 1½- to two-hour river cruises (1900/950Ft per adult/child under

12) daily at noon and 7.30pm from early May to mid-September. In the low season, from April to early May and mid-September to mid-October, only the evening cruise sails (1600/800Ft) and it's on Friday, Saturday and Sunday. A ticket with a meal on board costs 2800/1400Ft, except in the evening in high season when it's 3200/1600Ft and there's music and dancing on board.

Bus

BUDATOURS Map p224

☎ 353 0558, 374 7070; www.budatours.hu; VI Andrássy út 2; Ⓜ M1/2/3 Deák tér

Budatours runs nine city bus tours (4300/3000Ft per adult/student) daily in both open and covered coaches in July and August (between three and eight the rest of the year) from VI Andrássy út 3 across the street from its main office. It's a two-hour tour with one stop (Gellért Hill) and with taped commentary in 16 different languages.

CITYRAMA Map p222

☎ 302 4382; www.cityrama.hu; V Báthory utca 22; Ⓜ M3 Arany János utca

Cityrama offers three-hour city tours with three stops from 7000/3000Ft per adult/child under 12.

HUNGARY PROGRAM CENTRUM Map p224

☎ 317 7767, 06 20 944 9091; www.programcentrum.hu; V Erzsébet tér 9-10

With an office next to the Le Meridien Budapest hotel, this operator has similar tours to those offered by Cityrama, but they're a wee bit cheaper (eg 6500/3250Ft per adult/child for the three-hour city tour) – at least for adults.

QUEENYBUS Map p216

☎ 247 7159, 06 70 338 1159; queenybus@queenybus.hu; XI Törökbálinti út 28; 🚌 8

Queenybus has buses departing three times daily (10am, 11am and 2.20pm) from in front of the Basilica of St Stephen (Map p224; V Bajcsy-Zsilinszky út) for three-hour city tours (6000/3000/3200Ft per adult/child under 14/student, open deck 4300/1500/3000Ft).

Cycling

YELLOW ZEBRA BIKES Map p224

☎ 266 8777, 06 30 211 8861; www.yellowzebrabikes.com; V Sütő utca 2; Ⓜ M1/2/3 Deák Ferenc tér

Run by the same people behind Absolute Walking Tours (below), Yellow Zebra has cycling tours (5500/5000Ft per adult/student) of Budapest by day at 11am May to October with an additional departure at 4pm in July and August. Tours take in Heroes' Sq, City Park, inner Pest and Castle Hill and include the bike and a drink. They depart from in front of the yellow Calvinist church in V Deák Ferenc tér (Map p224) and last 3½ to four hours. There is an **Opera House branch** (Map p222; ☎ 269 3843; VI Lázár utca 16; Ⓜ M1 Opera), from where it also runs **City Segway Tours** (www.citysegwaytours.com), which though not on bicycles involve two-wheeled, electric-powered conveyances. Segway tours (12,500Ft), which follow an abbreviated version of the bike tour's Pest route and last three to 3½ hours, depart from the Opera branch at 10.30am daily year-round and at 6.30pm daily April to October. You must book 72 hours in advance via the web (24 hours ahead by phone) for these tours.

Walking

ABSOLUTE WALKING TOURS Map p224

☎ 266 8777, 06 30 211 8861; www.absolutetours.com; V Sütő utca 2; Ⓜ M1/2/3 Deák Ferenc tér

This very reliable outfit has, among other tours, a 3½-hour guided promenade (4000/3500Ft per adult/student or under-26) through City Park, central Pest and Castle Hill. Tours depart at 9.30am and 1.30pm daily from mid-May to September and at 10.30am daily the rest of the year from the steps of the yellow Calvinist church on V Deák Ferenc tér (Map p224). Cracker specialist tours include the Hammer & Sickle Tour (6000/5000Ft) and the Hungaro Gastro Food & Wine Tour (6500/5500Ft).

HUNGÁRIA KONCERT

☎ 317 2754, 201 5928; www.ticket.info.hu

Focusing on Budapest's Jewish heritage, this operator has a 2½-hour tour available at 10.30am and 1.30pm most weekdays year-round and at 11.30am on Sunday. The tour includes a visit to the Great and Orthodox Synagogues, the Jewish Museum, a walking tour of the ghetto and a nonkosher snack for 5600/5100Ft per adult/student (4900/4300Ft without the snack), including transport to the Great Synagogue. Tickets are available from locations throughout the city, including the **Duna Palota** (Map p224; V Zrínyi utca) entertainment centre and at the entrance to the **Great Synagogue** (Map p224; VII Dohány utca 2-8).

PAUL STREET TOURS

☎ 06 20 933 5240; taylorj@mail.datanet.hu

These very personal walking tours cover the Castle District (about two hours), less-explored areas of Pest, such as the Jewish Quarter and Andrássy út (two to three hours), the Little Ring Road, the parks and gardens of Budapest and shopping, with lots of anecdotal information on architecture and social history, especially life in and around the *udvar* (courtyards) of *fin-de-siècle* Pest. Tours are available by appointment year-round in English or Hungarian and cost €25 per hour regardless of size.

BUDA

Eating p94; Sleeping p154; Shopping p142

Leafy and unpolluted, Buda is more than just a 'pretty face' seen from the Pest side of the Danube. Its more majestic western side fronting the Danube contains some of Budapest's most important and historical landmarks (eg Castle Hill, the Citadella) and museums (eg National Gallery, Budapest History Museum) and, to the north, the original Roman settlement at Aquincum.

CASTLE HILL

Várhegy (Castle Hill; Map p220) is a limestone plateau 1km long and towering 170m above the Danube. It contains Budapest's most important medieval monuments and museums and is a Unesco World Hertage Site. It is the premier sight in the capital, and with its grand views and so many things to see, you should start here. Below is a 28km network of caves formed by thermal springs that were supposedly used by the Turks for military purposes, as air-raid shelters during WWII, and as a secret military installation during the Cold War.

The walled area consists of two distinct parts: the Old Town to the north, where commoners lived in the Middle Ages (the present-day owners of the coveted burgher houses here are anything but 'common'); and the Royal Palace, the original site of the castle built in the 13th century, now housing two important museums.

The easiest way to get to Castle Hill from Pest is to take bus 16 from Deák Ferenc tér to Dísz tér, midway between the Old Town and the Royal Palace. Much more fun, though, is to stroll across Chain Bridge and board the **Sikló** (uphill/downhill ticket adult 650/550Ft, child aged 3-14 flat fare 350Ft; 🕑 7.30am-10pm, closed 1st and 3rd Monday of each month), a funicular railway built in 1870 that ascends from Clark Ádám tér to Szent György tér near the Royal Palace.

Alternatively, you can walk up the Király lépcső, the 'Royal Steps' that lead northwest from Clark Ádám tér, or the wide staircase that goes to the southern end of the Royal Palace from I Szarvas tér.

Another option is to take metro M2 to Moszkva tér, walk up the steps in the northeastern part of the square and along I Várfok utca to the Vienna Gate; a minibus with a logo of a castle and labelled 'Várbusz' (or 'Dísz tér') follows the same route from the start of Várfok utca.

BUDA CASTLE LABYRINTH Map p220

Budavári Labirintus; ☎ 489 3280; www.labirintus.com; entrances at I Úri utca 9 & Lovas út 4; adult/child 1400/1100Ft; 🕑 9.30am-7.30pm; 🚌 16 or Várbusz

The labyrinth, a 1200m-long cave system some 16m under the Castle District, looks at how the caves have been used – from prehistoric times – in nine halls and chambers.

BUDA TRANSPORT

Bus 7 to Gellért Hill & the Tabán; 16 to Castle Hill; 27 to Gellért Hill & the Tabán; 34, 42 to Óbuda & Aquincum; 60 to Víziváros; 86 to Gellért Hill & the Tabán, Víziváros and Óbuda & Aquincum; 158 to Buda Hills; Várbusz to Castle Hill

Funicular Sikló to Castle Hill

HÉV To Víziváros and Óbuda & Aquincum

Metro M2 to Castle Hill, Víziváros and Buda Hills

Tram 1, 1/a to Óbuda & Aquincum; 4, 6 to Víziváros; 17 to Víziváros and Óbuda & Aquincum; 18 to Gellért Hill & the Tabán and Buda Hills; 19 to Gellért Hill & the Tabán and Víziváros; 47, 49 to Gellért Hill & the Tabán; 56 to Buda Hills

BUDA TOP FIVE

- Aquincum Museum (p59)
- Fishermen's Bastion (below)
- Hungarian National Gallery (right)
- Kiscelli Museum & Municipal Gallery (p60)
- Matthias Church (opposite)

The admission fee is very high by Budapest standards, but it's all good fun and a relief from the heat and the crowds above on a hot summer's day.

BUDAPEST HISTORY MUSEUM Map p220

Budapesti Történeti Múzeum; ☎ 225 7815, 375 7533; Royal Palace, Wing E; adult/student or child/family 900/450/1500Ft, audioguide 800Ft; 🕑 10am-6pm daily mid-May–mid-Sep, 10am-6pm Wed-Mon Mar–mid-May & mid-Sep–Oct, 10am-4pm Wed-Mon Nov-Feb; 🚌 16 or Várbusz

Also known as the Castle Museum (Vár Múzeum), the history museum traces the 2000 years of the city on three floors of rather jumbled exhibits. Restored palace rooms dating from the 15th century can be entered from the basement, which contains a display on the Royal Palace in medieval Buda. In the basement three vaulted halls, one with a magnificent door frame in red marble bearing the seal of Queen Beatrice and tiles with a raven and a ring (the seal of her husband King Matthias Corvinus), lead to the **Gothic Hall**, the **Royal Cellar** and the 14th-century **Tower Chapel**. On the ground floor is an exhibit entitled 'Budapest in the Middle Ages', as well as Gothic statues of courtiers, squires and saints discovered during excavations in 1974. The presentation on the 1st floor – 'Budapest in Modern Times' – traces the history of the city from the expulsion of the Turks in 1686 to Hungary's entry into the EU. On the 2nd floor you'll learn about Budapest from prehistoric times to the arrival of the Avars in the late 6th century.

FISHERMEN'S BASTION Map p220

Halászbástya; adult/child 330/165Ft; 🕑 9am-11pm; 🚌 16 or Várbusz

The bastion is a neo-Gothic masquerade that most visitors (and Hungarians) believe to be much older. But who cares? It looks medieval and still offers among the best views in Budapest. Built as a viewing platform in 1905 by Frigyes Schulek, the bastion's name was taken from the guild of fishermen responsible for defending this stretch of the wall in the Middle Ages. The seven gleaming white turrets represent the Magyar tribes that entered the Carpathian Basin in the late 9th century.

GOLDEN EAGLE PHARMACY MUSEUM Map p220

Arany Sas Patikamúzeum; ☎ 375 9772; I Tárnok utca 18; admission free; 🕑 10.30am-5.30pm Tue-Sun mid-Mar–Oct, 10.30am-3.30pm Tue-Sun Nov–mid-Mar; 🚌 16 or Várbusz

Just north of Dísz tér on the site of Budapest's first pharmacy (1681), this branch of the Semmelweis Museum of Medical History (p57) contains an unusual mixture of displays, including a mock-up of an alchemist's laboratory and a small 'spice rack' used by 17th-century travellers for their daily fixes of herbs.

HOUSE OF HUNGARIAN WINES Map p220

Magyar Borok Háza; ☎ 212 1030; www.winehouse.hu; I Szentháromság tér 6; wine tasting 3800Ft; 🕑 noon-8pm; 🚌 16 or Várbusz

This wine centre offers a crash course in Hungarian viticulture in the heart of the Castle District. But with over 700 wines on display from Hungary's 22 wine regions and up to 50 to try, 'crash' may soon become the operative word. Do what the pros do and try not to swallow.

HUNGARIAN NATIONAL GALLERY Map p220

Magyar Nemzeti Galéria; ☎ 201 9082, 06 20 439 7325; Royal Palace, Wings B, C & D; admission free, special exhibitions adult/child/family 1500/800/3000Ft; 🕑 10am-6pm Tue-Sun; 🚌 16 or Várbusz

The Hungarian National Gallery is an overwhelmingly large collection over four floors that traces the development of Hungarian art from the 10th century to the present day. The largest collections include medieval and Renaissance stonework, Gothic wooden sculptures and panel paintings, late Gothic winged altars, and late Renaissance and baroque art. Do not miss the restored altar of St John the Baptist from Kisszebes (now in Romania) or the 16th-century painted wooden ceiling in the next room.

The museum also has an important collection of Hungarian paintings and sculpture from the 19th and 20th centuries. You may not recognise many names, but keep an eye open for the harrowing depictions of war and the dispossessed by László Mednyánszky, the unique portraits by József Rippl-Rónai, the mammoth canvases by Tivadar Csontváry, the paintings of carnivals by the modern artist Vilmos Aba-Novák and works by the realist Mihály Munkácsy, the 'painter of the *puszta*' (Great Plain).

MATTHIAS CHURCH Map p220

Mátyás-templom; ☎ 355 5657; www.matyas-templom.hu; I Szentháromság tér 2; adult/child/family 600/300/1000Ft, audioguide 300Ft; 9am-5pm Mon-Fri, 9am-1pm Sat, 1-5pm Sun; 16 or Várbusz

Parts of Castle Hill's landmark church date back some 500 years, notably the carvings above the southern entrance. But basically the church (so named because King Matthias Corvinus married Beatrice here in 1474) is a neo-Gothic creation designed by the architect Frigyes Schulek in 1896.

The church has a colourful tiled roof and a delicate spire; the interior is remarkable for its stained-glass windows, frescoes and wall decorations by the Romantic painters Károly Lotz and Bertalan Székely. There are organ concerts in the church on certain evenings, continuing a tradition that began in 1867 when Franz Liszt's *Hungarian Coronation Mass* was first played here for the coronation of Franz Joseph and Elizabeth as king and queen of Hungary. A US$20 million restoration of the church undertaken by the government is expected to be complete in 2007.

Steps to the right of the main altar inside the church lead to the crypt. The **Matthias Church Collection of Ecclesiastical Art** (Mátyás-templom Egyházművészeti Gyűjteménye; ☎ 488 0717), which is included in the church admission fee and keeps the same hours, contains ornate monstrances, reliquaries, chalices and other church plate.

MEDIEVAL JEWISH PRAYER HOUSE

MAP p220

Középkori Zsidó Imaház; ☎ 225 7815; I Táncsics Mihály utca 26; adult/student or child 400/150Ft; 10am-5pm Tue-Sun May-Oct; 16 or Várbusz

With parts dating from the 14th century, this medieval Jewish house of worship contains documents and items linked to the Jewish community of Buda, as well as Gothic stone carvings and tombstones from the Great Synagogue (p68) in Pest.

HUNGARIAN MUSEUM OF COMMERCE & CATERING Map p220

Magyar Kereskedelmi és Vendéglátóipari Múzeum; ☎ 375 6249; I Fortuna utca 4; adult/child/family 400/200/1000Ft; 10am-5pm Wed-Fri, 10am-6pm Sat & Sun; 16 or Várbusz

The catering section of this museum, to the left as you enter the archway, contains an entire 19th-century cake shop in one of its three rooms, complete with a pastry kitchen. There are moulds for every occasion, a marble-lined icebox and an antique ice-cream maker. Much is made of the great confectioners Emil Gerbeaud of *cukrászda*

Royal Palace containing the Hungarian National Gallery (opposite), Castle Hill, from Széchenyi Chain Bridge (p57)

(café) fame and József Dobos, who gave his name to *Dobos torta* (p29). The commerce collection traces retail trade in the capital. Along with advertisements and electric toys that still work, there's an exhibit on the hyperinflation that Hungary suffered after WWII when a basket of money would buy no more than four eggs.

MILITARY HISTORY MUSEUM Map p220

Hadtörténeti Múzeum; ☎ 356 9522; I Tóth Árpád sétány 40; admission free; 🕒 10am-6pm Tue-Sun Apr-Sep, 10am-4pm Tue-Sun Oct-Mar; 🚌 16 or Várbusz

Loaded with weaponry from before the Turkish conquest, the Military History Museum also does a good job with uniforms, medals, flags and battle-themed fine art. Exhibits focus on the 1848–49 War of Independence and the Hungarian Royal Army under Admiral Miklós Horthy (1918–43).

TELEPHONY MUSEUM Map p220

Telefónia Múzeum; ☎ 201 8188; www.postamuzeum.hu; I Úri utca 49 & Országház utca 30; adult/child 200/100Ft; 🕒 10am-4pm Tue-Sun; 🚌 16 or Várbusz

This museum, set within a lovely backstreet garden, documents the history of the telephone in Hungary since 1881, when the world's first switchboard – a 7A1 Rotary still working and the centrepiece of the exhibition – was set up in Budapest. Other exhibits pay tribute to Tivadár Puskás, a Hungarian associate of Thomas Edison, and of the latter's fleeting visit to Budapest in 1891.

GELLÉRT HILL & THE TABÁN

Gellért-hegy (Gellért Hill; Map p220 and Map pp228–9), a 235m-high rocky hill southeast of the Castle District, is crowned with a fortress of sorts and the Independence Monument, Budapest's unofficial symbol. From Gellért Hill, you can't beat the views of the Royal Palace or the Danube and its fine bridges, and Jubilee Park on the south side is an ideal spot for a picnic. The Tabán (Map p220), the leafy area between Gellért and Castle Hills, and stretching northwest as far as Déli train station, is associated with the Serbs, who settled here after fleeing from the Turks in the early 18th century. Plaques on I Döbrentei utca mark the water level of the Danube during two devastating floods in 1775 and 1838.

This neighbourhood later became known for its restaurants and wine gardens – a kind of Montmartre for Budapest. Most of these burned to the ground at the turn of the 20th century. All that remains is a lovely little renovated building with a fountain designed by Miklós Ybl in 1879 known as the **Castle Garden Kiosk** (Várkert Kioszk; I Ybl Miklós tér 2-6), which was once a pump house for Castle Hill and is now a casino. The dilapidated steps and archways across the road, is all that is left of the **Castle Bazaar** (Várbazár) pleasure park.

Today Gellért Hill and the Tabán districts are given over to private homes, parks and three thermal spas that make good use of the hot springs gushing from deep below Gellért Hill: the recently renovated Rudas Baths (Map p224; p137) and the Gellért Baths (Map pp228–9; p137); the Rác Baths (Map p220), designed by Miklós Ybl around a much older Turkish bath, was still under renovation at the time of writing. If you don't like getting wet you can try a 'drinking cure' by visiting the **pump room** (*ivócsarnok*; Map p224; 🕒 11am-6pm Mon, Wed & Fri, 7am-2pm Tue & Thu), which is within sight of the Rudas Baths just below the western end of Elizabeth Bridge. A half-litre/litre of the hot smelly water – meant to cure whatever ails you – is just 15/25Ft.

CAVE CHAPEL Map pp228-9

Sziklakápolna; ☎ 385 1529; 🕒 9am-9pm; 🚊 47 or 49

This chapel on a small hill directly north of the landmark Gellért Hotel was built into a cave in 1926. It was the seat of the Pauline order until 1951 when the priests were arrested and imprisoned by the communists and the cave was sealed off. It was reopened and reconsecrated in 1992. Behind the chapel is the monastery, with its neo-Gothic turrets visible from Independence Bridge.

CITADELLA Map pp228-9

☎ 365 6076; www.citadella.hu; 🕒 24hr; 🚌 27

The Citadella atop St Gellért Hill is a fortress that never did battle. Built by the Habsburgs after the 1848–49 War of Independence to 'defend' the city from further insurrection, by the time it was ready in 1851 the political climate had changed and the Citadella had become obsolete. It was given to the city in the 1890s and parts of it were symbolically blown to pieces. Today

BUDAPEST'S BRIDGES

The city's bridges, both landmarks and delightful vantage points over the Danube, are stitches that have bound Buda and Pest together since well before the two were linked politically in 1873. There are a total of nine spans, including a railroad bridge, but the four in the centre stand head and shoulders above the rest.

Margaret Bridge (Margit híd; Map pp218–19) This span introduces the Big Ring Road to Buda. It is unique in that it doglegs in order to stand at right angles to the Danube at its confluence at the southern tip of Margaret Island. It was originally built by French engineer Ernest Gouin in 1876; the branch leading to the island was added in 1901.

Széchenyi Chain Bridge (Széchenyi lánchíd; Map p220) A twin-towered structure to the south, this is the city's oldest and arguably its most beautiful bridge. It is named in honour of its initiator, István Széchenyi (p42), but was actually built by Scotsman Adam Clark. When it opened in 1849, Chain Bridge was unique for two reasons: it was the first permanent dry link between Buda and Pest; and the aristocracy – previously exempt from all taxation – had to pay a toll like everybody else to use it.

Elizabeth Bridge (Erzsébet híd; Map p224) This gleaming white (though rather generic-looking) suspension bridge further downstream enjoys a special place in the hearts of many Budapesters as it was the first newly designed bridge to reopen after WWII (1964). (The original span, erected in 1903, was too badly damaged to rebuild.) Boasting a higher arch than the others, it offers dramatic views of both Castle and Gellért Hills and, of course, the more attractive bridges to the north and south.

Independence Bridge (Szabadság híd; Map pp228–9) Opened for the 1896 millenary exhibition, Independence Bridge has a *fin-de-siècle* cantilevered span. Each post of the bridge, which was originally named after Habsburg emperor Franz Joseph, is topped by a mythical *turul* bird (p37) ready to take flight. It was rebuilt in the same style in 1946.

the Citadella contains some big guns and dusty displays in the central courtyard, the new **1944 Waxworks** (1944 Panoptikum; ☎ 279 1963; admission 1200Ft; ⏲ 9am-9pm Mon-Fri, 8am-10pm Sat, 8am-9pm Sun) inside a WWII bunker, a hotel/hostel (p154), a restaurant and a dance club.

INDEPENDENCE MONUMENT

Map pp228-9

Szabadság-szobor; 🚌 27

The charming lady with the palm frond proclaiming freedom throughout the city from atop Gellért Hill is just east of the Citadella. Some 14m high, it was erected in 1947 in tribute to the Soviet soldiers who died liberating Budapest in 1945, but the victims' names in Cyrillic letters on the plinth and the statues of the Soviet soldiers were removed in 1992. In fact, the monument had been designed by the politically 'flexible' sculptor Zsigmond Kisfaludi Strobl much earlier for the ultraright government of Admiral Miklós Horthy. After the war, when procommunist monuments were in short supply, Kisfaludi Strobl passed it off as a memorial to the Soviets. If you walk west for a few minutes along Citadella sétány north of the fortress, you'll come to what is arguably the best **vantage point** in Budapest.

SEMMELWEIS MUSEUM OF MEDICAL HISTORY Map p220

Semmelweis Orvostörténeti Múzeum; ☎ 201 1577; I Apród utca 1-3; adult/child 300/150Ft; ⏲ 10.30am-5.30pm Tue-Sun mid-Mar–Oct, 10.30am-3.30pm Tue-Sun Nov–mid-Mar; 🚋 19

This museum traces the history of medicine from Graeco-Roman times through medical tools and implements and photographs, and yet another antique pharmacy makes an appearance. Ignác Semmelweis (1818–65), the 'saviour of mothers' who discovered the cause of puerperal (or childbirth) fever, was born in this house.

STATUES & BRIDGES

Szent Gellért tér faces **Independence Bridge** (Szabadság híd; Map pp228–9; 🚋 47 or 49), which opened for the millenary exhibition in 1896.

Looking down on **Elizabeth Bridge** (Erzsébet híd; Map p224; 🚌 7) from Gellért Hill is **St Gellért** (Map p220; 🚌 7), an Italian missionary invited to Hungary by King Stephen to convert the natives. The monument marks the spot from where the bishop was hurled to his death in a spiked barrel in 1046 by pagan Hungarians resisting the new faith.

North of the bridge and through the underpass is a **statue of Elizabeth** (Map p224; 🚌 7), the Habsburg empress and Hungarian queen and the consort of Franz Joseph much beloved by Magyars because, among other things, she learned to speak Hungarian. Sissi, as she was affectionately known, was assassinated by an Italian anarchist in Geneva in 1898.

VÍZIVÁROS

The suburb of Víziváros (Watertown; Map p220) is the narrow area between the Danube and Castle Hill that widens as it approaches Óbuda to the north and Rózsadomb (Rose Hill) to the northwest, spreading west to Moszkva tér, one of Buda's main transport hubs. Under the Turks many of the district's churches were used as mosques, and baths were built, one of which is still functioning.

Víziváros begins at Clark Ádám tér, that is named after the 19th-century Scottish engineer who supervised the building of the Széchenyi Chain Bridge (p57), leading east from the square. Clark also designed the all-important **tunnel** *(alagút)* under Castle Hill (p53), which took eight months to carve out of the limestone. The curious sculpture, which looks like a elongated doughnut, hidden in the bushes to the south is the **0km stone**; all Hungarian roads to and from the capital are measured from this exact spot.

FŐ UTCA

86

Fő utca is the 'Main Street' running through Víziváros and dates from Roman times. At the former **Capuchin church** (Map p220; I Fő utca 30-32), used as a mosque during the Turkish occupation, you can see the remains of two Islamic-style ogee-arched doors and windows on the southern side. Around the corner there's the seal of King Matthias Corvinus – a raven and a ring – and the little square with the delightful **Louis Fountain** (Lajos kútja; 1904; Map p220) is called **Corvin tér**. The Eclectic building on the north side is the **Buda Concert Hall** (Budai Vigadó; Map p220; Corvin tér 8). The **Iron Stump** (Vastuskó; Map p220; cnr I Vám utca & Iskola utca) to the north is the odd-looking tree trunk into which itinerant artisans and merchants would drive a nail to mark their visit.

Batthyány tér (Map p220), a short distance to the northeast, is the centre of Víziváros and the best place to snap a picture of the Parliament building across the river. In the centre of this rather shabby square is the entrance to both metro M2 and the HÉV suburban line to Szentendre. On the southern side is **St Anne's Church** (Szent Ana templom; Map p220; II Batthyány tér 7), with one of the most eye-catching baroque interiors of any church in Budapest.

A couple of streets north is **Nagy Imre tér**, with the enormous former **Military Court of Justice** (Map pp218–19; II Fő utca 70-78) on the northern side. Here Imre Nagy and others were tried and sentenced to death in 1958 (p47). It was also the site of the notorious **Fő utca prison** where many other victims of the regime were incarcerated and tortured.

The **Király Baths** (Király Gyógyfürdő; Map pp218–19; II Fő utca 82-86), parts of which date from 1580, is one block to the north (see p136). Across pedestrianised Ganz utca is the Greek Catholic **St Florian Chapel** (Szent Florián kápolna; Map pp218–19; II Fő utca 88-90), built in 1760 and dedicated to the patron saint of firefighters.

FOUNDRY MUSEUM Map pp218-19

Öntödei Múzeum; ☎ 202 5011, 201 4370; II Bem József utca 20; admission free; 9am-5pm Tue-Sun; 4 or 6

This museum is housed in the Ganz Machine Works foundry that was in use until the 1960s, and the massive ladles and cranes still stand, anxiously awaiting use. The exhibits include cast-iron stoves, bells and street furniture.

FRANKEL LEÓ ÚT Map pp218-19

17

At Bem József tér, Fő utca turns into Frankel Leó út, a tree-lined street of antique shops and boutiques. At its northern end is the **Lukács Bath** (Lukács Gyógyfürdő; II Frankel Leó út 25-29), which caters to an older and quite serious crowd of thermal enthusiasts (see p136). A short distance north and tucked away in an apartment block is the **Újlak Synagogue** (Újlaki zsinagóga; ☎ 326 1445; II Frankel Leó út 49), built in 1888 and the only functioning synagogue left on the Buda side.

GÜL BABA'S TOMB Map pp218-19

Gül Baba Türbéje; ☎ 326 0062; II Türbe tér 1; adult/child 500/250Ft; 10am-6pm Mar-Oct, 10am-4pm Nov-Feb; 17

This overly reconstructed tomb contains the remains of one Gül Baba, an Ottoman Dervish who took part in the capture of Buda in

Gül Baba statue, Víziváros

1541, and is known in Hungary as the 'Father of Roses'. The tomb is a pilgrimage place for Muslims, especially from Turkey, and you must remove your shoes before entering the tomb. There's a pleasant café here with fine views. To reach the tomb from Török utca, which runs parallel to Frankel Leó út, walk west along steep (and cobbled) Gül Baba utca to the set of steps just past No 16. You can also reach here along Mecset utca, which runs north from Margit tér.

MILLENNIUM PARK Map pp218-19

Millenáris Park; ☎ 438 5312; www.millenaris.hu; II Kis Rókus utca 16-20 & Lövőház utca 37; 🕑 6am-1am; Ⓜ M2 Moszkva tér

One of the more successful urban redevelopment projects on either side of the Danube in the past decade, this 'park' is a large landscaped complex behind the Mammut shopping mall comprising fountains, ponds, little bridges, a theatre and the **Millennium Exhibition Hall** (Millenáris Kiállítócsarnok; ☎ 438 5335; admission varies; 🕑 10am-6pm or 8pm), which hosts some unusual cultural exhibitions.

ÓBUDA & AQUINCUM

Ó means 'ancient' in Hungarian; as its name suggests, Óbuda (Map pp226–7) is the oldest part of Buda. The Romans established Aquincum, a key military garrison and civilian town north of here at the end of the 1st century AD (see p36), and it became the seat of the Roman province of Pannonia Inferior in AD 106. When the Magyars arrived, they named it Buda, which became Óbuda when the Royal Palace was built on Castle Hill and turned into the real centre.

Most visitors on their way to Szentendre (p170) on the Danube Bend are put off by what they see of Óbuda from the highway or the HÉV commuter train. Prefabricated housing blocks seem to go on forever, and the Árpád Bridge flyover splits the heart of the district (Flórián tér) in two. But behind all this are some of the most important Roman ruins in Hungary, noteworthy museums and small, quiet neighbourhoods that still recall *fin-de-siècle* Óbuda.

Aquincum (Map pp226–7), the most complete Roman civilian town in Hungary and now a museum, had paved streets and fairly sumptuous single-storey houses with courtyards, fountains and mosaic floors, as well as sophisticated drainage and heating systems. Not all that is apparent today as you walk among the ruins, but you can see its outlines as well as those of the big public baths, market, an early Christian church and a temple dedicated to the god Mithra, the chief deity of a religion that once rivalled Christianity in its number of believers (see p61).

AQUINCUM MUSEUM Map pp226-7

Aquincumi Múzeum; ☎ 250 1650, 430 1081; www.aquincum.hu; III Szentendrei út 139; archaeological park adult/child 400/150Ft, park & museum adult/child/family 700/300/1200Ft; 🕑 park/museum 9/10am-6pm Tue-Sun May-Sep, 9/10am-5pm Tue-Sun 15-30 Apr & Oct; HÉV Aquincum

In the centre of what remains of the Roman civilian settlement, the Aquincum Museum tries to put the ruins in perspective, with some success. Most of the big sculptures and stone sarcophagi are outside to the left of the museum or behind it in the lapidary. Keep an eye open for the replica of a 3rd-century portable organ called a *hydra* (and the mosaic illustrating how it was played), pottery moulds, floor mosaics from the governor's palace across the river on Óbuda Island and a mock-up of a Roman bath.

HERCULES VILLA Map pp226-7

Herkules Villa; ☎ 250 1650; III Meggyfa utca 19-21; admission free; 🕑 10am-6pm Tue-Sun May-Sep, 10am-5pm Tue-Sun 15-30 Apr & Oct; 🚍 86

Hercules Villa, in the middle of a vast housing estate northwest of Fő tér, is the name given to some reconstructed Roman ruins. The name is derived from the astonishing 3rd-century floor mosaics of Hercules' exploits found in what was a Roman villa.

IMRE VARGA EXHIBITION HOUSE

Map pp226-7

Varga Imre Kiállítóháza; ☎ 250 0274; III Laktanya utca 7; adult/child 500/250Ft; 10am-6pm Tue-Sun; 86

This exhibition space includes sculptures, statues, medals and drawings by Varga (1923–), one of Hungary's foremost sculptors. Like others before him, notably Zsigmond Kisfaludi Strobl (see p57), he seems to have sat on both sides of the fence politically for decades – sculpting Béla Kun and Lenin as dextrously as he did St Stephen, Béla Bartók and even Imre Nagy (see p66). A short distance southwest of the museum is more of Varga's work: a group of metal sculptures of rather worried-looking women holding umbrellas in the middle of the road.

KASSÁK MUSEUM Map pp226-7

☎ 368 7021; III Fő tér 1; admission free, temporary exhibitions adult/child 150/100Ft; 10am-6pm Tue-Sun; 86

Sharing the same building as the Vasarely Museum (right) but facing the inner courtyard, the Kassák Museum contains some real gems of early-20th-century avant-garde art as well as the complete works of the artist and writer Lajos Kassák (1887–1967). It is a three-hall art gallery on the 1st floor.

KISCELLI MUSEUM & MUNICIPAL GALLERY Map pp226-7

Kiscelli Múzeum; ☎ 388 8560, 250 0304; III Kiscelli utca 108; adult/child/family 600/300/1000Ft; 10am-6pm Tue-Sun Apr-Oct, 10am-4pm Nov-Mar; 17

Housed in an 18th-century monastery, later a barracks that was badly damaged in WWII and again in 1956, the exhibits at this museum southwest of Flórián tér attempt to tell the story (from the human side) of Budapest since liberation from the Turks. The museum counts among its best displays a complete 19th-century apothecary moved here from Kálvin tér, ancient signboards advertising shops and other concerns and rooms furnished with Empire, Biedermeier and Art Nouveau furniture and bric-a-brac. The **Municipal Gallery** (Fővárosi Képtár), with its impressive art collection (József Rippl-Rónai, Lajos Tihanyi, István Csók, Béla Czóbel etc), is upstairs.

ROMAN MILITARY AMPHITHEATRE

Map pp226-7

Római Katonai Amfiteátrum; III Pacsirtamező utca; admission free; 24hr; 86

Built in the 2nd century for the Roman garrisons, this amphitheatre about 800m south of Flórián tér could accommodate up to 15,000 spectators and was larger than the Colosseum in Rome. The rest of the military camp extended north to Flórián tér. Archaeology and classical-history buffs taking the 86 bus to Flórián tér should descend at III Nagyszombat utca. HÉV passengers should get off at Tímár utca.

VASARELY MUSEUM Map pp226-7

☎ 388 7551; III Szentlélek tér 6; admission free, temporary exhibitions adult/child 400/200Ft; 10am-5.30pm Tue-Sun; 86

In the crumbling Zichy Mansion, this museum (part of the Museum of Fine Arts; p71) contains the works of Victor Vasarely (or Vásárhelyi Győző before he emigrated to Paris in 1930), the late 'father of op art'. The works, especially ones like *Dirac* and *Tlinko-F*, are excellent and fun to watch as they swell and move around the canvas. On the 1st floor are exhibits of works by Hungarian artists working abroad.

ZSIGMOND KUN FOLK ART COLLECTION Map pp226-7

Kun Zsigmond Népművészeti Gyűjtemény; ☎ 368 1138; III Fő tér 4; adult/child 300/200Ft; 10am-6pm Tue-Sun; 86

This charming small museum displays folk art amassed by a wealthy ethnographer in his 18th-century townhouse. Most of the pottery and ceramics are from Mezőtúr near the Tisza River, but there are some rare Moravian and Swabian pieces as well as Transylvanian furniture and textiles. The attendants are very proud of the collection so be prepared for some lengthy explanations. And don't ask about the priceless tile stove that a workman knocked over a couple of years back (unless you want to see a grown man cry).

BUDA HILLS

With 'peaks' reaching over 500m, a comprehensive system of trails and no lack of unusual conveyances, the Buda Hills (Map p216) make up what is the city's playground, and they're a welcome respite from hot, dusty Pest in the warmer months. Indeed, some well-heeled Budapest families have summer homes here. If you're planning to ramble, take along a copy of Cartographia's 1: 30,000 *A Budai-hegység* map (No 6; 900Ft), available from bookshops and newsstands throughout the city. Apart from the Béla Bartók Memorial House (right), there are very few sights per se, though you might want to poke your head into one of the Buda Hills' several caves (p138).

With all the unusual transport options, heading for the hills is more than half the fun. From the Moszkva tér metro station on the M2 line in Buda, walk west along Szilágyi Erzsébet fasor for 10 minutes (or take tram 18 or 56 for two stops) to the circular high-rise **Hotel Budapest** (Map p216; II Szilágyi Erzsébet fasor 47). Directly opposite is the terminus of the **Cog Railway** (Fogaskerekű vasút; ☎ 355 4167; admission 1 BKV ticket or adult/child 170/85Ft; 🕑 up 5am-11pm, down 5.20am-11.30pm). Built in 1874, the cog climbs for 3.6km in about 16 minutes to Széchenyi-hegy (427m), one of the prettiest residential areas in the city.

At Széchenyi-hegy, you can stop for a picnic in the park south of the old-time station or board the narrow-gauge **Children's Railway** (Gyermekvasut; ☎ 397 5394; www.gyermekvasut.com; adult/child 300/ 100Ft; 🕑 10am-5pm Mon-Fri, 9.45am-5.30pm Sat & Sun mid-Mar–late Oct, 10am-4pm Tue-Fri, 10am-5pm Sat & Sun late Oct–mid-Mar), two minutes to the south on Hegyhát út. The railway was built in 1951 by Pioneers (socialist Scouts) and is staffed entirely by schoolchildren aged 10 to 14 – with the exception of the engineer. The little train chugs along for 12km, terminating at Hűvösvölgy (Chilly Valley). There are walks fanning out from any of the stops along the way, or you can return to Moszkva tér on tram 56 from Hűvösvölgy. The train operates about once an hour (every 45 minutes at the weekend in peak season).

A more interesting way down from the hills, though, is to get off at János-hegy, the fourth stop on the Children's Railway and the highest point (527m) in the hills. About 700m due east is the **chair lift** (*libegő;* ☎ 394 3764; adult/child 500/200Ft; 🕑 9.30am-5pm mid-May–mid-Sep, 9.30am-4pm mid-Sep–mid-May), which will take you down to Zugligeti út. (Note the chair lift is closed on the Monday of every even-numbered week.) From here bus 158 returns to Moszkva tér (last one is just after 10.15pm).

BÉLA BARTÓK MEMORIAL HOUSE

Map p216

Bartók Béla Emlékház; ☎ 394 2100; II Csalán út 29; adult/child 500/250Ft; 🕑 10am-5pm Tue-Sun; 🚌 29

North of Szilágyi Erzsébet fasor but still very much in the Buda Hills, this recently renovated house is where the great composer resided from 1932 until 1940, when he emigrated to the USA. Among other things on display is the old Edison recorder

MITHRA & THE GREAT SACRIFICE

Mithraism, the worship of the god Mithra, originated in Persia. As Roman rule extended into Asia, the religion became extremely popular with traders, imperial slaves and mercenaries of the Roman army and spread rapidly throughout the empire in the 2nd and 3rd centuries AD. In fact, Mithraism was the principal rival of Christianity until Constantine came to the throne in the 4th century.

Mithraism was a mysterious religion with its devotees sworn to secrecy. What little is known of Mithra, the god of justice and social contract, has been deduced from reliefs and icons found in sanctuaries and temples, such as the one at Aquincum. Most of these portray Mithra clad in a Persian-style cap and tunic, sacrificing a white bull in front of Sol, the sun god. From the bull's blood sprout grain and grapes and from its semen animals. Sol's wife Luna, the moon, begins her cycle and time is born.

Mithraism and Christianity were close competitors partly because of the similarity in many of their rituals. Both involve the birth of a deity on 25 December, shepherds, death and resurrection, and a form of baptism. Devotees knelt when they worshipped and a common meal – a 'communion' of bread and water – was a regular feature of both liturgies.

(complete with wax cylinders) that Bartók used to record Hungarian folk music in Transylvania, as well as furniture and other objects he collected.

OUTER BUDA DISTRICTS

Worth a visit are a number of unusual sights further afield in southwest Buda. Whether you're into socialist icons, exquisite European furniture or tropical fish in formation, they're all an easy bus ride away.

NAGYTÉTÉNY CASTLE MUSEUM

Nagytétényi Kastélymúzeum; ☎ 207 5462, 207 0005; XXII Kastélypark utca 9-11; admission free, special exhibitions adult/child 600/300Ft; 🕑 10am-6pm Tue-Sun; 🚌 3 from XI Móricz Zsigmond körtér in Pest

In a baroque mansion in deepest south Buda, Nagytétény Castle Museum contains an exhibition from the Applied Arts Museum (p69) tracing the development of European furniture – from the Gothic to Biedermeier styles (approximately 1450 to 1850) – with some 300 items on display in more than two dozen rooms.

STATUE PARK Map p216

Szoborpark; ☎ 424 7500; www.szoborpark.hu; cnr XXII Szabadkai út & Balatoni út; adult/child 600/400Ft; 🕑 10am-dusk; 🚌 for Diósd-Érd

Home to more than 40 busts, statues and plaques of Lenin, Marx, Béla Kun and 'heroic' workers that have ended up on trash heaps in other former socialist countries, Statue Park is a truly mind-blowing place to visit. Ogle at the socialist realism and try to imagine that at least four of these monstrous monuments were erected as recently as the late 1980s; a few of them, including the Béla Kun memorial of our 'hero' in a crowd by fence-sitting sculptor Imre Varga (p60), were still in place when this author moved to Budapest in early 1992.

To reach this socialist Disneyland, take tram 19 from I Batthyány tér in Buda, tram 49 from V Deák Ferenc tér in Pest or red-numbered bus 7 from V Ferenciek tere in Pest to the terminus at XI Etele tér. From the square catch a yellow Volán bus from stand 7 to Diósd-Érd; you'll want to get off at the fifth stop.

A direct bus costing 1950/1350Ft per adult/child return departs from in front of the Le Meridien Budapest hotel on V Deák Ferenc tér daily at 11am year-round, with an extra departure at 3pm March to October and additional ones at 10am and 4pm in July and August.

TROPICARIUM-OCEANARIUM

☎ 424 3050; www.tropicarium.hu; XXII Nagytétényi út 37-45; adult/child 1700/1000Ft; 🕑 10am-8pm; 🚌 3 from XI Móricz Zsigmond körtér

This vast aquarium complex at the Campona shopping centre in south Buda measures 3000 sq metres and is apparently the largest in Central Europe. Don't expect just to see snazzy neon-coloured tropical examples, however; this place prides itself on its local specimens too.

MARGARET ISLAND

Sleeping p158

Neither Buda nor Pest though part of district XIII, 2.5km-long Margaret Island (Margitsziget; Map pp226–7 and Map pp218–19) in the middle of the Danube was always the domain of one religious order or another until the Turks arrived and turned what was then called the Island of Rabbits into – appropriately enough – a harem, from which all 'infidels' were barred. It's been a public park since the mid-19th century.

Like the Buda Hills, Margaret Island is not overly endowed with important sights and landmarks. But boasting a couple of large complexes, a thermal spa, gardens and shaded walkways, the island is a lovely place to head on a hot afternoon.

Margaret Island is a great spot for sports and other activities, and you could spend the entire day here cycling, swimming or just pampering yourself at the Danubius Grand Hotel Margitsziget (p158), one of the most modern spas in Budapest.

Margaret Island has two popular swimming pools on its western side. The first is the indoor/outdoor **Alfréd Hajós National Sports Pool** (Nemzeti Sportuszoda; Map pp218–19; XIII Margit-sziget), officially named after

MARGARET ISLAND TRANSPORT

Bus 26 to Árpád Bridge from Nyugati train station
Tram 4 or 6 to Margaret Bridge

Inline skaters, Margaret Island

the Olympic swimming champion and later architect Alfréd Hajós, who won the 100m and 1200m events at the first modern Olympiad in 1896 and who actually built the place. Further north is the renovated **Palatinus** (Map pp226–7; XIII Margit-sziget) complex of outdoor pools, huge water slides and *strand* (beaches). For more on these pools see p137 and p137.

You can hire a bicycle from one of several stands, including **Sétacikli** (Map pp218–19; ☎ 06 30 966 6453; 3-speed per half-hour/hour/day 400/600/1800Ft, pedal coach for 3/5 people per hour 1800/2700Ft; 🕒 10am-dusk Mar-Oct), next to the athletic stadium as you walk from Margaret Bridge. **Bringóhintó** (Map pp226–7; ☎ 329 2073, 06 30 881 0983; www.bringohinto.hu; mountain bike per half-hour/hour 590/990Ft, pedal coach for 4 people 1480/3380Ft, inline skates 880/1480Ft; 🕒 8am-dusk year-round) rents out equipment from the refreshment stand near the Japanese Garden in the northern part of the island.

A twirl around the island in one of the horse-drawn **carriages** (Map pp226–7), stationed just south of the Bringóhintó bike-rental stand, costs from about 2000Ft per person.

PEST

Eating p111; Sleeping p158; Shopping p143

While Buda can often feel like a garden, Pest is an urban jungle, with a wealth of architecture, museums, historic buildings and broad boulevards that are unmatched on the other side of the Danube. And while there's nothing like the Buda Hills here, there's no shortage of green 'lungs' either – City Park at the end of Andrássy út is the largest park in Budapest and is filled with various sights and diversions.

INNER TOWN

Belváros (Inner Town; Map p224) is the heart of Pest and contains the most valuable commercial real estate in the city. The area north of busy Ferenciek tere is particularly full of flashy boutiques and well-touristed bars and restaurants; you'll usually hear more German, Italian, Spanish and English spoken here than Hungarian.

The Inner Town contains four important 'centres': V Deák Ferenc tér, a busy square in the northeast corner of the Inner Town and the only place where all three metro lines (M1/2/3) converge; touristy V Vörösmarty tér, which is on the M1 metro at the northern end of V Váci utca; V Ferenciek tere on metro M3, which divides the Inner Town at Szabadsajtó út (Free Press Ave); and V Egyetem tér (University Sq), a five-minute walk south along V Károly Mihály utca from Ferenciek tere and 250m northwest of Kálvin tér on the M3 metro along leafy V Kecskeméti utca.

Semipedestrianised IX Ráday utca, which leads south from V Kálvin tér into Ferencváros, is full of cafés, clubs and restaurants where university students entertain themselves these days.

PEST TRANSPORT

Bus 7 to the Inner Town, 15 to the Inner Town, Inner North Town and Józsefváros & Ferencváros; 16, 105 to the Inner North Town

Metro M1 to the Inner Town, Northern Inner Town, Svent István & Terézváros, Erzsébetváros, Andrássy Út and City Park; M2 to the Inner Town, Northern Inner Town, Erzsébetváros, Józsefváros & Ferencváros and Andrássy Út; M3 to the Inner Town, Northern Inner Town, Svent István & Terézváros, Józsefváros & Ferencváros and Andrássy Út

Tram 2, 2/a to the Inner Town, Inner North Town and Svent István & Terézváros; 4, 6 to the Inner North Town, Svent István & Terézváros, Erzsébetváros, Józsefváros & Ferencváros and Andrássy Út; 47, 49 to Józsefváros & Ferencváros

Trolleybus 70, 72 to City Park; 74 to Erzsébetváros; 76, 78, 79 to Svent István & Terézváros and City Park

PEST TOP FIVE

- Basilica of St Stephen (right)
- House of Terror (p71)
- Hungarian State Opera House (p71)
- Museum of Fine Arts (p71)
- Parliament (opposite)

INNER TOWN PARISH CHURCH
Map p224

Belvárosi plébániatemplom; V Március 15 tér 2; 2 or 2/a

On the eastern side of Március 15 tér, sitting uncomfortably close to the Elizabeth Bridge flyover is where a Romanesque church was first built in the 12th century within a Roman fortress. You can still see a few bits of the fort, **Contra Aquincum**, in the small park to the north. The present church was rebuilt in the 14th and 18th centuries, and you can easily spot Gothic, Renaissance, baroque and even Turkish elements both inside and out.

UNDERGROUND RAILWAY MUSEUM
Map p224

Földalatti Vasúti Múzeum; 461 6500; 1 BKV ticket or adult/child 170/85Ft; 10am-5pm Tue-Sun Apr-Oct, 10am-4pm Tue-Sun Nov-Mar; M M1/2/3 Deák Ferenc tér

In the pedestrian subway beneath V Deák Ferenc tér and next to the main ticket window, the Underground Railway Museum traces the history of the capital's three underground lines and displays plans for the future. Much emphasis is put on the little yellow metro (M1), Continental Europe's first underground railway, which opened for the millenary celebrations in 1896 and was completely renovated for the millecentenary 100 years later.

NORTHERN INNER TOWN

The Northern Inner Town (Map p224 and Map p222), which is more accurately called Lipótváros (Leopold Town), is full of offices, government ministries, 19th-century apartment blocks and grand squares. Its confines are, in effect, Szent István körút to the north, V József Attila utca to the south, the Danube to the west and, to the east, V Bajcsy-Zsilinszky út, the arrow-straight boulevard that stretches from central Deák Ferenc tér and Nyugati tér, where Nyugati train station (Nyugati pályaudvar) is located.

BASILICA OF ST STEPHEN Map p224

Szent István Bazilika; 311 0839, 338 2151; V Szent István tér; 9am-5pm & 7-8pm Mon-Fri, 9am-1pm & 7-8pm Sat, 1-5pm & 7-8pm Sun; M M2 Arany János utca

Budapest's cathedral was built over the course of half a century and completed in 1905. Much of the interruption had to do with the fiasco in 1868 when the dome collapsed during a storm, and the structure had to be demolished and rebuilt from the ground up. The basilica is rather dark and gloomy inside, but take a trip to the top of the **dome** (adult/child 500/400Ft; 10am-4.30pm Apr & May, 9.30am-6pm Jun-Aug, 10am-5.30pm Sep & Oct), which can be reached by lift and 146 steps and offers one of the best views in the city.

To the right as you enter the basilica is a small **treasury** (*kincstár;* 9am-5pm Apr-Sep, 10am-4pm Oct-Mar) of ecclesiastical objects. Behind the main altar and to the left is the basilica's major drawing card: the **Holy Right Chapel** (Szent Jobb kápolna; 9am-4.30pm Mon-Sat, 1-4.30pm Sun May-Sep, 10am-4pm Mon-Sat, 1-4.30pm Sun Oct-Apr). It contains the Holy Right (also known as the Holy Dexter), the mummified right hand of St Stephen and an object of great devotion. It was returned to Hungary by Habsburg empress Maria Theresa in 1771 after it was discovered in a monastery in Bosnia. Like the Crown of St Stephen, it too was snatched by the bad guys after WWII but was soon, er, handed over to the rightful (ugh) owners.

English-language guided tours of the basilica (with/without dome visit 2000/1500Ft) depart weekdays at 9.30am, 11am, 2pm and 3.30pm and on Saturday at 9.30am and 11am.

ETHNOGRAPHY MUSEUM Map p222

Néprajzi Múzeum; 473 2400; www.hem.hu; V Kossuth Lajos tér 12; admission free, temporary exhibitions adult/child/family from 500/200/1000Ft; 10am-6pm Tue-Sun; M M2 Kossuth Lajos tér

Visitors are offered an easy introduction to traditional Hungarian life here, with thousands of displays in 13 rooms on the 1st floor. The mock-ups of peasant houses from the Őrség and Sárköz regions of Western and Southern Transdanubia are well done, and there are some priceless objects collected from Transdanubia. On the 2nd floor, most of the temporary exhibitions deal with other peoples of Europe and further afield. The building itself was designed in 1893 to house the Supreme Court; note the ceiling fresco of *Justice* by Károly Lotz.

PARLIAMENT Map p222

Országház; ☎ 441 4904, 441 4415; V Kossuth Lajos tér 1-3, Gate X; admission free for EU citizens, other nationalities adult/child 2300/1150Ft; English-language tours ⏲ 10am, noon, 1pm, 2pm & 6pm daily; Ⓜ M2 Kossuth Lajos tér

The Eclectic Parliament, designed by Imre Steindl and completed in 1902, has about 700 sumptuously decorated rooms but you'll only get to see three on a guided tour of the North Wing: the main staircase and Domed Hall, where the **Crown of St Stephen** (below), the nation's most important national icon, is on display, along with the ceremonial sword, orb and the oldest object among the coronation regalia, the 10th-century Persian-made sceptre with a crystal head depicting a lion; the Loge Hall; and the Congress Hall, where the House of Lords of the one-time bicameral assembly sat until 1944. The building is a blend of many architectural styles – neo-Gothic, neo-Romanesque, neobaroque – and overall works very well. Unfortunately what was spent on the design wasn't matched in the building materials. The ornate structure was surfaced with a porous form of limestone that does not resist pollution very well. Renovations began almost immediately after it opened and will continue until the building crumbles. Members of Parliament sit in the National Assembly Hall in the South Wing from February to June and again from September to December. Tours are available in six languages other than Hungarian and English.

LIFT US THIS DAY

One of the strangest public conveyances you'll ever encounter can still be found in a few office and government buildings in Budapest. They're the *körfogó* (rotator) lifts or elevators, nicknamed 'Pater Nosters' for their supposed resemblance to a large rosary. A Pater Noster is essentially a rotating series of individual cubicles that runs continuously. You don't push a button and wait for a door to open; you hop on just as a cubicle reaches floor level and you jump out – quickly – when you reach your desired floor. If you were wondering what happens at the top, stay on and find out. Don't worry – you'll live. The lift simply descends to the ground floor in darkness to begin its next revolution. The most central Pater Noster – that you may or may not be able to ride – is in the government building at V Vigadó utca 6 (Map p224).

ROOSEVELT TÉR Map p224

🚊 2 or 2/a

Roosevelt tér, named in 1947 after the long-serving (1933–45) American president, is at the foot of Chain Bridge and offers among the best views of Castle Hill in Pest. Reach it from Buda on bus 16 or 105.

On the southern end of the square is a **statue of Ferenc Deák**, the Hungarian minister largely responsible for the Compromise of

THE CROWN OF ST STEPHEN

Legend tells us that it was Asztrik, the first abbot of the Benedictine monastery at Pannonhalma in Western Transdanubia, who presented a crown to Stephen as a gift from Pope Sylvester II around the year 1000, thus legitimising the new king's rule and assuring his loyalty to Rome over Constantinople. It's a nice story but has nothing to do with the object on display in the Parliament building. That two-part crown, with its characteristic bent cross, pendants hanging on either side and enamelled plaques of the Apostles, dates from the 12th century. Regardless of its provenance, the Crown of St Stephen has become the very symbol of the Hungarian nation.

The crown has disappeared several times over the centuries – purloined or otherwise – only to reappear later. During the Mongol invasions of the 13th century, the crown was dropped while being transported to a safe house, giving it that slightly skewed look. More recently, in 1945, Hungarian fascists fleeing ahead of the Soviet army took the crown to Austria. Eventually it fell into the hands of the US army, which transferred it to Fort Knox in Kentucky. In January 1978 the crown was returned to Hungary with great ceremony – and relief. Because legal judgments had always been handed down 'in the name of St Stephen's Crown' it was considered a living symbol and had thus been 'kidnapped'.

Roosevelt tér and statue of Count István Széchenyi (p43)

1867, which brought about the Dual Monarchy of Austria and Hungary (p44). The statue on the western side is of an Austrian and a Hungarian child holding hands in peaceful bliss. The Magyar kid's hair is tousled and he is naked; the Osztrák is demurely covered by a bit of the patrician's robe and his hair neatly coifed.

The Art Nouveau building with the gold tiles to the east is **Gresham Palace** (V Roosevelt tér 5-6), built by an English insurance company in 1907. After a major overhaul, it now houses the sumptuous Four Seasons Gresham Palace Hotel (p159), arguably the city's finest hostelry. The **Hungarian Academy of Sciences** (Magyar Tudományos Akadémia; V Roosevelt tér 9), founded by Count István Széchenyi (p42), is at the northern end of the square.

STATUES & MONUMENTS Map p222

Southeast of V Kossuth Lajos tér is a **statue of Imre Nagy** (V Vértanúk tere; Ⓜ M2 Kossuth Lajos tér), the reformist communist prime minister executed in 1958 for his role in the Uprising two years earlier (p47). It was unveiled with great ceremony in the summer of 1996.

Further south from the same square is a new monument to Hungarian Jews shot and thrown into the Danube by members of the fascist Arrow Cross Party (p46) in 1944 entitled **Shoes on the Danube** (V Pesti alsó rakpart; tram 2 or 2/a) by sculptor Gyula Pauer. It's a simple affair – 60 pairs of old-style boots and shoes in cast iron, tossed higgledy-piggledy on a bank of the river – but it is one of the most poignant monuments yet unveiled in this city of so many tears. And when you've had your look around, considered how the authorities managed to round up so many Jews so very quickly – you mean there were actually snitches and informants among the brave and heroic souls of Budapest?!? – and wondered what it must have been like to hit the water, drowning, with a bullet in your guts, look up to open sky and do something the detainees of the 'glorious 1000-year' Reich could not do. Don't say, but shout: 'Never! Never! Never again!' Whoever wasn't listening 60 years ago just might have tuned in by now (but don't count on it).

SZABADSÁG TÉR Map p222

bus **15**

'Independence Square', one of the largest in the city, is a few minutes' walk northeast of Roosevelt tér. In the centre is a memorial to the Soviet army, one of the very few still left in Budapest.

At the eastern side of the square is the fortress-like **US Embassy** (V Szabadság tér 12), now cut off from the square by high metal fencing and concrete blocks. It was here that Cardinal József Mindszenty sought refuge after the 1956 Uprising and stayed for

15 years until departing for Vienna in 1971 (below). The embassy backs onto Hold utca (Moon St), which, until 1990, was named Rosenberg házaspár utca (Rosenberg Couple St) after the American husband and wife Julius and Ethel Rosenberg who were executed as communist spies in the USA in 1953.

On that street south of the embassy you'll find the sensational former **Royal Postal Savings Bank** (V Hold utca 4), a Secessionist extravaganza of colourful tiles and folk motifs built by Ödön Lechner (p21) in 1901. It is now part of the **National Bank of Hungary** (Magyar Nemzeti Bank; V Szabadság tér 8) next door, which has reliefs that illustrate trade and commerce through history: Arab camel traders, African rug merchants, Chinese tea salesmen – and the inevitable solicitor witnessing contracts.

SZENT ISTVÁN KÖRÚT & TERÉZVÁROS

Szent István körút (Map p222), the northernmost stretch of the Big Ring Road in Pest, runs in a westerly direction from Nyugati tér to Margaret Bridge and the Danube. It's an interesting street to stroll along, with many fine Eclectic-style buildings decorated with Atlases, reliefs and other details. The neighbourhood to the north of it, Újlipótváros (New Leopold Town; Map p222 and Map pp218–19), so called to distinguish it from Lipótváros (Leopold Town) in the Northern Inner Town – Archduke Leopold was the grandson of Habsburg empress Maria Theresa – is especially rewarding to explore on foot (p82).

Teréz körút carries on from Szent István körút after the Nyugati train station. The neighbourhood on either side of this section of the ring road - district VI - is known as Terézváros (Teresa Town; Map p222) and was named in honour of Maria Teresa. It extends as far as VI Király utca and the start of VII Erzsébet körút.

HOUSE OF HUNGARIAN PHOTOGRAPHERS Map p222

Magyar Fotográfusok Háza; ☎ 473 2666; VI Nagymező utca 20; adult/senior & student 500/200Ft; ⏲ 2-7pm Mon-Fri, 11am-7pm Sat & Sun; Ⓜ M1 Opera

The House of Hungarian Photographers is an extraordinary venue in the city's theatre district with top-class photography exhibitions. It is in delightful Mai Manó Ház, which was built in 1894 as a photo studio and has the bizarre meaning 'Modern Devil House'.

NYUGATI TRAIN STATION Map p222

Nyugati pályaudvar; ☎ 349 0115; VI Teréz körút 55-57; Ⓜ M3 Nyugati pályaudvar

The large iron and glass structure on Nyugati tér (known as Marx tér until the early 1990s) is the Nyugati train station, built in 1877 by the Paris-based Eiffel Company. In the early 1970s a train actually crashed through the enormous glass screen on the main façade when its brakes failed, coming to rest at the 4 and 6 tram line.

CARDINAL MINDSZENTY

Born József Pehm in the village of Csehimindszent near Szombathely in 1892, Mindszenty was politically active from the time of his ordination in 1915. Imprisoned under the short-lived regime of communist Béla Kun in 1919 and again when the fascist Arrow Cross came to power in 1944, Mindszenty was made archbishop of Esztergom (and thus primate of Hungary) in 1945 and cardinal the following year.

When the new cardinal refused to secularise Hungary's Roman Catholic schools under the new communist regime in 1948, he was arrested, tortured and sentenced to life imprisonment for treason. Released during the 1956 Uprising, Mindszenty took refuge in the US embassy on Szabadság tér when the communists returned to power. There he would remain until 1971.

As relations between the Kádár regime and the Holy See began to thaw in the late 1960s, the Vatican made several requests for the cardinal to leave Hungary, which he refused to do. Following the intervention of US president Richard Nixon, Mindszenty left for Vienna, where he continued to criticise the Vatican's relations with the regime in Hungary. He retired in 1974 and died the following year. But as he had vowed not to return to Hungary until the last Russian soldier had left Hungarian soil, Mindszenty's remains were not returned until May 1991. This was actually several weeks before that pivotal date.

ERZSÉBETVÁROS

The Big Ring Road slices district VII, also called Erzsébetváros (Elizabeth Town; Map p222 and Map p224), in half between two busy squares: Oktogon and Blaha Lujza tér. The eastern side is a rather poor area (though developing fast) with little of interest to travellers except the Keleti train station (Keleti pályaudvar; Map pp218–19) on Baross tér. The western side, bounded by the Little Ring Road, has always been predominantly Jewish, and this was the ghetto where Jews were forced to live behind wooden fences when the Nazis occupied Hungary in 1944.

GREAT SYNAGOGUE Map p224

Nagy zsinagóga; VII Dohány utca 2-8; admission 300Ft; 10am-5pm Mon-Thu, 10am-2pm Fri, 10am-2pm Sun mid-Apr–Oct, 10am-3pm Mon-Thu, 10am-2pm Fri, 10am-2pm Sun Nov–mid-Apr; M M2 Astoria

The Great Synagogue is the largest Jewish house of worship in the world outside New York City and can seat 3000 of the faithful. Built in 1859, it contains both Romantic-style and Moorish architectural elements. Concerts are held here in summer.

In an annexe of the synagogue is the **Jewish Museum** (Zsidó Múzeum; ☎ 342 8949; VII Dohány utca 2; synagogue & museum adult/student & child 1000/400Ft; same), which contains objects related to religious and everyday life, and an interesting handwritten book of the local Burial Society from the 18th century. The Holocaust Memorial Room relates the events of 1944–45, including the infamous mass murder of doctors and patients at a hospital on Maros utca. English-language tours (adult/student & child 1900/1600Ft) are available hourly from 10.30am to 1.30pm or 3.30pm Monday to Thursday and 10.30am to 12.30pm Friday and Sunday.

On the synagogue's north side, the **Holocaust Memorial** (Map p224; VII Wesselényi utca) stands over the mass graves of those murdered by the Nazis in 1944–45. On the leaves of the metal 'tree of life' are the family names of some of the 400,000 victims.

HUNGARIAN ELECTROTECHNOLOGY MUSEUM Map p224

Magyar Elektrotechnikai Múzeum; ☎ 322 0472; VII Kazinczy utca 21; admission free; 11am-5pm Tue-Sat; M M2 Astoria

This place doesn't sound like everyone's cup of tea, but the staff are very enthusiastic and some of the exhibits are unusual enough for a visit. Its collection of 19th-century generators, condensers, motors and – egad – the world largest supply of electricity-consumption meters is not very inspiring, but the staff will show you how the alarm system of the barbed-wire fence between Hungary and Austria once

RAOUL WALLENBERG, RIGHTEOUS GENTILE

Of all the 'righteous gentiles' honoured by Jews around the world, the most revered is Raoul Wallenberg, the Swedish diplomat and businessman who rescued as many as 35,000 Hungarian Jews during WWII.

Wallenberg, who came from a long line of bankers and diplomats, began working in 1936 for a trading firm whose president was a Hungarian Jew. In July 1944 the Swedish Foreign Ministry, at the request of Jewish and refugee organisations in the USA, sent the 32-year-old Wallenberg on a rescue mission to Budapest as an attaché to the embassy there. By that time, almost half a million Jews in Hungary had been sent to Nazi death camps.

Wallenberg immediately began issuing Swedish safe-conduct passes (called 'Wallenberg passports') from the former Swedish embassy (Map pp228–9; Minerva utca 3a/b; 27) on Gellért Hill, which bears a plaque attesting to the heroism of Wallenberg and the less well-known diplomats Carl-Ivan Danielsson (1880–1963) and Per Anger (1913–2002). He also set up a series of 'safe houses' flying the flag of Sweden and other neutral countries where Jews could seek asylum. He even followed German 'death marches' and deportation trains, distributing food and clothing and actually pulling some 500 people off the cars along the way.

When the Soviet army entered Budapest in January 1945, Wallenberg went to report to the authorities but in the wartime confusion was arrested for espionage and sent to Moscow. In the early 1950s, responding to reports that Wallenberg had been seen alive in a labour camp, the Soviet Union announced that he had in fact died of a heart attack in 1947. Several reports over the next two decades suggested Wallenberg was still alive, but none was ever confirmed. Many believe Wallenberg was executed by the Soviets, who suspected him of spying for the USA. A statue called the *Serpent Slayer* in honour of Raoul Wallenberg by Pál Pátzay stands in XIII Szent István Park (Map pp218–19).

worked. There's also a display on the nesting platforms that the electric company kindly builds for storks throughout the country so they won't try to nest on the wires and electrocute themselves.

MIKSA RÓTH MEMORIAL HOUSE

Map pp218-19

Róth Miksa Emlékház; ☎ 341 6789, 413 6147; VII Nefelejcs utca 26; adult/child 200/100Ft; ⏲ 2-6pm Tue-Sat; Ⓜ M2 Keleti pályaudvar

This fabulous museum exhibits the work of the eponymous Art Nouveau stained-glass maker Róth (1865–1944) on two floors of the house and workshop where he lived and worked from 1911 until his death. Less well known are the master's stunning mosaics. Roth's dark brown, almost foreboding, living quarters stand in sharp contrast to the lively, technicolour creations that emerged from his workshop.

JÓZSEFVÁROS & FERENCVÁROS

From Blaha Lujza tér, the Big Ring Road runs through district VIII, also called Józsefváros (Joseph Town; Map p222 and Map pp218–19). The western side of the district transforms itself from a neighbourhood of lovely 19th-century townhouses and villas around the Little Ring Road to a large student quarter. East of the boulevard is the once rough-and-tumble district so poignantly described in the Pressburger brothers' *Homage to the Eighth District* (p23), and where much of the fighting in October 1956 took place. Today it is being developed at breakneck speed and the reverberation of pile-drivers is constant.

The neighbourhood south of Üllői út is Ferencváros (Francis Town; Map pp218–19 and Map pp228–9), home of the city's most popular football team, Ferencvárosi Torna Club (Ferencváros; p140), and many of its tough, green-and-white-clad supporters.

APPLIED ARTS MUSEUM Map pp218-19

Iparművészeti Múzeum; ☎ 456 5100; www.imm.hu; IX Üllői út 33-37; admission free, temporary exhibitions adult/child 600/300Ft; ⏲ 10am-6pm Tue-Sun; Ⓜ M3 Ferenc körút

This stunning building, designed by Ödön Lechner and decorated with Zsolnay ceramic tiles, was completed for the Millenary Exhibition (1896) but was badly damaged during WWII and again in 1956. The galleries of the Applied Arts Museum, which surround a central hall of white marble supposedly modelled on the Alhambra in southern Spain, usually contain a wonderful array of Hungarian furniture dating from the 18th and 19th centuries, Art Nouveau and Secessionist artefacts, and objects related to the history of trades and crafts (glass making, bookbinding, gold-smithing, leatherwork etc). However, the last time we visited there were only temporary exhibitions on display and the permanent collections were closed. Nice way to rake in the dosh; instead, visit the museum's European furniture exhibit at **Nagytétény Castle Museum** (p62).

HOLOCAUST MEMORIAL CENTER

Map pp228-9

Holokauszt Emlékközpont; ☎ 455 3348; www.hdke.hu; IX Páva utca 39; admission free; ⏲ 10am-6pm Tue-Sun; Ⓜ M3 Ferenc körút

This centre, housed in a striking modern building in a working-class neighbourhood of Ferencváros, opened in 2004 on the 60th anniversary of the start of the holocaust in Hungary. Both a museum and an educational foundation, the centre displays pages from the harrowing 'Auschwitz Album', an unusual collection of photographs documenting the transport, internment and extermination of Hungarian Jews that was found by a camp survivor after liberation. In the central courtyard, a sublimely restored synagogue designed by Leopold Baumhorn and completed in 1924 hosts temporary exhibitions.

HUNGARIAN NATIONAL MUSEUM

Map p224

Magyar Nemzeti Múzeum; ☎ 338 2122, 317 7806; www.mnm.hu; VIII Múzeum körút 14-16; admission free, temporary exhibitions adult/child 700/350Ft; ⏲ 10am-6pm Tue-Sun; 🚋 47 or 49

The National Museum contains Hungary's most important collection of historical relics in a large neoclassical structure purpose-built in 1847. On the 1st floor exhibits trace the history of the Carpathian Basin from earliest times to the arrival of the Avars during the 9th century; 2nd-floor displays deal with the Magyar people to 1849 and Hungary in the 19th and 20th centuries.

Look out for: the enormous 3rd-century Roman mosaic from Balácapuszta, near Veszprém in Central Transdanubia, at the foot of the central staircase; the crimson silk royal coronation robe (or mantle) stitched by nuns at Veszprém; the reconstructed 3rd-century Roman villa from Pannonia; the treasury room with pre-Conquest gold jewellery; a second treasury room with later gold objects (including the 11th-century Monomachus crown); a stunning baroque library; and Beethoven's Broadwood piano.

HUNGARIAN NATURAL HISTORY MUSEUM Map pp228-9

Magyar Természettudományi Múzeum; ☎ 210 1085; www.nhmus.hu; VIII Ludovika tér 2-6; admission free, temporary exhibitions adult/child 1000/600Ft; 10am-6pm Wed-Mon; M M3 Klinikák

Just one metro stop southeast of the Ferenc körút station, the Natural History Museum has lots of hands-on interactive displays over three floors. The geological park in front of the museum is well designed and there's an interesting exhibit focusing on both the natural resources of the Carpathian Basin and the flora and fauna of Hungarian legends and tales.

LUDWIG MUSEUM OF CONTEMPORARY ART Map pp228-9

Kortárs Művészeti Múzeum; ☎ 555 3444; www.ludwigmuseum.hu; IX Komor Marcell utca 1; admission free, temporary exhibitions adult/child 1000/500Ft; 10am-6pm Tue, Fri & Sun, noon-6pm Wed, noon-8pm Thu, 10am-8pm Sat; 2

Budapest's most important collection of contemporary art has moved from the Royal Palace on Castle Hill to the palatial (and equally controversial) **Palace of Arts** (Művészetek Palotája; p131) opposite the National Theatre. The museum is the only one collecting and exhibiting international contemporary art, and shows works by American, Russian, German and French artists from the past 50 years and Hungarian, Czech, Slovakian, Romanian, Polish and Slovenian works from the 1990s onward.

NATIONAL THEATRE Map pp228-9

Nemzeti Színház; ☎ 476 6800; www.nemzetiszinhaz.hu; IX Bajor Gizi park 1; 2

The National Theatre by the Danube in southwestern Ferencváros opened in 2002 to much controversy. The design, by architect Mária Siklós, is supposedly 'Eclectic' to mirror other great Budapest buildings of that style (Gellért Hotel, Gresham Palace, Parliament). But in reality it is a pick-and-mix jumble sale of classical and folk motifs, porticoes, balconies and columns on the outside that just does not work and certainly will date fast. But then they said that about the Parliament building in 1902. Particularly odd is the ziggurat-like structure outside whose ramps lead to nowhere.

ZWACK UNICUM MUSEUM & VISITOR CENTRE Map pp228-9

Zwack Unicum Múzeum és Látogató Központ; ☎ 476 2383; www.zwackunicum.hu in Hungarian; IX Dandár utca 2; adult/child 1500/850Ft; 1-5pm Mon-Fri; 2

If you really can't get enough of Unicum, the thick brown medicinal-tasting bitter aperitif made from 40 herbs and weighing in at 42% alcohol – and supposedly named by Franz Joseph himself (see p30), visit this very commercial museum tracing the history of the product since it was first made in 1790 and inviting visitors to buy big at its *mintabolt* (sample store).

ANDRÁSSY ÚT

Andrássy út (Map pp218–19 and Map p222), listed as a Unesco World Heritage Site, starts a short distance north of Deák Ferenc tér and stretches for 2.5km to the northeast, ending at Hősök tere and Városliget, Pest's sprawling 'City Park'. Andrássy út is such a pretty boulevard and there's so much to enjoy en route that the best way to see it is on foot (p86), though the M1 metro runs beneath Andrássy út from Deák Ferenc tér as far as the City Park if you tire out.

ASIAN ART MUSEUMS Map pp218-19

M M1 Bajza utca

The Andrássy út area has two fine museums devoted to Asian arts and crafts within easy walking distance of one another. The **Ferenc Hopp Museum of East Asian Art** (Hopp Ferenc Kelet-Ázsiai Művészeti Múzeum; ☎ 322 8476; VI Andrássy út 103; adult/child 400/200Ft; 10am-6pm Tue-Sun) is in the former villa of its benefactor and namesake. Founded in 1919, the museum has a good collection of Indonesian *wayang* (shadow) puppets, Indian statuary and Lamaist sculpture and scroll paintings from Tibet.

Most of the Chinese and Japanese collection of ceramics and porcelain, textiles and sculpture is housed in the **György Ráth Museum** (Ráth György Múzeum; ☎ 342 3916; VI Városligeti fasor 12; adult/child 400/250Ft; 🕑 10am-6pm Tue-Sun), in a gorgeous Art Nouveau residence a few minutes south down Bajza utca.

FRANZ LISZT MEMORIAL MUSEUM

Map p222

Liszt Ferenc Emlékmúzeum; ☎ 322 9804; VI Vörösmarty utca 35; adult/child 400/250Ft; 🕑 10am-6pm Mon-Fri, 9am-5pm Sat; Ⓜ M1 Vörösmarty utca

This museum is in the building where the great composer lived in a 1st-floor apartment from 1881 until his death in 1886. The four rooms are filled with his pianos (including a tiny glass one), the composer's table, portraits and personal effects.

HOUSE OF TERROR Map p222

Terror Háza; ☎ 374 2600; www.terrorhaza.hu; Andrássy út 60; adult/child 1200/600Ft; 🕑 10am-6pm Tue-Fri, 10am-7.30pm Sat & Sun; Ⓜ M1 Vörösmarty utca

This museum, housed in the same building that served as headquarters of the dreaded ÁVH secret police (p47), purports to focus on the crimes and atrocities committed by both Hungary's fascist and Stalinist regimes, but the latter, particularly the years after WWII leading up to the 1956 Uprising, gets the lion's share of the exhibition space (almost three dozen rooms, halls and corridors over three floors). The tank in the central courtyard is a jarring introduction, and the wall displaying many of the victims' photos speaks volumes. But even more harrowing are the reconstructed prison cells and the final Perpetrators' Gallery, featuring photographs of the turncoats, spies, torturers and 'cogs-in-the-wheel', many of them still alive, who allowed or caused these atrocities to take place.

Millenary Monument, Hősök tere

HUNGARIAN STATE OPERA HOUSE

Map p222

Magyar Állami Operaház; ☎ 332 8197; www.operavisit.hu; VI Andrássy út 22; adult/student 2400/1200Ft; 🕑 English-language tours 3pm & 4pm; Ⓜ M1 Opera

The neo-Renaissance Hungarian State Opera House, among the city's most beautiful buildings, was designed by Miklós Ybl in 1884. If you cannot attend a concert or an opera, join one of the guided tours, which usually includes a brief musical performance. Tickets are available from the souvenir shop on the eastern side of the building facing Hajós utca.

MILLENARY MONUMENT Map pp218-19

Ezeréves Emlékmű; Ⓜ M1 Hősök tere

In the centre of Hősök tere (Heroes' Sq), which is at the northern end of Andrássy út and in effect forms the entrance to City Park, is this 36m-high pillar backed by colonnades to the right and left. Topping the pillar is the Angel Gabriel, who is holding the Hungarian crown and a cross. At the base are Árpád and the six other Magyar chieftains who occupied the Carpathian Basin in the late 9th century. The 14 statues in the colonnades are of rulers and statesmen – from King Stephen on the left to Lajos Kossuth on the right. The four allegorical figures atop are (from left to right): Work and Prosperity; War; Peace; Knowledge and Glory.

MUSEUM OF FINE ARTS Map pp218-19

Szépművészeti Múzeum; ☎ 469 7100, 363 2675; www.szepmuveszeti.hu; XIV Dózsa György út 41; admission free, temporary exhibitions adult/child 1200/600Ft; 🕑 10am-5.30pm Tue-Sun; Ⓜ M1 Hősök tere

The city's outstanding collection of foreign art works is housed in this renovated building dating from 1906. The Old Masters collection is the most complete, with thousands of works from the Dutch and Flemish, Spanish, Italian, German, French and British schools between the 13th and 18th centuries, including seven paintings by El Greco. Other sections include Egyptian and Graeco-Roman artefacts and 19th- and 20th-century paintings, watercolours, graphics and sculptures, including some important impressionist works. Free tours of key galleries are available in English at 11am Tuesday to Friday.

MŰCSARNOK Map pp218-19

Palace of Art; ☎ 460 7014, 363 2671; www.mucsarnok.hu; XIV Dózsa György út 37; 3-D film adult/child 1000/500F, exhibitions & film 1500/500Ft; 🕑 10am-6pm Tue-Sun; Ⓜ M1 Hősök tere

Műcsarnok is the among the city's largest exhibition spaces and hosts temporary exhibitions of works by Hungarian and foreign artists in fine and applied art, photography and design. Concerts are sometimes staged here as well. A 3-D film that whisks you around Hungary in 25 minutes (with commentary available in seven languages) is screened continuously from 10am to 5pm Tuesday to Sunday mid-March to September and from 10am to 4.30pm Friday to Sunday from October to mid-March.

POSTAL MUSEUM Map p224

Postamúzeum; ☎ 269 6838; VI Andrássy út 3; adult/child 200/150Ft; 🕑 10am-6pm Tue-Sun; Ⓜ M1 Bajcsy-Zsilinszky út

The museum exhibits the contents of original 19th-century post offices – old uniforms and coaches, those big curved brass horns etc – that probably won't do much for you. But the museum is housed in the seven-room apartment of a wealthy late-19th-century businessman and is among the best-preserved in the city.

ZOLTÁN KODÁLY MEMORIAL MUSEUM Map p222

Kodály Zoltán Emlékmúzeum; ☎ 352 7106; VI Kodály körönd 1; adult/child 200/100Ft; 🕑 10am-4pm Wed, 10am-6pm Thu-Sat, 10am-2pm Sun; Ⓜ M1 Kodály körönd

In the flat where the great composer lived from 1924 until his death in 1967 is the Zoltán Kodály Memorial Museum, with four rooms bursting with furniture, furnishings and other personal items. One room is devoted to Kodály's manuscripts.

CITY PARK

Városliget (City Park; Map pp218–19) is Pest's green lung, an open space measuring almost a square kilometre that hosted most of the events during Hungary's 1000th anniversary celebrations in 1896. It's not so cut and dried, but in general museums lie to the south of XIV Kós Károly sétány, while activities of a less cerebral nature – including the Municipal Great Circus (opposite), Funfair Park (opposite) and Széchenyi Baths (p136) – are to the north.

CITY ZOO & BOTANICAL GARDEN

Map pp218-19

Városi Állatkert és Növénykert; ☎ 273 4900, 363 3701; www.zoobudapest.com; XIV Állatkerti út 6-12; adult/child/student/family 1300/900/1000/4100Ft; 🕑 9am-6.30pm Mon-Thu, 9am-7pm Fri-Sun May-Aug, 9am-5.30pm Mon-Thu, 9am-6pm Fri-Sun Apr & Sep, 9am-5pm Mon-Thu, 9am-5.30pm Fri-Sun Mar & Oct, 9am-4pm daily Nov-Feb

The large zoo and Botanical Garden, a five-minute walk northeast of Hősök tere along Állatkerti út, has a collection of some 3700 animals (big cats, rhinos, hippopotamuses), but some visitors come here just to look at the Secessionist animal houses built in the early part of the 20th century, such as the **Elephant House** (1912) with pachyderm heads in beetle-green Zsolnay ceramic and the **Palm House** (admission 300Ft extra, including aquarium), which was erected by the Eiffel Company of Paris.

HUNGARIAN AGRICULTURAL MUSEUM Map pp218-19

Magyar Mezőgazdasági Múzeum; ☎ 422 0765, 363 50997; www.mmgm.hu; XIV Vajdahunyad sétány; admission free, temporary exhibitions adult/child 550/300Ft; 🕑 10am-5pm Tue-Sun mid-Feb–mid-Nov, 10am-4pm Tue-Fri, 10am-5pm Sat & Sun mid-Nov–mid-Feb; Ⓜ M1 Hősök tere

This rather esoteric museum is housed in the stunning baroque wing of Vajdahunyad Castle, built for the 1896 millenary celebrations on the little island in the park's lake and modelled after a fortress in Transylvania (but with Gothic, Romanesque and baroque wings and additions to reflect architectural styles from all over Hungary). Here you'll find Europe's largest collection of things agricultural (fruit production, cereals, wool, poultry, pig slaughtering, viticulture etc).

BUDAPEST FOR CHILDREN

Budapest abounds in places and sights that will delight children, and there is always a special child's entry rate to paying attractions (though ages of eligibility may vary).

Kids love transport and the city's many unusual forms of conveyance – from the **Cog** and **Children's Railways** (p61) in the Buda Hills and the **Sikló** (p53) funicular climbing up to Castle Hill to the trams, trolleybuses and little M1 metro – will fascinate and entertain. And don't forget the **Transport Museum** (below). It has got an embarrassment of hands-on displays for kids of all ages.

Specific places to take children include the following:

Budapest Eye (Budapest Kilátó; Map p222; ☎ 238 7623; VI Váci út 1-3; adult/child/student & senior/family 3000/1000/2000/6000Ft; 🕑 10am-10pm Sun-Thu, 10am-midnight Sat & Sun; Ⓜ M3 Nyugati pályaudvar) This attraction exaggerates just a titch when it claims 'The Budapest Eye is to Budapest what the Eiffel Tower is to Paris and the London Eye to London'. Huh? In reality, it's just a hot-air balloon tethered to ropes in a lot between the Nyugati train station and the West End City Center mall that is allowed to ascend to 150m for some hair-raising views over Budapest. But the kids will love it.

Budapest Puppet Theatre (Budapesti Bábszínház; Map p222; ☎ 342 2702, 321 5200; www.budapest-babszinhaz.hu; VI Andrássy út 69; tickets 500-1100Ft; Ⓜ M1 Vörösmarty utca) The puppet theatre, which usually doesn't require fluency in Hungarian, presents shows designed for children on weekdays (usually at 10am or 10.30am and 4pm) and folk programmes for adults occasionally in the evening.

Funfair Park (Vidámpark; Map pp218–19; ☎ 363 8310, 363 2660; www.vidampark.hu; XIV Állatkerti körút 14-16; under/over 120cm free/300Ft, rides 300-600Ft; 🕑 10am-8pm daily Jul & Aug, 11am-7pm Mon-Fri, 10am-8pm Sat & Sun May & Jun, 11am-6.30pm Mon-Fri, 10am-7pm Sat & Sun Apr & Sep, 11am-6pm Mon-Fri, 10am-6.30pm Sat & Sun Mar & Oct; Ⓜ M1 Széchenyi fürdő) This 150-year-old luna park sits on 2.5 hectares of land next to the Municipal Great Circus. There's a couple of dozen thrilling rides, including the heart-stopping Ikarus Space Needle, the looping Star roller coaster and the Hip-Hop freefall tower, as well as go-karts, dodgem cars and a carousel built in 1906.

Municipal Great Circus (Fővárosi Nagycirkusz; Map pp218–19; ☎ 344 6008, 343 8300; www.maciva.hu in Hungarian; XIV Állatkerti körút 7; adult 1200-1900Ft, child 900-1500Ft; Ⓜ M1 Széchenyi fürdő) Performances at Budapest's circus, Europe's only permanent big top, are at 3pm from Wednesday to Sunday, with additional shows at 10.30am on Saturday and Sunday and at 7pm on Saturday.

Palace of Miracles (Csodák Palotája; Map pp218–19; ☎ 350 6131; www.csodapalota.hu; XIII Váci út 19; adult/child/family 800/700/2300Ft; 🕑 10am-6pm Jul & Aug, 9am-5pm Mon-Fri, 10am-6pm Sat & Sun Sep-Jun; Ⓜ M3 Lehel tér) This is a wonderfully thought-out interactive playhouse for children of all ages with 'smart' toys and puzzles, most of which have a scientific bent.

Planetarium (Map pp228–9; ☎ 263 1811, 265 0725; www.planetarium.hu in Hungarian; X Népliget; adult/child 940/840Ft; 🕑 shows 9.30am, 11am, 1pm, 2.30pm & 4pm Tue-Sun; Ⓜ M3 Népliget) This large planetarium has star shows as well as 3-D films and cartoons.

STATUES & MONUMENTS Map pp218-19

City Park boasts a number of notable statues and monuments. Americans (and collectors of greenbacks) will be amused to see a familiar face in the park south of the lake. The **statue of George Washington** (Washington György sétány) was erected by Hungarian Americans in 1906. The little church opposite Vajdahunyad Castle (ie the agricultural museum) is called **Ják Chapel** (Jáki kápolna) because its intricate portal was copied from the 13th-century Abbey Church in Ják in Western Transdanubia.

The statue of the hooded figure south of the chapel is that of **Anonymous**, the unknown chronicler at the court of King Béla III who wrote a history of the early Magyars. Note the pen with the shiny tip in his hand; writers (both real and aspirant) touch it for inspiration.

TRANSPORT MUSEUM Map pp218-19

Közlekedési Múzeum; ☎ 273 3840; XIV Városligeti körút 11; admission free, temporary exhibitions adult/child 400/200Ft; 🕑 10am-5pm Tue-Fri, 10am-6pm Sat & Sun May-Sep, 10am-4pm Tue-Fri, 10am-5pm Sat & Sun Oct-Apr; trolleybus 72 or 74

In an old and a new wing, this museum has scale models of ancient trains (some of which still run), classic late-19th-century automobiles and lots of those old wooden bicycles called 'bone-rattlers'. There are a few hands-on exhibits and lots of show-and-tell from the attendants. Outside are pieces from the original Danube bridges that were retrieved after the bombings of WWII and a café in an old MÁV coach. The museum's air and space-travel collection is housed in the **Aviation Museum** (Repülési Múzeum; Map pp218–19; ☎ 363 4016; XIV Zichy Mihály utca 14; admission free; 10am-5pm Tue-Fri, 10am-6pm Sat & Sun mid-May–mid-Oct; trolleybus 72) in the nearby Petőfi Csarnok (p133).

OUTER PEST DISTRICTS

Unusual sights and museums in several of Pest's outer districts will be of interest to lager louts, train spotters, rock hounds and necrophiliacs.

DREHER BREWERY & BEER MUSEUM

Dreher Sörmúzeum; ☎ 432 9700, 432 9850; www.dreher.hu; X Jászberényi utca 7-11; museum/museum & film/museum, film & beer tasting 300/800/1300Ft; 9am-6pm Mon-Fri, 10am-4pm Sat & Sun; M M3 Örs vezér tere then bus 85

Budapest's – and Hungary's – largest beer maker has a museum at its brewery where you can look at displays of brewing and bottling over the centuries, watch a film about beer-making and/or get stuck into a generous tasting session. The brewery is about 7km east of the city centre.

HUNGARIAN RAILWAY HISTORY PARK Map pp226-7

Magyar Vasúttörténeti Park; ☎ 428 0180, 450 1497; www.lokopark.hu; XIV Tatai út 95; adult/child/family 900/300/1800Ft; 10am-6pm Tue-Sun Apr-Oct, 10am-3pm Tue-Sun Nov–mid-Dec & mid-Mar–Apr; bus 30, tram 14

This mostly outdoor museum contains more than 100 locomotives (most of them still working) and an exhibition on the history of the railroad in Hungary. There's a wonderful array of hands-on activities – mostly involving getting behind the wheel – for kids. From early April to late October a vintage diesel train leaves Nyugati train station for the park four times a day at 9.45am, 10.45am, 1.45pm and 3.45pm and returns at 1.13pm and 3.13pm. The fare is included in the admission price.

KEREPES CEMETERY Map p216

Kerepesi temető; ☎ 333 9125, 314 1269; Fiumei út 16; 7am-8pm May-Jul, 7am-7pm Apr & Aug, 7am-6pm Sep, 7am-5pm Oct-Mar; tram 24

About 500m southeast of Keleti station is the entrance to Budapest's equivalent of Highgate or Père Lachaise cemeteries, which was established in 1847. Some of the mausoleums in this 56-hectare necropolis, which is also called the National Graveyard (Nemzeti Sírkert), are worthy of a pharaoh, especially those of statesmen and national heroes such as Lajos Kossuth, Ferenc Deák and Lajos Batthyány. Other tombs are quite moving (eg those of the actress Lujza Blaha and the poet Endre Ady). Plot 21 contains the graves of many who died in the 1956 Uprising. Near the huge mausoleum for party honchos, which is topped with the words 'I lived for Communism, for the people', is the simple grave of János Kádár, who died in 1989 (p48). Near the entrance is the new **Tribute Museum** (Kegyeleti Múzeum; 10am-3pm Mon-Thu, 10am-1pm Fri, every 2nd Sat & Sun in Jul & Aug), which looks (grimly) at the Hungarian way of death.

NEW MUNICIPAL CEMETERY

Új Köztemető; ☎ 265 2458; X Kozma utca; 8am-7pm; tram 28

This huge city cemetery, reached by tram from Blaha Lujza tér, is where Imre Nagy, prime minister during the 1956 Uprising, and 2000 others were buried in unmarked graves (plots 300–301) after executions in the late 1940s and 1950s. Today, the area has been turned into a moving **National Pantheon** and is about a 30-minute walk from the entrance; follow the signs pointing the way to '300, 301 parcela'. At peak periods you can take a microbus marked 'temető járat' around the cemetery or hire a taxi at the gate.

Walking Tours

Walking Tours

Budapest is a city made for walking and there are sights around every corner – from a brightly tiled gem of an Art Nouveau building to peasant women from the countryside hawking their homemade *barack lekvár* (apricot jam) or colourful embroidery at the markets or outside metro stations.

The following eight tours include sights and attractions described elsewhere in this guide, as well as additional significant features; the walks are really designed for those with more time or an interest in seeing the city in greater depth. Don't worry about doing every tour or even finishing each one; linger as long as you like in a museum or market that takes your fancy, do a little shopping or even visit one of the city's fine thermal spas along the way.

CASTLE CAPER

You can start your tour of Várhegy (Castle Hill; p53) by walking up Várfok utca from Moszkva tér to **Vienna Gate 1** (Bécsi kapu), the medieval entrance to the Old Town, which was rebuilt in 1936 to mark the 250th anniversary of the retaking of the castle from the Turks. The gate is not all that huge, but when Budapest children are loquacious or noisy, their parents tell them: 'Your mouth is as big as the Vienna Gate!'.

The large building to the west with the superb majolica-tiled roof contains the **National Archives** (**2**; Országos Levéltár; Bécsi kapu tér 2-4), built in 1920. Across the square, which was a weekend market in the Middle Ages, a **Lutheran church 3** with the words 'A Mighty Fortress is Our God' written in Hungarian marks the start of Táncsics Mihály utca. On the west side of the square, there's an attractive group of **burgher houses 4**; No 7 has four medallions of classical poets and philosophers, and No 8, a curious round corner window.

Táncsics Mihály utca is a narrow street of little houses painted in lively hues and adorned with statues. Many have plaques with the word *műemlék* (memorial) attesting to their historical associations. In the entrances to many of the courtyards, you'll notice lots of *sedilia* – stone niches dating as far back as the 13th century. Some historians think they were used as merchant stalls, while others believe servants cooled their heels here while their masters (or mistresses) paid a visit to the occupant.

The **medieval Jewish prayer house 5** (p55), dating partly from the 14th century, contains a small museum. Across the road to the southeast at Táncsics Mihály utca 9 is where **Lajos Kossuth was imprisoned 6** from 1837 to 1840. The controversial **Hilton Budapest 7** (p154), which incorporates parts of a medieval Dominican church and a baroque Jesuit college, is further south. Have a look at the little **red hedgehog relief 8** above the doorway at the house on Hess András tér 3, which was an inn in the 14th century.

If you walk north from Hess András tér along Fortuna utca, you'll soon reach the interesting **Hungarian Museum of Commerce and Catering 9** (p55). This street leads back into Bécsi kapu tér, but if you continue west along Petermann bíró utca you'll reach Kapisztrán

A STREET BY ANY OTHER NAME

After WWII, most streets, squares and parks were renamed after people, dates and political groups that have since become anathema to an independent and democratic Hungary. From April 1989, names were changed at a pace and with a determination that some people felt was almost obsessive; Cartographia's *Budapest Atlas* lists almost 400 street name changes in the capital alone. Sometimes it was just a case of returning a street or square to its original (perhaps medieval) name – from Lenin útja, say, to Szent korona útja (Street of the Holy Crown). Other times the name is new.

The new (or original) names are now in place after more than a decade and a half, the old street signs with a red 'X' drawn across them have all but disappeared and virtually no one refers to Ferenciek tere (Square of the Franciscans), for example, as Felszabadulás tér (Liberation Sq), which honoured the Soviet army's role in liberating Budapest in WWII.

tér, named after John Capistranus (1386–1456), a charismatic Franciscan monk who raised an entire army for János Hunyadi (p40) in his campaign against the Turks. He was canonised in 1724 and is known as St John of Capistrano.

The large white building to the north of the square houses the **Military History Museum 10** (p56). Around the corner, along the so-called Anjou Bastion (Anjou bástya), with displays detailing the development of the cannon, lies the turban-topped **tomb 11** of Pasha Abdi Arnaut Abdurrahman (1615–86), the last Turkish Grand Vizier of Budapest, who was killed here on the day Buda was liberated. 'He was a heroic foe,' reads the tablet in Hungarian, 'may he rest in peace.'

The big steeple on the south side of Kapisztrán tér, visible for kilometres to the west of Castle Hill, is the **Mary Magdalene Tower** (**12**; Magdolna-torony; I Kapisztrán tér), the reconstructed spire of an 18th-century church. The church, once reserved for Hungarian speakers in this district (German speakers worshipped at Matthias Church), was used as a mosque during the Turkish occupation and was destroyed in an air raid in 1944.

WALK FACTS

Start II Moszkva tér
End I Szarvas tér
Distance 3.5km
Duration Two hours (or more)
Transport (M) M2 (start); (tram) 18, (bus) 86 (end)
Fuel Stop Ruszwurm café (p125)

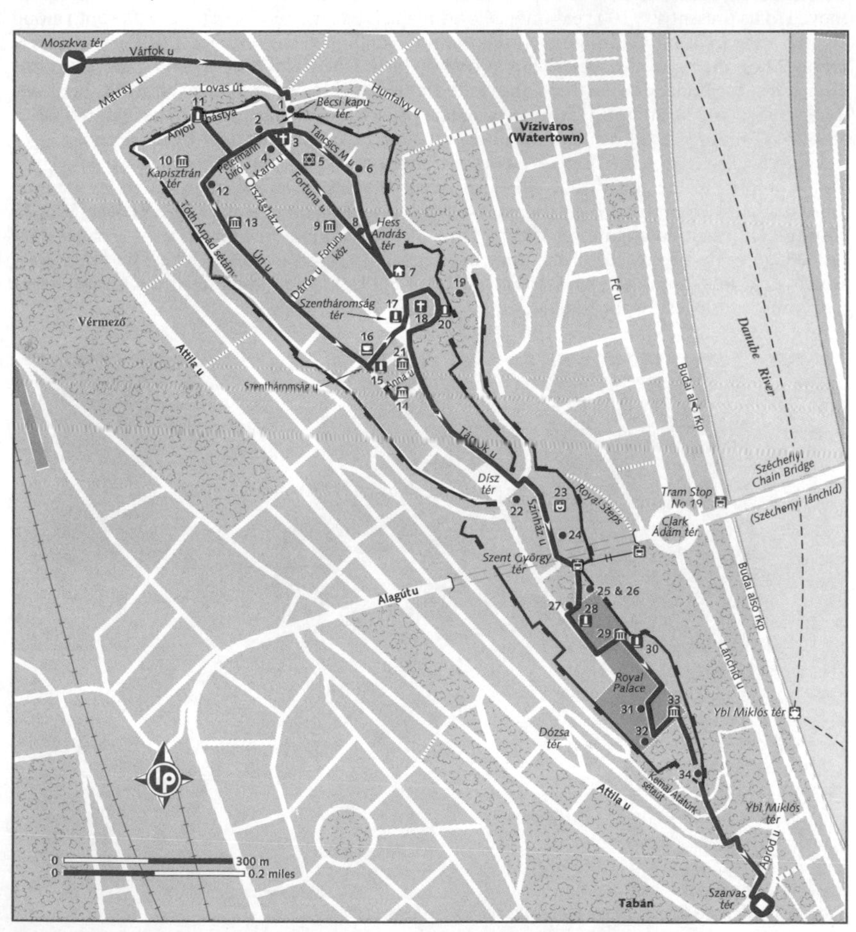

From Kapisztrán tér, walk southeast on Országház utca, keeping an eye open for the sedile in the glassed-in entrance to No 9 and the medieval houses painted white, terra cotta and lime at Nos 18, 20 and 22.

Úri utca, the next parallel street to the west, has some interesting courtyards, especially No 19 with a sundial and what looks like a tomb. There are more Gothic sedilia at Nos 32 and 40; if the gates are locked there's a peephole to look through. The **Telephony Museum 13** (p56) is housed in an old Clarist monastery. At No 9 of the same street is the entrance to the touristy **Buda Castle Labyrinth 14** (p53). Returning to I Szentháromság utca, on the corner you'll pass a mounted **statue of András Hadik 15**, a Hussar field marshal in the wars against the Turks. If you're wondering why the steed's brass testicles are so shiny, well, it's a student tradition in Budapest to give them a stroke before taking an exam. For a coffee-and-cake break, try **Ruszwurm 16**.

In the centre of I Szentháromság tér to the northeast there's a **statue of the Holy Trinity** (**17**; Szentháromság szobor), another one of the 'plague pillars' put up by grateful (and healthy) Buda citizens in the early 18th century. The square is dominated by Castle Hill's two most famous sights: **Matthias Church 18** (Mátyás templom; p55) and **Fishermen's Bastion 19** (Halászbástya; p54) just beyond it. In front of the bastion is an ornate equestrian **statue of St Stephen 20** by Alajos Stróbl.

The **Golden Eagle Pharmacy 21** (p54), a short distance to the southwest and just before Dísz tér, probably looks exactly the way it did in Buda Castle in the 16th century, though it was moved to its present site 100 years later. Continue to Dísz tér, then from here walk south along Színház utca to Szent György tér. Along the way you'll pass the bombed-out **former Ministry of Defence 22** on the right, a casualty of WWII and, during the Cold War, NATO's supposed nuclear target for Budapest. Further south and on the left is the **National Dance Theatre 23** (Nemzeti Táncszínház; p135), built in 1736 as a Carmelite church and monastery, and the restored **Sándor Palace 24** (Sándor palota), which now houses the offices of the president of the republic.

From Szent György tér there are two entrances to the **Royal Palace** (Budavári palota), the large complex to the south that has been burned, bombed, razed, rebuilt and redesigned at least a half-dozen times over the past seven centuries. The first is via the **Habsburg Steps 25** through an ornamental gateway dating from 1903. Flanking the steps is a large **statue of the turul 26**, an eagle-like totem of the ancient Magyars (p37), erected in 1905. The other way, which we'll take, is via **Corvinus Gate 27**, with its big black raven symbolising King Matthias Corvinus, southwest of the square.

Statue of András Hadik (above), a hero of the wars against the Turks, Castle Hill

The first part of the palace (Wing A) is currently empty since the Ludwig Museum of Contemporary Art (p70) has relocated to Pest. In the middle of the square and facing the entrance, a **statue of a Hortobágy csikós 28** (cowboy) in full regalia breaks a mighty *bábolna* steed, a sculpture that won international recognition for its creator, György Vastagh, at the Paris World Exhibitions of 1900 and 1901.

To reach one of two entrances to the **Hungarian National Gallery 29** (p54), walk under the little archway south of Wing B to the square facing the Danube for Wing C, or walk under the massive archway protected by four snarling lions to Wing D. Those choosing the former will enter what was once the palace terrace and gardens. Just in front of Wing C stands a **statue of Eugene of Savoy 30** (1663–1736), who wiped out the last Turkish army in Hungary at the Battle of Zenta in 1697. Designed by József Róna 200 years later, it is considered to be the finest equestrian statue in the capital.

Whichever route you take, you'll pass the large, Romantic-style **Matthias Fountain 31** (Mátyás kút), to the west and facing the palace's large northwestern courtyard, which portrays the young king Matthias Corvinus in hunting garb. To his right below is Szép Ilona (Beautiful Helen), a protagonist of a Romantic ballad by the poet Mihály Vörösmarty. Apparently the poor girl fell in love with the dashing 'hunter' and, upon learning his true identity and feeling unworthy, she died of a broken heart. The rather smug-looking fellow with the shiny foot below to the left is Galeotto Marzio, an Italian chronicler at Matthias' court. The middle of the king's three dogs was blown up during the war; canine-loving Hungarians – and most are – quickly had an exact copy made.

If you want to bail out of the tour and leave Castle Hill altogether now, there's a lift (elevator; 100Ft) to the right of the Lion Court archway that will take you down to Dózsa tér and the stop for bus 16 for Pest.

In Wing F of the palace on the west side of Lion Court is the **National Széchenyi Library 32** (p190), which contains codices and manuscripts, a large collection of foreign newspapers and a copy of everything published in Hungary or the Hungarian language. It was founded by Count Ferenc Széchenyi (1754–1820), father of István Széchenyi (p42), who endowed it with 15,000 books and 2000 manuscripts. The **Budapest History Museum 33** (p54) is in Wing E.

You can walk through the history museum and exit through the rear doors without buying a ticket. Have a look around the castle walls and enter the palace gardens. **Ferdinand Gate 34** under the conical Mace Tower will bring you to a set of steps. These descend to Szarvas tér in the Tabán district, from where you can take tram 18 south to XIII Gellért tér or bus 86 north to Margit körút.

ÓBUDA'S MADE FOR WALKIN'

Begin this walking tour of Óbuda (p59) in **Flórián tér 1**, which is split in two by the Árpád Bridge flyover and encircled by mammoth housing blocks. It is not the best introduction to Óbuda, but it remains the district's historic centre.

In the subway below this massive square are Roman objects that have been discovered in the area (many of them, sadly, are now vandalised and tagged in graffiti), including the **Baths Museum** (**2**; Fürdő Múzeum; ☎ 250 1650; admission free; 🕑 10am-6pm Tue-Sun May-Sep, 10am-5pm Tue-Sun 15-30 Apr & Oct). Still more Roman ruins, including a reconstructed temple, can be found in the park that is above the subway.

Dominating the easternmost side of III Flórián tér is the yellow baroque **Óbuda Parish Church** (**3**; Óbudai plébániatemplom; III 168 Lajos utca), which was built in 1749 and dedicated to Sts Peter and Paul. There's a massive rococo pulpit inside. To the southeast, the large neoclassical building beside the Corinthia Aquincum Hotel is the **former Óbuda Synagogue** (**4**; Óbudai zsinagóga; III Lajos utca 163), dating from 1821. It now houses sound studios for Hungarian Television (MTV).

WALK FACTS

Start III Flórián tér
End Aquincum
Distance 4.5km
Duration Three hours
Transport HÉV Árpád híd, 🚌 86 from Buda, 🚆 from Pest (start); HÉV Aquincum (end)
Fuel Stop Új Sípos Halászkert (p97)

Two contiguous squares lying east of Flórián tér – **Szentlélek tér 5** (Holy Spirit Sq), a transport hub, and **Fő tér 6** (Main Sq), a quiet restored square of baroque houses, public buildings and restaurants – contain Óbuda's most important museums. To reach them, walk north on Budai alsó rakpart and under the flyover.

In the former Zichy Mansion is the **Vasarely Museum 7** (p60), devoted to the works of the 'father of op art', the late Victor Vasarely. In the back of the same building facing the courtyard (enter at Fő tér 1) is the **Kassák Museum 8** (p60) of early-20th-century avant-garde art. Take advantage of outdoor seating for a snack at **Új Sípos Halászkert 9**.

Walking northeast from the square, you'll see a group of odd metal **sculptures of women 10** under umbrellas in the middle of the road. It is an installation by the prolific Imre Varga, whose work is shown at the **Imre Varga Exhibition House 11** (p60) in a charming townhouse nearby.

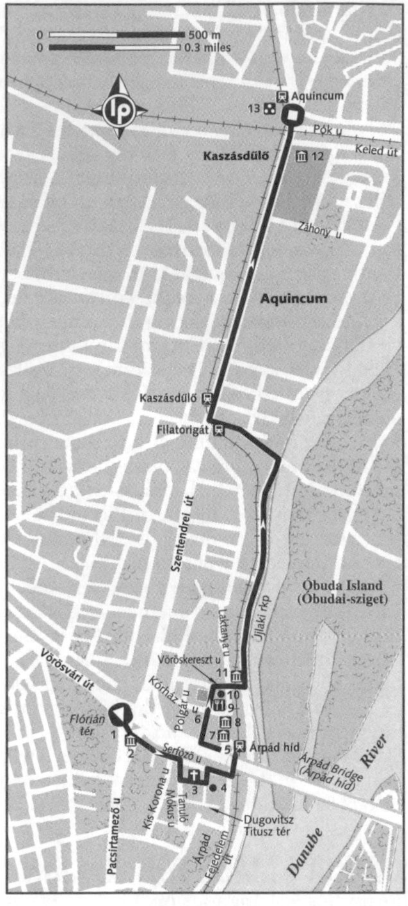

If you want to continue on to Aquincum (p59), the most complete Roman civilian town in Hungary and now an indoor and outdoor museum, don't walk but hop on bus 34 or 43 heading north from III Szentlélek tér or catch the HÉV suburban train from Árpád híd for three stops, and alight at the Aquincum station. A Roman aqueduct used to pass this way from a nearby spring, and remains have been preserved in the central reservation (median strip) of III Szentendrei út. The prosperous town's heyday was in the 2nd and 3rd centuries, lasting until the Huns and assorted other hordes came and ruined everything. The **Aquincum Museum 12** (p59) is well worth the trip.

Across Szentendrei út to the northwest is the **Roman Civilian Amphitheatre 13** (Római polgári amfiteátrum), about half the size of the one reserved for the garrison (p60). Much is left to the imagination, but you can still see the small cubicles where lions were kept and the 'Gate of Death' to the west through which slain gladiators were carried.

MARGARET ISLAND HOPPER

Begin your tour of Margit-sziget (Margaret Island; p62) by heading north from the tram stop (4 or 6) on Margaret Bridge. In the flower-bedded roundabout 350m to the north is the **Centennial Monument 1** (Centenariumi emlékmű), unveiled in 1973 to mark the union of Buda, Pest and Óbuda 100 years before. Three decades ago was an entirely different era in Budapest, and the sculptor filled the strange split cone with all sorts of socialist and nationalist symbols. They remain – as if contained in a time capsule that's been cracked open.

Walking along the central road, you'll pass two popular swimming pools on the west side. The first is the very serious **Alfréd Hajós National Sports Pool 2** (Hajós Alfréd Nemzeti Sportuszoda; p137). To the north is the recently renovated **Palatinus 4** (p137) complex. This place is an absolute madhouse on a hot summer afternoon but it's always a good place to watch Hungarians at play.

Just before you reach the Palatinus (and almost in the exact geographical centre of the island) you'll pass the ruins of a **Franciscan church and monastery 3** (Ferences templom és kolostor), including a large tower and wall dating from the late 13th century. The Habsburg archduke Joseph built a summer residence here when he inherited the island in 1867. It was later converted into a hotel that ran until 1949.

In the north-central north part of the island, an **open-air theatre** (**5**; *szabadtéri színpad;* ☎ 340 4883) is used for opera, plays and concerts in summer. An octagonal **water tower 6** *(víztorony)*, erected in 1911, rises 66m above the theatre. The tower now houses the **Lookout Gallery** (Kiállító Galéria; ☎ 340 4520; adult/child 200/100Ft; 🕑 11am-7pm May-Oct), which exhibits some interesting folk craft and contemporary art on the ground floor. The main reason for entering is to climb the 153 steps for a stunning 360-degree view of the island, Buda and Pest from the cupola terrace.

Due east is the former **Dominican convent 7** (Domonkos kolostor) constructed by Béla IV whose scribes played an important role in the continuation of Hungarian scholarship. Its most famous resident was Béla's daughter, St Margaret (1242–71). According to the story, the king promised to commit his daughter to a life of devotion in a nunnery if the Mongols were driven from the land. They were and she was – at nine years of age. Still, she seemed to enjoy it – if we're to believe the *Lives of the Saints* – especially the mortification-of-the-flesh parts. St Margaret, only canonised in 1943, commands something of a cult following in Hungary. A red-marble sepulchre cover surrounded by a wrought-iron grille marks her original resting place, and there's a much visited shrine with ex-votives nearby.

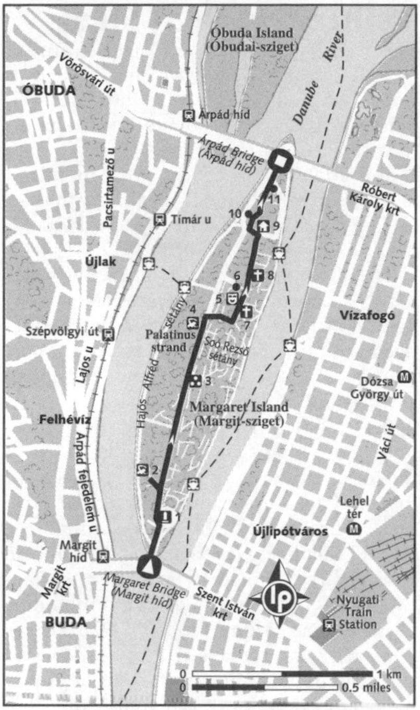

WALK FACTS

Start Margaret Bridge
End Árpád Bridge
Distance 3km
Duration Two hours
Transport 🚋 4 or 6 (start); 🚌 26, 🚋 1 (end)

Some 200m north is the reconstructed-Romanesque **Premonstratensian Church 8** (Premontre templom), dedicated to St Michael and originally dating back to the 12th century. Its 15th-century bell is real enough, though; it mysteriously appeared one night in 1914 under the roots of a walnut tree that had been knocked over in a storm. It was probably buried there by monks at the time of the Turkish invasion.

The Romans used the thermal springs bubbling below the northeastern part of the island both as drinking water and therapy and so do modern Magyars. Margitszigeti Krisztályvíz (Margaret Island Crystal Water), one of the more popular brands of mineral water in Hungary, is sourced and bottled here, and the thermal spa at the **Danubius Grand Hotel Margitsziget 9** (p136) to the northeast is one of the cleanest and most modern in Budapest.

The attractive **Japanese Garden 10** (Japánkert), at the northwestern end of the island, has koi, carp and lily pads in its ponds, a small wooden bridge and a waterfall. The raised gazebo to the north is called the **Musical Fountain 11** (Zenélőkút), a replica of one in Transylvania. A tape plays chimes and tinny snatches of a folk song on the hour. From here walk to Árpád Bridge and the bus stop.

IN THE STEPS OF ST STEVE

This walking tour of Szent István körút (p67), not particularly long or demanding, begins in XIII Jászai Mari tér, which is split in two by the foot of Margaret Bridge on the Pest side. Two buildings of very different styles and functions face the square. The modern building south of the square is nicknamed the **White House** (**1**; V Széchenyi rakpart 19), the former headquarters of the Central Committee of the Hungarian Socialist Workers' Party. It now contains the offices of the members of the nearby Parliament. To the north is an elegant block of flats called **Palatinus House** (**2**; XIII Pozsonyi út 2), built in 1912.

WALK FACTS

Start XIII Jászai Mari tér
End V Erzsébet tér
Distance 3km
Duration 2½ hours
Transport (tram) 4 or 6 (start); (M) M1/2/3 Deák Ferenc tér (end)
Fuel Stop Okay Italia (p115)

The area to the north of Szent István körút is known as Újlipótváros (New Leopold Town). It is a wonderful neighbourhood with tree-lined streets, antique shops, boutiques and a few cafés and is vaguely reminiscent of uptown Manhattan. It was upper middle class and Jewish before the war (and remains essentially so today, with the odd ex-communist boss thrown in for good measure), and many of the 'safe houses' organised by the Swedish diplomat Raoul Wallenberg (p68) during WWII were here. A street named after this heroic man, two blocks to the north, bears a commemorative plaque. Along the bank of the river is a rarity for Budapest: a row of **Bauhaus apartments 3**. They may not look like much today after decades of bad copies, but they were the bee's knees when they were built in the late 1920s. East of the apartments is **Szent István Park 4**, where a **statue of Raoul Wallenberg 5** doing battle with a snake (evil) was erected in 1999. It is titled *Kígyóölő* (Serpent Slayer) and replaces one created by sculptor Pál Pátzay that was mysteriously removed the night before its unveiling in 1948.

Return along Pozsonyi út to Szent István körút, which is an interesting street to stroll along; as elsewhere on the Big Ring Road, most of the Eclectic-style buildings were erected in the last part of the 19th century. Don't hesitate to explore the inner courtyards here and further on – if Dublin is celebrated for its doors and London for its squares, Budapest is known for its lovely *udvarok*.

This stretch of the boulevard is also good for shopping. The **Szőnyi Antikváriuma 6** (p148), a second-hand and antiquarian bookshop, is excellent for browsing – it has old prints and maps in the chest of drawers at the back. **Falk Miksa utca 7**, the next street on the right and running south, is loaded with pricey antique shops. You can get an idea of what Hungarians are off-loading these days from the secondhand **BÁV shop 8** (p147).

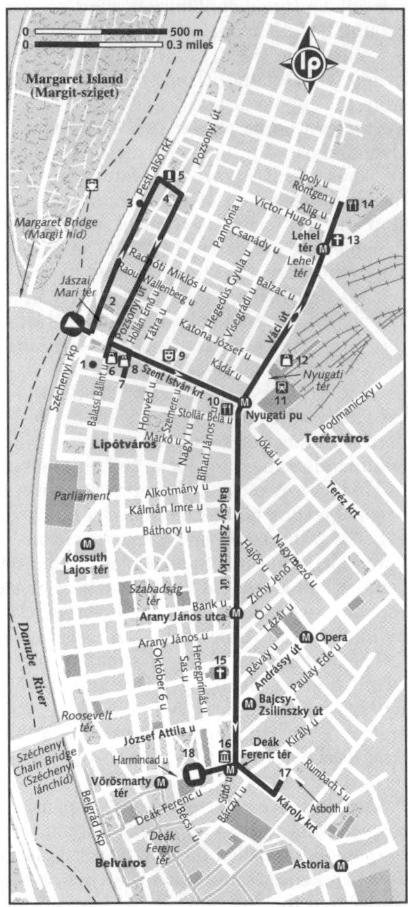

Eighteenth-century Nyugati train station (p67), Terézváros, built by the Eiffel Company of Paris

The attractive little theatre roughly in the middle of this section of the Big Ring Road is the **Comedy Theatre 9** (p134). Right on Nyugati tér, **Okay Italia 10** is a good place to replenish for the rest of the tour.

You might recognise the large iron and glass structure on Nyugati tér (known as Marx tér until 1989) if you arrived by train. It's the **Nyugati train station 11** (Nyugati pályaudvar), dating from the end of the 19th century. The old restaurant room to the right now houses one of the world's most elegant McDonald's.

If you look north up Váci út from Nyugati tér, beyond the new **West End City Centre 12** shopping mall, you may catch sight of the twin spires of the **Lehel church 13** (XIII Lehel tér) a 1933 copy of the 13th-century Romanesque church (now in ruins) at Zsambék, 33km west of Budapest. The monstrosity that is **Lehel Csarnok 14** (p93) is nearby.

If you're feeling energetic, walk south through Nyugati tér and along Bajcsy-Zsilinszky út for about 800m to the **Basilica of St Stephen 15** (p64). The street ends at busy Deák Ferenc tér. In the subway below, near the entrance to the metro, you'll find the **Underground Railway Museum 16** (p64).

In the early part of the 20th century, big foreign insurance companies built their offices here, with some huge ones still standing. **Madách Imre út 17**, running east from Károly körút, the start of the Little Ring Road, was originally designed to be as large and grand a boulevard as nearby Andrássy út. But WWII nipped that plan in the bud, and it now ends abruptly and rather self-consciously after just two blocks. Much of **Erzsébet tér 18** is now given over to a park since the international bus station was moved to Népliget and the National Theatre opened its doors along the Danube in Ferencváros and not here, as originally planned.

ELIZABETH TOWN TAILORED TOUR

This walking tour of Erzsébetváros (p68), or Elizabeth Town, which takes you through the old Jewish Quarter and up along Rákóczi út to the Keleti train station, begins in Liszt Ferenc tér, where you'll find the **Ferenc Liszt Academy of Music 1** (Liszt Zeneakadémia; p131) at the southeastern end. There are always tickets (some very cheap) available to something – perhaps a recital or an early Saturday morning rehearsal.

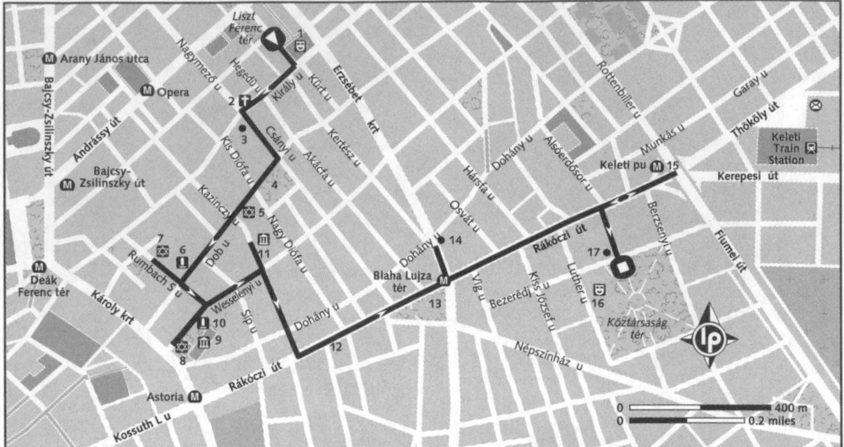

If you walk southwestwards along Király utca you'll pass the **Church of St Teresa 2**, built in 1811 and containing a massive neoclassical altar and chandelier and, diagonally opposite, a lovely **neo-Gothic house 3** at No 47 built in 1847. **Klauzál tér 4**, the heart of the old Jewish Quarter, is a couple of streets to the southeast over Dob utca.

The square and its surrounding streets retain a feeling of prewar Budapest. Signs of a continued Jewish presence are still evident – in a kosher bakery at Kazinczy utca 28, the Kővári butcher's at Dob utca 35, the Fröhlich cake shop and café (p125) which has old Jewish favourites, at Dob utca 22 and wigmakers at Kazinczy utca 32.

There are about half a dozen synagogues and prayer houses in the Erzsébetváros district, and these were reserved for different sects and ethnic groups: conservatives, the Orthodox, Poles, Sephardics and so on. The **Orthodox Synagogue** (**5**; Ortodox zsinagóga; VII Kazinczy utca 29-31), which is also accessed from Dob utca 35, was built in 1913 for Budapest's Orthodox community, and the Moorish **Rumbach Sebestyén utca Synagogue** (**7**; Rumbach Sebestyén utcai zsinagóga; VII Rumbach Sebestyén utca 11) in 1872 by Austrian Secessionist architect Otto Wagner for the conservatives. Between the two synagogues there's an unusual antifascist **monument to Carl Lutz** (**6**; VII Dob utca 12), a Swiss consul who, like Raoul Wallenberg, provided Jews with false papers in 1944. It portrays an angel on high sending down a long bolt of cloth to a victim.

WALK FACTS

Start VI Liszt Ferenc tér
End Keleti metro station
Distance 4km
Duration 3½ hours
Transport Ⓜ M1 Oktogon (start); Ⓜ M2 Keleti pályaudvar (end)
Fuel Stop Kádár (p120)

Façade of the Great Synagogue (p68), Erzsébetváros

No synagogue compares with the **Great Synagogue 8** (p68), which also contains the **Jewish Museum 9** (p68). Outside the front of the synagogue a plaque notes that Theodore Herzl, the father of modern Zionism, was born at this site in 1860. The **Holocaust Memorial Center 10** p69) is on the northern side of the synagogue. and faces Rumbach Sebestyén utca. The **Hungarian Electrotechnology Museum 11** (p68), a personal favourite, is a short distance to the north.

Rákóczi út 12, a busy shopping street to the south, leads to **Blaha Lujza tér 13**, named after a leading 19th-century stage actress. The subway (underpass) below is one of the liveliest in the city, with hustlers, beggars, peasants selling their wares, musicians and, of course, pick-pockets. Just north of the square is the Art Nouveau **New York Palace** (**14**; New York Palota; VII Erzsébet körút 9-11), erstwhile home of the celebrated New York Café (New York Kávéház; see boxed text, p126), scene of many a literary gathering over the years. It has now been almost completely restored and will soon reopen as a hotel.

Rákóczi út ends at Baross tér and the **Keleti train station 15** (Keleti pályaudvar). It was built in 1884 and renovated a century later. To the southwest in huge VIII Köztársaság tér is the city's 'other' opera house, the ugly **Erkel Theatre 16** (p133). From the outside, you'd never guess it was built in 1911. On the same square you'll find the **former Communist Party headquarters** (**17**; VIII Köztársaság tér 26-27), from which members of the secret police were dragged and shot by demonstrators on 30 October 1956. It now houses the main offices of the 'reformed' MSZP.

WORKING THROUGH THE VIII & IX DISTRICTS

Begin the walking tour of the traditionally working-class districts of Józsefváros and Ferencváros (p69) in **Rákóczi tér 1**, the only real square right on the Big Ring Road and as good a place as any get a feel for these areas. The square is the site of a busy **market hall 2** (*vásárcsarnok;* p93), erected in 1897 and renovated in the early 1990s after a bad fire.

Across József körút, Bródy Sándor utca runs west from Gutenberg tér – with a lovely **Art Nouveau building** (**3**; VIII Gutenberg tér 4) to the **former Hungarian Radio headquarters** (**4**; Magyar Rádió; VIII Bródy Sándor utca 5-7), where shots were first fired on 23 October 1956. Beyond it is the **Italian Institute of Culture** (**5**; VIII Bródy Sándor utca 8), which once housed the erstwhile House of Commons and appears on the reverse of the 20,000Ft

WALK FACTS

Start VIII Rákóczi tér
End Applied Arts Museum
Distance 3.5km
Duration Three hours
Transport 4 or 6 (start); M3 Ferenc körút (end)
Fuel Stop Darshan Udvar (p124)

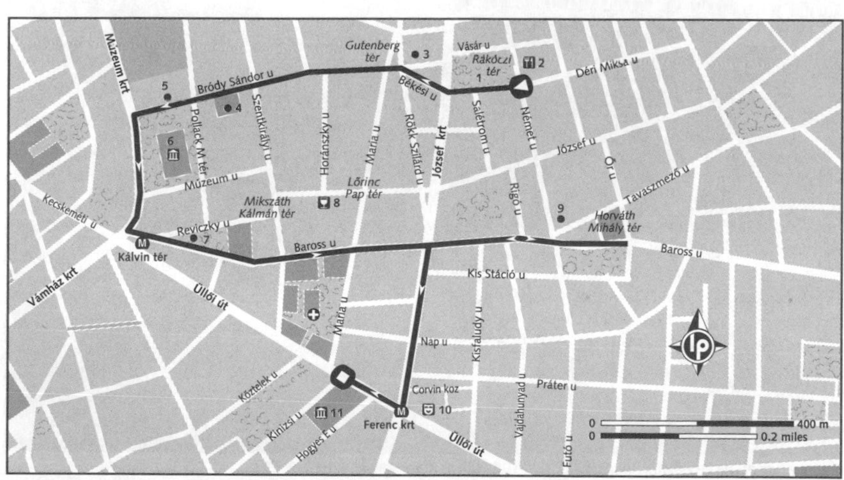

note, and the **Hungarian National Museum 6** (p69). You may enjoy walking around the museum gardens, laid out in 1856. The column to the left of the museum entrance once stood at the Forum in Rome. Have a look at some of the villas and public buildings on Pollack Mihály tér behind the museum and the white wrought-iron gate in the centre.

Walk south to Kálvin tér and follow Baross utca and Reviczky utca eastwards to the **Ervin Szabó Central Library 7** (p190), built between 1887 and 1894 and exquisitely renovated in recent years. With its gypsum ornaments, gold tracery and enormous chandeliers, you'll never see another public reading room like it. Take time out for a refreshment in the terrace café of **Darshan Udvar 8**, just beyond Mikszáth Kálmán tér.

Further east along Baross utca, across the Big Ring Road, the old **Telephone Exchange building** (**9**; VIII Horváth Mihály tér 18), built in 1910, has reliefs of classical figures using the then newfangled invention, the telephone. The Art Deco **Corvin Film Palace 10** (Corvin Filmpalota; p133), at the southern end of Kisfaludy utca in the middle of a square flanked by Regency-like houses, has been restored to its former glory.

West of here is Hungary's answer to London's Victoria and Albert Museum: the **Applied Arts Museum 11** (p69). In fact, the London museum was the inspiration when this museum was founded in 1864.

ANDRÁSSY AMBLE

Andrássy út (p70) splits away from Bajcsy-Zsilinszky út about 200m to the north of V Deák Ferenc tér. This section of Andrássy út is lined with plane trees – cool and pleasant on a warm day. The first major point is the **Hungarian State Opera House 1** (p71). The interior, which can be visited on a tour, is particularly lovely and sparkles following a total overhaul undertaken in the 1980s.

Opposite the Opera House, the so-called **Drechsler House** (**2**; VI Andrássy út 25) was designed by Art Nouveau master builder Ödön Lechner in 1882. Until recently it housed the Hungarian State Dance Institute but it now stands empty, another victim of 'development' that never happened. For something even more magical, walk down Dalszínház utca to the **New Theatre** (**3**; Új Színház; ☎ 351 1406; VI Paulay Ede utca 35), a Secessionist gem embellished with monkey faces, globes and geometric designs that opened as the Parisiana music hall in 1909.

Concert hall of the neo-Renaissance Hungarian State Opera House (p71), Andrássy út

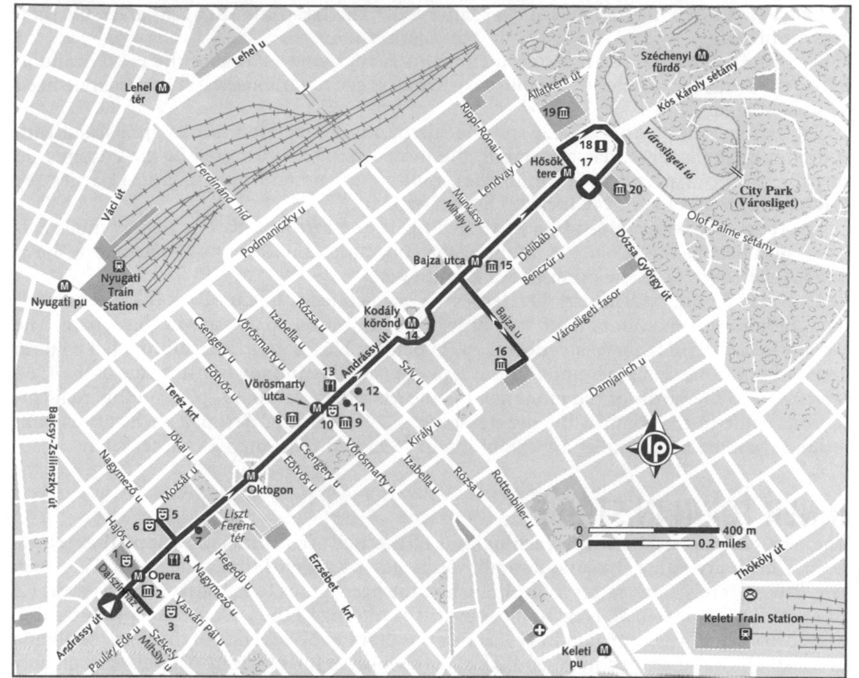

The old-world café **Művész 4** (p126) is in the next block. The following cross street is Nagymező utca, 'the Broadway of Budapest', counting a number of theatres, including the **Budapest Operetta 5** (p133) at No 17 and, just opposite, the **Thália** (**6**, ☎ 331 0500; VI Nagymező utca 22-24), lovingly restored in 1997.

On the right-hand side of the next block, the **Fashion House** (**7**; Divatcsarnok; VI Andrássy út 39), the fanciest emporium in town when it opened as the Grande Parisienne (or Párisi Nagyaruház in Hungarian) in 1912, contains the ornate Ceremonial Hall (Díszterem) on the mezzanine floor, a room positively dripping with gilt, marquetry and frescoes by Károly Lotz. It is currently being redeveloped so it may be closed when you pass by.

WALK FACTS

Start Opera metro station
End VI Hősök tere
Distance 2.6km
Duration Two hours (or more)
Transport Ⓜ M2 Opera (start); Ⓜ M1 Hősök tere (end)
Fuel Stop Művész (p126) or Lukács (p126) cafés

Andrássy út meets the Nagykörút – the Big Ring Road – at Oktogon, a busy intersection full of fast-food places, shops, honking cars and pedestrians. Just beyond it, the former secret police building, which now houses the **House of Terror 8** (p71), has a ghastly history, for it was here that many activists of every political persuasion was out of fashion before and after WWII were taken for interrogation and torture. The walls were apparently double thickness to mute the screams. A plaque on the outside of this house of shame reads in part: 'We cannot forget the horror of terror, and the victims will always be remembered'. The **Franz Liszt Memorial Museum 9** (p71) is diagonally opposite.

Along the next two blocks you'll pass some very grand buildings housing such institutions as the **Budapest Puppet Theatre 10** (p73) at No 69, the **Academy of Fine Arts** (**11**; Magyar Képzőművészeti Egyetem; VI Andrássy út 71) next door and the headquarters of **MÁV** (**12**;

V Andrássy út 73), the national railway, after that. The **Lukács café 13** (p126) and cake shop is just opposite.

The next square (more accurately a circus) is **Kodály körönd 14**, one of the most beautiful in the city, with the façades of the four neo-Renaissance townhouses still in desperate need of a massive face-lift.

The last stretch of Andrássy út and the surrounding neighbourhoods are packed with stunning old mansions that are among the most desirable addresses in the city. It's no surprise to see that embassies, ministries, multinationals and even political parties (eg FIDESZ-MPP at VI Lendvay utca 28) have moved in.

The **Ferenc Hopp Museum of East Asian Art 15** (p70) is in the former villa of its eponymous collector and benefactor at No 103. More of the collection is on display at the nearby **György Ráth Museum 16** (p71), a few minutes' walk southwest.

Andrássy út ends at **Hősök tere 17** (Heroes' Sq), which leads to City Park (p72). The city's most flamboyant monument and two of its best exhibition spaces are in the square. The **Millenary Monument 18** (Ezeréves emlékmű; p71) defines Hősök tere. Beneath the tall column and under a stone slab is an empty coffin representing the unknown insurgents of the 1956 Uprising. To the north of the monument is the **Museum of Fine Arts 19** (p71) and its rich collection, while to the south is the ornate **Műcsarnok 20** (Palace of Art; p72), which was built around the time of the millenary exhibition in 1896 and renovated a century later.

INNER TOWN IN STRIDE

The best place to start a wide-reaching tour of the Belváros (Inner Town; p63) is **Egyetem tér 1** (University Sq), a five-minute walk south along Károlyi Mihály utca from Ferenciek tere. The square's name refers to the branch of the prestigious **Loránd Eötvös Science University** (**2**; ELTE; V Egyetem tér 1-3). Next to the university building to the west is the **University Church 3**, a lovely baroque structure built in 1748. Over the altar inside is a copy of the Black Madonna of Częstochowa so revered in Poland. The church is often full of young people – presumably those who haven't tickled András Hadik's horse (see p78) on Castle Hill.

Just north of Egyetem tér, the **Petőfi Literary Museum** (**4**; Petőfi Irodalmi Múzeum; ☎ 317 3611; V Károlyi Mihály utca 16; adult/child 280/140Ft; ⏲ 10am-6pm Tue-Sun) is housed in the sublimely renovated neoclassical **Károly Palace 5** (Károlyi Palota; 1840), which also houses a centre for contemporary literature, library, concert/lecture hall and terrace restaurant in the courtyard.

Southwest of Egyetem tér, at the corner of Szerb utca and Veres Pálné utca, stands the **Serbian Orthodox church** (**6**; Szerb ortodox templom; V Szerb utca 2-4; admission 260Ft; ⏲ 9.30am-1pm & 2-5pm), built by Serbs fleeing the Turks in the 17th century. The iconostasis is worth a look.

There are a couple of interesting things to see along **Veres Pálné utca 7**, which runs north to south just west of Egyetem tér. For example, the building at No 19 has bronze reliefs above the 2nd floor illustrating various periods of construction in the capital in the 18th, 19th and early 20th centuries. At the corner of Papnövelde utca and Cukor utca, the stairwells of the enormous **Apáczai Gimnázium** (**8**; V Papnövelde utca 4-10) elementary school (1913) is topped with little Doric temples on either side of the roof symbolising culture and learning. A few steps north is **Szivárvány köz 9** (Rainbow Alley), the narrowest and shortest street in Budapest. The building with the multicoloured tiled dome and north of the alley is the **Loránd Eötvös University Library** (**10**; Egyetemi könyvtár; V Ferenciek tere 6).

The best way to see the posher side of the Inner Town is to walk up pedestrian Váci utca, the capital's premier – and most expensive – shopping street, with designer clothes, expensive jewellery shops, pubs and some bookshops for browsing. This was the total length of Pest in the Middle Ages. To gain access from Ferenciek tere, walk through **Párisi Udvar** (**11**; Parisian Court; V Ferenciek tere 5), a gem of a Parisian-style arcade built in 1909, out onto tiny Kigyó utca. Váci utca is immediately to the west.

Make a little detour off Váci utca by turning east on Haris köz – once a privately owned street – and continue across Petőfi Sándor utca to **Kamermayer Károly tér 12** a lovely little square with shops, an arty café and, in the centre, a statue of Károly Kamermayer (1829–97), united Budapest's first mayor.

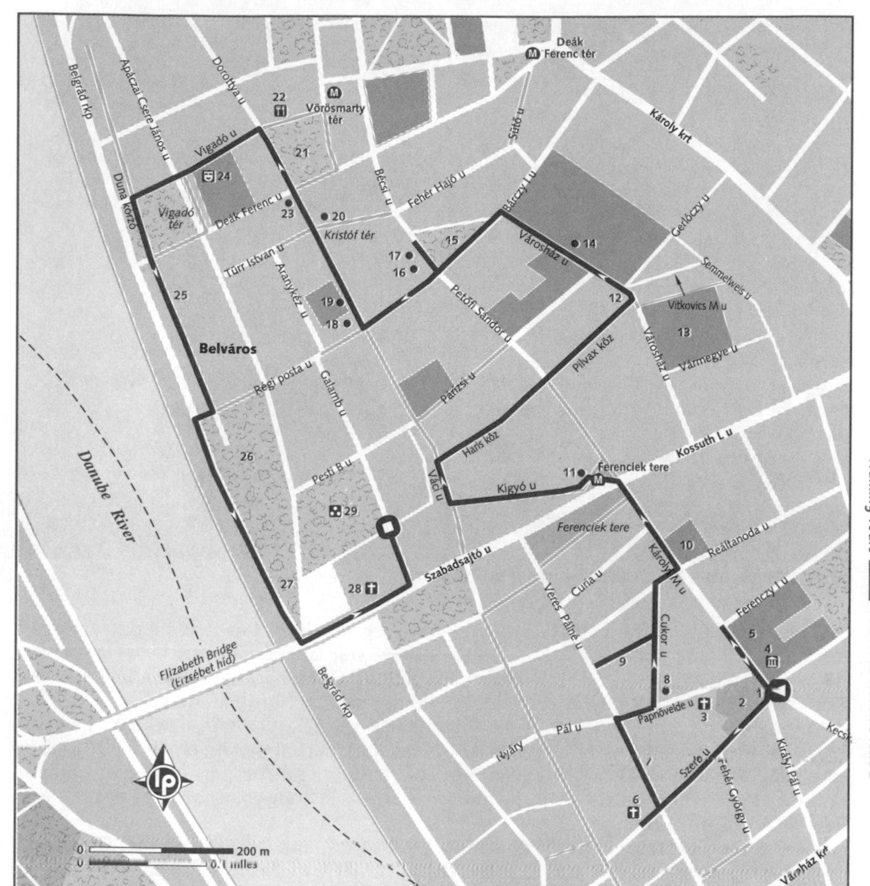

On the southeastern corner of the square is the **Pest county hall** (**13**; Pest Megyei Önkormánzat Hivatal; V Városház utca 7) – the city of Budapest is located in the county of Pest – a large neoclassical building with inner three courtyards. North of the square is the 18th-century **municipal council office** (**14**; Fővárosi Önkormánzat Hivatal; V Városház utca 9-11), or city hall, a rambling red and yellow structure that is the largest baroque building in the city.

WALK FACTS

Start V Egyetem tér
End V Március 15 tér
Distance 2.3km
Duration Two hours
Transport (M) M3 Ferenciek tere (start and end)
Fuel Stop Gerbeaud café (p125)

Szervita tér 15 is at the northwestern end of Városház utca. Naturally there's the requisite baroque church (Szervita templom; 1732) presiding over the square, but much more interesting are the buildings that stand to the west. You would probably never guess, but the **Rózsavölgyi House** (**16**; V Szervita tér 5) apartment block was built in 1912, and is a wonderful example of early Modernism. Two doors away is the former **Török Bank House 17** (p20); have a look up to the gable to see its marvellous mosaic. You can return to Váci utca via Régiposta utca.

Elegant afternoon tea at the famous Gerbeaud café (p125), Belváros

Many of the buildings on Váci utca are worth a closer look, but as it's a narrow street you'll have to crane your neck or walk into one of the side lanes for a better view. **Thonet House** (**18**; V Váci utca 11/a) is another masterpiece built by Ödön Lechner (1890), and a flower shop called **Philanthia** (**19**; V Váci utca 9) has an original Art Nouveau interior.

At the top of Váci utca, across from Kristóf tér with the little **Fishergirl Well 20**, is a brick outline of the foundations of the Vác Gate (Váci kapu), part of the old city wall. The street leads into **Vörösmarty tér 21**, a large square of smart shops, galleries, cafés and an outdoor market of stalls selling tourist schlock, and artists who will draw your portrait or caricature. Suitable for framing (maybe).

In the centre is a statue of the 19th-century poet after whom Vörösmarty tér was named. It is made of Italian marble and is protected in winter by a bizarre plastic 'iceberg' that kids love sliding on. The first – or last – stop of the little yellow metro line (M1) is also in the square, and at the northern end is **Gerbeaud 22** (p125), Budapest's most famous café and cake shop.

South of Vörösmarty tér is the sumptuous **Bank Palace** (**23**; Bank Palota; V Deák utca 5), built in 1915 and now housing the Budapest Stock Exchange. The **Pesti Vigadó 24** (p131) concert hall dating from the mid-19th century faces the river to the west of Vörösmarty tér. Before proceeding, have a look (if open) in the foyer at V Vigadó utca 6, which has one of those strange conveyances called Pater Noster lifts (p65).

A pleasant way to return to Ferenciek tere is via the **Duna korzó 25**, the riverside 'Danube Embankment' between Chain and Elizabeth Bridges and above Belgrád rakpart. It's full of cafés, musicians and handicraft stalls and leads into **Petőfi tér 26**, named after the poet of the 1848–49 War of Independence and the scene of political rallies (both legal and illegal) over subsequent years. **Március 15 tér 27**, which marks the date of the outbreak of the revolution, abuts it to the south. Here you'll find the **Inner Town parish church 28** (p64) and, in the small park to the north, what's left of the **Contra Aquincum 29** Roman fort.

Eating

Eating

Budapest is currently undergoing something of a restaurant revolution. Stodgy and heavy Hungarian food (p26) is being 'enlightened', brought up to date and rechristened as *kortárs magyar konyha* (modern Hungarian cuisine) at many midrange and upmarket restaurants; judging from the bookings at the establishments serving it, it's here to stay. At the same time, a fair few vegetarian (or partially vegetarian) restaurants have opened up in recent years and more 'regular' restaurants have a greater selection of 'real' vegetarian dishes – not just fried cheese and stuffed mushroom caps. And ethnic food – from Middle Eastern and Greek to takeaway Thai and Chinese – has become very popular. It all makes a very nice change from the not-too-distant days when munching on a cheeseburger at McDonald's was an attractive alternative to tussling with an overcooked *bécsiszelet* (Wiener schnitzel) in yet another smoky *vendéglő* (small restaurant) where the waiters just didn't want to know.

If looking for something cheap and cheerful, international fast-food places abound in Budapest (Oktogon is full of them), but old-style *önkiszolgáló* (self-service restaurants), the mainstay of both white- and blue-collar workers in the old regime are fast disappearing.

More interesting places for local colour and better value in the long run are the wonderful little restaurants called *étkezde,* canteens not unlike British 'cafs' that serve simple dishes that change every day. A meal should easily cost under 1000Ft. You'll find *gyors kinai büfé* (Chinese fast-food 'buffets') serving uninspired but cheap rice and noodle dishes everywhere in Budapest. Traditional coffee houses and newly popular teahouses are primarily known for their teas and coffees, but sometimes serve cakes and light meals as well. These are listed in the Drinking section of the Entertainment chapter.

Opening Hours & Reservations

Most restaurants are open from 10am or 11am to 11pm or midnight; if there are no times listed under a particular entry in this chapter, you can assume the place will be open between those hours. It's always best to arrive by 9pm or 10pm (at the latest), though, to ensure being served.

It is advisable to book tables at medium-priced to expensive restaurants.

How Much?

Very roughly, a two-course sit-down meal for one person with a glass of wine or beer for under 2500Ft in Budapest is 'budget' (though you can eat 'cheaply' for less than that), while a 'moderate' meal will cost up to 5000Ft. There's a big jump to an 'expensive' meal (5000Ft to 7500Ft), and 'very expensive' is anything above that. Most restaurants offer a good-value *menü* (set menu) of two or three courses at lunch.

Tipping

The way you tip in restaurants here is unusual. You never leave the money on the table – this is considered both stupid and rude – but tell the waiter how much you're paying in total. If the bill is, say, 2700Ft, you're paying with a 5000Ft note and you think the waiter deserves a gratuity of around 10%, first ask if service is included (some restaurants add it to the bill automatically, which makes tipping unnecessary). If it isn't, say you're paying 3000Ft or that you want 2000Ft back.

It is not unknown for waiters to try to rip you off once they see you are a foreigner. They may try to bring you an unordered dish or make a 'mistake' when tallying the bill. If you think there's a discrepancy, ask for the menu and check the bill carefully. If you've been taken for more than 15% or 20% of the bill, call for the manager. Otherwise just don't leave a tip.

Self-Catering

Budapest counts some 20 large food markets, most of them in Pest. They are usually open from 6am or 6.30am to 6pm weekdays and to 2pm on Saturday. Monday is always very quiet (if the market is open at all). Supermarkets and 24-hour shops selling everything from cheese and cold cuts to cigarettes and beer abound on both sides of the Danube. Fresh food is generally sold by weight or by piece *(darab)*. When ordering by weight, you specify by kilos or *deka* (decagrams – 50dg is equal to 0.5kg or a little more than 1lb).

BUDA

One of the largest and most central food markets in Buda is the **Fény utca market** (Map pp218–19; II Fény utca; 6am-6pm Mon-Fri, 6am-2pm Sat; M M2 Moszkva tér) next to the Mammut shopping mall (p143). **Kaiser's Szupermarket** (Map pp228–9; cnr XI Október 23 utca & XI Bercsényi utca; 7am-8pm Mon-Fri, 7am-4pm Sat, 8am-3pm Sun; 4) is a good-sized supermarket south of XI Béla Bartók út, and a shop called **Ezred Nonstop** (Map p220; I Attila utca 57; 24hr; 78) is open around the clock.

PEST

Two of the most central (though not the most colourful or well-stocked) markets are **Rákóczi tér market** (Map pp218–19; VIII Rákóczi tér 8; 6am-4pm Mon, 6am-6pm Tue-Fri, 6am-1pm Sat; 4 or 6) and, near V Szabadság tér, **Hold utca market** (Map p222; V Hold utca 11; 6am-5pm Mon, 6.30am-6pm Tue-Fri, 6.30am-2pm Sat; M M3 Arany János utca).

Large supermarkets are everywhere in Pest, including **Match** (Map p222; VIII Rákóczi út 50; 6am-9pm Mon-Fri, 7am-8pm Sat, 7am-3pm Sun; M M3 Blaha Lujza tér) facing Blaha Lujza tér, with a **district VI branch** (Map p222; VI Andrássy út 30; 7am-8pm Mon-Fri, 7am-6pm Sat; M M1 Opera) at the corner with VI Nagymező utca; **Kaiser's Szupermarket** (Map p222; VI Nyugati tér 1-2; 7am-8pm Mon-Sat, 7am-4pm Sun; M M3 Nyugati pályaudvar), opposite the Nyugati train station; and **Rothschild** (Map p222; XIII Szent István körút 4; 6am-8pm Mon-Fri, 7am-6pm Sat, 9am-5pm Sun; 4 or 6), with a good supply of kosher products and a **district VI branch** (Map p222; VI Teréz körút 19; 24hr; 4 or 6).

There are nonstop shops open very late or even 24 hours throughout Pest, including the **Nyugati ABC** (Map p222; track 13, Nyugati train station; 24hr; M M3 Nyugati pályaudvar); the **Keleti Sarok** (Map pp218–19; VIII Baross tér 3; 6am-midnight; M M2 Keleti pályaudvar) near the Keleti train station; and the **Mini Coop** (Map p222; VI Nagymező utca 60; 24hr; M M1 Opera).

BUTTERFLY Map p222

VI Teréz körút 20; 90Ft per scoop; 10am-7pm Mon-Fri, 10am-2pm Sat; M M1 Oktogon

This place – and *not* the pastry shop next door, which is called Vajassütemények boltja – is *the* place in Pest for ice cream, as you'll be able to deduce from the queues outside.

LEHEL CSARNOK Map pp218-19

Lehel Market; XIII Lehel tér; 6am-6pm Mon-Fri, 6am-2pm Sat, 6am-1pm Sun; M M3 Lehel tér

One of Pest's more interesting traditional markets, Lehel Csarnok is housed in a hideous boat-like structure, which was designed by László Rajk, son of the communist minister of the interior executed for 'Titoism' in 1949. This is apparently his revenge.

MEZES KUCKO Map p222

Honey Nook; XIII Jászai Mari tér 4; 10am-6pm Mon-Fri year-round, 9am-1pm Sat Oct-May; 4 or 6

The place to go if you've got the urge for something sweet; its nut-and-honey cookies (180Ft per 10dg) are to die for, and the colourful gingerbread hearts (400Ft to 600Ft) make excellent gifts.

NAGY TAMÁS Map p224

Big Tom; 317 4268; V Gerlóczy utca 3; 9am-6pm Mon-Fri, 9am-1pm Sat; M M1/2/3 Deák Ferenc tér

Budapest's best cheese shop stocks more than 200 varieties of Hungarian and imported cheeses; ask for the Hungarian *kecskesajit* (goat's cheese) made by an eccentric theatre critic.

NAGYCSARNOK Map p224

Great Market; IX Vámház körút 1-3; 6am-5pm Mon, 6am-6pm Tue-Fri, 6am-2pm Sat; 47 or 49

This is Budapest's biggest market, though it has become a bit of a tourist trap since it was renovated for the millecentenary in 1996. Still, plenty of locals head here for fruit and vegetables, deli items, fish and meat. There are good food stalls on the west side of the 3rd level.

BUDA

Buda can't claim anything close to the same number of restaurants as Pest can but what it does have are high-quality, very atmospheric dining venues. From romantic spots with spectacular views and live piano music up on Castle Hill to the little neighbourhood eateries of Óbuda, so long established they make a cameo in Hungarian literature, restaurants on this side offer great food and romance.

CASTLE HILL

CAFÉ PIERROT

Map p220 Hungarian, International

375 6971; I Fortuna utca 14; soups 990-1190Ft, starters 1590-2980Ft, mains 2690-5890Ft; 11am-midnight; 16

This very stylish and long-established café-cum-bar-cum-restaurant is one of the very few places to be recommended on Castle Hill. The décor is, well – what else? – clownish and there's live piano music nightly. The food is Hungo-hybrid and quite good, and staff are exceptionally friendly.

Subdued lighting, Aranyszarvas (right), Gellért Hill

RIVALDA Map p220 International

489 0236; I Színház utca 5-9; starters 975-1800Ft, mains 3000-4500Ft; 11.30am-11.30pm; 16

An international café-restaurant in an old convent next to the National Dance Theatre with some modern Hungarian favourites, Rivalda has a thespian theme and a delightful garden courtyard. This is the second of very few places we'd choose to visit in the generally touristy and expensive Castle District. The menu changes frequently and the wine list is among the best.

GELLÉRT HILL & THE TABÁN

ARANYSZARVAS Map p220 Hungarian

375 6451; I Szarvas tér 1; soups 150-890Ft, starters 1100-2900Ft, mains 2180-3500Ft; noon-11pm; 86

Set in an 18th-century inn literally at the foot of Castle Hill, the 'Golden Stag' serves up – guess what? – game dishes. There's piano music Thursday to Saturday in the evening, and the covered outside terrace in summer, when grills are available, is inviting. Vegetarians will give this place a wide berth and head for nearby Éden.

ÉDEN Map p220 Vegetarian

375 7575; I Döbrentei utca 9; soups 590-690Ft, mains 990-1790Ft; noon-11pm Sun-Thu; 86

This place in a mid-18th-century townhouse below Castle Hill must have the classiest location of any vegetarian restaurant anywhere. Seating is in the 1st-floor dining room and, in warmer months, in the pleasant courtyard. Note that Éden is closed on Friday and Saturday.

MARCELLO Map pp228-9 Italian

466 6231; XI Bartók Béla út 40; soup 450Ft, pizza & pasta 820-950Ft, mains 1680-2880Ft; noon-10pm Mon-Sat; 49

Popular with students from the nearby university since it was founded some 15 years ago, this father-and-son-owned operation just down the road from XI Gellért tér offers reliable Italian fare at affordable prices. The salad bar (small/large 580/780Ft) is good value and the lasagne (950Ft) almost legendary in these parts.

TABÁNI TERASZ Map p220 Hungarian

☎ 201 1086; I Apród utca 10; soups & starters 690-890Ft, mains 1850-2750Ft; ⌚ 11.30am-midnight; 🚌 86

This charming terrace restaurant at the foot of Castle Hill is giving the long-established Aranyszarvas (opposite) a run for its money. It's a modern take on the same, with less calorific Hungarian dishes and an excellent wine selection. The candle-lit cellar is a delight in winter.

VÍZIVÁROS

KACSA Map pp218-19 Hungarian

☎ 201 9992; II Fő utca 75; soups 450-750Ft, starters 800-2300Ft, mains 1200-3600Ft; ⌚ noon-midnight; 🚌 86

'Duck' is the place to go, well, 'quackers', though you need not restrict yourself to just dishes with a bill (2200Ft to 2800Ft). It's a fairly elegant place, with art on the walls and piano music in the evening so dress appropriately. Fresh ingredients but stuffy service and pricey wines.

LE JARDIN DE PARIS Map p220 French

☎ 201 0047; II Fő utca 20; soups 900-1900Ft, starters 1500-3000Ft, mains 1950-4650Ft; ⌚ noon-midnight; 🚌 86

A regular haunt of staff from the French Institute across the road (who should know *la cuisine française*), 'The Parisian Garden' is housed in Kapisztory House, a wonderful old townhouse abutting an ancient castle wall. The back garden ablaze in fairy lights is enchanting in summer. Try the home-made pâtés and the brasserie-style steak and chips.

MALOMTÓ

Map pp218-19 Hungarian, International

☎ 336 1830; II Frankel Leó utca 48; soups 750-1100Ft, starters 1400-2100Ft, mains 2400-4200Ft; ⌚ noon-10pm; 🚊 17

The 'Mill Lake', north of Margit körút and just across from the Lukács Baths, is a welcome arrival, with up-to-date, fresh décor and an inspired menu of modern Hungarian and international – especially game and seafood – dishes, many with an Asian spin. But its major draw is its unique position on the edge of a tiny lake filled with water lilies and croaking green frogs; a seat on the terrace in the warmer months is not just recommended it's mandatory.

TOP FIVE BUDA RESTAURANTS

- Malomtó (left)
- Maligán (p96)
- Kisbuda Gyöngye (p96)
- Tabáni Terasz (left)
- Le Jardin de Paris (left)

MAROS SÖRÖZŐ Map pp218-19 Slovakian

☎ 212 3746; XII Maros utca 16; soups 310-600Ft, starters 650-1450Ft, mains 910-2270Ft; ⌚ 11am-11pm; 🚊 61

This brasserie just northwest of Déli train station serves some of the best (and most generous) Slovakian dishes in town. Try the *sztrapacska* (potato dumplings; 1070Ft) with smoked ham or the beef in red wine with noodles which, of course, must be washed down with Zlatý Bažant (Golden Pheasant) draught beer.

MARXIM Map pp218-19 Italian

☎ 316 0231; II Kis Rókus utca 23; pizza 590-1250Ft, pasta 620-890Ft; ⌚ noon-1am Mon-Thu, noon-2am Fri & Sat, 6pm-1am Sun; Ⓜ M2 Moszkva tér

A short walk (very logically) from Moscow Sq, this odd place is a hangout for teens who have added a layer of their own graffiti to the communist memorabilia and kitsch. OK, we all know Stalin *szuksz,* but it's still a curiosity for those who appreciate the Gulag, Lenin and Red October pizzas and the campy Stalinist décor.

MONGOLIAN BARBECUE

Map pp218-19 Asian

☎ 212 1859; XII Márvány utca 19/a; buffet before 5pm 2590Ft, after 5pm & weekends 4390Ft; ⌚ noon-5pm & 6pm-midnight; 🚊 61

South of Moszkva tér, this restaurant is another one of those all-you-can-eat pseudo-Asian places where you choose the raw ingredients and legions of cooks stir-fry it for you. The difference here is that as much beer and wine as you can sink is included in the price. During summer there's also seating in an attractive, tree-filled courtyard. Don't expect gourmet cuisine but if you're hungry (and thirsty) and skint, head here.

TOP FIVE ASIAN RESTAURANTS

- Seoul House (below)
- Új Lanzhou (below)
- Nefrit (opposite)
- Fuji (opposite)
- Kama Sutra (p113)

SEOUL HOUSE Map p220 Korean

☎ 201 9607; I Fő utca 8; soups 400-1000Ft, rice & noodle dishes 2200Ft, mains 2100-2700Ft; noon-3pm & 6-11pm Mon-Sat; 86

This place serves excellent Korean food, from barbecue grills to *kimchi* (pickled spicy cabbage) dishes. Not the most atmospheric place in town and service is rather grim but, well, that makes it all very authentic.

SZENT JUPÁT

Map pp218-19 Hungarian, Late Night

☎ 212 2923; II Retek utca 16; soups 360-550Ft, mains 1490-1990Ft; noon-6am; M M2 Moszkva tér

Szent Jupát is the classic late-night choice for solid Hungarian fare – consider splitting a dish with a friend. It's just north of Moszkva tér and opposite the Fény utca market so within easy striking distance of both Buda and Pest.

ÚJ LANZHOU Map pp218-19 Chinese

☎ 201 9247; II Fő utca 71; soups 290-340Ft, starters 390-990Ft, mains 1290-2390Ft; 11.30am-11pm; 86

They say that the 'New Lanzhou' is not as authentic as its miniscule sister-restaurant **Lanzhou** (Map pp218–19; ☎ 314 1080; VIII Luther utca; 11:30am-11pm; M M2 Keleti pályaudvar) over in Pest, but you could have fooled us. This place is also more stylish and closer to the real world so no doubt it will be a winner.

ÓBUDA & AQUINCUM

KÉHLI Map pp226-7 Hungarian

☎ 368 0613; III Mókus utca 22; soups 580-880Ft, starters 980-2880Ft, mains 1480-6280Ft; noon-midnight; 86

A rustic but stylish place in Óbuda, Kéhli has some of the best traditional Hungarian food. In fact one of Hungary's best-loved writers, the novelist Gyula Krúdy (1878–1933), who lived in nearby Dugovits Titusz tér, moonlighted as a restaurant critic and enjoyed Kéhli's bone marrow on toast (980Ft as a starter – and better than it sounds!) so much he included it in one of his novels.

KISBUDA GYÖNGYE Map pp226-7 Hungarian

☎ 368 6402; III Kenyeres utca 34; soups 880-1180Ft, starters 920-2980Ft, mains 2380-4880Ft; noon-midnight Mon-Sat; 60

This is a favourite traditional and very eccentric Hungarian restaurant in Óbuda; the antique-strewn dining room and attentive service manage to create a *fin-de-siècle* atmosphere. Try the excellent goose-liver dishes (around 3400Ft) and more pedestrian things like *csirke paprikás* (chicken paprika; 2380Ft). The roving fiddler sometimes gets in the way; ignore him.

LEROY CAFÉ Map pp226-7 International

☎ 439 1698; III Bécsi út 63; soups 590-890Ft, starters 1280-1780Ft, mains 2150-3750Ft; 1pm-midnight; 86

Like the other branches of this ever-expanding chain, including a **Pest branch** (Map p222; ☎ 411 0915; VI Liszt Ferenc tér 10; noon-midnight; M M1 Oktogon), this café-restaurant serves international cuisine that is not especially inspired but is of a certain standard – and there just when you've ordered one too many pints of Dreher. Pasta dishes (1550Ft to 2250Ft) are always good blotter. The large terrace fills up (and stays that way) very early in the warm weather.

MAHARAJA Map pp226-7 Indian

☎ 250 7544; III Bécsi út 89-91; starters 450-1500Ft, mains 1500-4000Ft; noon-11pm; 17

This Óbuda institution was the first Indian restaurant to open in Budapest. It specialises in northern Indian dishes and has never been the best in town, but it does manage some mean samosas. It recently opened a branch called **City Maharaja** (Map p222; ☎ 351 1289; VII Csengery utca 24; noon-11pm; 4 or 6) in Pest's Erzsébetváros.

MALIGÁN Map pp226-7 Hungarian, Wine

☎ 240 9010; III Lajos utca 38; soups 650-980Ft, starters 1450-1950Ft, mains 1950-3500Ft; noon-11pm; 86

No-one but no-one takes their wine as seriously as the folk at Maligán, a fabulous cellar wine restaurant in Óbuda. It's become a firm favourite, and nothing is more enjoyable than eating course after course of extremely well-prepared modern Hungarian cuisine with 4cL of excellent wine recommended by the waiter-sommelier. Try the tenderloin of *mangalica* (a form of pork; 1950Ft) roasted with morel sauce or sirloin of grey cattle with onion duck-liver ragout (1800Ft). There are regularly scheduled blind wine tastings (www.malign.hu).

MENNYEI ÍZEK Map pp226-7 Korean, Chinese

☎ 388 6430; Pacsirtamező utca 13; dishes 490-990Ft; noon-9pm; 86

That's 'Celestial Tastes' to you… This little Korean-Chinese hole in the wall serves excellent and very cheap dishes such as spicy pork with eggplant and lots of the hot pickled cabbage called *kimchi*. It's a great place for refuelling en route to/from Aquincum.

ROZMARING Map pp226-7 Hungarian

☎ 367 1301; III Árpád fejedelem útja 125; soups 690-950Ft, starters 790-1650Ft, mains 1290-3950Ft; noon-midnight Mon-Sat, noon-9pm Sun; HÉV Tímár utca

You probably wouldn't come all the way up here for the food – it's uninspired Hungarian at best – but the flower-bedecked covered terraces at 'Rosemary' (as in the herb) that look onto the Danube and the western side of Margaret Island (the water tower just visible above the trees) are a delight in summer.

ÚJ SÍPOS HALÁSZKERT

Map pp226-7 Hungarian

New Piper Fisher's Garden; ☎ 388 8745; III Fő tér 6; soups 950-1950Ft, starters 1200-2100Ft, mains 1650-3300Ft; noon-midnight; 86

This lovely, very traditional restaurant in Óbuda faces (and, in the warmer weather, has outside seating in) the district's most beautiful square, which is worth the trip in itself. Try the *halászlé* (fish soup; from 950Ft). Service is very good here.

WASABI Map pp226-7 Japanese

☎ 430 1056; III Szépvölgyi út 15; lunch Mon-Fri 2990Ft, Sat & Sun 3990Ft, dinner daily 3990Ft; 11am-11pm; 86

The sushi conveyor belt has finally arrived in Budapest and has headed straight for Óbuda. There are more than five dozen items to choose from, fish is flown in fresh every other day and the restaurant has minimalist décor and a very cool feel. A winner.

BUDA HILLS

ARCADE Map pp218-19 International

☎ 225 1969; XII Kiss János altábornagy utca 38; soups 790Ft, starters 850-2450Ft, mains 2690-4990Ft; noon-4pm & 6pm-midnight Mon-Sat; 59

This distant (we're talking kilometres here) cousin of Café Kör (p112) in Buda's well-heeled district XII southwest of the Déli train station has superb and very creative international cuisine, a much coveted leafy terrace set between two converging roads and seamless service. Dress up. There's an excellent wine list.

FUJI Map p216 Japanese

☎ 325 7111; II Csatárka út 54; set meals 2500-5800Ft; noon-11pm; 29

Above Rózsadomb (the poshest area of Budapest) in district II and on the corner of Zöldlomb utca and Zöldkert út, Fuji is a long way to schlep for sushi, sashimi and sukiyaki. But this is the most authentic Japanese game in town, judging from the repeat clientele who nip in for noodles and more.

NÁNCSI NÉNI Hungarian

Auntie Nancy; ☎ 397 2742; II Ördögárok út 80; meals per person about 4000Ft; noon-11pm; 56

Auntie Náncsi, any loopy old lady in Hungarian, is a perennial favourite with Hungarians and expats alike and very much of a sound mind. Housed in a wood-panelled cabin in Hűvösvölgy, the restaurant specialises in game in autumn and winter. In summer it's the lighter fare and garden seating that attract.

NEFRIT Map pp218-19 Chinese

☎ 213 9039; XII Apor Vilmos tér; soups & starters 390-1680Ft, mains 1220-2660Ft; noon-midnight; 59

This Chinese restaurant housed in a small villa on the way to the Buda Hills is popular with diplomats who like what purports to be authentic Cantonese and Szechuan cuisines. The dim sum (610Ft to 850Ft), hard to find in Budapest, is acceptable and some of the seafood dishes quite good. Service is particularly prompt.

REMÍZ Map p216 Hungarian, International

☎ 275 1396; II Budakeszi út 5; soups 780-1240Ft, starters 980-2620Ft, mains 1980-3220Ft; 🕑 9am-midnight; 🚊 56

Next to an old tram depot *(remíz)* in the Buda Hills, this virtual institution kitted out in retro décor remains excellent for its grilled dishes, especially the ribs (1980Ft to 2880Ft), competitive prices and verdant garden terrace. The portions are huge and the service is flawless.

SZÉP ILONA

Map p216 Hungarian, International

☎ 275 1392; II Budakeszi út 1-3; soups 420-800Ft, starters 600-2210Ft, mains 1000-3470Ft; 🕑 11.30am-10pm; 🚊 56

This old favourite in the Buda Hills and opposite the Remíz is the place to come for heavy, indigenous Hungarian and other dishes at very modest prices. The name refers to the 'Beautiful Helen' of poet Mihály Vörösmarty's ballad who falls in love with a dashing 'hunter' who turns out to be the young king Matthias Corvinus (see p79). It's a sad story.

CHEAP EATS – BUDA

DÉLI KINAI GYORSÉTTEREM

Map pp218-19 Chinese

☎ 355 4565; XII Alkotás utca 1/a; starters 140-300Ft, mains 730-1720Ft; 🕑 9am-10.30pm; Ⓜ M2 Déli pályaudvar

This very cheap Chinese place just opposite the Déli train station is suitable for a last-minute feed before you head off.

FORTUNA ÖNKISZOLGÁLÓ

Map p220 Hungarian, Self-Service

Fortune Self-Service Restaurant; ☎ 375 2401; I Fortuna utca 4; soups 200-300Ft, mains 500-700Ft; 🕑 11.30am-2.30pm Mon-Fri; 🚌 16

You'll find cheap and fast weekday lunches in the Castle District at this place, a very basic but clean and cheerful self-service restaurant. Reach it via the stairs on the left side as you enter the Fortuna Passage.

GASZTRÓ HÚS-HENTESÁRU

Map pp218-19 Butcher's Shop

☎ 212 4159; II Margit körút 2; dishes from 250Ft; 🕑 7am-6pm Mon, 6am-7pm Tue-Fri, 6am-1pm Sat; 🚊 4 or 6

Opposite the first stop of trams 4 and 6 on the west side of Margaret Bridge, this place with the unappetising name of Gastro Meat and Butcher Products is a traditional butcher shop also serving cooked sausages and roast chicken, which is common in Hungary.

IL TRENO Map pp218-19 Italian

☎ 356 2846; II Retek utca 12; pizzas 820-1790Ft, pasta 990-1290Ft; 🕑 10.30am-11pm; Ⓜ M2 Moszkva tér

With a cheap set menu (950Ft), a half-dozen branches throughout the city and a thriving takeaway service (☎ 814 1414), 'The Train' (its first branch was opposite Déli train station) is one of the most popular pizzerias in town. Seating at this branch is in the neighbouring Trombitás restaurant or, in warmer months, in a positive oasis of a courtyard off busy Moszkva tér.

ÍZ-É FALODA

Map pp218-19 Hungarian, Self-Service

☎ 345 4130, 238 0282; II Lövőház utca 12; soups 250-380Ft, mains 320-590Ft; 🕑 11am-6pm Mon-Fri, 11am-4pm Sat; Ⓜ M2 Moszkva tér

The 'Drink-Eat Snack Bar' is a clean, modern and cheap self-service place in Fény utca market next to the Mammut shopping mall. It has excellent *főzelék* (see p29) dishes.

NAGYI PALACSINTÁZÓJA

Map pp218-19 Hungarian, Late Night

Granny's Palacsinta Place; ☎ 201 5321; I Hattyú utca 16; set menus 780-1060Ft; 🕑 24hr; Ⓜ M2 Moszkva tér

This place, with branches in **Buda** (Map p220; ☎ 212 4866; I Batthyány tér 5; 🕑 24hr; Ⓜ M2 Batthyány tér), **Óbuda** (Map pp226–7; ☎ 212 4866; III Záhony utca 2; 🕑 24hr; 🚌 34) and still another across the river in **Pest** (Map p224; ☎ 418 0721; V Petőfi Sándor tér 17-19; 🕑 24hr; Ⓜ M1/2/3 Deák Ferenc tér) with Internet access does Hungarian pancakes – both savoury (218Ft to 398Ft) and sweet (118Ft to 398Ft) varieties – round the clock. It's always packed.

(Continued on page 111)

1 *Széchenyi Chain Bridge (p57) crosses the Danube to Buda* **2** *The New York Palace (p85) and its café, in Erzsébetváros, hosted famous names of the past* **3** *Ödön Lechner–designed Applied Arts Museum (p69), Feréncváros* **4** *Art Nouveau feature, Lindenbaum apartment block (p21), Terézváros*

1 *Well-prepared Imre Varga installation (p60), Óbuda* **2** *Evening peace descends over Széchenyi Chain Bridge (p57) and Castle Hill (p53)* **3** *Fishermen's Bastion (p54), Castle Hill, commands a view over Budapest* **4** *Colourful medieval houses (p78) in the Castle District of Buda* **5** *Decorative tiles, Gül Baba's Tomb, Víziváros (p58)*

1 World Heritage–listed Andrássy út (p70) **2** *Stained glass creation of Miksa Róth (p69)* **3** *Art Nouveau lines flow in the central hall of the Applied Arts Museum (p69), Jozsefváros* **4** *Statue of reformist prime minister Imre Nagy (p66) on Vértanúk tere, Lipótváros*

1 *Elizabeth (foreground) and Széchenyi Chain Bridges (p57) link Buda and Pest* **2** *Grand dome of Parliament (p65), Lipótváros* **3** *Tram along the banks of the Danube* **4** *Entrance detail of Mücsarnok (Palace of Art) exhibition space (p72), City Park*

1

1 *Leisure for body and mind Széchenyi Thermal Baths (p136), City Park* **2** *Art Nouveau dome, Gellért Thermal Baths (p136), Gellért Hill* **3** *Medieval dolphin handle, Király Thermal Baths (p136), Buda* **4** *Outdoor swimming pools of the Széchenyi Baths complex (p136), City Park* **5** *Bathing in cathedral-like grandeur of Gellért Thermal Baths (p136), Gellért Hill*

1 *West End City Centre shopping mall (p148), Central Pest* **2** *Club Vittula (p129), Erzsébetváros* **3** *The finest of décor and cakes at Lukács café (p126), Andrássy út* **4** *Szőnyi Antikváriuma (p148), Lipótváros, is the place for antiquarian books*

1 *Cosy dining, Menza restaurant (p114), Újlipótváros* **2** *Budapest's biggest market, Nagycsarnok (p94), Belváros* **3** *The Mellow Mood group's flagship Marco Polo Hostel (p163), Erzsébetváros* **4** *Signalling the delights of Frici Papa Kifőzdéje restaurant (p119), Erzsébetváros*

1

1 *Priceless manuscripts and a ceiling masterpiece at Eger's baroque Lyceum (p176)* **2** *View over the rooftops of Eger to the Minorite church, from the city's 40m minaret (p176)* **3** *Szentendre (p170) scenes captured in ceramic* **4** *Ornate Trinity Column (1751) and Veszprém Cathedral (right; p174)* **5** *Cycling the cobbled streets of Eger (p175)*

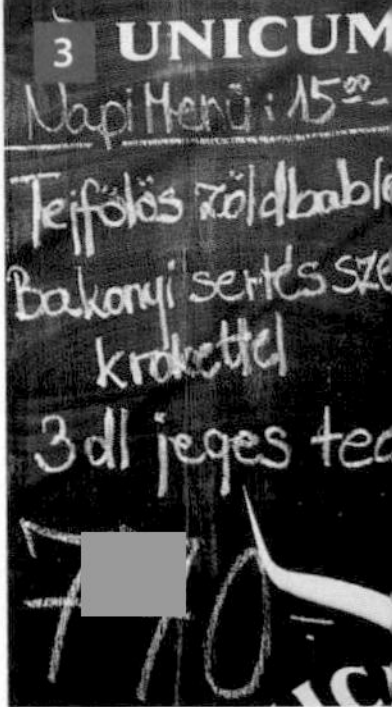

1 *Topical wall adornments at Firkász restaurant (p114), Újlipótváros* **2** *Recommendations available at La Boutique des Vins (p146), Belváros* **3** *Restaurant chalkboard menu with daily specials* **4** *Tempting delicatessen fare, Nagycsarnok market (p94), Belváros*

(Continued from page 98)

TOLDI ÉTKEZDE

Map pp218-19 Hungarian, Étkezde

☎ 214 3867; I Batthyány utca 14; starters 160-390Ft, mains 689-980Ft; 🕑 11am-4pm Mon-Fri; 🚌 39

This little eatery just west of Fő utca is the place to come if you're in search of Hungarian comfort food at lunchtime (weekdays only). Unusually for this kind of place, there are at least a half-dozen real vegetarian dishes to choose from.

PEST

Pest offers a much wider range of restaurants than Buda does – especially when it comes to things like ethnic cuisine. Not always as sophisticated as those across the Danube, Pest-side eateries are often more relaxed and (it must be said) hipper.

INNER TOWN

BANGKOK HOUSE Map p224 Thai

☎ 266 0584; V Só utca 3; soups & Thai salads 550-2250Ft, mains 1450-4550Ft; 🕑 noon-11pm; 🚊 47 or 49

Bangkok House is done up in kitsch, Asian-esque décor that recalls takeaway places on any British high street or American strip mall. But the Thai- and Laotian-inspired dishes are acceptable in a city where Southeast Asian restaurants are at a premium, and the staff is friendly. There's a tourist menu (1460Ft) available from noon to 4pm.

FATÁL Map p224 Hungarian

☎ 266 2607; V Váci utca 67; soups 580-890Ft, dishes 1890-2190Ft; 🕑 11.30am-2am; 🚊 47 or 49

This place serves massive Hungarian meals on *fatal* (wooden platters) or in iron cauldrons in three rustic rooms. And follow the rules: bring your appetite and its friends; avoid the noisy backroom; and book in advance.

KÁROLYI ÉTTEREM Map p224 Hungarian

☎ 328 0240; V Károlyi Mihály utca 16; soups 600-650Ft, starters 1050-1800Ft, mains 2450-3350Ft; 🕑 10am-11pm; 🚌 15

This place beckons not so much for the food (though it is decent enough) but for its location in the renovated Károly Palace (Károlyi Palota) near ELTE university. It has a wonderful terrace in the palace courtyard open in the warmer months and the menu has lots of options for vegetarians.

KÁRPÁTIA Map p224 Hungarian

☎ 317 3596; V Ferenciek tere 7-8; starters 800-2000Ft, mains 2800-5900Ft; 🕑 11am-11pm; Ⓜ M3 Ferenciek tere

A veritable palace of *fin-de-siècle* design dating back 120 years that has to be seen to be believed, the 'Carpathia' serves almost modern Hungarian and Transylvanian specialities in both its restaurant and cheaper pub, and there is a lovely covered garden terrace. This is the place to hear authentic *csárdás* Gypsy music.

KÉPÍRÓ Map p224 French

☎ 266 0430; V Képíró utca 3; soups 900-1100Ft, starters 1450-2950Ft, mains 2200-3950Ft; 🕑 noon-3pm & 6pm-midnight Mon-Fri, 6pm-midnight Sat & Sun; Ⓜ M3 Kálvin tér

Using the old word for 'painter', this restaurant is one of the more stylishly appointed eateries in town, with provocative frescoes on the walls and canned jazz. The food is French classical (it gets a red Michelin mention), the service professional and there is a decent selection of vegetarian dishes.

MOMOTARO RAMEN Map p222 Asian

☎ 269 2037; V Széchenyi utca 16; noodles 900-1700Ft, mains 1100-2500Ft; 🕑 11am-10pm; 🚌 15

This is a favourite pit stop for noodles – especially the soup variety – when *pálinka* had been a-flowing the night before. But it's also good for dumplings and more substantial dishes, including the odd Szechuan one.

ÓCEÁN BÁR & GRILL Map p224 Seafood

☎ 266 1826; V Petőfi tér 3-5; soups 900-1250Ft, starters 990-2790Ft, mains 2490-5450Ft; 🕑 noon-midnight; 🚊 2 or 2/a

We'd like to say this place has made quite a splash in Budapest but we're afraid we'd be arrested by the pun police. Still, it's making waves with its fresher-than-fresh seafood flown in daily from Scandinavia, congenial décor and wonderful fishmonger's/delicatessen (enter from Régiposta utca; 🕑 10am-9pm). We'll come back for the curried crabmeat soufflé and the boiled lobster (1990Ft per 100g) but we do wish they'd remove that aquarium. There's a three-course set lunch for 5000Ft.

SPOON Map p224 International

☎ 411 0933; off V Vigadó tér; mains 2690-4500Ft; noon-midnight; 2 or 2/a

If you like the idea of dining on the high waters but still remaining tethered to the bank (just in case) Spoon's for you. It serves international cuisine amid bright and breezy surrounds and the choices for vegetarians are great. You can't beat the views of the castle and Chain Bridge. It also does sushi (300Ft to 900Ft), hand rolls (880Ft to 3000Ft) and sashimi (2550Ft to 4800Ft).

SUSHI AN Map p224 Japanese

☎ 317 4239; V Harmincad utca 4; sushi per piece 300-600Ft, hand rolls 900-1400Ft, sets 1900-3900Ft; noon-10pm; M M1/2/3 Deák Ferenc tér

This tiny sushi bar next to the British embassy in central Pest is great for sushi and sashimi but even better for Japanese sets served with miso soup. But there's not much more room in here than space to swing a cat.

TAVERNA PIREUS REMBETIKO Map p224 Greek

☎ 266 0292; V Fővám tér 2-3; starters 590-1590Ft, mains 1690-2290Ft; noon-midnight; 47 or 49

Overlooking a patch of green and facing the Great Market Hall, this place serves reasonably priced and pretty authentic Greek fare. Rembetiko is a folk music school and a style of traditional Greek music; there are live performances on Friday and Saturday evening. The courtyard is tempting in summer.

TRATTORIA TOSCANA Map p224 Italian

☎ 327 0045; V Belgrád rakpart 13; starters 990-3200Ft, pasta & pizza 1350-2690Ft, mains 1500-3390Ft; noon-midnight; 15

Hard by the Danube, this trattoria serves rustic and very authentic Italian and Tuscan food, including *ribollito alla chiantigiana,* a hearty vegetable soup stewed with *cannelini* (white Tuscan beans) and Parmesan cheese. The focaccia is excellent too.

VEGETARIUM Map p224 Vegetarian

☎ 484 0848; V Cukor utca 3; soups & starters 490-760Ft, mains 950-1500Ft; 11.30am-10pm Mon-Sat; M M3 Ferenciek tere

A basement restaurant just off Egyetem tér, the Vegetarium, Budapest's (and Hungary's) oldest meat-free restaurant, serves vegetarian and organic food of the old style but there are lots of choices for vegans here too. Set lunch is a snip at just 650Ft.

NORTHERN INNER TOWN

CAFÉ KÖR Map p224 International

☎ 311 0053; V Sas utca 17; salads 730-2110Ft, mains 1590-3190Ft; 10am-10pm Mon-Sat; 15

Just behind the Basilica of St Stephen, the 'Circle Café' is a great place for a light meal at any time, including late breakfast (460Ft to 590Ft). Salads, desserts and daily specials are always recommended, and there are more ambitious three/four-course wine-tasting menus for 4900/6900Ft.

CAFÉ MOKKA Map p224 International

☎ 328 0081; V Sas utca 4; soups 890-960Ft, dishes 2450-5950Ft; noon-midnight; 15

The name of the game here is 'ethno-cuisine' (don't know either), with a mish-mash of dishes; you'll virtually need a map and compass to read the menu. But we love the space and the great African theme and there's a good wine list. The three-course set menu (7000Ft) with wine is good value.

GOVINDA Map p224 Vegetarian

☎ 269 1625, 473 1309; V Vigyázó Ferenc utca 4; soups 350Ft, dishes 240-450Ft; noon-9pm Mon-Sat; 15

As well as wholesome salads, soups and desserts, Govinda serves up a daily set menu plate (small/large 1280/1600Ft). Run by a Buddhist and blessed by the Dalai Lama when it was first opened, the restaurant is in a basement near Chain Bridge.

GRESHAM KÁVÉHÁZ Map p224 International

☎ 268 5110; Four Seasons Gresham Palace Hotel, V Roosevelt tér 5-6; soup 1200Ft, starters 1600-3200Ft, mains 2600-3900Ft; 6.30am-11.30pm Mon-Fri, 7am-11.30pm Sat, noon-10pm Sun; 2 or 2/a

Hotel coffee shops – even ones that masquerade as proper restaurants and call themselves PPHRs (popular-priced hotel restaurants) in the hospitality trade – don't usually make the grade as far as we are concerned but this one in a stunning newly renovated hotel is worth its weight in majolica tiles. There's live jazz every Thursday, Friday and Saturday from 7pm.

IGUANA Map p222 Mexican

☎ 331 4352; V Zoltán utca 16; starters 430-1590Ft, mains 1890-3990Ft; 🕑 11.30am-12.30am; 🚍 15

Iguana serves decent-enough Mexican food (not a difficult task in this cantina-free desert of a town), but it's hard to say whether the pull is the chilli (1050Ft to 1490Ft), the enchilada and burrito combination *platos* (2090Ft to 2290Ft) or the frenetic and very boozy 'we-party-every-night-style' atmosphere.

KAMA SUTRA Map p224 Indian

☎ 373 0092; V Október 6 utca 19; starters 450-899Ft, mains 1200-2800Ft; 🕑 11am-11pm; 🚍 15

This new arrival is a welcome one indeed: decent curries and tandoor dishes in upbeat surrounds in the very heart of town. Try the samosas (450Ft) and chicken vindaloo (1600Ft). It's definitely a cut above the usual curry-house atmosphere and the perfect place for a meal before moving on for the evening.

LA FONTAINE Map p224 French

☎ 317 3715; V Mérleg utca 10; starters 1190-2990Ft, mains 1990-6990Ft; 🕑 noon-2.30pm Mon-Fri, 7-10.30pm daily; 🚍 15

'The Fountain' is a Parisian-style 'café-théâtre', with more of the former than the latter. The relatively simple brasserie food is good, especially the leg of lamb and the steak *frîtes*. There is also a much wider choice of fish dishes than one would normally find in such a restaurant.

LOU LOU Map p224 French

☎ 312 4505; V Vigyázó Ferenc utca 4; soups 800Ft, starters 1600-2800Ft, mains 2300-4400Ft; 🕑 noon-3pm & 7-11pm Mon-Fri, 7-11pm Sat; 🚍 15

One of the most popular places with expatriate *français* in Budapest is this bistro with excellent daily specials. Two signature dishes are the marinated grilled breast of duck with orange and Arabica coffee sauce (3100Ft) and the rack of lamb with garlic and *haricots verts* (3600Ft).

TOP FIVE PEST RESTAURANTS

- Óceán Bár & Grill (**p111**)
- Menza (p114)
- Múzeum (p117)
- Fausto (p115)
- Vörös és Fehér (p118)

TOM-GEORGE Map p224 International

☎ 266 3525; V Október 6 utca 8; soups 680-1680Ft, starters 1650-3580Ft, mains 2500-6200Ft; 🕑 noon-midnight; 🚍 15

Let's be honest. What's the point of eating in a place that could be in London or New York when in Budapest? This über-trendy and overdecorated place is the venue of the moment and not an unpleasant spot. It's just that the menu is all over the place – contemporary Hungarian, Argentine steaks (3200Ft to 7600Ft) and sushi (420Ft to 1400Ft) is not fusion it's confusion – and the service is as attitudinous as a film star being IDed. Set lunch is 1350Ft.

ÚJLIPÓTVÁROS & TERÉZVÁROS

ALHAMBRA Map p222 Spanish, Moroccan

☎ 354 1068; VI Jókai tér 3; starters 790-1980Ft, mains 890-2490Ft; 🕑 noon-midnight Mon-Fri, 6pm-midnight Sat & Sun; Ⓜ M1 Oktogon

This place, which almost certainly has taken inspiration from the celebrated Moro restaurant in London, serves Spanish food with a North African twist as well as straightforward Moroccan dishes such as couscous and tajines. The décor is decidedly more Moorish than the dishes, though, which also include Spanish things like empanadas (790Ft to 890Ft) and paella (2100Ft to 2600Ft). Set midweek lunch is 980Ft.

ARTICSÓKA Map p222 Mediterranean

☎ 302 7757; VI Zichy Jenő utca 17; soups 690-1300Ft, starters 1260-2950Ft, mains 2920-6000Ft; 🕑 11am-midnight; Ⓜ M3 Arany János utca

Charming Articsóka is tastefully decorated and has an atrium, roof-top terrace and a theatre that can accommodate 100 people. There's live music every second week of the month, and the atmosphere should win a prize. The food is more Hungo-Med than

Italian (but heading in that general direction). Pasta dishes (1400Ft to 2200Ft) are especially recommended.

FIRKÁSZ Map pp218-19 Hungarian

☎ 450 1118; Tátra utca 18; soups 590-790Ft, starters 1150-1690Ft, mains 1990-3600Ft; 🕑 noon-midnight; 🚌 15

Set up by former journalists (the name means 'hack' in Hungarian), Firkász is a retro Hungarian restaurant with lovely old mementos on the walls, excellent home cooking and a great wine list. And you can't beat the location in Újlipótváros. Would that they were all like this…

MARQUIS DE SALADE
Map p222 International

☎ 302 4086; VI Hajós utca 43; soups & salads 800-1700Ft, mains 2500-3400Ft; 🕑 11am-1am; trolleybus 72 or 73

This is a serious hybrid of a place, with dishes from Russia and Azerbaijan as well as Hungary. There are lots of quality vegetarian choices, too, in the basement restaurant. And, by the way, it's not just about *salade*.

MENZA Map p222 Hungarian

☎ 413 1482; VI Liszt Ferenc ter 2; soups 590-650Ft, starters 990-1390Ft, mains 1390-2790Ft; 🕑 10am-midnight; Ⓜ M1 Oktogon

On Budapest's most lively square, this upmarket Hungarian restaurant takes its name from the Hungarian for a drab school canteen – something it is anything but. Book a table; it's fabulously stylish and always packed by diners who come for the simply but perfectly cooked Hungarian classics with a modern spin. Weekday two-course set lunches are a snip at 790Ft.

MÓRI KISVENDÉGLŐ
Map pp218-19 Hungarian Jewish, Étkezde

☎ 349 8390; XIII Pozsonyi út 39; dishes 480-1500Ft; 🕑 10am-8pm Mon-Thu, 10am-3pm Fri; trolleybus 76 or 79

Sample some of the best home-cooked Hungarian Jewish food in Budapest at this simple *borozó* (wine bar) and restaurant, a short walk north of Szent István körút. But, as the owner warns our 'dear readers', get here by 3pm if you want to eat the famous *főzelék*.

MOSSELEN Map p222 Belgian

☎ 452 0535; www.mosselen.hu; XIII Pannónia utca 14; soup 610Ft, starters 1290-2100Ft, mains 1890-3390Ft; 🕑 noon-midnight; 🚌 15

This pleasant pub-restaurant in Újlipótváros serves Belgian (and some Hungarian) specialities, including its namesake, mussels, and has a wide selection of Belgian beers, including some of the fruit-flavoured ones. A beer tasting of six costs 1650Ft and there is a good snacks menu (990Ft to 1340Ft).

Spinoza Café (p116), a restaurant complete with art gallery and theatre in Erzsébetváros

OKAY ITALIA Map p222 Italian

☎ 349 2991; XIII Szent István körút 20; pizza 1320-1790Ft, pasta 1460-2290Ft, mains 1680-3050Ft; 🕓 11am-midnight Mon-Fri, noon-midnight Sat & Sun; 🚊 4 or 6

Okay is a perennially popular place run by Italians with a full range of dishes with a nearby **branch** (Map p222; ☎ 332 6960; V Nyugati tér 6; Ⓜ M3 Nyugati pályaudvar) that serves just pasta and pizza, which is what most people come for in any case. Both restaurants have terraces.

PESTI VENDÉGLŐ Map p224 Hungarian

☎ 266 3227; VI Paulay Ede utca 5; soups 350-650Ft, starters 490-1350Ft, mains 1250-1750Ft; 🕓 11am-11pm; Ⓜ M1/2/3 Deák tér

Here is a great choice for someone trying traditional Hungarian specialities for the first time. This very popular family-run and clean eatery close to Deák tér offers a lighter take on standard Hungarian favourites, and the staff is very welcoming and helpful.

POZSONYI KISVENDÉGLŐ

Map pp218-19 Hungarian

☎ 329 2911; XIII Radnóti Miklós utca 38; soups 350-520Ft, starters 680-850Ft, mains 750-1350Ft; 🕓 11am-midnight; trolleybus 76 or 79

Visit this neighbourhood restaurant on the corner of Pozsonyi út offering the ultimate local experience: gargantuan portions of standard Hungarian favourites, rock-bottom prices and a cast of local characters. There's a bank of tables on the pavement in summer and simple set weekday menus for 550Ft.

TROFÉA GRILL

Map pp218-19 International, Buffet

☎ 270 0366; XIII Visegrádi utca 50/a; lunch/dinner Mon-Thu 2200/3000Ft, lunch & dinner Fri-Sun 3600Ft; 🕓 noon-midnight Mon-Fri, 11.30am-midnight Sat, 11.30am-9pm Sun; Ⓜ M3 Lehel tér

When you really could eat a horse (which might be there somewhere), head for the Troféa. It's an enormous buffet of more than 100 cold and hot dishes over which diners swarm like bees while being observed by the cooks from their kitchen. Considering there's goose liver and salmon on the table (at least for a while) it's good value.

VOGUE Map pp218-19 South Slav

☎ 350 7000, 06-30 942 5027; XIII Újpesti alsó rakpart 1; soups 650-1000Ft, starters 700-2000Ft; 🕓 11am-1am; trolleybus 76 & 79

This fine old vessel moored off XIII Szent István Park in Újlipótváros and opposite the eastern side of Margaret Island has fine views south to Margaret and Széchenyi Chain Bridges and – unusually – you can also take in both sides of the river. The food is Serbian and other South Slav – *čevapčiči* (spicy meatballs), *pljeskavica* (spicy meat patties) and *ražnjiči* (shish kebab) – always grilled and always in large portions.

ERZSÉBETVÁROS

AL-AMIR Map p224 Middle Eastern

☎ 352 1422; VII Király utca 17; meze 650-850Ft, mains 1490-2300Ft; 🕓 noon-11pm; Ⓜ M1 Bajcsy-Zsilinszky út

Arguably the most authentic Middle Eastern (in this case, Syrian) place in town and light years from the gyros and falafel places found along the Big Ring Road (p119).

Al Amir too has a window selling takeaway gyros (500Ft) and falafels (450Ft), but we're talking quality here.

CARMEL PINCE Map p224 Jewish

☎ 322 1834, 342 4585; VII Kazinczy utca 31; soups 380-900Ft, starters 600-2200Ft, mains 1400-3000Ft; 🕓 noon-11pm; trolleybus 74

Decidedly *not* kosher – signs outside will warn you of that fact in six living languages – but the 'Carmel Cellar' has authentic Ashkenazi specialities such as gefilte fish (800Ft), *matzo*-ball soup (700Ft) and a *cholent* almost as good as the one Aunt Goldie used to make. There's live *klezmer* music (see p19) on Thursday evening. A three-course tourist menu (1800Ft) is available daily from noon to 6pm.

FAUSTO Map p224 Italian

☎ 269 6806; VII Dohány utca 5; soups 1300-3300Ft, starters 2400-4200Ft, mains 3200-6400Ft; 🕓 noon-3pm & 7pm-11pm Mon-Sat; trolleybus 74

Still the most upmarket (and expensive) Italian restaurant in town, Fausto has brilliant pasta dishes, daily specials and desserts; there are lots of choices for vegetarians. The yellow walls and antique furniture provide an elegant touch and the Italian wine selection is huge. It remains one of the most pleasant dining experiences in Budapest.

HANNA Map p224 Kosher

☎ 342 1072; VII Dob utca 35; lunch per person 3000Ft; 8am-3.30pm Mon-Thu, 8am-10pm Fri, 11am-2pm Sat, 8am-2pm Sun; 4 or 6

Housed upstairs in an old school in the Orthodox Synagogue complex, this simple eatery is as soulless as the devil himself, but if you answer to a Higher Authority on matters culinary, it is another option for kosher food at lunchtime only. (On the Sabbath meals are available later but you must pay for them in advance.)

KINOR DAVID Map p224 Kosher

☎ 512 8783; VII Dohány utca 10; soup 800-1300Ft, mains 2800-3200Ft; 11am-11pm Mon-Fri & Sun, noon-2pm Sat; trolleybus 74

Budapest's largest kosher restaurant, 'David's Harp' is a cut above the usual and serves dinner as well. There are special fish dishes (3000Ft to 4500Ft) and Israeli treats (2600Ft to 3100Ft) as well. Pay in advance for Friday dinner and Saturday lunch.

MAGDALENA MERLO
Map p222 Hungarian, Italian

☎ 322 3278; VII Király utca 59; starters 460-520Ft; mains 1190-2190Ft; 10am-midnight; 4 or 6

This restaurant, conveniently catty-cornered from the Ferenc Liszt Academy of Music , serves an odd mix of Hungarian and Italian dishes. What's more, since it was the Svejk (from Jaroslav Hašek's satirical novel *The Good Soldier Svejk*) for many years it has retained a page of 'nostalgic' Czech and Slovak dishes (895Ft to 1390Ft) for those who can't let go of the memories.

SHALIMAR Map p222 Indian

☎ 352 0297; VII Dob utca 50; starters 690-1680Ft, mains 1720-2480Ft; noon-4pm & 6pm-midnight; 4 or 6

Shalimar is a rather tired-looking place serving tandoori, tikka and kebab dishes that taste like they've come via southern Hungary (there's got to be paprika in there somewhere) rather than India, but at least it's a fix when you need it. We're told the chef's from Nepal, which may explain the hybrid tastes. Still the mutton biryani (2480Ft) is a force to be reckoned with and vegetarian dishes (1050Ft to 1460Ft) are plentiful.

SPINOZA CAFÉ Map p224 International

☎ 413 7488; VII Dob utca 15; starters 1190-1490Ft, mains 1590-2990Ft; 11am-11pm; 47 or 49

This very attractive café-restaurant in the Jewish district has become a personal favourite both for meals and as a chill-out zone. The venue includes both an art gallery and theatre, where events take place from May to September, along with a restaurant and coffee house. The food is an unusual (but successful) hybrid of Hungarian, Dutch and Jewish; try the signature chicken with honey and garlic or the roast goose leg with apple and red cabbage. There's live music on Thursday from 7pm.

JÓZSEFVÁROS & FERENCVÁROS

BIOPONT Map p222 Vegetarian

☎ 266 4601; VIII Krúdy utca 7; soups 290Ft, dishes 380-660Ft; 10am-10pm Mon-Fri, noon-10pm Sat & Sun; 4 or 6

In the Darshan Udvar complex (p124), this is a pleasant place for a meatless organic meal, with all dishes available in both full and half-portions. There are also 'bio' sandwiches (320Ft) and pizzas (800Ft to 1290Ft) if you just want a snack. The attached Samadhi Spiritual Centre hosts all sorts of programmes, classes and lectures.

CSÜLÖK CSÁRDA Map pp218-19 Hungarian

☎ 210 7897; VIII Berzsenyi utca 4; soups 350-690Ft, starters 790-1500Ft, mains 990-2290Ft; noon-11pm Mon-Fri, 5-11pm Sat & Sun; M M2 Keleti pályaudvar

The rough-and-ready 'Pork Knuckle Inn' serves just that and other country specialities in enormous quantities in a cellar restaurant. Slide into one of the wooden booths and order a plate to share before you board your train at the nearby Keleti station.

FÜLEMÜLE Map p222 Hungarian, Jewish

☎ 266 7947; VIII Kőfaragó utca 5; soups 570-590Ft, starters 790-2700Ft, mains 1300-3700Ft; noon-11pm; 7

This quaint Hungarian restaurant that looks like time stood still just before WWII is quite a find in deepest Józsefváros and well worth the search. Dishes mingle Hungarian and international tastes with some old-style Jewish favourites.

MÚZEUM Map p224 Hungarian

☎ 338 4221, 267 0375; VIII Múzeum körút 12; soups 700-800Ft, starters 1400-3400Ft, mains 2400-4400Ft; noon-midnight Mon-Sat; 47 or 49

This is the place to come if you want to really dine in style. Múzeum is a café-restaurant that is still going strong after more than a century at the same location near the National Museum. The food is excellent and reliable, if not particularly inventive, and there is a good-value, three-course set menu (2600Ft) that is available noon to 4pm.

PATA NEGRA Map p224 Spanish

☎ 215 5616; IX Kálvin tér 8; tapas 250-650Ft, plates 500-1200Ft; 11am-midnight Mon-Wed, 11am-1am Thu & Fri, noon-1am Sat, noon-midnight Sun; M M3 Kálvin tér

The 'Black Foot' – it's a special kind of Spanish cured ham – is a new cellar-like Spanish tapas bar and restaurant at the (almost) top of trendy Ráday utca. There are good cheese and excellent wine selections, and it's very vegetarian-friendly.

PINK CADILLAC

Map pp218-19 Italian

☎ 216 1412; IX Ráday utca 22; pizzas 720-1890Ft, set menu 2500Ft; 11am-12.30am Sun-Thu, 11am-1am Fri & Sat; 15

More of an upbeat 1950s diner than a pizzeria, the Pink Cadillac still reigns supreme on IX Ráday utca after all this time. If you don't like the surrounds, have it delivered to Paris Texas (that's a pub next door and not some one-horse town in the Lone Star State; p124). There's a set menu for 2500Ft.

SHIRAZ Map pp218-19 Middle Eastern

☎ 218 0881; IX Ráday utca 21; starters & salads 750-1450Ft, mains 1400-3200Ft; noon-midnight; 15

A 'Persian' restaurant with carpets and hookahs loaded with apple, peach and strawberry tobacco (990Ft) to lure in the punters. The food is tasty but not particularly substantial and most are stew-like in form and taste.

TOP FIVE OLD-STYLE HUNGARIAN RESTAURANTS

- Firkász (p114)
- Kéhli (p96)
- Náncsi Néni (p97)
- Kárpátia (p111)
- Móri Kisvendéglő (p114)

SOUL CAFÉ Map p224 International

☎ 217 6986; IX Ráday utca 11-13; starters 590-1890Ft, mains 1980-2980Ft; noon-1am; M M3 Kálvin tér

One of the better choices along a street full of so-so restaurants and iffy cafés, the Soul has inventive Continental food and décor. You can order anything from a sandwich (850Ft) or a pizza (890Ft to 1500Ft) to a full meal, including many vegetarian dishes (590Ft to 1890Ft). It has a great terrace.

STEX ALFRED

Map pp218-19 Hungarian, Late Night

☎ 318 5716; VIII József körút 55-57; starters 450-1990Ft, mains 950-3000Ft; 8am-6am; M M3 Ferenc körút

A big, noisy place that's open almost 24 hours, the Stex is north of the Applied Arts Museum. The menu offers soups, sandwiches, pasta, fish and meat dishes as well as vegetarian choices (750Ft to 890Ft). It transforms into a lively bar late at night. Best of all, there's breakfast (350Ft to 910Ft).

TAIWAN Map pp228-9 Chinese

☎ 215 1236; IX Gyáli út 3/b; soups 395-880Ft, mains 960-2250Ft; noon-midnight; M M3 Nagyvárad tér

In the same building as the Fortuna Hotel (p164) in south Ferencváros, this mammoth Chinese restaurant (think airline hangar – in red) may seem a long way to go for a bit of rice but it's one of the few places in Budapest that does decent dim sum.

VÖRÖS POSTAKOCSI

Map p224 Hungarian

☎ 217 6756; IX Ráday 15; soups 750-900Ft, starters 990-2190Ft, mains 1590-3600Ft; 11.30am-midnight; 15

What was for over three decades a more than forgettable eatery serving

Vörös és Fehér restaurant and bar (below), Andrássy út

Hungarian stodge and overlooked by all but the bravest or most desperate of diners in Ferencváros has remerged Phoenix-like as a trendy retro Hungarian restaurant. If you want a take on how modern Hungarians think they used to eat when times were tougher (and less health-conscious), visit the 'Red Postal Coach'.

ANDRÁSSY ÚT

GOA Map p224 International

☎ 302 2570; VI Andrássy út 8; soups 850-1150Ft, starters 950-2250Ft, mains 2550-4500Ft; 🕑 noon-midnight; Ⓜ M1 Bajcsy-Zsilinszky út

This new, very well-dressed kid on the block is *the* place at the 'mo to be seen to be 'A' (as in list). It's the trendiest place in town and the food is very good. The salads (1450Ft to 2150Ft) are especially recommended.

NAPFÉNYES ÍZEK Map pp218-19 Vegetarian

☎ 351 5649; VII Rózsa utca 39; soups 450-850Ft, pasta & pizza 1190-1490Ft, mains 1190-1650Ft; 🕑 10am-11pm Mon-Fri, noon-10.30pm Sat & Sun; trolleybus 73 or 76

'Sunny Tastes' is a bit out of the way (unless you're staying near Andrássy út, but the wholesome foods and the speciality cakes are worth the trip out here. There is an organic shop where you can stock up on both packaged and baked goods, including excellent cakes. Set lunches are a bargain at 490Ft to 990Ft.

PREMIER

Map pp218-19 Hungarian, International

☎ 342 1768; VI Andrássy út 101; soups 950-1850Ft, starters 1600-3700Ft, mains 2200-4200Ft; 🕑 11am-11pm; Ⓜ M1 Bajza utca

In the hallowed Art Nouveau-influenced halls of the Hungarian Journalists' Association and just far enough from the House of Terror for our comfort, the Premier attracts a motley crew of media types and diplomats from nearby embassies and consulates with its Hungarian comfort food and international dishes. Check out the stained glass.

VÖRÖS ÉS FEHÉR

Map p222 Hungarian, Wine

☎ 413 1545; VI Andrássy út 41; soups 650-950Ft, starters 1450-1950Ft, mains 1650-4300Ft; 🕑 11am-midnight; Ⓜ M1 Oktogon

The 'Red and White' is all about wine – Hungarian to be precise – and here you can order from the top of the shelf by the 0.1L to sip and compare. The menu is brief but has come into its own in recent years. It hasn't eclipsed the wine but it certainly plays a greater role than it did. The pork dishes are superb.

CITY PARK

BAGOLYVÁR Map pp218-19 Hungarian

☎ 468 3110; XIV Állatkerti út 2; soups 500-880Ft, mains 1330-2400Ft; 🕑 noon-11pm; Ⓜ M1 Hősök tere

With reworked Hungarian classics that make it a winner, the 'Owl's Castle' attracts the Budapest cognoscenti, who leave its sister restaurant next door, Gundel, to the expense-account brigade. It's staffed entirely by women – in the kitchen, at tables and in front of house. (We don't know either.) There's a three-course set menu for 3620Ft.

HAN KUK GUAN Map pp218-19 Korean

☎ 460 0838; XIV Ilka utca 22; dishes 850-2250Ft; 🕑 noon-10pm Mon-Sat; trolleybus 75 or 77

No-one is going to be able to tell you what a Korean joint is doing way out in district XIV southeast of City Park, but who cares? It's about as authentic as you'll find. Try any of the barbecues or the *p'ajon* (green onion pancakes) served with seafood.

ROBINSON Map pp218-19 International

☎ 422 0222; XIV Városligeti tó; soups 790-890Ft, starters 1990-2890Ft, mains 2790-4800Ft; 🕑 noon-4pm & 6pm-midnight; Ⓜ M1 Hősök tere

Inside leafy City Park, Robinson is the place to secure a table on the lakeside terrace on a warm summer's evening. There are excellent starters like sliced goose liver (2890Ft) and homemade venison pâté to begin the dining experience. Mains include *fogas* (Balaton pike-perch; 3790Ft), grilled tuna and smoked duck breast cooked on lava stones.

CHEAP EATS – PEST

CENTRAL EUROPEAN UNIVERSITY CAFETERIA Map p224 Self-Service

☎ 327 3000; V Nádor utca 9; soups 190-235Ft, mains 380-495Ft; 🕑 11.30am-4pm Mon-Fri; 🚌 15

The *caféteria* at the conveniently located Central European University is open to all and also serves pizza (220ft to 250Ft).

DURCIN Map p224 Sandwiches

☎ 267 9624; VI Bajcsy-Zsilinszky út 7; sandwiches 120-140Ft; 🕑 8am-6pm Mon-Fri, 9am-1pm Sat, 8am-noon Sun; Ⓜ M1/2/3 Deák tér

This is the place to go for bite-sized open-face sandwiches as well as soups (510Ft to 590Ft) and salads (890Ft to 990Ft). There is also a **Northern Inner Town branch** (Map p224; ☎ 332 9348; V Október 6 utca 15; 🕑 8am-6pm Mon-Fri, 8am-1pm Sat; 🚌 15) as well as a **Buda branch** (Map pp218–19; ☎ 438 3104; II Retek utca 18; 🕑 8am-6pm Mon-Fri, 8am-1pm Sat; Ⓜ M2 Moszkva tér) behind the Mammut shopping mall.

FALAFEL FALODA
Map p222 Vegetarian, Israeli

☎ 267 9567; VI Paulay Ede utca 53; small/large sandwiches 400/600Ft, salads 520-700Ft; 🕑 10am-8pm Mon-Fri, 10am-6pm Sat; trolleybus 70 or 78

This inexpensive place just down from Budapest's theatre district has Israeli-style nosh. You pay a fixed price to stuff a piece of pita bread or fill a plastic container from a great assortment of salads. It also has a good variety of soups (270Ft to 310Ft).

FŐZELÉK FALÓ Map p222 Hungarian, Étkezde

☎ 266 6398; VI Nagymező utca 18; dishes 280-450Ft; 🕑 9am-10pm Mon-Fri, 10am-7pm Sat; Ⓜ M1 Opera

Some people say that this *étkezde*, which keeps relatively extended hours, is the best in town. It's very convenient to the bars of Liszt Ferenc tér and the music academy, but is always busy and it seems like there's never a place to sit down.

FRICI PAPA KIFŐZDÉJE
Map p222 Hungarian, Étkezde

☎ 351 0197; VI Király utca 55; soups 280-440Ft, mains 430-530Ft; 🕑 11am-9pm Mon-Sat; 🚊 4 or 6

'Papa Frank's Canteen' is larger and more modern than most *étkezde*. Excellent *főzelék* dishes are 290Ft to 340Ft.

HÁROM TESTVÉR
Map p222 Middle Eastern, Self-Service

☎ 342 2377; VII Erzsébet körút 17; salads 350-450Ft, gyros & kebabs 500-900Ft; 🕑 9am-3am; 🚊 4 or 6

Great any time but especially for a late-night snack or post-club bit of blotter, the 'Three Brothers' have branches throughout Pest, including a **Szent István körút branch** (Map p222; ☎ 329 2951; XIII Szent István körút 20-22; 🕑 9am-3am Sun-Wed, 9am-4am Thu, 9am-5am Fri & Sat; 🚊 4 or 6) and a **Teréz körút branch** (Map p222; ☎ 312 5835; VI Teréz körút 60-62; 🕑 9am-3am; 🚊 4 or 6).

HOLLY Map p222 Hungarian, Étkezde

☎ 772 0895; cnr VI Jókai utca 24; soups & starters 280-380Ft, mains 410-560Ft; 11.30am-6pm Mon-Thu, 11.30am-4pm Fri; 4 or 6

This very popular new *étkezde* is an excellent place for lunch or an early evening meal. There are daily specials and the menu changes every week.

KÁDÁR Map p222 Hungarian, Étkezde

☎ 321 3622; X Klauzál tér 9; soups 400Ft, mains 580-1100Ft; 11.30am-3.30pm Tue-Sat; 4 or 6

Located in the heart of the Jewish district, Kádár is probably the most popular and authentic *étkezde* you will find in town. Unfortunately, it closes for most of the month of August.

KISHARANG Map p224 Hungarian, Étkezde

☎ 269 3861; V Október 6 utca 17; soups 145-230Ft, mains 290-850Ft; 11am-8pm Mon-Fri, 11.30am-4.30pm Sat & Sun; 15

The central 'Little Bell' is an *étkezde* that is on the top of the list with students and staff of the nearby Central European University. The daily specials are something to look forward to and the retro décor is a bit of fun.

NAGY FAL Map p224 Chinese

☎ 353 4021; V Nádor utca 20; dishes 410-1595Ft; 9.30am-10pm Mon-Fri, 10.30am-10pm Sat & Sun; 15

This cheap and cheerful Chinese place has a seemingly endless menu of dishes to eat in or take away. It's all pretty samey stuff but it's a budget Asian option in the heart of town.

PICK HÁZ Map p222 Hungarian, Self-Service

☎ 331 7783; V Kossuth Lajos tér 9; sandwiches & salads 140-180Ft, mains 210-580Ft; 8am-4pm Mon-Fri; M M2 Kossuth Lajos tér

Next to M2 Kossuth Lajos tér metro station, this self-service eatery is above the famous salami manufacturer's central showroom, just opposite the Parliament building.

SOHO PALACSINTABÁR
Map p222 Hungarian

VI Nagymező utca 21; pancakes 198-480Ft; 9am-3am Mon-Wed, 9am Thu-3am Mon; M M1 Opera

It may not be as popular as the Nagyi Palacsintázója chain (p98), but the Soho can provide a fix of *palacsinta* (Hungarian-style pancakes) till the wee hours just as effortlessly. Try the more unusual pancake varieties like Mexican. Open non-stop from Thursday to Monday morning.

SZERÁJ Map p222 Middle Eastern, Self-Service

☎ 311 6690; XIII Szent István körút 13; salads & meze 200-400Ft, mains 1100-1250Ft; 9am-5am; 4 or 6

This is a very inexpensive self-service Turkish place for felafels and kebabs (700Ft), with some 10 varieties on offer. Szeráj is open late.

Entertainment

Entertainment

For a city of its size, Budapest has a huge choice of things to do and places to go after dark – from opera and folk dancing to jazz and meat-market clubs. It's almost never difficult getting tickets or getting in; the hard part is deciding what to do.

What's On

Your best sources of information for what's on in the city are the weekly freebie **PestiEst** (www.est.hu in Hungarian), published every Thursday and available from bars, cinemas and fast-food joints, and the more thorough weekly – with everything from clubs and films to art exhibits and classical music – **Pesti Műsor** (Budapest Program; www.pestimusor.hu in Hungarian), also called PM Program Magazin, available from newsstands every Thursday for 149Ft. The English-language weekly *Budapest Sun* also lists events and concerts in its useful Style supplement.

Other freebies include the vastly inferior (though English- and German-language) *Programme in Hungary/in Ungarn* and its scaled-down monthly version for the capital, *Budapest Panorama*. The free *Koncert Kalendárium*, published monthly (bimonthly in summer), has more serious offerings: concerts, opera, dance etc. A welcome arrival is *Mr Gordonsky's Budapest City Spy Map*, a hip little publication with all sorts of insider's tips. It's available free at pubs and bars.

Internet Resources

The best overall website for happenings in Budapest is **BTO** (www.budapestinfo.hu), though you might also try **Visitors' Guide Budapest** (www.visitorsguide.hu). Budapest Week (www.budapestweek.com) has events, music and movie listings. **Budapest Sun Online** (www.budapestsun.com) is similar but also has local news, interviews and features. A positive favourite and useful in all respects is **Pestiside** (www.pestiside.hu), subtitled 'The Daily Dish of Cosmopolitan Budapest'. It's an acerbic and often very funny take on the capital and includes lots of listings and reviews of what's on.

Tickets & Reservations

The most important and/or useful booking agencies in Budapest include those listed below. You can book almost everything online through www.jegymester.hu or www.kulturinfo.hu.

The **Central Ticket Office** (Map p224; Központi Jegyiroda; ☎ 267 9737, 267 1267; VI Andrássy út 15; ⏲ 10am-6pm Mon-Fri; Ⓜ M1 Opera) is the busiest theatrical ticket agency, with tickets to plays and other events at theatres around Budapest. Visit the **Symphony Ticket Office** (Map p222; Szimfonikus Jegyiroda; ☎ 302 3841; VI Nagymező utca 19; ⏲ 10am-7pm Mon-Fri; Ⓜ M1 Opera) for tickets to the philharmonic and other classical-music concerts.

Ticket Express (Map p224; ☎ information 312 0000, reservations 06 30 303 0999; www.tex.hu; VI Andrássy út 18; ⏲ 9.30am-6.30pm Mon-Fri; Ⓜ M1 Opera) is the largest ticket-office network in the city with eight outlets, including a **Józsefváros branch** (Map p222; ☎ 334 0369; MCD Zeneáruház, VIII József körút 50; ⏲ 9.30am-6.30pm Mon-Fri; 🚊 4 or 6).

Nightlife Strips & Neighbourhoods

There are no concentrated nightlife areas on the Buda side, unless you count sedate (some might say comatose) Castle Hill or the rather dispersed **II Moszkva tér** (Map pp218–19; Ⓜ M2 Moszkva tér). The Pest side, on the other hand, has all sorts of strips – from the ultratouristed **V Duna korzó** (Map p224; 🚊 2 or 2/a), along the river, with pricey (and very ordinary) eateries and watering holes, to leafy **VI Andrássy út** (Map p224; Ⓜ M1/2/3 Deák Ferenc utca) – always a sophisticated choice for a night out. But the two main areas are über-trendy

VI Liszt Ferenc tér (Map p222; Ⓜ M1 Oktogon), where you'll have to duel to the death for a spot under the plane trees, and **IX Ráday utca** (Map p224; Ⓜ M3 Kálvin tér), a rather subdued (some might say dull) semipedestrianised street in Józsefváros full of pubs and bars.

DRINKING

BARS

Budapest (and particularly Pest) is loaded with pubs and bars and there are enough to satisfy every taste. For popular outdoor venues in season, beyond the pubs and bars with terraces along VI Liszt Ferenc tér and up and down IX Ráday utca, see the boxed text, p129.

Buda

ERZSÉBET HÍD ESZPRESSZÓ Map p220

☎ 214 2785; I Döbrentei tér 1; ⏲ 10am-10pm; 🚊 19 or 🚌 86

If you're in the mood for a relaxing drink in simple surrounds, the 'Elizabeth Bridge Espresso Bar' is a wonderful old dive with a large terrace and views of the bridge. Most people call it Platán in honour of the big plane tree sheltering the outdoor tables.

KISRABLÓ Map pp228-9

☎ 209 1588; XI Zenta utca 3; ⏲ 11am-2am Mon-Sat, noon-2am Sun; 🚊 18, 19, 47 or 49

This pub is close to the university and to many of the hostels mentioned in this guide and is thus very popular with students. But don't be misled; it's an attractive and well-run place.

LÁNCHÍD SÖRÖZŐ Map p220

☎ 214 3144; I Fő utca 4; ⏲ 10am-midnight; 🚌 86

The 'Chain Bridge Pub', at the southern end of Fő utca, has a wonderful retro Magyar feel to it, with old movie posters and advertisements on the walls and red-checked cloths on the tables. Friendly service too.

OSCAR AMERICAN BAR Map pp218-19

☎ 212 8017; I Ostrom utca 14; ⏲ 5pm-2am Mon-Thu, 5pm-4am Fri & Sat year-round, 5pm-2am Sun Nov-May only; Ⓜ M2 Moszkva tér

The décor is cinema-inspired – film memorabilia on the wood-panelled walls, leather directors' chairs – and the beautiful crowd often act like they're on camera. Not to worry – the potent cocktails (some 150, in fact) go down a treat. There's music most nights.

POCO LOCO Map pp218-19

☎ 326 1357; II Harcsa utca 1; ⏲ 11am-midnight; 🚊 17

At the corner of Harcsa utca and Frankel Leó út on the way to Óbuda, this one-time seamy place has cleaned up its act; however, it still remains interesting. There's live music some nights.

Pest

ACTION BAR Map p224

☎ 266 9148; V Magyar utca 42; ⏲ 9pm-4am; Ⓜ M3 Kálvin tér

The name of this gay bar says it all. Take the usual precautions and have a ball. Strippers and dancers make appearances every night from about midnight.

BECKETTS Map p222

☎ 311 1033; V Bajcsy-Zsilinszky út 72; ⏲ 10am-1am Sun-Thu, 10am-3am Fri & Sat; Ⓜ M3 Nyugati pályaudvar

Of the capital's ubiquitous 'Irish' pubs, this is the best (and largest) of the lot, with all-day breakfast (1600Ft) as well as sandwiches (850Ft to 1700Ft) and salads (1200Ft to 1300Ft). The new cocktail bar in the rear is an additional plus.

CAFÉ EKLEKTIKA Map p224

☎ 266 1226; V Semmelweis utca 21; ⏲ noon-midnight Mon-Fri, 5pm-midnight Sat & Sun; 🚊 47 or 49

While there are no specifically lesbian bars in Budapest, Café Eklektika – love the name and the concept – comes the closest and attracts a very mixed crowd. Lots of canned jazz and the like.

CHA CHA CHA Map p224

☎ 215 0545; ⏲ 8am-3am Mon-Thu, 10am-4am Fri & Sat Sep-May, 9am-11pm Jun-Aug; Ⓜ M3 Kálvin tér

In the underpass/subway at the Kálvin tér metro, this is a campy/groovy café-bar with distressed-looking furniture, a very unusual – and we're talking *Star Wars* here – crowd, and bopping from the end of the week. It's a great place to meet people, and it probably gets busier here in the wee hours than the entire station does during the day.

CHAMPS SPORT BAR Map p224

☎ 413 1655; VII Dohány utca 20; ☎ noon-midnight Sun-Thu, noon-2am Fri & Sat; M M2 Astoria
Owned by five Olympic medallists (swimmer, runners, pentathlete), Champs is the place for sports fans and the vicarious, with two huge screens and 35 TVs. There's a wide choice of low-fat 'fitness meals' along with the less healthy favourites of armchair athletes.

COXX PUB Map p222

☎ 344 4884; VII Dohány utca 38; 9pm-4am Sun-Thu, 9pm-5am Fri & Sat; 7 or 7/a
This gay cellar bar with the in-your-face name has a DJ and small dance floor, but it's more of a pub than a club. There's a **gallery and Internet café** (noon-4am Mon-Fri, 9pm-4am Sat & Sun) at street level just to let you know this place has a serious side too.

DARSHAN UDVAR Map p222

☎ 266 5541; VIII Krúdy utca 7; 11am-1am Mon-Fri, 6pm-1am Sat & Sun; 4 or 6
This cavernous complex of two bars, a restaurant and a courtyard-terrace vegetarian café with décor that combines Euro-techno with Eastern flair is a great escape from the bars of VI Liszt Ferenc tér and IX Ráday utca. In fact, Krúdy utca may be poised to take over as Budapest's next after-hours strip. There are pizzas (880Ft to 1500Ft) and pasta dishes (550Ft to 1050Ft) as well as more substantial mains (1290Ft to 2500Ft) to accompany the liquid offerings.

FEHÉR GYŰRŰ Map p222

☎ 312 1863; V Balassi Bálint utca 27; 1pm-midnight Mon-Thu, 1pm-1am Fri & Sat, 5pm-midnight Sun
The 'White Ring' has always been a firm favourite and it's still not clear why. Perhaps it's because it is opposite the 'White House' (p82) and it's always fun to spot MPs. More likely it's because there are so few pubs in this area.

TOP FIVE DRINKING SPOTS

- Café Ponyvaragény (p127)
- Gerlóczy Kávéház (p127)
- Két Szerecsen (p128)
- Darshan Udvar (left)
- Oscar American Bar (p123)

JANIS PUB Map p224

☎ 266 2619; V Királyi Pál utca 8; 4pm-2am Mon-Thu, 4pm-3am Fri & Sat; M M3 Kálvin tér
Close to the university, this ever-popular pub is a shrine to the late, great Janis 'Pearl' Joplin and usually a stop for a quick one or two on the way to somewhere else. But some linger here for the choice of five imported beers on draught and the darts.

KULTIPLEX Map pp218-19

☎ 219 0706; IX Kinizsi utca 28; 10am-5am; M M3 Ferenc körút;
This huge complex has something for everyone – performance space, cinema, grill restaurant, great DJs, theme parties – and a simple inside/outside bar, where you can enjoy an unreconstructed drink.

MYSTERY BAR Map p222

☎ 312 1436; V Nagysándor József utca 3; 4pm-4am Mon-Fri, 6pm-4am Sat & Sun; M M3 Arany János utca
This miniscule gay neighbourhood bar with draped muslin and Greek statuary also moonlights as an Internet café (p189) and is just the ticket for boyz who want to log on and get off.

PARIS TEXAS Map pp218-19

☎ 218 0570; IX Ráday utca 22; 10am-1am Sun & Mon, 10am-3am Tue-Sat; M M3 Kálvin tér
A coffee-house feel, with old sepia-tinted photos on the walls and pool tables. Nurse a cocktail from the huge list and order a pizza from Pink Cadillac (p117) next door.

PICASSO POINT Map p222

☎ 312 1727; VI Hajós utca 31; noon-midnight Mon-Wed, noon-2am Thu & Fri, 4pm-2am Sat; M M3 Arany János utca
A stalwart of the Budapest entertainment scene, Picasso Point is a laid-back place for a drink and good for meeting people. Great décor.

PÓTKULCS Map p222

☎ 269 1050; VI Csengery utca 65/b; ⏲ 5pm-1.30am Sun-Wed, 5pm-2.30am Thu-Sat; Ⓜ M3 Nyugati pályaudvar

The 'Spare Key' is a wonderful little drinking venue, with a varied menu of live music from 9.30pm most nights and *táncház* (p131) at 8pm every Tuesday. The small central courtyard is a wonderful place to chill out in summer.

SZIMPLA Map p222

☎ 321 9119, 321 5880; VII Kertész utca 48; ⏲ 10am-2am Sep-May, noon-midnight Jun-Oct; 🚋 4 or 6

This is a distressed-looking, very unflashy three-floor venue – the name says it all – and it's just a hop, skip and a tumble from the stilettos south of Liszt Ferenc tér. There's live music three nights a week.

TRADITIONAL CAFÉS

Old-style cafés, some of which date back as much as a century and a half, abound in Budapest and some of them are classic examples of their type. They were the centre of social life and in them alliances were formed and momentous events plotted. For more, see boxed text, p126. The majority are in Pest, but Buda can lay claim to several good examples.

Buda

ANGELIKA Map p220

☎ 212 3784; I Batthyány tér 7; cakes 310Ft; ⏲ 9am-2am; Ⓜ M2 Batthyány tér

Angelika is a charming café attached to an 18th-century church, with a lovely terrace overlooking the Danube. The food (salads from 490Ft to 1490Ft, sandwiches from 750Ft to 850Ft) is just so-so; come here for the cakes and the views.

AUGUSZT Map pp218-19

☎ 356 8931, 316 3817; II Fény utca 8, 1st fl; cakes 150-350Ft; ⏲ 10am-6pm Tue-Fri, 9am-6pm Sat; Ⓜ M2 Moszkva tér

Tucked away on the 1st floor of a building behind the Fény utca market and Mammut shopping mall, this is the original Auguszt café (there are imitators) and only sells its own shop-made cakes, pastries and biscuits.

DAUBNER CUKRÁSZDA Map pp226-7

☎ 335 2253; II Szépvölgyi út 50; cakes 150-400Ft; ⏲ 9am-7pm; 🚌 86

A bit far-flung, tis true, and you can only nibble on the hoof here; there are no seats. But it gets rave reviews from locals and expats alike and has won the Best of Budapest award for best cake shop.

RUSZWURM Map p220

☎ 375 5284; I Szentháromság utca 7; cakes 190-440Ft; ⏲ 9am-8pm; 🚌 16 or Várbusz

This is the perfect place for coffee and cakes in the Castle District, though it can get pretty crowded and it's almost always impossible to get a seat.

Pest

CENTRÁL KÁVÉHÁZ Map p224

☎ 266 4572, 266 2110; V Károlyi Mihály utca 9; cakes 290-350Ft; ⏲ 8am-midnight; Ⓜ M3 Ferenciek tere

This grande dame, which reopened a few years ago after extensive renovations, is still jostling to reclaim her title as the place to sit and look intellectual in Pest. It serves meals (mains 1990Ft to 3590Ft) as well as lighter fare such as sandwiches (750Ft to 1190Ft), omelettes (890Ft to 990Ft) and, of course, cakes and pastries.

FRÖHLICH Map p224

☎ 267 2851; VII Dob utca 22; cakes 350-500Ft; ⏲ 9am-8pm Mon-Thu, 7.30am-6pm Fri, 10am-6pm Sun; trolleybus 74

This ancient cake shop and café in the former ghetto makes and sells old Jewish favourites such as *flódni*, a three-layer cake with apple, walnut and poppy-seed fillings, and *kindli*, cookies with nuts or poppy seeds.

GERBEAUD Map p224

☎ 429 9020; V Vörösmarty tér 7-8; cakes 580-850Ft; ⏲ 9am-9pm; Ⓜ M1 Vörösmarty tér

This is the most famous of the famous cafés in Budapest – bar none. Founded in 1858, it has been a fashionable meeting place for the city's elite on the northern side of Pest's busiest square since 1870. A visit is mandatory. It also does continental breakfast (2880Ft) and sandwiches (1300Ft to 2500Ft).

MY CAFÉ, MY CASTLE

Café life has a longer (and arguably more colourful) history in Budapest than in any other city in Europe. The Turks introduced coffee to Hungary in the early 16th century, and the coffee house was an essential part of the social scene here long before it had even made an appearance in Vienna or Paris. In the final decades of the Austro-Hungarian Empire, Budapest had some 600 cafés.

Budapest cafés were a lot more than just places to drink coffee that was 'black like the devil, hot like hell and sweet like a kiss' as they used to say. In them, momentous events were plotted or took place, great alliances formed and rivalries spawned, *chefs d'œuvre* written or sketched. To the English aphorism about the sanctity of one's house, the great writer Dezső Kosztolányi had a reply in his essay *Budapest, City of Cafés*: '*Az én kávéházam, az én váram*' (My café is my castle).

The Budapest café of the 19th century embodied the progressive liberal ideal that people of all races and classes could mingle under one roof, and acted as an incubator for Magyar culture. Combining the neighbourliness of a local pub, the bonhomie of a gentlemen's club and the intellectual activity of an open university, coffee houses were places to relax, gamble, work, network, do business and debate.

Or start revolutions... On the morning of 15 March 1848, the future novelist Mór Jókai stood on a table on the Pilvax Café in the Inner Town to proclaim the demands of the Hungarian nation. The so-called Youth of March then took over a printing shop two streets away to print copies of their *Twelve Points* (p43) and marched to the National Museum. The rest, as they say, is history.

Different cafés catered to different groups. Actors preferred the Pannónia and businessmen the Orczy while cartoonists frequented the Lánchíd and stockbrokers the Lloyd. But the two most important in terms of the city's cultural life were the Japán and the New York.

The Café Japán at VI Andrássy út 45 – now, fittingly, Írók Boltja (the Writers' Bookshop; p150) – was a favourite haunt of artists and architects and attracted the likes of Kosztka Tivadar Csontváry, József Rippl-Rónai, Pál Merse Szinyei and Ödön Lechner. The New York Café, which opened in 1894 at VII Erzsébet körút 9-11 and quickly became the city's most celebrated literary café, hosted virtually every Hungarian writer of note at one time or another – from Kosztolányi and Endre Ady to Gyula Krúdy and Ferenc Molnár. Molnár, playwright-in-residence at the Comedy Theatre, famously threw the key to the New York into the Danube the night the café opened so that it would never close. And that's just what it did, remaining open round the clock 365 days a year for decades.

But all good things must come to an end, and the depression of the 1930s, WWII and the dreary days of communism conspired against grand old cafés in favour of the cheap (and seldom cheerful) *eszpresszó*. By 1989 and the return of the Republic of Hungary only about a dozen remained and since then even the New York, where the influential literary magazine *2000* was edited right up into the 1990s, has been turned into a swanky five-star hotel.

Nowadays you're more likely to find young Budapesters drinking a beer or a glass of wine at one of the new modern cafés. It's true – the café *is* very much alive in Budapest. It's just reinvented itself, that's all.

HAUER CUKRÁSZDA Map pp218-19

☎ 323 1476; VIII Rákóczi út 47-49; cakes 150-350Ft; 9am-10pm; M M2 Blaha Lujza tér

This Art Deco (but frayed) café is often overlooked in favour of its sexier cousins, and is a real find for that. The cakes may not be Gerbeaud-quality, but it feels local and real.

LUKÁCS Map p222

☎ 302 8747; VI Andrássy út 70; cakes 200-500Ft; 9am-8pm Mon-Fri, 10am-8pm Sat & Sun; M M1 Vörösmarty utca

This café is dressed up in the finest of divine decadence – all mirrors and gold and soft piano music (on weekday evenings) with a nonsmoking section too. The selection of cakes is small but good; try the creamy *Lukács szelet* (Lukács slice).

MŰVÉSZ Map p222

☎ 352 1337; VI Andrássy út 29; cakes 280-480Ft; 9am-11.45pm; M M1 Opera

Almost opposite the State Opera House, the 'Artist' is a more interesting place to people-watch than most cafés (especially from the terrace), though its cakes are not what they used to be, with the exception of the *almás torta* (apple cake). It's been here since 1898.

SZALAI Map p222

☎ 269 3210; V Balassi Bálint utca 7; cakes 150-320Ft; 9am-7pm Wed-Mon; 2 or 2/a

This humble little cake shop in the Northern Inner Town and just north of Parliament probably has the best cherry strudel in the capital (though its cream cakes go down a treat as well).

MODERN CAFÉS

A new breed of café – all polished chrome, halogen lighting and straight lines – now co-exists with the more traditional cafés. There are a few of these in Buda but the lion's share is in Pest, especially in VI Liszt Ferenc tér. There are also a few on IX Ráday utca and in V Szent István tér behind the Basilica of St Stephen. Almost all do food, some complete meals, as well as serve hot and cold drinks.

Buda

CAFÉ MIRÓ Map p220

☎ 201 5573; I Úri utca 30; 9am-midnight; bus 16 or Várbusz

A personal favourite in the Castle District; Miró has Med-coloured walls and furniture, snacks, cakes (300Ft to 470Ft) and main courses (1790Ft to 2890Ft) and local artwork and photography on the walls. It's open on two sides. There's also a Pest branch called **Miró Grande** (Map p222; ☎ 321 8666; VI Liszt Ferenc tér 9; 10am-2am; M M1 Oktogon).

CAFÉ PONYVARAGÉNY Map pp228-9

☎ 209 5255; XI Bercsényi utca 5; 10am-midnight Mon-Sat, 2pm-midnight Sunday; tram 18, 19, 47 or 49

The 'Pulp Fiction' is a great new place that's supposed to be a local secret but – alas – is no longer. The old books and fringed lampshades are a nice touch and the coffee (230Ft to 645Ft) is some of the best in town.

Pest

BALLET CIPŐ Map p222

☎ 269 3114; VI Hajós utca 14; 8am-1am Mon-Fri, 10am-midnight Sat & Sun; M M1 Opera

The pretty little 'Ballet Slipper' in the theatre district and just behind the opera house is a delightful place to stop for a rest and refreshment or to have a light meal (dishes 800Ft to 1500Ft).

BIRDLAND Map p222

☎ 413 7983; VI Liszt Ferenc tér 7; 9am-1am; M M1 Opera

This new venue at the southern end of Liszt Ferenc tér is surprisingly bereft of jazz despite its name. It is, however, the ideal spot to catch strains from musicians practising music at the academy just opposite. The food (starters 950Ft to 1750Ft, mains 1450Ft to 2750Ft) gets good reports.

CAFÉ CSIGA Map pp218-19

☎ 210 0885; VIII Vásár utca 2; 11am-1pm Mon-Sat Oct-May, 6am-1am Mon-Sat Jun-Sep; tram 4 or 6

This very popular, eclectically decorated café-cum-bar just opposite the Rákóczi tér market attracts a mixed, arty crowd.

CAFÉ VIAN Map p222

☎ 268 1154; VI Liszt Ferenc tér 9; 9am-1am; M M1 Oktogon

This comfortable café – all done up in warm peach tones and serving breakfast all day – remains the anchor tenant on the sunny side of 'the tér' and the court of Pest's arty aristocracy.

CASTRO BISZTRÓ Map pp228-9

☎ 215 0814; IX Ráday utca 35; 9am-midnight Mon-Thu, 9am-1am Fri, 2pm-1am Sat, 2pm-midnight Sun; bus 15

This eclectic place has a mixed clientele, Serbian dishes and chilli (990Ft to 1780Ft) on its menu and a few terminals for logging on to the Internet (100Ft for 10 minutes). It's one of the few places on the strip that is crowded all year.

GERLÓCZY KÁVÉHÁZ Map p224

☎ 235 0953; V Gerlóczy utca 1; 7am-11pm Mon-Fri, 8am-11pm Sat & Sun; tram 47 or 49

This wonderful retro-style café looks out onto one of Pest's most attractive little squares and serves excellent snacks and light meals (690Ft to 1790Ft), including a cheese plate sent over from the excellent Nagy Tamás (p93) cheese shop around the corner.

Café Ponyvaragény (left), Tabán

INCOGNITO CAFÉ Map p222

☎ 342 1471; VI Liszt Ferenc tér 3; ⌚ noon- midnight Mon-Wed, noon-2am Thu-Sat, 2pm-midnight Sun

The 'Unknown' is hardly that. It was the first café to open on what everyone now calls 'the tér', way back in 1994, and it's still low-key and going strong.

KÉT SZERECSEN Map p222

☎ 343 1984; VI Nagymező utca 14; ⌚ 8am-1am Sun-Thu, 9am-1am Fri & Sat

Not on the square but close enough, the very relaxed 'Two Moors' serves both main meals (starters from 690Ft to 1100Ft, mains 1250Ft to 3190Ft) and decent breakfasts (590Ft to 680Ft till 11am) as well as coffee.

NEGRO Map p224

☎ 302 0136; V Szent István tér 11; ⌚ 8am-midnight Sun, 8am-1am Mon-Wed, 8am-3am Thu & Fri, 8am-4am Sat; Ⓜ M3 Arany János utca

This stylish café just behind the basilica (views!) attracts Budapest's über-trendy crowd, dressed to the nines (or did we see 10s too?) and sipping the latest concoction. Breakfasts are a snip at 320Ft to 910Ft.

TEAHOUSES

Teahouses serving every imaginable type of tea and tisane have become very trendy in Budapest in recent years and they're often quite stylish places.

Buda

DEMMER'S TEAHÁZ Map pp218-19

☎ 345 4150; II Lövőház utca 12; ⌚ 9.30am-7.30pm; Ⓜ M2 Moszkva tér

This cosy little teahouse next to the Mammut shopping mall is the place to come in Buda if you're serious about your cuppa cha (180Ft to 400Ft). There's also a **Pest branch** (Map p222; ☎ 302 5674; VI Podmaniczky utca 14; ⌚ 11am-9pm Mon-Sat, 1-9pm Sun; Ⓜ M3 Nyugati pályaudvar).

Pest

1000 TEA Map p224

☎ 337 8217; V Váci utca 65; ⌚ noon-9pm Mon-Sat; 🚌 15

In a small courtyard off lower Váci utca, this is the place if you want to sip a soothing blend made by tea-serious staff and lounge on pillows in a Japanese-style tearoom. You can also sit and sip on the tea chests in the courtyard. There's a shop here too.

MOZAIK TEAHÁZ Map p224

☎ 266 7001; VI Király utca 18; ⌚ 10am-10.30pm Mon-Fri, 1-10.30pm Sat & Sun Oct-May, 11am-10.30pm Mon-Fri, 4-10.30pm Sat & Sun Jun-Sep; 🚋 4 or 6

An eclectic – note the mosaic of a satyr outside – rarity among Budapest teahouses: non–New Age music played and smoking permitted.

TEAHÁZ A VÖRÖS OROSZLÁNHOZ Map p222

☎ 269 0579; VI Jókai tér 8; ⌚ 11am-11pm Mon-Fri, 3-11pm Sat, 5-11pm Sun; Ⓜ M1 Oktogon

This serene place with quite a mouthful of a name (it just means 'Teahouse at the Sign of the Red Lion') just north of Liszt Ferenc tér is quite serious about its teas (480Ft to 630Ft). There's also a **Ráday utca branch** (Map p224; ☎ 215 2101; IX Ráday utca 9; ⌚ 11am-11pm Mon-Sat, 3pm-11pm Sun).

CLUBBING

Like everywhere else, clubs in Budapest do not really get off the ground until well after Cinderella's coach has turned into a pumpkin – or even later. Budapest's hottest DJs include Palotai, Naga and Yonderboy.

ANGEL Map p222

☎ 351 6490; VII Kazinczy utca 2; ⌚ 10pm-5am Fri-Sun; Ⓜ M2 Astoria

Angel, also known by its Hungarian name, Angyal, is Budapest's flagship gay club even since its big move in 2005 after something like a decade. It welcomes girls on Friday and Sunday but boyz only on Saturday.

BANK DANCE HALL Map p222

☎ 06 20 344 4888; VI Teréz körút 55; ⌚ 10pm-4am Sun-Thu, 10pm-5am Fri & Sat; Ⓜ M3 Nyugati pályaudvar

In the southern wing of Nyugati train station next to McDonald's, this positively enormous disco has rhythm and blues on the 1st floor, house and trance on the 2nd, Dance on the 3rd and funk-house (a Hungarian thing) on the 4th. Lots of young suburban types reeking of cologne and on the prowl.

THE HEAT IS ON

During Budapest's (usually) very long and very hot summer, what are called *kertek,* literally 'gardens' but in Budapest any outdoor spot that has been converted into an entertainment zone (including courtyards and any available stretch along the river), have been emptying out even the most popular indoor bars and clubs since 1999. The venues (and their locations) can change from year to year and a definitive list is usually not available until about May; the best single source of information is the Pestiside website (www.pestiside.hu). Some of the places listed under Bars (p123) and under Clubbing (opposite) have their own outside equivalent, and there are 'gardens' that only blossom in summer. Some of the more popular ones in recent years include those listed below.

Café del Rio (Map pp228–9; ☎ 06 30 297 2158; www.rio.hu in Hungarian; XI Goldman György tér 1; 🕒 2pm-4.30am; 🚋 4 or 6) On the northern side of Petőfi Bridge on the Buda side, Rio is stylish but not up itself, with a pseudo tropical/carnival theme.

Cha Cha Cha Terasz (Map pp218–19; ☎ 215 0545; www.chachacha.hu in Hungarian; XIII Margit-sziget; 🕒 4pm-4am; 🚌 26, 🚋 4 or 6) In the stadium at the southern tip of Margaret Island, Cha Cha Cha Terasz is an attitude-free venue with great music and dance space.

Holdudvar (Map p224; ☎ 485 5270; VIII Múzeum körút 6-8; Ⓜ M2 Astoria; 🕒 8am-4am) This large courtyard on the grounds of the ELTE, the city's largest university, has a predictably split personality: earnest and coffee-drinking, wild and out of control.

Mokka Cuka (Map pp226–7; ☎ 453 2120; www.mokkacuka.hu; III Óbuda Hajógyári-sziget; 🕒 2pm-4am; HÉV Filatorigát) On the island that attracts the capital's beautiful people, Mokka Cuka is a leading outdoor underground venue showcasing great indie DJs.

Szimpla Kert (Map p222; ☎ 06 20 248 1968, 321 5880; www.szimpla.hu; VII Kazinczy 14; 🕒 noon-midnight; trolleybus 74) One of the capital's first 'gardens', Szimpla is just that – a simple, low-key affair that keeps itself to itself.

Szóda Udvar (Map p87; ☎ 461 0007; V József nádor tér 1; Ⓜ M1/2/3 Deák Ferenc tér; 🕒 2pm-4am) This rather well-heeled venue – a former bank headquarters – pulls in a rather subdued crowd that lets loose on the basement dance floor in the wee hours.

Zöld Pardon (Map pp228–9; www.zp.hu in Hungarian; XI Goldman György tér; 🕒 9am-6am; 🚋 4 or 6) What bills itself as the 'world's longest summer festival' is a rocker's paradise just opposite the Café del Rio.

CLUB BOHEMIAN ALIBI Map pp228-9

☎ 06 20 314 1959; IX Üllői út 45-47; 🕒 4pm-4am Sun-Thu, 9pm-4am Fri & Sat; Ⓜ M3 Ferenc körút

This gay club attracts ladies and gentlemen and anything in between. It's the preferred watering hole of Budapest's burgeoning TV population, so if you're into cross-dressing or cross-dressers, this is the place.

CLUB VITTULA Map p222

☎ 06 20 527 7069; VII Kertész utca 4; 🕒 6pm-dawn Sep-Jun; Ⓜ M2 Blaha Lujza tér, 🚋 4 or 6

Probably the best place to get drunk and dance in Budapest at the moment, with cutting-edge DJs and cheap Slovakian blond (beer that is). Need we say more?

KAMÉLEON Map pp218-19

☎ 345 8547; Mammut II, 4th fl, II Lövőház utca 2-6; 🕒 5pm-midnight Sun-Thu, 5pm-3am Fri & Sat; Ⓜ M3 Moszkva tér

This throbbing club in the newer wing of Buda's massive Mammut shopping mall is a true 'chameleon', with a different party in the swing every night of the week – from La Noche Cubana on Friday to live bands on Monday.

KÖZGÁZ PINCE KLUB Map pp218-19

☎ 215 4359, 218 6855; IX Fővám tér 8; 🕒 9pm-5am Tue-Sat; 🚋 47 or 49

With few frills and cheap covers at the Economics University, this is the pick-up venue of choice for many a student and there's plenty of dance room. Beware: the bouncers bite, and avoid Wednesday unless you like karaoke.

PIAF Map p222

☎ 312 3823; VI Nagymező utca 25; 🕒 7pm-6am; Ⓜ M3 Arany János utca, trolleybus 70 or 78

Piaf is the place to go when everything else slows down. There's dancing and action well into the new day. Most of the action – and characters – are in the smoky cavern below.

SARK CAFÉ Map p222

☎ 06 30 282 9625; VII Klauzál tér 14; ⏲ 10am-3am Sun-Thu, 10am-5am Fri & Sat; 🚊 4 or 6

This popular alternative music pub and club on three floors has a big cellar with a dance floor where bands occasionally perform. It's all a bit student-clubbish, though.

SÜSS FÉL NAP Map p222

☎ 374 3329; V Honvéd utca 40; ⏲ 5pm-5am; 🚊 4 or 6

Attracting a student crowd, this cellar club hosts lots of student bands and visiting talent. It's a lot of fun and less expensive than many of the other clubs. It's one of the few places in town offering a two-for-one happy hour (5pm to 8pm).

TRAFÓ BÁR TANGÓ Map pp228-9

☎ 456 2049; IX Liliom utca 41; ⏲ 6pm-4am; Ⓜ M3 Ferenc körút

In the basement of the Trafó House of Contemporary Arts (p134), what's also called Tütü Tangó is one place that attracts arty (ie less booze, more smoke) types and their hangers-on.

UPSIDE DOWN Map p222

☎ 06 20 982 2884; V Podmaniczky tér 1; ⏲ 8pm-4am or 5am; Ⓜ M3 Arany János utca

Below a coffee shop of the same name on the southern side of Podmaniczky tér, this is one of the hottest new gay clubs in town.

WEST BALKAN CLUB BAR Map pp218-19

☎ 371 1807; VIII Kisfaludy utca 36; ⏲ noon-dawn; Ⓜ M3 Ferenc körút

This place without a sign has something for everyone – from live music and/or DJ to bars in the garden and films on the big screen. Bit alternative.

MUSIC

CLASSICAL

The *Koncert Kalendárium* (p122) highlights all concerts in Budapest monthly, and most nights you'll have several to choose from. As well as the city's main concert halls listed below, many museums and other venues feature chamber music including the Old Music Academy, where the Franz Liszt Memorial Museum (p71) is housed; Béla Bartók Memorial House (p61); the Military History Museum (p56); the Műcsarnok (p72); the Kiscelli Museum (p60); and the Hungarian Academy of Sciences (p66).

Organ recitals are best heard in the city's churches, including Matthias Church (p55), St Anne's Church (p58), the Basilica of St Stephen (p64) and the Inner Town Parish Church (p64).

GAY & LESBIAN VENUES

What a difference a decade and a half makes! With only a couple of sleazy – actually scary – dives full of Romanian and Transylvanian hustlers a mere 15 years ago, Budapest now counts upwards of 20 gay venues and can lay claim to being Central Europe's gayest city. For useful websites, organisations and other information, see p188.

Budapest's flagship gay club is **Angel** (p128) but you'll probably do better starting the evening off at **Mystery Bar** (p124) or **CoXx Pub** (p124). There's a lot to say for **Club Bohemian Alibi** (p129) – though we can't think of anything just now – and if you're feeling frisky head for **Action Bar** (p123). Another great club is **Upside Down** (left).

Choices are more limited for girlz but there's always **Café Eklektika** (p123) and Angel (above) on Friday and Sunday nights if they don't mind a mixed scene. Lesbian parties are held on the first Friday of the month at **Jailhouse** (p132) and on the last Saturday of the month at a bar called **Candy** (Map p224; ☎ 789 2130; V Kossuth Lajos utca 17; Ⓜ M2 Astoria).

BUDAPEST CONGRESS CENTRE

Map pp218-19

Budapesti Kongresszusi Központ; ☎ information 372 5700, tickets 372 5429; www.bcc.hu; XII Jagelló út 1-3; 🚌 8 or 112

This modern conference centre in Buda moonlights as a concert hall and has recently undergone a major renovation – supposedly to improve its poor acoustics. Big-ticket galas and opening nights are frequently held here.

DUNA PALOTA Map p224

Danube Palace; ☎ 235 5500, 317 2790; V Zrínyi utca 5; 🚌 15

This elaborate 'palace' diagonally opposite the main Central European University building hosts light classical music and touristy musical revues in summer. Its biggest drawcard is its folk-dance performances (p135).

FERENC LISZT ACADEMY OF MUSIC
Map p222

Liszt Zeneakadémia; ☎ 342 0179; www.zeneakademia.hu; VI Liszt Ferenc tér 8; ticket office 10am-8pm Mon-Fri, 2-8pm Sat & Sun; M M1 Oktogon

A block southeast of Oktogon, what's usually just called the 'music academy' was built in 1907. It attracts students from all over the world and is one of the top venues for concerts. The interior, with large and small concert halls richly embellished with Zsolnay porcelain and frescoes, is worth a look even if you're not attending a performance.

ÓBUDA SOCIETY Map pp226-7

Óbudai Társaskör; ☎ 250 0288; www.obudaitarsaskor.hu; III Kis Korona utca 7; HÉV Tímár utca, bus 86

This very intimate venue surrounded by appalling Óbuda housing estates takes its music very seriously and hosts recitals and some chamber orchestras.

PALACE OF ARTS Map pp228-9

Művészetek Palotája; ☎ information 555 3000, tickets 555 3301; www.mupa.hu; IX Komor Marcell utca; ticket office 1-6pm Mon-Sat, 10am-3pm Sun; tram 2 or 2/a

The main concert halls in this palatial new arts centre by the Danube and just opposite the National Theatre are the 1700-seat **National Concert Hall** (Nemzeti Hangversenyterem) and the smaller **Festival Theatre** (Fesztivál Színház), accommodating up to 450 people. Both are purported to have the best acoustics in Budapest.

PESTI VIGADÓ Map p224

V Vigadó tér 2; ☎ 318 9903, 318 9167; V Vigadó tér 2; M M1 Vörösmarty tér, tram 2 or 2/a

This Romantic-style hall built in 1865 and facing the Danube to the west of Vörösmarty tér is a popular venue for concerts, dance performances and other cultural events. It was badly damaged during WWII and, though the original style of the exterior was retained, the interior is all new and has been recently renovated.

FOLK & TRADITIONAL

Authentic *táncház*, literally 'dance house' but really folk-music workshops, are held at various locations throughout the week, but less often in summer. Times and venues change frequently; consult one of the publications mentioned on p122 or check out the website of the Dance House Guild (www.tanchaz.hu). The best local *klezmer* (p19) is the Budapest Klezmer Band. See the band's website (www.budapestklezmer.hu) for concert dates and venues.

Two cultural houses in Buda have frequent folk programmes. The Folklór Centrum in the **Municipal Cultural House** (Fővárosi Művelődési Háza; Map pp228–9; ☎ 203 3868; XI Fehérvári út 47; tram 41 or 47), presents folk music every Friday at 7.30pm and a children's dance house hosted by the incomparable Muzsikás (p19) every Tuesday from 5pm to 6.30pm. The **Marczibányi tér Cultural Centre** (Marczibányi téri Művelődési Központ; Map pp218–19; ☎ 212 0803, 212 2820; II Marczibányi tér 5/a; tram 4, 6 or 49) has Hungarian, Moldavian and Slovakian dance and music every Wednesday starting from 8pm. Certain bars, including Pótkulcs (p125) also have dance house one or two nights a week.

ALMÁSSY TÉR RECREATION CENTRE
Map pp218-19

Almássy téri Szabadidő Központ; ☎ 352 1572; VII Almássy tér 6; trolleybus 74

This venue west of Keleti train station has just about anything that's in and/or interesting, from rock and blues to jazz, but especially folk music. There's Hungarian dance house every second Saturday at 7.30pm.

ARANYTÍZ CULTURAL CENTRE
Map p224

Aranytíz Művelődési Központ; ☎ 354 3400, 311 2248; V Arany János utca 10; bus 15

With programmes from 5pm on Saturday and frequently running to well after 2am, this gleaming new cultural centre in the Northern Inner Town hosts the incomparable Kalamajka Táncház.

FONÓ BUDA MUSIC HOUSE
Map pp228-9

Fonó Budai Zeneház; ☎ 206 5300; www.fono.hu; XI Sztregova utca 3; tram 41 or 47

Fonó Buda has regular programmes at 8pm on Wednesday and the second Friday of each month as well as concerts by big-name bands throughout each month; it's one of the best venues in town for this sort of thing. Consult the website for more details.

JAZZ & BLUES

COLUMBUS JAZZKLUB Map p224

☎ 266 9013; www.majazz.hu; V Pesti Alsó rakpart; noon-midnight; 2 or 2/a

On a boat moored in the Danube just north of V Vigadó tér opposite the Budapest Inter-Continental Hotel, this club has transformed itself from being 'just another Irish pub' to a jazz club of note, with big-name local and international bands.

COTTON CLUB Map p222

☎ 354 0886; www.cottonclub.hu; VI Jókai utca 26; noon-midnight Mon-Sat; 4 or 6

This centrally located restaurant and nightclub with the predictable gangster-and-moll décor (complete with cigar room) has live jazz – let's say jazz lite – nightly at 7.30pm or 8pm, with additional concerts at 10.30pm on Friday and Saturday. Starters are 1590Ft to 1990Ft and mains 1790Ft to 3890Ft; three-course set menus come in at 5260Ft and 7360Ft.

FAT MO'S MUSIC CLUB Map p224

☎ 267 3199; V Nyáry Pál utca 11; noon-2am Mon & Tue, noon-3am Wed, noon-4am Thu & Fri, 6pm-4am Sat, 6pm-2am Sun; M M3 Ferenciek tere, 15

With a speakeasy Prohibition theme and enough beer and booze to fill Bonnie and Clyde (with bullets, that is), FM's has live jazz (and sometimes country) from 9pm or 9.30pm daily. DJs take over at midnight Thursday to Saturday.

JAZZ GARDEN Map p224

☎ 266 7364; V Veres Pálné utca 44/a; 6pm-1am Sun-Thu, 6pm-2am Fri & Sat; 47 or 49

This is a sophisticated venue with traditional, vocal and Latin jazz and odd décor – a faux cellar 'garden' with street lamps and a night 'sky' bedecked with blinking stars. Book a table (starters 1420Ft to 2250Ft, mains 2250Ft to 3490Ft) in the dining room; music starts here at 9.30pm.

SATCHMO Map p222

☎ 302 2654; V Nádor utca 29; 11.30am-1am; M M2 Kossuth Lajos tér

As its subtitle 'Amerikai Kreol Jazztaurant' would suggest, this club-restaurant with big windows just round the corner from Szabadság tér serves up 'American' Creole cuisine (lots of spices, shellfish and 'blackened' things for 1400Ft to 2900Ft) and live jazz music courtesy of Mr Louis Armstrong from Thursday to Saturday nights.

ROCK & POP

A38 HAJÓ Map pp228-9

☎ 464 3940; www.a38.hu; XI Műegyetem rakpart; 4pm-midnight Tue-Sat, 4pm-midnight Sun & Mon; 4 or 6

Moored on the Buda side just south of Petőfi Bridge, the 'A38 Ship' is a decommissioned Ukrainian stone hauler from 1968 that has been reinvented as a party venue. It's so cool it's hot in summer and the hold, well, rocks throughout the year.

GÖDÖR KLUB Map p224

☎ 06 20 943 5464; Erzsébet tér; 9am-late; M 1/2/3 Deák Ferenc tér

This new arrival in the old bus bays below Elizabeth Sq in central Pest is a real mixed bag, offering everything from folk and jazz but especially rock.

JAILHOUSE Map pp228-9

☎ 06 30 989 4905, 218 1368; IX Tűzoltó utca 22; 10pm-5am Fri & Sat; M M3 Ferenc körút

This tiny venue with a friendly atmosphere has underground DJs and live music. It's an excellent place to part ways from the usual choice of venues. It hosts a lesbian night on the first Friday of the month.

LASER THEATRE Map pp228-9

Lézer Színház; ☎ 263 0871, 281 2211; www.lezerszinhaz.hu; X Népliget; adult/student 2090/1590Ft; performances 7.30pm Mon-Sat; M M3 Népliget

At the Planetarium in Népliget, the Laser Theatre has a mixed bag of video (some 3D) concerts with laser and canned music featuring the likes of Madonna, Pink Floyd, Queen, Mike Oldfield, Vangelis and Enigma, and performances by Carmina Burana. Very low tech and old hat but fun in a retro kind of way.

M4 MUSIC CLUB Map p222

☎ 322 0006; VII Dohány utca 22; 6pm-5am; M M2 Astoria

A particularly smoky place named after the illusory fourth metro line that still refuses to get dug or built or started, M4 has both live music (pop, rock, soul, funk) and DJs.

ROCK & POP MEGAVENUES

Budapest counts a trio of venues for big-name local and international acts, all of them in Pest and within walking distance of one another.

Budapest Sportaréna (Mapp pp218–19; ☎ 422 2600; www.budapestarena.hu; XIV Stefánia út 2; Ⓜ M2 Stadionok) Near Keleti train station, this new arena named after the Hungarian pugilist László Papp is where the likes of Phil Collins, Duran Duran, Simply Red and Jo Cocker warble.

Kisstadion (Map pp218–19; ☎ 471 4306, 251 1222; XIV Szabó József utca 1; 🚌 7, trolleybus 72 or 75) This venue is smaller than the nearby Budapest Sportaréna and thus something of an elephants' graveyard (think, Rod Stewart) for international acts.

Petőfi Csarnok (Map pp218–19; ☎ 363 3730, 251 7266; www.petoficsarnok.hu; XIV Zichy Mihály út 14; 🕑 ticket office 9am-7pm Mon-Fri, 10am-7pm Sat & Sun; Ⓜ M1 Széchenyi fürdő, trolleybus 72 or 74) The city's main youth centre, the PC is in City Park and the place for smaller rock concerts (Jamiroquai, Yngwie Malmsteen etc).

TŰZRAKTÁR Map pp228-9

☎ 06 70 523 1593; http://tuzrakter.hu; IX Tűzoltó utca 54-56; 🕑 5pm-3am; Ⓜ 3 Klinikák

The 'Fire Warehouse', an abandoned factory building, and its big courtyard plays host to all sorts of cultural and party events.

WIGWAM ROCK & BLUES CLUB

Map pp228-9

☎ 208 5569; XI Fehérvári utca 202; 🕑 8pm-5am; 🚊 41 or 47

This place with the wacky name (did the Sioux do Elvis before his time?) is one of the best of its kind in Hungary and hosts some big-name Hungarian rock and blues bands on Friday and Saturday nights.

OPERA

BUDAPEST OPERETTA Map p222

Budapesti Operettszínház; ☎ 472 2030, 312 4866; www.operettszinhaz.hu; VI Nagymező utca 17; 🕑 ticket office 10am-7pm Mon-Fri, 1-7pm Sat & Sun; Ⓜ M1 Opera

This theatre presents operettas, which are always a riot, especially campy ones like the *Queen of the Csárdás* by Imre Kálmán, with their OTT staging and costumes.

ERKEL THEATRE Map pp218-19

Erkel Színház; ☎ 333 0540; VIII Köztársaság tér 30; 🕑 ticket office 11am-7pm Tue-Fri, 11am-3pm Sat, 10am-1pm & 4-7pm Sun; Ⓜ M2 Keleti pályaudvar, 🚌 7 or 7/a

Budapest's modern (and ugly) second opera house is southwest of Keleti train station. Tickets are sold just inside the main door.

HUNGARIAN STATE OPERA HOUSE

Map p222

Magyar Állami Operaház; ☎ information 353 0170, tickets 332 7914; www.opera.hu; VI Andrássy út 22; 🕑 ticket office 11am-7pm Mon-Sat, 4-7pm Sat & Sun; Ⓜ M1 Opera

The gorgeous neo-Renaissance opera house should be visited at least once – to admire the incredibly rich decoration inside as much as to view a performance and hear the perfect acoustics. Visits are guided.

CINEMAS

Some 26 *mozi* (movie houses) show English-language films with Hungarian subtitles. Consult the listings in the *Budapest Sun* newspaper, *PestiEst* or *Pesti Műsor* (p122).

Be aware that many foreign films are dubbed into Hungarian, so try asking the ticket seller if the film retains the original soundtrack and has Hungarian subtitles (*feliratos*) or is dubbed (*szinkronizált* or *magyarul beszélő*). The latter is often abbreviated as 'mb' in listings.

CORVIN FILM PALACE Map pp218-19

Corvin Filmpalota; ☎ 459 5050; VIII Corvin köz 1; Ⓜ M3 Ferenc körút

This place saw a lot of action during the 1956 Uprising and led a revolution of a different sort four decades later – the introduction of state-of-the-art sound systems and comfortable seating. It has now has been fantastically renovated and is worth a visit. Note the two wonderful reliefs outside and the monument to the 'Pesti srácok', the heroic 'kids from Pest' who fought and died here in '56.

MŰVÉSZ Map p222

☎ 332 6726; VI Teréz körút 30; Ⓜ M1 Oktogon, 🚊 4 or 6

The 'Artist' shows, appropriately enough, artsy and cult films, but not exclusively so.

Uránia National Cinema (below), Józsefváros

ÖRÖKMOZGÓ FILM MUSEUM Map p222

Örökmozgó Filmmúzeum; ☎ 342 2167; VII Erzsébet körút 39; 🚊 4 or 6

Part of the Hungarian Film Institute, this cinema (whose mouthful of a name vaguely translates as 'moving picture') shows an excellent assortment of foreign classic films in their original languages.

SZINDBÁD Map p222

☎ 349 2773; XIII Szent István körút 16; 🚊 4 or 6

This place, named after the seminal (and eponymous) 1971 film by director Zoltán Huszárik and based on the novel by Gyula Krúdy (p23), shows good Hungarian and foreign films with subtitles. Very occasionally the show is on a video projector, which makes for a less-than-pleasurable night out at the movies.

URÁNIA NATIONAL CINEMA Map p222

Uránia Nemzeti Filmszínház; ☎ 486 3413; VIII Rákóczi út 21; 🚌 7 or 7/a

This all-Art Deco/neo-Moorish extravaganza is another tarted-up film palace. It has an excellent café on the 1st floor, which is an attraction in itself.

THEATRE

COMEDY THEATRE Map p222

Vígszínház; ☎ information 329 2340, tickets 329 3920; XIII Szent István körút 14; 🕑 ticket office 10am-6pm Mon-Thu, 10am-5pm Fri; 🚊 4 or 6

The attractive little theatre roughly in the middle of the Szent István körút section of the Big Ring Road is the venue for comedies and musicals. When it was built in 1896, the new theatre's location was criticised for being too far out of the city.

INTERNATIONAL BUDA STAGE

Map p216

IBS; ☎ 391 2525; www.ibs-b.hu; II Tárogató út 2-4; 🚊 56, 🚌 29

This theatre is a more recent arrival and further afield at the foot of the Buda Hills, with occasional performances – often comedies – in English.

JÓZSEF KATONA THEATRE Map p224

Katona József Színház; ☎ 318 3725; www.szinhaz.hu/katona; V Petőfi Sándor utca 6; 🕑 ticket office 10am-7pm Mon-Fri, 2-7pm Sat & Sun; Ⓜ M3 Ferenciek tere

The József Katona Theatre is the best known in Hungary and is a public theatre supported mainly by the city of Budapest. Its studio theatre, Kamra, has among the best troupes in the country.

MERLIN THEATRE Map p224

☎ 318 9338, 266 4632; www.merlinszinhaz.hu; V Gerlóczy utca 4; Ⓜ M1/2/3 Deák Ferenc tér, 🚊 47 or 49

This theatre in the heart of Pest stages numerous plays in English, often performed by the theatre's own Atlantis Company or the local Madhouse troupe. It's usually pretty serious stuff, with little scenery and few props.

NATIONAL THEATRE Map pp228-9

Nemzeti Színház; ☎ information 476 6800, reservations 476 6868; www.nemzetiszinhaz.hu; IX Bajor Gizi park 1; 🕑 ticket office 10am-6pm Mon-Fri, 2-6pm Sat & Sun; 🚊 2 or 2/a

This rather eclectic venue is the place to go if you want to brave a play in Hungarian or just check out the bizarre and very controversial architecture (see p70).

DANCE

CLASSICAL & MODERN

Budapest's two so-so ballet companies – the Hungarian National and the Hungarian Festival Ballet troupes – perform at the Opera House, the Erkel Theatre (p133) and the National Dance Theatre (opposite).

CENTRAL EUROPE DANCE THEATRE Map pp218-19

Közép-Európa Táncszínház; ☎ 342 7163, 06 30 526 1024; www.cedt.hu; VII Bethlen Gábor tér 3; trolleybus 74 or 78

This pan-European theatre has some fine contemporary dance performances; enter from VII István út.

MU SZÍNHÁZ Map pp228-9

☎ 466 4627, 209 4014; www.mu.hu in Hungarian; XI Kőrösy József utca 17; tram 4

Virtually everyone involved in the Hungarian dance scene got their start at this place in the business in south Buda, where the cutting edge of modern dance can still be enjoyed.

TRAFÓ HOUSE OF CONTEMPORARY ARTS Map pp228-9

Trafó Kortárs Művészetek Háza; ☎ information 456 2045, tickets 215 1600; www.trafo.hu; IX Liliom utca 41; M M3 Ferenc körút

The best stage on which to see modern dance is Trafó, which presents the cream of the crop, including a good pull of international acts.

FOLK

The 30 dancers of the **Hungarian State Folk** Ensemble (Magyar Állami Népi Együttes) perform at the **Buda Concert Hall** (Budai Vigadó; Map p220; ☎ 201 3766; I Corvin tér 8; bus 86, tram 19) in Buda on Tuesday, Thursday and Sunday from May to mid-October and on Saturday and/or Sunday only during the rest of the year. In addition the **Rajkó Folk Ens**emble (Rajkó Népi Együttes) stages folk-dance performances at the Budapest Puppet Theatre (p73) on Saturday and the Duna Folk Ensemble (Duna Népi Együttes) dances at the Duna Palota (p130) just off Roosevelt tér in Pest on Monday and Wednesday. The 1½-hour programmes by these groups begin at 8pm, and tickets cost from 4600/4200Ft per adult/student. Contact **Hungaria Koncert** (☎ 317 2754, 201 5928; www.ticket.info.hu) for information and bookings for any of the above groups.

Many people attend *táncház* evenings (p131) to learn the folk dances that go with the music, and you can become part of the programme as well instead of merely watching others perform.

NATIONAL DANCE THEATRE Map p220

Nemzeti Táncszínház; ☎ information 201 4407, tickets 375 8649; www.nemzetitancszinhaz.hu; I Színház utca 1-3; ⏲ ticket office 1-6pm; bus 16 or Várbusz

The National Dance Theatre on Castle Hill hosts at some point every troupe in the city, including the two ballet companies and the Honvéd Ensemble – one of the city's best folk troupes and now experimenting with modern choreography as well.

ACTIVITIES

HEALTH & FITNESS

Thermal Baths

Budapest lies on the geological fault separating the Buda Hills from the Great Plain; more than 30,000 cu metres of warm to scalding – 21°C to 76°C – mineral water gush forth daily from some 120 thermal springs. As a result, the city is a major spa centre and 'taking the waters' at one of the many *gyógyfürdő* (thermal baths) or spa swimming pools is a real Budapest experience. Some baths date from Turkish times, others are Art Nouveau wonders, and still others are spic-and-span modern establishments.

At thermal baths, depending on the number of patrons, you will sometimes be given a number and will have to wait until it is called or appears on the electronic board. All baths and pools have cabins or lockers. Find one, get changed in it (or beside it) and call the attendant. He or she will lock the door with your clothes inside, write the time on a chalkboard on the door and hand you a numbered tag to tie on your costume. Note: In order to prevent theft lest you lose or misplace the tag, the number is not the same as the one on the locker, so commit the locker number to memory.

Though some of the local spas and baths look a little rough around the edges, they are clean and the water is changed regularly. You might consider taking along a pair of plastic sandals or flip-flops, however. Most bathhouses now require you to wear a bathing suit and no longer distribute those strange drawstring loincloths. Most of them hire out swimming costumes (around 800Ft) if you don't have your own.

Generally, entry to those baths without a deposit or voucher system (such as the Gellért, Lukács and Széchenyi Baths) allows you to stay for two hours on weekdays and 1½ hours at weekends, though this rule is not always enforced. Most of the baths offer a full range of serious medical treatments plus services such as massage (1900/2700Ft for 15/30 minutes) and pedicure (2000Ft). Specify what you want when buying your ticket.

Please note that some baths become gay venues on male-only days – especially the Király. Not much actually goes on except for some intensive cruising, but those not into it may feel uncomfortable.

An excellent source of information is the Budapest Spas and Hot Springs website: www.spasbudapest.com.

GELLÉRT Map pp228-9

Gellért Gyógyfürdő; ☎ 466 6166; XI Kelenhegyi út; admission 1600Ft; ⏲ 6am-7pm Mon-Fri, 6am-5pm Sat & Sun May-Sep, 6am-7pm Mon-Fri, 6am-2pm Sat & Sun Oct-Apr; 🚊 18, 19, 47 or 49

Soaking in this Art Nouveau palace, open to both men and women in separate sections, has been likened to taking a bath in a cathedral. The pools maintain a constant temperature of 44°C, and the water, high in calcium, magnesium and hydrogen carbonate, is good for pains in the joints, arthritis and blood circulation. The entrance fee is actually a kind of deposit; you get back 700/400/200Ft if you leave within two/three/four hours before 3pm and 500/200Ft if you exit within two/three hours after 3pm.

KIRÁLY Map pp218-19

Király Gyógyfürdő; ☎ 202 3688, 201 4392; II Fő utca 84; admission 1100Ft; ⏲ men 9am-8pm Tue, Thu & Sat, women 7am-6pm Mon, Wed & Fri; 🚌 60 or 86

The four pools here, with water temperatures of between 26°C and 40°C, are genuine Turkish baths erected in 1570 and have a wonderful skylit central dome.

LUKÁCS Map pp218-19

Lukács Gyógyfürdő; ☎ 326 1695; II Frankel Leó út 25-27; admission deposit locker/cabin 1500/1700Ft; ⏲ 6am-7pm daily May-Sep, 6am-7pm Mon-Fri, 6am-5pm Sat & Sun Oct-Apr; 🚊 17, 🚌 60 or 86

Housed in a sprawling, 19th-century complex, the Lukács Baths are popular with older, very keen spa aficionados and include everything from thermal and mud baths (temperatures 22°C to 40°C) to a swimming pool. The thermal baths are open to men on Tuesday, Thursday and Saturday and women on Monday, Wednesday and Friday. You get back 500/300/100Ft in you leave two/three/four hours after you enter.

RUDAS Map p224

Rudas Gyógyfürdő; ☎ 356 1322, 356 1010; I Döbrentei tér 9; admission deposit with cabin 2000Ft; ⏲ men 6am-8pm Mon-Thu, 6am-5pm Fri & Sun, mixed 10pm-4am Fri & Sat, 8am-5pm Sun; 🚊 18 or 19, 🚌 7 or 86

These recently renovated baths are the most Turkish of all in Budapest, built in 1566, with an octagonal pool, domed cupola with coloured glass and massive columns. It's a real zoo on mixed Friday and Saturday nights, when bathing costumes are compulsory. On men's days only you get back 700/400Ft if you leave two/three hours after you enter.

SZÉCHENYI Map pp218-19

Széchenyi Gyógyfürdő; ☎ 363 3210; XIV Állatkerti út 11; admission deposit before/after 3pm 2300/1400Ft; ⏲ 6am-7pm; Ⓜ M1 Széchenyi fürdő

The Széchenyi baths complex in the northern end of City Park is unusual for three reasons: its immense size (a dozen thermal baths and three swimming pools); its bright, clean look; and its water temperatures (up to 38°C), which really are what the wall plaques say they are. It is open to both men and women at all times and you get back 800/500/200Ft on your deposit if you leave within two/three/four hours before 3pm and 600/300Ft if you exit within two/three hours after 3pm.

THERMAL BATH Map pp226-7

☎ 889 4737; XIII Margit-sziget; admission weekday/weekend 5200/6300Ft; ⏲ 6.30am-9.30pm; 🚌 26

This bath is a modern-style thermal spa in the Danubius Grand Hotel Margitsziget (p158) on leafy Margaret Island. The baths are open to men and women in separate sections.

Swimming

Hungarians are keen swimmers and Budapest boasts dozens of *uszoda* (pools), both indoor and outdoor. They're always excellent places to get in a few laps (if indoor), cool off on a hot summer's day (if outdoor) or watch all the posers strut their stuff (both).

The system inside is similar to that at the baths (see p135) except that instead of a cabin or cubicle, there are sometimes just lockers. Many pools require the use of a bathing cap, so bring your own or wear the plastic one provided or sold for a nominal fee. Most pools hire bathing suits and towels.

Following are the best outdoor and indoor pools in the city. Some are attached to thermal baths reviewed previously; others are part of hotel wellness centres.

ALFRÉD HAJÓS Map pp218-19

☎ 450 4214, 340 4946; XIII Margit-sziget; adult/child 900/550Ft; outdoor pools 6am-7pm daily May-Sep, indoor pools 6am-7pm Mon-Fri, 6am-5pm Sat & Sun Oct-Apr; 4 or 6, 26

The one indoor and three outdoor pools here form the National Sports Pool, where Olympic swimming and water-polo teams train.

BÉLA KOMJÁDI Map pp218-19

☎ 212 2750; II Árpád fejedelem útja 8; adult/child 900/550Ft; 6am-7pm; 17, 60 or 86

This pool is used by very serious swimmers and fitness freaks so don't come here for fun and games.

CSILLAGHEGY Map pp226-7

☎ 250 1533; III Pusztakúti út 3; adult/child 1000/800Ft; 9am-7pm daily mid-May–Sep, 7am-7pm Mon-Fri, 7am-5pm Sat, 7am-6pm Sun Sep–mid-May; HÉV Csillaghegy

This popular swimming complex north of Óbuda is the oldest open-air bathing area in Budapest. There are three pools in a 90-hectare terraced park; in winter they are covered by a heated canvas tent.

DAGÁLY Map pp226-7

☎ 452 4500; XIII Népfürdő utca 36; adult deposit with/without cabin 1800/1500Ft, child deposit 1300Ft; outdoor pools 6am-7pm daily May-Sep, indoor pools 6am-7pm Mon-Fri, 6am-5pm Sat & Sun Oct-Apr; M M3 Árpád híd, 1

This huge complex has a total of 10 pools, with plenty of grass and shade. If you leave the complex two/three hours after entering you get 500/300Ft back.

GELLÉRT Map pp228-9

☎ 466 6166; XI Kelenhegyi út; deposit to swimming pool & thermal baths with locker/cabin 2500/3000Ft, after 5pm daily May-Sep, after 5pm Mon-Fri & after 2pm Sat & Sun Oct-Apr 2400/2800Ft; 6am-7pm daily May-Sep, 6am-7pm Mon-Fri, 6am-5pm Sat & Sun Oct-Apr; 18, 19, 47 or 49

The indoor pools at the Gellért Baths are the most beautiful in Budapest. The outdoor pools (open May to September) have a wave machine and landscaped gardens.

HÉLIA Map pp218-19

☎ 889 5800; XIII Kárpát utca 62-64; admission before/after 3pm Mon-Fri 3500/4500Ft, Sat & Sun 4900Ft; 7am-10pm; M M3 Dózsa György út, trolleybus 79

This ultramodern swimming and spa centre in the four-star Danubius Hélia Hotel boasts three pools, sauna and steam room.

LUKÁCS Map pp218-19

☎ 326 1695; II Frankel Leó út 25-27; deposit locker/cabin 1500/1700Ft; 6am-7pm daily May-Sep, 6am-7pm Mon-Fri, 6am-5pm Sat & Sun Oct-Apr; 17, 60 or 86

Use of the three swimming pools at the Lukács Baths is included in the general admission and the hours are the same.

PALATINUS Map pp226-7

☎ 340 4505; XIII Margit-sziget; adult/child locker 1500/1300Ft, admission with cabin 1900Ft; 10am-6pm Mon-Fri, 9am-7pm Sat & Sun May & Jun, 9am-7pm daily Jul & Aug; 26

The largest series of pools in the capital, the 'Palatinus Beach' complex on Margaret Island has a total of 11 pools (two or three with thermal water), wave machines, water slides etc.

RÓMAIFÜRDŐ Map pp226-7

☎ 388 9740; III Rozgonyi Piroska utca 2; adult/child locker 1200/1000Ft, admission with cabin 1600Ft; 9am-7pm May-Aug; HÉV Rómaifürdő, 34

The outdoor cold-water thermal pools here are in a leafy area of Óbuda just north of Aquincum.

RUDAS Map p224

☎ 356 1322, 356 1010; I Döbrentei tér 9; admission with locker/cabin 1000/1200Ft; 6am-6pm Mon-Fri, 6am-1pm Sat & Sun; 18 or 19, 7 or 86

The indoor pools at the Rudas Baths close to the river were built by the Turks in 1566 and retain a strong Turkish atmosphere.

SZÉCHENYI Map pp218-19
☎ 363 3210; XIV Állatkerti út 11; deposit before/after 3pm 2300/1400Ft; 6am-7pm; Ⓜ M1 Széchenyi fürdő
Use of the three enormous thermal swimming pools at the Széchenyi Baths is included in the general admission fee.

Gyms & Fitness Clubs

A daily ticket into the **thermal bath and pools** (p136) at the Danubius Grand Hotel Margitsziget includes use of the fitness room and machines. Independent gyms and fitness clubs worth a bend and a stretch include **Astoria Fitness Centre** (Map p222; ☎ 343 1140; V Dohány utca 32; adult/student day ticket 1100/900Ft; 6.30am-10pm Mon-Fri, 9.30am-6pm Sat; Ⓜ M2 Astoria), with a nearby **branch** (Map p224; ☎ 317 0452; V Károly körút 4; 6.30am-11pm Mon-Fri, 10am-6pm Sat & Sun; Ⓜ M2 Astoria); **Arnold Gym** (Map p80; ☎ 250 4259; III Szépvölgyi út 15; two visits 2000Ft; 7am-11pm Mon-Fri, 9am-10pm Sat & Sun; HÉV Szépvölgyi út, 86); and **A&TSA Fitness Club** (Map p220; ☎ 488 7220; I Pálya utca 9; to 4pm/full day 1400/1900Ft; 7am-11pm Mon-Fri, 9am-9pm Sat & Sun; 105).

OUTDOOR ACTIVITIES

Cycling

Parts of Budapest, including City and Népliget Parks, Margaret Island and the Buda Hills, are excellent places for cycling. At present dedicated bike lanes in the city total about 140km, including the path along Andrássy út, but that is expected to double in the next decade.

For information and advice on cycling, contact the very helpful **Hungarian Cyclists' Club** (MK; ☎ 206 6223, 06 30 922 9052; www.kerosz.hu) or the **Hungarian Bicycle Touring Association** (MKTSZ; Map p222; ☎ 311 2467; mktsz@dpg.hu; VI Bajcsy-Zsilinszky út 31, 2nd fl; Ⓜ M3 Arany János utca). See p52 for information about joining a city tour by bike.

Frigoria publishes a number of helpful guides and maps, including one called *Kerékparral Budapest környékén* (By Bike around Budapest; 2200Ft) that takes in the surrounding areas and describes 30 different routes. The tourist offices distribute the free, but less ambitious, *Budapest & Surroundings Bicycle Route Map,* with 20 recommended tours that range in length from 24km to 177km.

Bicycles can be transported on the HÉV, all Mahart boats and the Cog and Children's Railways but not on the metro, buses or trams.

There are a couple of places to rent bicycles on Margaret Island (p63) but these are just for twirling round the island. Bikes to hire for touring further afield include the long-established and very reliable **Yellow Zebra Bikes** (Map p224; ☎ 266 8777, 06 30 211 8861; www.yellowzebrabikes.com; V Sütő utca 2; 1hr/half-day/full day hire 500/2000/3000Ft; Ⓜ M1/2/3 Deák Ferenc tér; 10am-6pm Nov-Mar, 9am-8pm Apr-Oct), with an **Opera House branch** (Map p222; ☎ 269 3843; VI Lázár utca 16; 10am-5pm Nov-Mar, 9.30am-7.30pm Apr-Oct; Ⓜ M1 Opera); **Budapest Bike** (Map p222; ☎ 06 30 944 5533; www.budapestbike.hu; VII Wesselényi utca 18; 2hr/half-day/full day hire 600/1500/3000Ft; 9am-midnight; 4 or 6, trolleybus 74), with a **Chain Bridge branch** (Map p224; ☎ 06 30 944 5533; V Lánchíd; 9am-midnight May-Sep; 2 or 2a) open only in summer; and **Bike Base** (Map p222; ☎ 269 5983, 06 70 625 8501; www.bikebase.hu; VI Podmaniczky utca 19; 1-/2-/3-day hire €8/12/16; 9am-7pm; Ⓜ M3 Nyugati pályaudvar).

Boating

The best place for canoeing and kayaking in Budapest is on the Danube at Romai-part; take the HÉV suburban line to Rómaifürdő and walk east towards the river. Two reliable places to rent kayaks and/or canoes are **Óbuda Sport Club** (ÓSE; Map pp226–7; ☎ 240 3353; III Rozgonyi Piroska utca 28; canoes per day 1400Ft; 8am-6pm) and the **KSH boat club** (Map pp226–7; ☎ 368 8967; III Királyok útja 31; 1-/2-person kayak per day 1300/1500Ft, 3-/4-person canoe per day 1800/1900Ft; 8am-6pm mid-Apr–mid-Oct).

Caving

Budapest has several caves, two of which can be visited on walk-through guided tours in Hungarian. Most of the hostels offer 4½-hour caving excursions for 2500Ft to **Mátyáshegy Cave** (Mátyáshegyi-barlang; Map pp226–7), a cave opposite the Pálvölgy, usually commencing at 4pm on Monday, Wednesday and Friday.

PÁLVÖLGY CAVE Map pp226-7

Pálvölgyi-barlang; ☎ 325 9505; II Szépvölgyi út 162; adult/child 750/450Ft; ⌚ hourly tours 10am-4pm Tue-Sun; 🚌 65 from Kolosy tér in Óbuda

The second-largest cavern in Hungary, 'Paul Valley' Cave is noted for both its stalactites and its bats. The 500m route involves climbing some 400 steps and a ladder so it may not be suitable for children or the elderly.

SZEMLŐHEGY CAVE Map pp226-7

Szemlőhegyi-barlang; ☎ 325 6001; II Pusztaszeri út 35; adult/child 650/400Ft; ⌚ 10am-4pm Wed-Mon; 🚌 29 from III Kolosy tér

This is Budapest's most beautiful cave, with stalactites, stalagmites and weird grape-like formations. It's about 1km southeast of Pálvölgy Cave.

Horse Riding

The nonprofit **Hungarian Equestrian Tourism Association** (MLTSZ; Map p224; ☎ 456 0444; www.equi.hu; IX Ráday utca 8) can provide you with a list of recommended riding schools that are within striking distance of Budapest. **Pegazus Tours** (Map p224; ☎ 317 1644; www.pegazus.hu; V Ferenciek tere 5) organises riding programmes as does the highly respected **Favorit Lovarda** (☎ 257 1065, 06 30 966 9992; XVI Mókus utca 23; HÉV Szabadságtelep) in the northeastern Csömör district.

PETNEHÁZY LOVASCENTRUM

☎ 397 5048, 06 20 588 3571; petnehazy@net.hu; II Feketefej utca 2-4; ⌚ 9am-4pm Sat & Sun; 🚌 63 from Hűvösvölgyi út

One of the closest places to the city is this long-established riding centre at Adyliget near Hűvösvölgy, west of Budapest. By the time you read this it may have resumed lessons, paddock practice and trail riding, which were put on hold while Hungary introduced a new system of rating riding schools. In the meantime there are pony rides (1500Ft per quarter-hour) for the kiddies and carriage rides (15,000Ft per half-hour for 8 people).

Skating

Bringóhintó (p63) on Margaret Island rents out inline skates for 880/1480Ft per half/full hour.

GÖRZENÁL ROLLER-SKATING PARK

Map pp226-7

Görzenál Görkocsolya Park; ☎ 250 4800; III Árpád fejedelem útja 125; admission weekdays/weekends 400/600Ft; ⌚ 9am-7.30pm; HÉV Tímár utca

This outdoor roller-skating rink and karting track across from the Danube in Óbuda rents skates (500Ft) as well as protective equipment such as gloves, shin and elbow guards (100Ft per set).

CITY PARK ICE-SKATING RINK

Map pp218-19

Városligeti Műjégpálya; ☎ 364 0013; XIV Olof Palme sétány 5; admission weekdays/weekends 360/720Ft; ⌚ 9am-1pm & 4-8pm Mon-Fri, 10am-2pm & 4-8pm Sat & Sun

In winter this huge outdoor skating rink operates on the western edge of the lake in City Park. If you want to avoid the seasonal crowds, visit on weekday mornings.

Tennis & Squash

There are some three dozen tennis clubs in Budapest usually charging between 2700Ft and 4500Ft per hour for use of their courts (clay and/or green set). Among the best are the **Városmajor Tennis Academy** (Map p216; ☎ 202 5337; XII Városmajor utca 63-69; ⌚ 7am-10pm Mon-Fri, 7am-7pm Sat & Sun; 🚌 28); **Szépvölgyi Tennis Centre** (Szépvölgyi Teniszcentrum; Map pp226–7; ☎ 388 1591; III Virág Benedek utca 39-41; ⌚ 7am-10pm; 🚌 65 from Kolosy tér in Óbuda); and **Pasarét Sport Centre** (Pasaréti Sportcentrum; Map p216; ☎ 212 52 46; II Pasaréti út 11-13; ⌚ 7am-10pm Mon-Fri, 9am-9pm Sat & Sun; 🚌 5).

For squash, book a court at any of the following: A&TSA Fitness Club (opposite) for 2400Ft to 4000Ft per hour; Arnold Gym (opposite) for 1950Ft to 2950Ft; or **Top Squash** (Map pp218–19; ☎ 345 8193; II Lövőház utca 2-6; court rental 2300-4500Ft; ⌚ 7am-11pm Mon-Fri, 8am-9pm Sat & Sun; Ⓜ M2 Moszkva tér, 🚋 4 or 6) on the 4th floor of the Mammut I shopping mall.

WATCHING SPORT

Hungarians love attending sporting matches as well as watching them on TV. The most popular spectator sports are football and water polo, though horse racing and motor racing also have their fans.

For its size and population, Hungary has done extremely well in the Olympics. It finished 13th overall at both the 2004 Olympic Games in Athens and the ones in Sydney in 2000, with exactly the same number of medals: 17 (eight gold, six silver and three bronze). At the 1996 games in Atlanta, it placed 12th with 21 medals and at Barcelona in 1992 the ranking was eighth with 30 medals.

Football

Hungary's descent from being on top of the heap of European football to a *béka segge alatt* – literally, 'under the arse of the frog' as the Hungarians describe something *really* far down – remains one of life's great mysteries. Hungary's defeat of the England team both at Wembley (6–3) in 1953 and at home (7–1) the following year, are still talked about as if the winning goals were scored yesterday.

There are four premier league football teams in Budapest out of a total 12 playing nationwide, including Kispest-Honvéd, which plays at the city's **József Bozsik Stadium** (☎ 282 9791, 282 9789; XIX Új temető út 1-3; bus 36), southeast of the centre, accommodating 15,000 spectators; MTK at **Hungária Stadium** (Map pp218–19; ☎ 219 0300; VIII Salgótarjáni utca 12-14; tram 1 or 1/a), to the east of Kerepes Cemetery, for 8000 people; and UTE at **UTE Stadium** (☎ 369 7333; IV Megyeri út 13; bus 47 or 96), in Újpest, with room for 15,000 fans.

But no club dominates Hungarian football like Ferencváros (FTC), which is the country's loudest and brashest team, and its only hope. You either love the Fradi boys in their green and white or you hate them. You can watch them play at the **FTC Stadium** (Map pp228–9; ☎ 215 1013; IX Könyves Kálmán körút 26; Ⓜ M3 Népliget), near Népliget Park, with space for 18,000. The daily *Nemzeti Sport* (National Sport; 99Ft), available from newsstands everywhere, has the game schedules.

Horse Racing

The descendants of the nomadic Magyars are keen on horse racing. **Kincsem Park** (Map p216; ☎ 433 0522; www.kincsempark.com; X Albertirsai út 2; Ⓜ M2 Pillangó utca), which was recently renovated, is the place to go for both *ügető* (trotting) and *galopp* (flat racing). Schedules can change but in general three trotting meetings of 10 to 11 races take place each week, usually at 3pm on Saturday and Sunday and at 4pm or 5pm on Wednesday year-round. Flat racing usually takes place from 2pm on Thursday and Sunday between May and early November.

Motor Racing

Reintroduced in 1986 following a hiatus of half a century, the **Formula 1 Hungarian Grand Prix** (☎ 28-444 444; www.hungaroring.hu) is part of the World Championship Series that takes place at the Hungaroring at Mogyoród, 24km northeast of Budapest, in August. Practice is on the Friday, the qualifying warm-up on Saturday and the race begins after morning practice at 2pm on Sunday. The only seats with views of the starting grid are Super Gold ones and cost €400 for the weekend; cheaper are Gold (€300 to €320), which are near the pit lane, and Silver (€225 to €250) tickets. Standing room costs €110 for the weekend, €100 for Sunday.

Water Polo

The **Hungarian Water Polo Association** (MVLSZ; ☎ 412 0041; www.waterpolo.hu in Hungarian) is based at the Alfréd Hajós National Sports Pool (p137) on Margaret Island and matches take place here and at two other pools – the Béla Komjádi (p137) in Buda and the **BVSC** (Map pp218–19; ☎ 251 3888; XIV Szőnyi út 2; trolleybus 74 or 74/a) in Pest from September to May. If you want to see a match or watch the lads in training in summer, call the MVLSZ for times and dates or get someone to check schedules for you in *Nemzeti Sport* newspaper.

Shopping

Shopping

Shops in Budapest are well stocked and the quality of the products is generally high. Traditional markets stand side by side with mammoth shopping malls and old-style umbrella or button makers can be found next to cutting-edge fashion boutiques.

Books and folk-music tapes and CDs are affordable, and there's an excellent selection, especially of popoular classical music. Traditional items include folk embroidery and ceramics, pottery, wall hangings, painted wooden toys and boxes, dolls, all types of basketry, and porcelain (especially from Herend and Zsolnay). Feather or goose-down pillows and duvets (comforters) are of exceptionally high quality and are second only to the Siberian variety.

Foodstuffs that are expensive or difficult to buy elsewhere – goose liver (both fresh and potted), saffron, dried forest mushrooms, jam (especially the apricot variety), prepared meats like Pick salami, the many types of paprika – make nice gifts (as long as you're allowed to take them home). Some of Hungary's 'boutique' wines (p30) make good and relatively inexpensive gifts. A bottle of six-*puttonyos* Tokaji Aszú dessert wine always goes down a treat. Fruit-flavoured *pálinka* (brandies) are a stronger option.

Shopping Streets & Areas

Some streets or areas in Budapest specialise in certain goods or products. For example, antique shops line V Falk Miksa utca (Map p222) in Pest and, to a lesser extent, II Frankel Leó út (Map pp218–19) in Buda. V Múzeum körút (Map p224) in Pest has a string of antiquarian and secondhand bookshops. Central (and very high-rent) V Váci utca (Map p224) is chock-a-block with both top-end boutiques and tourist schlock.

In the mid-1990s Budapest began to go mall crazy, and at last count the city had at least a dozen, both in the centre of town and on the fringes. However, 'mall' may not properly describe what the Hungarians call *bevásárló és szorakoztató központ* (shopping and amusement centres); here you'll find everything from designer salons, more traditional shops and dry cleaners to food courts, casinos, cinemas and live bands. It's a place to spend the entire day, much as you would just about anywhere in the globalised world of the third millennium.

Some people consider a visit to one of Budapest's flea markets – the famous Ecseri Piac (p150) or the smaller one in City Park (p150) – a highlight, not just as a place to indulge their consumer vices but as the consummate Budapest experience. If you don't have time to get to either or it's the wrong day of the week, check any of the BÁV stores (p147).

Opening Hours

Very generally speaking, retail shops and department stores are open 10am to 6pm Monday to Friday and 10am to 1pm on Saturday. In summer, some private retail shops close early on Friday and at least part of August.

BUDA

CASTLE HILL

HEREND Map p220 Porcelain & Glassware

☎ 225 1050; www.herend.com; I Szentháromság utca 5; ⌚ 10am-6pm Mon-Fri, 9am-1pm Sat & Sun; 🚌 16 or Várbusz

For both contemporary and traditional fine porcelain, there is no other place to go but Herend, Hungary's answer to Wedgwood. Among the most popular motifs produced by the company is the Victoria pattern of butterflies and wildflowers designed for the eponymous British queen during the mid-19th century. There's also a more central **Belváros branch** (Map p224; ☎ 317 2622; V József nádor tér 11; ⌚ 10am-6pm Mon-Fri, 9am-1pm Sat; Ⓜ M1 Vörösmarty tér) of this Hungarian icon.

HOUSE OF HUNGARIAN WINES
Map p220 Food & Drink
Magyar Borok Háza; ☎ 212 1030, 212 1031; www.winehouse.hu; I Szentháromság tér 6; ⌚ noon-8pm; 🚌 16 or Várbusz
This popular tourist attraction (p54) in the Castle District also has a huge selection of wines to buy.

HUNGARICUM Map p220 Folk Art & Souvenirs
☎ 487 7306; I Fortuna utca 1; ⌚ 9am-9pm; 🚌 16 or Várbusz
This shop, conveniently located in the Castle District, sells quality Hungarian handicrafts as well as foodstuffs (eg potted goose liver and honey), wines and brandies.

VÍZIVÁROS

BUDAPEST WINE SOCIETY
Map pp218-19 Food & Drink
☎ 212 2569; www.bortarsasag.hu; I Batthyány utca 59; ⌚ 10am-8pm Mon-Fri, 10am-6pm Sat; Ⓜ M2 Moszkva tér
The society has several retail outlets, including one on trendy **IX Ráday utca** (Map p224; ☎ 219 5647; IX Ráday utca 7; ⌚ noon-8pm Mon-Fri, 10am-3pm Sat; Ⓜ M2 Moszkva tér), where serious oenophiles should head. No-one but no-one knows Hungarian wines like these guys do. There are free tastings on Saturday afternoon.

HEREND VILLAGE POTTERY
Map pp218-19 Porcelain & Glassware
☎ 356 7899; II Bem rakpart 37; ⌚ 9am-5pm Mon-Fri, 9am-noon Sat; Ⓜ M2 Batthyány tér
An alternative to what some might call prissy and overwrought Herend porcelain is the hard-wearing Herend pottery and dishes decorated with bold fruit patterns sold here. You can also enter from II Fő utca 61.

MAMMUT Map pp218-19 Shopping Mall
☎ 345 8020; II Lövőház utca; ⌚ 8am-11pm; Ⓜ M2 Moszkva tér
The two 'Mammoths' (Mammut I and Mammut II) – side by side in Buda – are true 'shopping and amusement centres', with almost as many fitness centres, billiard parlours, dance clubs and cafés as shops. They attract the Buda middle class in droves.

TAXES & REFUNDS

If you're not a resident of the EU, you can get a ÁFA (VAT or sales tax) refund, provided you have spent more than 50,000Ft in any one shop and take the goods out of the country (and the EU) within 90 days. For more information see p193.

SPORTHORGÁSZ
Map pp218-19 Sporting Goods
Sport Angler; ☎ 06 70 383 8825; II Bem József utca 8; ⌚ 8am-6pm Mon-Fri, 8am-1pm Sat; 🚌 86, 🚋 4 or 6
This is the place to come for rods, reels, flies and anything else it takes to get you out fishing.

TIMPANON Map pp226-7 Antiques
☎ 250 5547; III Nagyszombat utca 3; ⌚ 10am-6pm Mon-Fri; HÉV Tímár utca, 🚌 60
This seldom noticed shop in Óbuda sells antique Hungarian folk art of every shape and size: mangle boards, woodcarvings, chests etc. But don't expect any bargains. An early 19th-century *tulipán láda* (trousseau chest with tulips painted on it) from the Félvidék area of Transylvania will cost you around 130,000Ft. There's a Buda branch called **Almárium** (Map p220; ☎ 250 5547; I Attila utca 65; 🚌 5).

OUTER BUDA DISTRICTS

MOM PARK Map pp218-19 Shopping Mall
☎ 487 5501; XII Alkotás út 53; ⌚ 8am-11pm; 🚋 61
South Buda's biggest mall has both office and retail space, including a nine-screen cinema, recreation centre and in-house brewery pub.

PEST

INNER TOWN

ARTEN STÚDIÓ Map p224 Fine Art
☎ 266 3127; V Váci utca 25; ⌚ 10am-6.30pm Mon-Fri, 10am-6pm Sat; Ⓜ M3 Ferenciek tere
This fine-art gallery is somewhat commercial with lots of bric-a-brac but also shows works by such modern Hungarian artists as Ápád Müller and Endre Szász. Enter from Pesti Barnabás utca.

TOP FIVE SHOPS FOR FOLK ART

- Timpanon (p143)
- Holló Atelier (right)
- Intuita (right)
- Hungaricum (p143)
- Folkart Centrum (below)

BABAKLINIKA Map p224 Toys

☎ 267 2445; V Múzeum körút 5; 10am-5pm Mon-Fri, 9.30am-12.30pm Sat; M M2-Astoria

Just down the street from the Astoria metro station, the 'Doll Clinic' specialises in selling (and repairing) handmade dolls and other toys.

BALOGH KESTYŰ

Map p224 Fashion & Clothing

☎ 266 1942; V Haris köz 2; 10am-6pm Mon-Fri, 10.30am-1pm Sat; M M3 Ferenciek tere

If he can have a pair of bespoke shoes (p146), why can't she have a pair of custom-made gloves (and remember, ladies – the longer, the sexier)? You'll get them here at 'Balogh Gloves' – and there's any number of materials to choose from.

BELVÁROSI AUKCIÓSHÁZ

Map p224 Antiques & Auction House

☎ 267 3539; V Váci utca 36; 10am-6pm Mon-Fri, 10am-4pm Sat; M M3 Ferenciek tere

The ' Inner Town Auction House' usually has themed auctions (jewellery, artwork and graphics, furniture and carpets etc) at 5pm on Monday from September to June but is open for viewing throughout the week.

FOLKART CENTRUM

Map p224 Folk Art & Souvenirs

☎ 318 5840; V Váci utca 58; 10am-7pm; 15, 47 or 49

Also called 'Népművészet', the Folkart is a large shop where everything Magyar-made is available – folk costumes, dolls, painted eggs, embroidered tablecloths – and prices are clearly labelled. The staff are helpful and will advise. A similar place but even bigger is the **Folkart Kézművészház** (Folkart Artisan House; Map p224; ☎ 318 5143; V Régi posta utca 12; 10am-7pm Mon-Fri, 10am-4pm Sat; M M3 Ferenciek tere) further north on the same street.

HEPHAISTOS Map p224 Household Goods

☎ 266 1550; V Molnár utca 27; 11am-6pm Mon-Fri, 10am-2pm Sat; 47 or 49

Named after the Greek god of smiths and metalworkers, this shop has a zany collection of furniture, fittings and household goods, including many made of wrought iron, a medium in which the Hungarians have traditionally excelled.

HOLLÓ ATELIER Map p224 Folk Art & Souvenirs

☎ 317 8103; V Vitkovics Mihály utca 12; 10am-6pm Mon-Fri, 10am-noon Sat; M M1/2/3 Deák Ferenc tér

Off the northern end of Váci utca, this place has attractive folk art with a modern look and remains a personal favourite for buying gifts.

INTUITA Map p224 Folk Art & Souvenirs

☎ 266 5864; V Váci utca 67; 11am-6pm Mon-Fri, 10am-2pm Sat; 15

You're not likely to find painted eggs and *pálinka* (brandy) at this gift shop, but it does stock handmade glass, ceramics, bound books etc that are all modern versions of traditional Hungarian folk craft.

KÖZPONTI ANTIKVÁRIUM

Map p224 Antiquarian & Secondhand Books

☎ 317 3514; V Múzeum körút 13-15; 10am-6.30pm Mon-Fri, 10am-2pm Sat; M M2 Astoria

For antique and secondhand books in Hungarian, German and English, try the 'Central Antiquarian Bookshop', which was established in 1885 and is the largest of its kind in Budapest.

MAGMA Map p224 Household Goods

☎ 235 0277; V Petőfi Sándor utca 11; 10am-5pm Mon-Fri, 10am-3pm Sat; M M3 Ferenciek tere

In the centre of the Belváros, this showroom focuses on Hungarian design and designers – with everything from glassware and porcelain to textiles and furniture.

MONARCHIA Map p224 Fashion & Clothing

☎ 318 3146; V Szabadsajtó út 6; M M3 Ferenciek tere

This fashion house stocks funky one-off and made-to-measure items that have a distinctly Magyar stamp. There are branches in the **West End City Centre** (☎ 238 7172; p148) and **Duna Plaza** (☎ 239 4248; p150) malls.

NÁRAY TAMÁS Map p224 Fashion & Clothing

☎ 266 2473; V Károlyi Mihály utca 12; ⏰ noon-8pm Mon-Fri, 10am-2pm Sat; Ⓜ M3 Ferenciek tere

The principal outlet for Hungary's most celebrated and controversial designer, the Paris-trained Tamás Náray, stocks elegant ready-to-wear fashion and accessories for women and also accepts tailoring orders.

PORCELÁNHÁZ Map p224 Porcelain & Glassware

☎ 266 3165; V Váci utca 45; ⏰ 10am-6pm Mon-Fri, 10am-3pm Sat; Ⓜ M3 Ferenciek tere

This is the shop to source colourful pottery from Hődmezővásárhely in southeastern Hungary, a centre of that craft for hundreds of years.

RED BUS SECONDHAND BOOKSTORE

Map p224 Antiquarian & Secondhand Books

☎ 337 7453; V Semmelweis utca 14; www.redbus-budapest.hu; ⏰ 11am-6pm Mon-Fri, 10am-2pm Sat; Ⓜ M2 Astoria

Below the popular hostel of that name is the top shop in town for used (as opposed to antiquarian) English-language books.

RÓZSAVÖLGYI ÉS TÁRSA Map p224 Music

☎ 318 3312; V Szervita tér 5; ⏰ 9.30am-7pm Mon, Tue, Thu & Fri, 10am-7pm Wed, 10am-5pm Sat; Ⓜ M1/2/3 Deák Ferenc tér

This music shop is a good choice for CDs and tapes of traditional folk music.

SELENE LOVAS BOLT

Map p224 Sporting Goods

☎ 266 0143; V Irányi utca 7; ⏰ 10am-6pm Mon-Fri, 9am-1pm Sat; Ⓜ M3 Ferenciek tere

Selene sells everything and anything you might need to kit both you and a horse out for riding.

SZÁMOS MARCIPÁN Map p224 Food & Drink

☎ 317 3643; V Párizsi utca 3; ⏰ 10am-7pm; Ⓜ M3 Ferenciek tere

'Many Kinds of Marzipan' sells just that – in every shape and size imaginable. Its ice cream (100Ft per scoop) is another major draw here.

TANGÓ CLASSIC Map p224 Fashion & Clothing

☎ 267 6647; www.tangoclassic.hu; V Váci utca 8; Ⓜ M1 Vörösmarty tér

Tangó stocks exclusive women's suits, blazers, jackets, evening attire and accessories with a Hungarian twist. There's also a **district V branch** (Map p224; ☎ 318 4394; V Apáczai Csere János utca 3; Ⓜ M1 Vörösmarty tér) nearby.

THOMAS SABO Map p224 Jewellery

☎ 328 0557; www.thomassabo.com; V Kristóf tér 6; ⏰ 10am-7pm; Ⓜ M1 Vörösmarty tér

This Germany-based jewellery design company with Hungarian roots specialises in exquisite modern pieces in sterling silver.

Folk art and souvenirs on sale at Holló Atelier (opposite), Belváros

VASS Map p224 Fashion & Clothing
☎ 318 2375; www.vass-shoes.hu; V Haris köz 2; 10am-6pm Mon-Fri, 10am-2pm Sat; M M3 Ferenciek tere
A traditional shoemaker that stocks both ready-to-wear and cobbles to order, Vass has a reputation that goes back to 1896 and some people travel to Hungary just to have their footwear made here.

ZSOLNAY Map p224 Porcelain & Glassware
☎ 266 6305; V Váci utca 19-21; 10am-7pm; M M3 Ferenciek tere
For both contemporary and traditional fine eosin porcelain from Pécs, try this place.

NORTHERN INNER TOWN

BESTSELLERS Map p224 Books
☎ 312 1295; V Október 6 utca 11; 9am-6.30pm Mon-Fri, 10am-5pm Sat, 10am-4pm Sun; M M1/2/3 Deák Ferenc tér
Still top of the pops for English-language bookshops in Budapest is the recently expanded Bestsellers, which has novels, travel guides and lots of Hungarica as well as a large selection of magazines and newspapers.

CENTRAL EUROPEAN UNIVERSITY BOOKSHOP Map p224 Books
☎ 327 3096; V Nádor utca 9; 10am-6pm Mon-Fri; 15
Under the same management as Pendragon (opposite), the two-floor bookshop at the Central European University has a good selection of academic and business titles with a regional focus as well as some secondhand stock.

KÓDEX Map p222 Books
☎ 428 1010; V Honvéd utca 5; 9am-6pm Mon-Fri; M M2 Kossuth Lajos tér
At Kódex you'll find Hungarian books on the ground floor and foreign books on the 1st floor, along with a decent selection of classical and jazz CDs.

LA BOUTIQUE DES VINS
Map p224 Food & Drink
☎ 317 5919; www.malatinszky.hu; V József Attila utca 12; 10am-6pm Mon-Fri, 10am-3pm Sat; M M1/2/3 Deák Ferenc tér
Owned and operated by the former sommelier at the exclusive Gundel restaurant, 'The Wine Shop' has an excellent selection

PERMISSION GRANTED

Budapest's antique shops and auction houses are magnets for bargain hunters. Those with a trained eye may find the treasures of tomorrow at some of the modern galleries today, but purchases still require you to reach deep into the pocket – at least for the credit card.

Any item over 50 years old requires a permit from the Ministry of Culture for export; this involves a visit to a museum expert (see the following), photos of the piece and a National Bank form with proof-of-purchase receipts. Companies that will take care of all this for you and ship the piece(s) include **First European Shipping** (☎ 06 20 933 5240, 06 20 264 0424; www.firsteuropeanshipping.com) and **Move One** (☎ 213 0018; www.moveone.info). Be aware that most art shippers won't take a job for under US$450, so if the piece is small enough and not really valuable, consider taking it in your suitcase. First European Shipping quotes a price of about US$850 for obtaining export customs clearance, crating and air-freighting a small chest of drawers to JFK International Airport in New York.

If you're in a DIY mood, the following are the museums and other offices you must contact for valuations and permits in order for your purchase to be allowed out of the country.

Applied Arts Museum (Map pp218–19; ☎ 217 5222; IX Üllői út 33-37) For antique furniture, porcelain, glass and carpets.

Ethnography Museum (Map p222; ☎ 473 2400; V Kossuth Lajos tér 12) For folk art and handicraft items.

Hungarian National Gallery (Map p220; ☎ 201 9082; Wings B & D, Royal Palace, I Szent György tér) For pictorial works by Hungarian artists.

Museum of Fine Arts office (Map pp218–19; ☎ 302 1785; VI Szondi utca 77) For foreign paintings, sculptures and other works of art.

National Széchenyi Library (Map p220; ☎ 224 3700; Wing F, Royal Palace, I Szent György tér) For books, printed matter, written music, hand-written items dating from before 1957.

of Hungarian wines. Ask the staff to recommend a bottle.

NÁDORTEX Map p224 Household Goods

☎ 317 0030; V József nádor tér 12; 10am-6pm Mon-Fri; M M1 Vörösmarty tér

Goose-feather or down products such as pillows (from 12,000Ft) or duvets (comforters; from 22,000Ft) are of excellent quality in Hungary and a highly recommended purchase. Nádortex, small but reliable, has some of the best prices; a pure down 'summer' (ie 500g per sq metre) measuring 200cm x 220cm costs 38,000Ft.

NYUGAT ANTIKVÁRIUM

Map p222 Antiquarian & Secondhand Books

☎ 311 9023; V Bajcsy-Zsilinszky út 34; 10am-5.30pm Mon-Fri; M M3 Arany János utca

The 'West Antiquarian Bookshop' stocks both foreign- and Hungarian-language titles.

SZENT ISTVÁN KÖRÚT & TERÉZVÁROS

AJKA KRISTÁLY

Map p222 Porcelain & Glassware

☎ 332 4541; VI Teréz körút 50; M M3 Nyugati pályaudvar

Established in 1878, Ajka has Hungarian-made lead-crystal pieces and stemware. Most of it is very old fashioned but there are some more-contemporary pieces.

ANNA ANTIKVITÁS Map p222 Antiques

☎ 302 5461; V Falk Miksa utca 18-20; 4 or 6

Anna is the place to go if you're in the market for embroidered antique tablecloths and bed linen. They're stacked up all over the shop.

BÁV Map p222 Antiques

Bizományi Kereskedőház és Záloghitel; ☎ 325 2600, 473 0666; www.bav.hu; XIII Szent István körút 3; 10am-6pm Mon-Fri, 9am-1pm Sat; 4 or 6

This chain of pawn and secondhand shops, with a number of branches around town, is always a fun place to comb for trinkets and treasures; check out this branch for chinaware, textiles and artwork. Other stores include the **VI Andrássy út branch** (Map p222; ☎ 342 9143; VI Andrássy út 43; M M1 Opera) for old jewellery, watches and silver; the **V Bécsi utca branch** (Map p224; ☎ 318 4403; V Bécsi utca 1-3; M M1/2/3 Deák Ferenc tér) for knick-knacks, porcelain and glassware; and the **II Margit körút branch** (Map pp218–19; ☎ 315 0417; II Margit körút 4; 4 or 6) for furniture, lamps and fine porcelain.

TOP FIVE BOOKSHOPS

- Bestsellers (opposite)
- Szőnyi Antikváriuma (p148)
- Libri Könyvpalota (p149)
- Központi Antikvárium (p144)
- Írók Boltja (Writers' Bookshop; p150)

DÁRIUS Map p222 Antiques

☎ 311 2603; V Falk Miksa utca 24-26; 4 or 6

This shop, which handles furniture, paintings, glass and porcelain, is among the best on V Falk Miksa utca.

HAAS & CZJZEK

Map p222 Porcelain & Glassware

☎ 311 4094; www.porcelan.hu; VI Bajcsy-Zsilinszky út 23; 10am-7pm Mon-Fri, 10am-3pm Sat; M M3 Arany János utca

In the vicinity of the Basilica of St Stephen, this chinaware and crystal shop sells Zsolnay as well as more affordable Hungarian-made Hollóháza and Alföldi porcelain.

JÁTÉKSZEREK ANNO Map p222 Toys

☎ 302 6234; VI Teréz körút 54; 10am-6pm Mon-Fri, 9am-1pm Sat; M M3 Nyugati pályaudvar

The wonderful little 'Anno Playthings' shop near Nyugati train station sells finely made reproductions of antique wind-up and other old-fashioned toys.

KIESELBACH GALÉRIA Map p222 Fine Art

☎ 269 3148; www.kieselbach.hu; V Szent István körút 5; 10am-6pm Mon-Sat; 4 or 6

This is without a doubt the best source in the city for Hungarian painting and there are frequent auctions.

PENDRAGON Map pp218-19 Books

☎ 340 4426; XIII Pozsonyi út 21-23; 10am-6pm Mon-Fri, 10am-2pm Sat; 4 or 6, trolleybus 76 or 79

While this 'English bookshop', which takes its name from the legend of King Arthur, has an excellent selection of English books and guides (including Lonely Planet titles), most Anglophones will have a hard time making themselves understood here.

PINTÉR ANTIK Map p222 Antiques

☎ 311 3030; www.pinterantik.hu; V Falk Miksa utca 10; 🕑 10am-6pm Mon-Fri, 10am-2pm Sat; 🚊 4 or 6

With a positively enormous antique showroom measuring 1800 sq metres in a series of cellars near the Parliament, Pintér has everything from furniture and chandeliers to oil paintings and china, and is the best around for browsing.

SZŐNYI ANTIKVÁRIUMA

Map p222 Antiquarian & Secondhand Books

☎ 311 6431; www.szonyi.hu; V Szent István körút 3; 🕑 10am-6pm Mon-Fri, 9am-1pm Sat; 🚊 4 or 6

This long-established antiquarian bookshop has an excellent selection of antique prints and maps (look in the drawers) as well as books.

WAVE MUSIC Map p224 Music

☎ 331 0718; VI Révay köz 2; 🕑 11am-7pm Mon-Fri, 11am-3pm Sat; Ⓜ M1 Bajcsy-Zsilinszky út

Wave is another excellent outlet for both Hungarian and international indie music.

WEST END CITY CENTRE

Map p222 Shopping Mall

☎ 238 7777; VI Váci út 1; 🕑 8am-11pm; Ⓜ M3 Nyugati pályaudvar

In central Pest, this Goliath of a shopping complex has everything you could possibly want or need, with 400 shops, telecom outlets, large indoor fountains, the hair-raising Budapest Eye (p73) and the 230-room Hilton West End (p160).

ERZSÉBETVÁROS

BILLERBECK Map p222 Household Goods

☎ 322 3606; www.billerbeck.hu; VII Dob utca 49; 🕑 10am-6pm Mon-Fri, 9.30am-1pm Sat; 🚊 4 or 6

With several branches around town, Billerbeck has a large selection of feather and goose-down duvets and other bedding and helpful staff.

CIÁNKÁLI Map pp218-19 Fashion & Clothing

☎ 341 0540; www.majomketrec.hu; VII Dohány utca 94; 🕑 10am-7pm Mon-Fri, 10am-2pm Sat; trolleybus 74

Whatever your 'drag' of choice happens to be – 1960s camp to leather or military – the folks at this antifashion emporium of used and vintage clothes will have you kitted out before you can say 'Trick or Treat!'.

Antique bookshop Szőnyi Antikváriuma (above), Újlipótváros

CONCERTO HANGLEMEZBOLT
Map p224 Music
☎ 268 9631; VII Dob utca 33; 🕑 noon-7pm Mon-Fri, noon-4pm Sun; Ⓜ M2 Astoria
For classical CDs, tapes and vinyl, try the wonderful 'Concerto Record Shop', which is always full of hard-to-find treasures.

LEKVÁRIUM Map p222 Food & Drink
☎ 321 6543; VII Dohány utca 39; 🕑 10am-6pm Mon-Fri, 10am-2pm Sat; Ⓜ M2 Blaha Lujza tér
This little speciality shop stocks homemade jams, bottled fruit and honey, wine from the Siklós and Villány regions of southern Hungary and fruit-flavoured brandies. It is *the* place to visit if you haven't been able to pick up a jar or two of Hungary's greatest edible contribution to humanity – traditionally made *lekvár* (fruit jam), especially the apricot variety – at a food market (p93).

LIBRI KÖNYVPALOTA Map p222 Books
☎ 267 4844; VII Rákóczi út 12; 🕑 10am-7.30pm Mon-Fri, 10am-3pm Sat; Ⓜ M2 Astoria
Spread over two floors, the huge 'Book Palace' has a selection of English-language novels, art books, guidebooks, maps, music, and a café and Internet access on the 1st floor. For books in English and other languages specifically on Hungarian subjects, a more useful branch is **Libri Stúdium** (Map p224; ☎ 318 5680; V Váci utca 22; 🕑 10am-7pm Mon-Fri, 10am-3pm Sat & Sun; Ⓜ M3 Ferenciek tere).

JÓZSEFVÁROS & FERENCVÁROS

IGUANA Map p222 Fashion & Clothing
☎ 317 1627; VIII Krúdy utca 9; 🕑 10am-7pm Mon-Fri, 10am-2pm Sat; 🚊 4 or 6
Iguana sells vintage leather, suede and velvet pieces from the 1950s, '60s and '70s, plus its own trousers, skirts and shirts. There's a **district IX branch** (Map pp228–9; ☎ 215 3475; IX Tompa utca 1; 🕑 10am-7pm Mon-Fri, 10am-2pm Sat; Ⓜ M3 Ferenc körút).

MAGYAR PÁLINKA HÁZ
Map p222 Food & Drink
Hungarian Pálinka House; ☎ 338 4219; www.magyarpalinkahaza.hu; VIII Rákóczi út 17; 🕑 9am-7pm Mon-Sat; Ⓜ M2 Astoria
If you're into Hungarian *pálinka*, the exquisite brandy flavoured with everything from apricot and sour cherry to raspberry, make a beeline for this place. They stock hundreds of varieties.

CLOTHING SIZES

Measurements approximate only, try before you buy

Women's Clothing						
Aus/UK	8	10	12	14	16	18
Europe	36	38	40	42	44	46
Japan	5	7	9	11	13	15
USA	6	8	10	12	14	16
Women's Shoes						
Aus/USA	5	6	7	8	9	10
Europe	35	36	37	38	39	40
France only	35	36	38	39	40	42
Japan	22	23	24	25	26	27
UK	3½	4½	5½	6½	7½	8½
Men's Clothing						
Aus	92	96	100	104	108	112
Europe	46	48	50	52	54	56
Japan	S		M	M		L
UK/USA	35	36	37	38	39	40
Men's Shirts (Collar Sizes)						
Aus/Japan	38	39	40	41	42	43
Europe	38	39	40	41	42	43
UK/USA	15	15½	16	16½	17	17½
Men's Shoes						
Aus/UK	7	8	9	10	11	12
Europe	41	42	43	44½	46	47
Japan	26	27	27½	28	29	30
USA	7½	8½	9½	10½	11½	12½

MONARCHIA BORÁSZATI
Map pp218-19 Food & Drink
☎ 456 9817; www.magyarborok.hu; IX Kinizsi utca 30-36; 🕑 noon-7pm Mon-Fri, 10am-6pm Sat; Ⓜ M3 Ferenc körút
Just opposite the Applied Arts Museum, Monarchia has an extensive selection from both established and new Hungarian vintners, but the best on offer are those bottled under its own label.

NAGYCSARNOK
Map p224 Folk Art & Souvenirs, Food & Drink
IX Vámház körút 1-3; 🕑 6am-5pm Mon, 6am-6pm Tue-Fri, 6am-2pm Sat; 🚊 47 or 49
The 'Great Market' is Budapest's biggest food market but, because it has been attracting tourists ever since it was renovated for the millecentenary in 1996, it now has dozens of stalls on the 1st floor's south side selling

Hungarian folk costumes, dolls, painted eggs, embroidered tablecloths, carved hunting knives and so on. At the same time, gourmets will appreciate the Hungarian and other treats – shrink-wrapped and potted foie gras and goose-liver pâté (2200/4400Ft for 100/200g), a good selection of dried mushrooms, garlands of dried paprika (600Ft to 800Ft), souvenir sacks and tins of paprika powder (290Ft to 650Ft), and as many kinds of honey (from 450Ft) and types of wine as you'd care to name – available on the ground floor at a fraction of what they would cost in the shops on nearby Váci utca.

ANDRÁSSY ÚT

BIBLIOTÉKA ANTIKVÁRIUM

Map p224 Antiquarian & Secondhand Books

☎ 475 0240; www.bibliotekaantikvarium.hu; VI Andrássy út 2; ⏲ 10am-6pm Mon-Fri, 9am-1pm Sat; Ⓜ M1/2/3 Deák Ferenc tér

The Bibliotéka at the start of VI Andrássy út is a bit of a jumble sale but always worth a once over for possible treasures.

ÍRÓK BOLTJA Map p222 Books

Writers' Bookshop; ☎ 322 1645; VI Andrássy út 45; Ⓜ M1 Oktogon, 🚋 4 or 6

For Hungarian authors in translation, including many of those mentioned on p21, this is the place to go.

LISZT FERENC ZENEMŰBOLT

Map p222 Music

☎ 322 4091; VI Andrássy út 45; Ⓜ M1 Oktogon

Next to the Writers' Bookshop, the 'Ferenc Liszt Music Shop' has mostly classical CDs, tapes and vinyl as well as books of local interest and very scary staff.

CITY PARK

CITY PARK FLEA MARKET

Map pp218-19 Flea Market

Városligeti Bolhapiac; ☎ 363 3730, 251 7266; www.bolhapiac.com; XIV Zichy Mihály út; ⏲ 7am-2pm Sat & Sun; 🚋 1 or 1/a, trolleybus 70, 72 or 74

This is a huge outdoor flea market – a kind of Hungarian boot or garage sale – held next to the Petőfi Csarnok (p133) in City Park. The usual diamonds-to-rust stuff is on offer – from old records and draperies to candles, honey and herbs. Sunday is the better day.

OUTER PEST DISTRICTS

CHINESE MARKET Map pp226-7 Flea Market

Kinai piac; XIII Fáy utca 60; ⏲ 7am-6pm; 🚋 14

A rather unusual place, this is essentially a series of stalls run by Chinese, Vietnamese and Thais that offer the usual array of knock-off designer clothing and cosmetics, cigarettes and liquor of dubious provenance. There are some decent (read authentic) Asian food stalls here too.

DUNA PLAZA Map pp226-7 Shopping Mall

☎ 465 1666; XIII Váci út 178; ⏲ 8am-11pm; Ⓜ M3 Gyöngyösi utca

This is second only to West End City Centre in size, with three floors of 120 clothing and shoe shops, a multiplex cinema with a dozen screens, bowling lanes, an ice-skating rink and the requisite Greek *taverna*.

ECSERI PIAC Flea Market

☎ 282 9563; XIX Nagykőrösi út; ⏲ 8am-4pm Mon-Fri, 6am-3pm Sat, 8am-1pm Sun; 🚌 54

Often just called the *piac* (market), this is one of the biggest and best flea markets in Central Europe, selling everything from antique jewellery and Soviet army watches to old musical instruments and Fred Astaire–style top hats. Saturday is the best day to go. To get there, take bus 54 from Boráros tér in Pest near Petőfi Bridge or, better yet, the red express bus 54 from the Határ utca stop on the M3 metro line and get off at the Fiume utca stop. Then follow the crowds over the pedestrian bridge.

MOUNTEX Map pp218-19 Sporting Goods

☎ 239 6050; XIII Váci út 19; ⏲ 10am-7pm Mon-Fri, 10am-2pm Sat; Ⓜ M3 Lehel tér

This huge emporium on two levels with branches throughout the city (and country for that matter) carries all the gear you'll need for hiking, climbing, camping and so on.

Sleeping

Sleeping

Accommodation in Budapest runs the gamut from hostels in converted flats and private rooms in far-flung housing estates to luxury *pensions* in the Buda Hills and five-star properties charging upwards of €300 a night for a double. The low season for hotels runs roughly from mid-October or November to March (not including the Christmas and New Year holidays). The high season is the rest of the year – a lengthy seven months or so – when prices can increase substantially. Almost without exception the rate quoted for hostel and hotel accommodation includes breakfast. If you're driving, parking at many of the central Pest hotels will be difficult.

Accommodation Styles

HOSTELS

Accommodation at Budapest's *ifjúsági szállók* (youth hostels) is available year-round, but during the university summer holidays (generally mid-June or July to late August) the number of hostels increase exponentially. During this time, private outfits rent vacant dormitories from the universities and turn them into hostels. Competition is fierce and there are several hostel operators, so you can afford to shop around a bit.

Dormitory accommodation in both year-round and summer hostels cost from 2000Ft to 5000Ft per person, depending on room size; doubles are 6000Ft to 12,000Ft. High season usually means April to October. A Hostelling International (HI) card or equivalent (p187) is not required at any hostel in Budapest, but it will sometimes get you a discount of up to 10% or an extra night's stay; make sure to ask beforehand.

Hostels usually provide laundry facilities (between 1000Ft and 1500Ft for a wash and dry), a fully equipped kitchen, storage lockers, TV lounge, no curfew or age limit and computers for accessing the Internet (free or about 10Ft per minute). A useful website is www.youthhostels.hu.

While you can go directly to all the hostels mentioned under Cheap Sleeps in this chapter, the Express (p195) and Mellow Mood (p195) travel agencies are the best outfits for information about budget accommodation. In fact, the latter, which is affiliated with HI, runs three hostels and five budget hotels year-round as well as a half-dozen hostels that are open in summer only, mostly in Buda. It also maintains three kiosks at Keleti train station (Map pp218–19): **Platform 9 kiosk** (☎ 353 2722; 7am-6pm); **Rail/bus office** (☎ 461 0948; 6am-10pm) along platform 6; and **U Tours travel agency** (☎ 303 9818; 7am-8pm) at the end of platform 6. Staff make bookings and can advise you about or arrange transport from there.

Another major player in the competitive world of Budapest summer hostels is **Universum** (☎ 06-28 558 900; www.universumyouthhostels.hu), which has accommodation at one year-round hotel and hostel in Pest and three hostels – all with fridges in the rooms, safes and washer-dryers – in the vicinity of the University of Technology and Economic Sciences (Map pp228–9) in Buda and a **Keleti train station booking office** (7am to 8pm) next to platform 9.

> **BOOK ACCOMMODATION ONLINE**
>
> For more accommodation reviews and recommendations by Lonely Planet authors, check out the online booking service at www.lonelyplanet.com. You'll find the true, insider lowdown on the best places to stay. Reviews are thorough and independent. Best of all, you can book online.

HOTELS

Hotels, called *szállók* or *szállodák*, can be anything from the rapidly disappearing run-down old socialist-era hovels to luxurious five-star palaces.

A cheap hotel will usually be more expensive than a private room in Budapest, but it may be the answer if you're only staying one night or if you arrive too late to get a private room through an agency. Two-star hotels usually have rooms with a private bathroom; it's almost always on the hall in a one-star place. Three- and four-star hotels can be excellent value compared with those in other European countries.

PENSIONS

Budapest has scores of *panziók (pensions),* most of them are in the outskirts of Pest or in the Buda Hills and not very convenient unless you have your own (motorised) transport. *Pensions* are popular with Germans and Austrians who like the homey atmosphere and the better breakfasts. Often *pensions* can cost as much as a moderate hotel, although there are some worthwhile exceptions.

PRIVATE ROOMS

Hungary's *fizetővendég szolgálat* ('paying-guest service') is a great deal and still relatively cheap, but with the advent of *pensions* it's not as widespread as it once was. Private rooms in Budapest generally cost from 4500Ft to 6000Ft for a single, 6500Ft to 8000Ft a double, and 8000Ft to 15,000Ft for a small apartment. There's usually a 30% supplement on the first night if you stay less than three nights. To get a room in the centre of town, you may have to try several offices. You might need an indexed city map (p190) to find the block where your room is located, though.

Individuals on the streets outside the main train stations may offer you a private room, but their prices are usually higher than those asked by the agencies, and there is no quality control. They vary considerably and cases of travellers being promised an idyllic room in the centre of town, only to be taken to a dreary, cramped flat in some distant suburb are not unknown. On the other hand, we've received dozens of letters extolling the virtues of the landlords who readers have dealt with directly in this way. You really have to use your own judgment here. Until you suss out the pitfalls, you're probably better off getting a room from an agency.

The tourist offices in Budapest do not arrange private accommodation, but will send you to a travel agency like **To-Ma** (Map p224; ☎ 353 0819; www.tomatour.hu; V Október 6 utca 22; 🕑 9am-noon & 1-8pm Mon-Fri, 9am-5pm Sat-Sun; Ⓜ M1/2/3 Deák Ferenc tér). Among the best places to try for private rooms are **Ibusz** (p195) and **Vista** (p195) as well as **U Tours** (opposite) in Keleti train station.

After hours, try the mostly unhelpful **Non-stop Hotel Service** (Map p224; ☎ 266 8042, 318 3925; www.non-stophotelservice.hu; V Apáczai Csere János utca 1; 🕑 9am-10pm; Ⓜ M1 Vörösmarty tér) near the Budapest Marriott Hotel.

SERVICED APARTMENTS

Budapest is chock-a-block with serviced apartments and apartment hotels. They all have private bathrooms and usually kitchens – at the very least. Some are positively luxurious (eg Millennium Court in Pest; p159) while others are bare-bones (eg Peter's Apartments in Pest; p161).

Price Ranges

In this book budget accommodation – hostels, private rooms, some *pensions* and cheap hotels – is anything for two people (double or twin) under 12,000Ft (€49), midrange (usually *pensions* and hotels) is 12,500Ft (€50) to 25,000Ft (€102) and top end is anything over 25,500Ft (€104). Because of the changing value of the forint, many hotels quote their rates in euros. In such cases, we have followed suit. We quote the high-season rates here, but during the low season tariffs can be as much as 30% less.

The price quoted should be the price you pay, but it's not as cut-and-dried in Budapest. Travel agencies generally charge a small fee for booking a private room or other accommodation, and there's usually a surcharge if you stay for less than three nights (at least on the first night). Budapest levies a 3% local tourist tax on those aged 18 to 70. Some top-end hotels in Budapest do not include the 15% VAT in their listed rack rates; make sure you read the fine print.

Longer-Term Rentals

After the changes of 1989, many families in Budapest were given the opportunity to buy – at very low rates – the flats they had been renting from the state since the 1950s. As a result, Budapest is full of fully paid-up flats waiting to be let.

Rental prices vary according to the condition of the property (naturally) and the district it's located in; the most expensive areas for renting are districts I, II and XII in Buda and districts V and XIII in Pest. Expect to pay at least 2000Ft per square metre in the leafy, sought-after neighbourhoods of Buda. In Pest, a flat in central district V will cost from 1500Ft to 2000Ft per square metre and from 1000Ft to 1500Ft in districts VI or VII. The diplomatic quarter west of City Park will cost as much as districts II and XII in Buda. The cheapest flats are to be found in the housing blocks of some of the more outlying districts (eg districts III and XXII in Buda and almost everything that is situated east of the Big Ring Road in Pest).

Your best source of information is the daily classifieds-only newspaper *Expressz* (99Ft), available from newsstands everywhere. These days, however, many of the advertisements are from agencies, which usually require you to pay 3000Ft up front for the address of the property. Monthly property magazines include *Ingatlan Magazin* (480Ft) and *Ingatlan Kavalkád* (296Ft). Since ads are always in Hungarian only – and the landlord is likely to be monolingual – you'll have to get a native speaker to help you. Some good websites for searching are the bilingual www.ingatlan.com and www.alfaapartments.com; www.alberlet .lap.hu is in Hungarian only.

BUDA

Options for accommodation in the Buda district are more limited than on the other side of the Danube River, but you will find a quite a few luxurious big-name hotels along with some small, atmospheric *pensions* and many hostels, especially the summer-only type.

CASTLE HILL

BURG HOTEL Map p220 Hotel

☎ 212 0269; www.burghotelbudapest.com; I Szentháromság tér 7-8; s/d €105/115, 2-person ste €127; 🚌 16 or Várbusz

This place with all the mod cons is in the Castle District, just opposite Matthias Church. The 26 rooms are no more than just ordinary but, as they say, location is everything.

HILTON BUDAPEST Map p220 Hotel

☎ 889 6600; www.budapest.hilton.com; I Hess András tér 1-3; s & d €130-190, with Danube view €160-210; 🚌 16 or Várbusz

Perched above the Danube on Castle Hill, the Hilton was built carefully in and around a 14th-century church and baroque college (though it still has its detractors). It has 322 disappointingly sombre rooms, with dark carpeting and low lighting but great views.

HOTEL ASTRA Map p220 Hotel

☎ 214 1906; www.hotelastra.hu; I Vám utca 6; s/d/ste €90/105/135; Ⓜ M2 Batthyány tér, 🚌 86

Tucked away in a small street just west of Fő utca and just below the castle is this hotel-cum-guesthouse, housed in a centuries-old townhouse. It has seven double rooms and three suites.

HOTEL KULTURINNOV Map p220 Hotel

☎ 224 8102, 06 20 544 5396; www.mka.hu; I Szentháromság tér 6; s/d/tr €64/80/100; 🚌 16 or Várbusz

A 16-room hotel in the neo-Gothic former Finance Ministry (1904), the Kulturinnov can't be beaten for location or price in the Castle District. The guestrooms, though clean and with private bathrooms, are not as nice as the opulent public areas of the hotel.

GELLÉRT HILL & THE TABÁN

CITADELLA HOTEL Map pp228-9 Hotel & Hostel

☎ 466 5794; www.citadella.hu; XI Citadella sétány; s & d with shared shower/shower/bathroom 10,000/11,000/12,000Ft; 🚌 27

This hotel in the fortress atop Gellért-hegy is pretty threadbare and though most of the dozen dark-wood guestrooms share facilities, they are extra large and retain some of their original features. The one dorm room with 14 beds is usually booked in advance. Be warned: this area is something of a tourist trap and you may feel more like a prisoner than a prince or princess here.

DANUBIUS GELLÉRT HOTEL

Map pp228-9 Hotel

☎ 889 5500; www.danubiusgroup.com/gellert; XI Szent Gellért tér 1; s €75-130, d €170-210, ste €270; tram 18, 19, 47 or 49

Budapest's *grande dame* is a 234-room four-star hotel with loads of character. Designed by Ármin Hegedűs in 1909 and completed in 1918, the hotel contains examples of the late Art Nouveau, notably the thermal spa with its enormous arched glass entrance hall and Zsolnay ceramic fountains in the bathing pools. The baths are free for guests, but overall its other facilities are forgettable. Prices depend on which way your room faces and what sort of bathroom it has.

HOTEL ORION Map p220 Hotel

☎ 356 8583; www.bestwestern-ce.com/orion; I Döbrentei utca 13; s/d/tr/ste €88/112/132/150; tram 18 or 19

Hidden away in the Tabán district, the Orion is a cosy place with a relaxed atmosphere and within easy walking distance of the castle. The 30 rooms are bright and of a good size.

TOP FIVE GRAND HOTELS

- Four Seasons Gresham Palace Hotel (p159)
- Danubius Gellért Hotel (left)
- Corinthia Grand Hotel Royal (p162)
- Le Meridien Budapest (p158)
- Danubius Grand Hotel Margitsziget (p158)

Cheap Sleeps

HOSTEL HILL Map pp228-9 Hostel

XI Ménesi út 5; r with 1/2/3 beds per person 6000/4000/3600Ft; open early Jul-Aug; tram 18, 19, 47 or 49, bus 7 or 7/a

On the way up to leafy Gellért Hill, this institutional-looking building has 170 beds, a sports ground and a swimming pool (admission 600Ft). It's a Mellow Mood hostel (p195).

HOSTEL LANDLER Map pp228-9 Hostel

☎ 463 3621; XI Bartók Béla út 17; dm 3400-3600Ft, d per person 3900Ft

At the foot of Gellért Hill with 280 beds, Universum's Landler has basic rooms for two to four people with washbasins and shared showers.

Matthias Church towers over the Hilton Budapest (opposite), Castle Hill

HOSTEL RÓZSA Map pp228-9 Hostel

☎ 463 4250; XI Bercsényi utca 28-30; d per person 3900Ft

Rózsa is another of the Universum group of hostels and has 111 double rooms with washbasins and shared showers.

HOSTEL SCHÖNHERZ Map pp228-9 Hostel

XI Irinyi József utca 42; r with 1/2/3 & 4 beds per person 5000/3000/2500Ft; early Jul-Aug; tram 4 or 6

In an 18-storey block with 600 beds, this Mellow Mood property (p195) has rooms with one to four beds, all with their own shower; toilets are on the hall.

HOSTEL UNIVERSITAS Map pp228-9 Hostel

XI Irinyi József utca 9-11; s/d per person 4000/2500Ft; early Jul-Aug; tram 4 or 6

With 500 beds, this Mellow Mood hostel is much more basic than the Schönherz, with just washbasins in the room and communal showers in the hallway. It has a real party atmosphere, though.

HOSTEL VÁSÁRHELYI Map pp228-9 Hostel

☎ 463 4326; XI Kruspér utca 2-4; dm 3800Ft, d per person 4200Ft

With a total of 500 beds, Universum's Hostel Vásárhelyi has rooms with two to four beds, all of which have private showers.

Art'otel Budapest (right), Víziváros

MARTOS HOSTEL Map pp228-9 Hostel

☎ 209 4883, 06 30 911 5755; reception@hotel.martos.bme.hu; XI Sztoczek József utca 5-7; s/d/tr/q/apt 4000/5000/7500/10,000/15,000Ft; tram 4 or 6

Though primarily a summer hostel with 200 beds, the independent Martos has around 20 beds available year-round. It's reasonably well located, near the Danube, and just a few minutes' walk from Petőfi Bridge.

VÍZIVÁROS

ART'OTEL BUDAPEST Map p220 Hotel

☎ 487 9487; www.artotel.hu; I Bem rakpart 16-19; s/d/ste €198/218/298, with Danube view €218/238/318; tram 19, bus 86

The Art'otel is a minimalist hotel that would not look out of place in London or New York. But what makes this 165-room place unique is that it cobbles together a seven-storey modern building (views of the castle and the Danube) and an 18th-century baroque building; they're separated by a leafy courtyard-cum-atrium.

CARLTON HOTEL Map p220 Hotel

☎ 224 0999; www.carltonhotel.hu; I Apor Péter utca 3; s/d/tr €90/115/126; bus 86

A total revamp at the start of 2005 has given this 95-room hotel at the foot of Castle Hill and at the end of a narrow cul-de-sac in Watertown (Víziváros) a cleaner, fresher look and an extra star.

HOTEL CSÁSZÁR Map pp218-19 Hotel

☎ 336 2640; www.csaszarhotel.hu; II Frankel Leó utca 35; s/d/q €42/53/84, ste €116; tram 17, bus 86

The 'Emperor' started life as a convent in the 1850s, which might explain the size of the 34 cell-like rooms. Request one of the larger superior rooms that look onto the outdoor Olympic-size pools of the huge Béla Komjádi swimming complex (p137).

HOTEL VICTORIA Map p220 Hotel

☎ 457 8080; www.victoria.hu; I Bem rakpart 11; s/d/tr €102/107/148; tram 19, bus 86

This hotel has 27 comfortable and spacious rooms with larger-than-life views of Parliament and the Danube. It gets special mention for its friendly service and facilities, despite its small size. The best rooms are on floors 7 to 9.

Cheap Sleeps

BÜRO PANZIÓ Map pp218-19 Pension

☎ 212 2929; http://buro-panzio.Internettudakozo.hu; II Dékán utca 3; s/d/tr/q 8000/12,000/16,000/20,000Ft; Ⓜ M2 Moszkva tér

Just off the northern side of Moszkva tér, this *pension* looks basic from the outside, but its 10 rooms are comfortable and have TVs and telephones. They were renovated in early 2005 so they still have that just-off-the-assembly-line look.

HOSTEL BAKFARK Map pp218-19 Hostel

II Bakfark Bálint utca 1-3; dm 3000Ft; mid-Jun–Aug; Ⓜ M2 Moszkva tér, 4 or 6

In a solid brick pile near Moszkva tér and below Castle Hill, this 80-bed Mellow Mood place has accommodation in dorm rooms with six beds.

BUDA HILLS

BEATRIX PANZIÓ Map p216 Pension

☎ 275 0550; www.beatrixhotel.hu; II Széher út 3; s/d/tr €60/65/75, apt €75-90; 56, 5

On the way up to the Buda Hills but still easily accessible by public transport, this is an attractive *pension* with 18 rooms available. Surrounding the *pension* is a lovely garden with a fish pond, sun terraces and a grill.

IBS GARDEN HOTEL Map p216 Hotel

☎ 274 2088; www.ibsgardenhotel.hu; II Tárogató út 2-4; s & d €59; 56, 29

This recently opened midrange hotel is west of the Danube as you head towards the Buda Hills. It has 100 rooms spread over five floors, and is an excellent option for those who want to be very close to the city but not exactly in it.

Cheap Sleeps

PAPILLON HOTEL Map pp218-19 Hotel

☎ 212 4750; www.hotels.hu/papillon; II Rózsahegy utca 3/b; s/d/tr €38/48/58, apt for 3/5 people per person €68/78; 4 or 6

One of Buda's best-kept accommodation secrets, this small 20-room hotel in Rózsadomb has a delightful back garden with a small swimming pool. There are also two apartments available in the block just across the road.

OUTER BUDA DISTRICTS

CHARLES HOTEL & APARTMENT Map p220 Serviced Apartment

☎ 212 9169; www.charleshotel.hu; I Hegyalja út 23; standard studio s €44-49, d €52-66, tr €64-90, executive studio €64-72, €72-89, €92-114, apt €72-158; 8 or 112

On the Buda side of the river and somewhat *on* the beaten track (a train line actually runs right past the place), the Charles has 70 'studios' (larger-than-average rooms) with tiny kitchens and weary-looking furniture, as well as two-room apartments. It also has bikes available for rent at 2000Ft per day.

CONGRESS PARK HOTEL FLAMENCO Map pp228-9 Hotel

☎ 889 5600; www.danubiusgroup.com/flamenco; XI Tas vezér utca 7; s & d €95-120, ste €150-220; 19 or 49

A rambling 355-room place, the Flamenco really has little to recommend it (faceless rectangular block, smallish rooms) except for its leafy location overlooking a park with Buda's 'Bottomless Lake' (Feneketlen-tó) and an excellent gym and fitness centre.

HOTEL VENTURA Map pp228-9 Hotel

☎ 208 1232; fax 208 1234; www.gerandhotels.hu/ventura.php; XI Fehérvári út 179; s €49-62, d €62-78, tr €81-99; 47 or 18

This hotel, all done up in various shades of blue, green and purple and with what can only be described as an enormous umbrella cage in the lobby, has 149 rooms spread over two buildings and a modern gym. It's off the beaten track but transport is good.

Cheap Sleeps

BACK PACK GUESTHOUSE Map pp228-9 Hostel

☎ 385 8946; www.backpackbudapest.hu; XI Takács Menyhért utca 33; dm 2500-3000Ft, d 7000Ft; black-numbered 7 or 7A, 19 or 49

A laid-back hostel in a colourfully painted suburban 'villa' in south Buda, the Back Pack Guesthouse is relatively small, with a mere 50 beds (large dormitories with between seven and 11 beds and small ones with four to five). There is a super garden in the back and a friendly, much-travelled manager.

HOTEL GRIFF JUNIOR
Map pp228-9 Hotel

☎ 203 2398; www.gerandhotels.hu/griff.php; XI Bartók Béla út 152; s/d/tr/q with washbasin & toilet €25/29/38/43, with shower €28/38/48/58; tram 19 or 49, bus red-numbered 7

With 126 rooms – a quarter of them with their own shower – at rock-bottom prices in a low-rise office block, this hotel next to the much larger and pricier Hotel Griff, with which it has no connection (except a confusion factor), is a great choice for those on a tight budget.

MARGARET ISLAND

Margaret Island has never done things by halves. Here you will have to make a choice between top-end luxury or, at the other end of the scale, budget accommodation.

DANUBIUS GRAND HOTEL MARGITSZIGET Map pp226-7 Hotel

☎ 889 4700; www.danubiusgroup.com/grandhotel; XIII Margit-sziget; s/d/ste €153/168/198; bus 26

Constructed in the late 19th century, this comfortable (rather than grand) and tranquil hotel has 164 rooms that boast all the mod cons you would want and is connected to the Danubius Thermal Hotel Margitsziget via a heated underground corridor, where you can take the waters for free.

Cheap Sleeps

HOTEL MARGITSZIGET Map pp218-19 Hotel

☎ 329 2949; www.hotelmsz.hu; XIII Margit-sziget; s €43-53, d €45-55; bus 26

This 11-room budget hotel in the centre of the island is surrounded by greenery and feels almost like a resort. Guests can use the tennis courts, swimming pool and sauna for free. Rooms 11 to 14 have balconies.

TOP FIVE BOUTIQUE & SMALLER HOTELS

- Art'otel Budapest (p156)
- Residence Izabella (p165)
- Andrássy Hotel (p164)
- Hotel Domina Fiesta (p162)
- Hotel Astra (p154)

PEST

Pest has the lion's share of accommodation in Budapest - with everything ranging from the five-star, palatial Four Seasons Gresham Palace Hotel to most of the city's cheapest hostels.

INNER TOWN

HOTEL ART Map p224 Hotel

☎ 266 2166; www.bestwestern.com; V Király Pál utca 12; s/d/tr €85/110/140; M M3 Kálvin tér

This Best Western property has Art Deco touches (including a pink façade) in the public areas, fitness centre and sauna, but the 32 guestrooms are, on the whole, quite ordinary except for the few that have separate sitting and sleeping areas. Rooms that are located on the 5th floor have mansard roofs.

HOTEL ERZSÉBET Map p224 Hotel

☎ 889 3700; www.danubiusgroup.com/erzsebet; V Károlyi Mihály utca 11-15; s €75-95, d €95-105; M M2 Ferenciek tere

One of Budapest's first independent hotels, the 'Elizabeth' is in a very good location in the centre of the university district and within easy walking distance of the pubs and bars of Ráday utca. But the 123 guestrooms – mostly twins spread across eight floors – are small and dark.

KEMPINSKI HOTEL CORVINUS
Map p224 Hotel

☎ 429 3777; www.kempinski-budapest.com; V Erzsébet tér 7-8; s €260-410, d €300-450, ste from €570; M M1/2/3 Deák Ferenc tér

Essentially for business travellers on hefty expense accounts, the Kempinski has European service, American efficiency and Hungarian charm. A recent (and very thorough) renovation has given both the hotel's public areas and 369 guestrooms and suites a fresh new look and colour scheme.

LE MERIDIEN BUDAPEST Map p224 Hotel

☎ 429 5500; www.budapest.lemeridien.com; V Erzsébet tér 9-10; s €235-385, d €275-425, ste from €360; M M1/2/3 Deák Ferenc tér

Le Meridien's public areas and 218 guestrooms spread over seven floors are dripping in brocade and French polished furniture (think royalty over rock star), and many consider it the city's top five-star property. It's next door to the Kempinski Corvinus.

LEÓ PANZIÓ Map p224 Pension

☎ 266 9041; www.leopanzio.hu; V Kossuth Lajos utca 2/a, 2nd fl; s/d/tr €66/82/08; Ⓜ M3 Ferenciek tere

This place would be a 'find' just on the strength of its central location but when you factor in the low cost, this B&B is a true 'discovery'. A dozen of its 14 immaculate rooms look down on busy Kossuth Lajos utca, but they all have double-glazing and are quiet.

MILLENNIUM COURT

Map p224 Serviced Apartment

☎ 235 1800; www.execapartments.com/buder; V Pesti Barnabás utca 4; 1-/2-bedroom apt from €145/195; Ⓜ M3 Ferenciek tere

A rather flash serviced apartment outfit in Pest with 108 serviced studio apartments measuring about 60 sq metres, one-bed apartments of 32 to 64 sq metres and two-bedroom ones of 57 to 87 sq metres. Stays of eight nights and more earn huge discounts. As part of the package, guests staying here get to use the facilities of the Budapest Marriott Hotel, which is just a block to the northwest.

Cheap Sleeps

DOWNTOWN HOSTEL Map p224 Hostel

☎ 266 4151; www.downtownhostel.com; V Királyi Pál utca 7, 1st fl; dm €10-12, d/tr per person €18/14; Ⓜ M3 Kálvin tér, 🚊 47 or 49

Accommodation at this reader-recommended hostel, in the centre of the university district and close to everything, is in dorm rooms with four or six beds as well as in doubles and triples. There's also a great kitchen here open round the clock and the tea is free.

GREEN BRIDGE HOSTEL Map p224 Hostel

☎ 266 6922; reservations@greenbridgehostel.com; V Molnár utca 22-24; dm €11-17, d/tr/q per person €25/19/18; Ⓜ M3 Kálvin tér

Few hostels truly stand out in terms of comfort, location and reception, but Green Bridge has it all – and in spades. With everything from doubles to an eight-person dormitory available, bunks are nowhere to be seen, it's on a quiet street just one block in from the Danube and coffee is on offer gratis throughout the day.

MELLOW MOOD CENTRAL GUESTHOUSE Map p224 Hostel

☎ 411 1310; www.mellowmoodhostel.com; V Bécsi utca 2; dm 4500-5000Ft, d/tr/q per person 6800/5700/5400Ft; Ⓜ M1/2/3 Deák Ferenc tér

This place will put you right in the heart of town. With 179 beds on four floors, it is the largest year-round hostel in Budapest so don't expect the personal treatment. The dorms have six to eight beds. Still, it's clean, upbeat and there's a 24-hour bar.

RED BUS HOSTEL Map p224 Hostel

☎ 266 0136; www.redbusbudapest.hu; V Semmelweis utca 14, 1st fl; dm 2800-3000Ft, s & d/tr 7900/11,000Ft; Ⓜ M2 Astoria

The Red Bus Hostel is a very friendly, central and well-managed place, with 28 beds in four large and airy rooms (four to five beds per room) as well as private rooms that sleep up to three people. The new branch, **Red Bus 2** (Map pp218–19; ☎ 321 7100; VII Szövetség utca 2, 2nd fl; dm 2800Ft; trolleybus 73, 74 or 76) has four rooms of four to five beds.

NORTHERN INNER TOWN

FOUR SEASONS GRESHAM PALACE HOTEL Map p224 Hotel

☎ 268 6000; www.fourseasons.com/budapest; V Roosevelt tér 5-6; s €250-740, d €280-770, ste from €950; Ⓜ M1 Vörösmarty tér, 🚌 15

This magnificent 179-room hotel has been created out of the long-derelict Art Nouveau Gresham Palace (1907). No expense was spared to piece back together the palace's Zsolnay tiles, famous wrought-iron Peacock Gates and splendid mosaics; the hotel is truly worthy of its name.

HOTEL HOLD Map p222 Hotel

☎ 472 0480; www.hotelhold.hu; V Hold utca 5; s/d €88/99, ste €121-165; Ⓜ M3 Arany János

The 'Moon' is an excellent choice if you want to stay in an affordable and romantic hotel right in the centre of town. The 28 rooms on two floors – there is no lift – look down onto a central covered courtyard or onto Hold utca.

STARLIGHT SUITEN HOTEL
Map p224 Serviced Apartment
☎ 484 3700; www.starlighthotels.com; V Mérleg utca 6; s/d ste €149/179; Ⓜ M1 Vörösmarty tér, 🚌 15
This very luxurious suite hotel with 54 units is primarily aimed at the German and Austrian business markets. The suites, which are uniform in layout, consist of a bedroom, living room and bathroom and range from 40 to 60 sq metres. There are no kitchens; the suites have microwave ovens only.

Cheap Sleeps

GARIBALDI GUESTHOUSE
Map p222 Guesthouse
☎ 302 3457, 06 30 951 8763; garibaldiguest@hotmail.com; V Garibaldi utca 5, 5th fl; s/d €28/32, apt per person €25-45; Ⓜ M2 Kossuth Lajos tér
Arguably the most welcoming hostel-cum-guesthouse in Budapest, the Garibaldi has five rooms with shared bathrooms and kitchen in a flat just around the corner from Parliament. The gregarious owner has at least a half-dozen other apartments available in the same building.

SZENT ISTVÁN KÖRÚT & TERÉZVÁROS

BOAT HOTEL FORTUNA
Map pp218-19 Hotel
☎ 288 8100; www.fortunahajo.hu; XIII Szent István Park, Pesti alsó rakpart; s/d/tr with washbasin €20/30/40, with shower €65/80/100; trolleybus 76 or 79
This 'boatel' in a one-time river ferry anchored in the Danube has 44 single and double rooms with shower and toilet at water level and 14 rooms with two or three beds and just washbasin below deck.

CITY HOTEL RING Map p222 Hotel
☎ 340 5450; www.taverna.hu/ring; XIII Szent István körút 22; s/d/tr €72/98/124; Ⓜ M3 Nyugati pályaudvar
This small, almost motel-like place with 39 rooms is on two floors of a *fin-de-siècle* building, but you'd never know that from the inside looking out. Some of the rooms look onto the busy ring road, others onto an attractive and very quiet courtyard.

HILTON WEST END Map p222 Hotel
☎ 288 5500; www.hilton.com; VI Váci út 1-3; s & d €170-225, ste €205-245; Ⓜ M3 Nyugati pályaudvar
The Hilton chain's more central 230-room property adjoins the massive West End City Centre shopping mall and offers every type of facility and food and beverage outlet imaginable (p148). The target here is very much the business market.

K+K HOTEL OPERA Map p224 Hotel
☎ 269 0222; www.kkhotels.com; VI Révay utca 24; s/d/ste from €168/209/336; Ⓜ M1 Opera
This upbeat, Austrian-owned place just behind the Hungarian State Opera House has 206 rooms spread over seven floors. They're on the smallish side and decorated in unusually cheerful colours – predominantly yellows, blues and reds – which raises the tenor of the whole place.

MEDOSZ HOTEL BUDAPEST
Map p222 Hotel
☎ 374 3000; www.medoszhotel.hu; VI Jókai tér 9; s/d/tr €55/65/75, ste from €93; Ⓜ M1 Oktogon
One of the most central cheaper hotels in Pest, the Medosz is just opposite the restaurants and bars of Liszt Ferenc tér. The 67 rooms are well worn but clean and have private bathrooms and satellite TV.

Four Seasons Gresham Palace Hotel (p159), Lipótváros

GAY STAYS

Connection Guest House (Map p224; ☎ 267 7104; www.connectionguesthouse.com; VII Király utca 41; s €45-60, d €50-70; Ⓜ M1 Opera)This very central gay *pension* above a leafy courtyard attracts a young crowd due to its proximity to nightlife venues. Two of the seven rooms share facilities on the corridor and rooms 6 and 7 face partially pedestrianised Király utca.

KM Saga Guest Residence (Map pp218-19; ☎ 217 1934; www.km-saga.hu; IX Lónyay utca 17, 3rd fl; s €38-63, d €50-75; Ⓜ M3 Kálvin tér, bus 15, tram 47 or 49) This unique place has five themed rooms, an eclectic mix of 19th-century furnishings and a hospitable, multilingual Hungarian-American owner. It's essentially a gay B&B but everyone is welcome. Two rooms share a bathroom. The **KM Saga II** (Map p224; ☎ 217 1934; IX Vámház körút 11, 6th fl; Ⓜ M3 Kálvin tér, tram 47 or 49) branch is somewhat more modern but less atmospheric and has three rooms with private bathrooms and a shared kitchen at the same rates.

NH BUDAPEST Map p222 Hotel

☎ 814 0000; www.nh-hotels.com; XIII Vígszínház utca 3; s & d €119-182; tram 4 or 6

There are 160 rooms spread out over this eight-floor purpose-built hotel and three rooms on each floor have a balcony. We especially like the location, behind the Comedy Theatre, the minimalist but welcoming and very bright atrium lobby and the helpful staff dressed in attractive black designer togs.

SYDNEY APARTMENT HOTEL

Map pp218-19 Serviced Apartment

☎ 236 8800, 236 8888; www.sydneyaparthotel.hu; XIII Hegedüs Gyula utca 52-54; studio €170, 1-bedroom apt €190-22, 2-bedroom apt €270-310; Ⓜ M3 Lehel tér, trolleybus 76, bus 15 or 133

This lovely property, hard by Váci út and the West End City Centre mall, has 97 tastefully furnished units of between 45 and 110 sq metres, a gorgeous courtyard garden, marble finishings throughout, classical music in the lobby and an indoor swimming pool and fitness centre. Special rates are available at the weekend and after a month's stay.

Cheap Sleeps

BEST HOSTEL Map p222 Hostel

☎ 332 4934; www.besthostel.hu; VI Podmaniczky utca 27, 1st fl; dm 3000Ft, d/q per person 4200/3600Ft; Ⓜ M3 Nyugati pályaudvar

This is a six-room hostel put together from several apartments with parquet floors, very high ceilings and big, airy rooms. It's a quiet place with a fair number of rules (no drugs, booze or tobacco), so don't expect to party here.

CATERINA HOSTEL Map p222 Hostel

☎ 269 5990, 06 20 992 8854; www.caterinahostel.hu; VI Teréz körút 30, 3rd fl; dm 2500-2800Ft Apr-Oct, s/d/t per person 6800/3400/3400Ft, 5-bed apt per person 3200Ft; Ⓜ M1 Oktogon

For a long time a key player on the Budapest budget accommodation scene, the Caterina Hostel has moved from Oktogon in the past year or so but continues to offer reliable and cheap accommodation in a 3rd-floor, 27-bed walk-up apartment that is above the celebrated Művész Cinema.

EASTSIDE HOSTEL Map p222 Hostel

☎ 06 70 574 0224; http://riversidebudapest.tripod.com; V Falk Miksa utca 24-26, 1st fl; dm €10, d €16; tram 4 or 6

This cosy hostel on Budapest's classy antique row is a wonderful place to stay and readers have highly recommended it. It has three rooms with between two and six beds (not a bunk bed in sight) and free Internet access. The six-bedded room has a small balcony and – wait for it – a sliver of a view of the Danube.

PETER'S APARTMENTS

Map pp218-19 Serviced Apartment

☎ 06 30 520 0400; www.peters.hu; XIII Victor Hugó utca 25-27; s/d/tr €42/52/55; Ⓜ M3 Lehel tér, bus 15, trolleybus 76

This budget place in Pest offers 20 studio apartments of approximately 20 sq metres in a basic but clean building at some rock-bottom prices. Some of the units have air-conditioning (which costs €8 extra) and balconies; all have TV. Prices are negotiable, especially during the low season and at weekends.

ERZSÉBETVÁROS

CARMEN MINI HOTEL Map p224 Pension

☎ 352 0798; carmen@axelero.hu; Károly körút 5/b, 2nd fl; s/d/tr €50/60/75; Ⓜ M1/2/3 Deák Ferenc tér

With nine rooms, the Carmen Mini Hotel is about the nearest you'll find to a B&B in Budapest. It's very close to Deák Ferenc tér and convenient to all forms of transport.

CORINTHIA GRAND HOTEL ROYAL Map p222 Hotel

☎ 479 4000; www.corinthia.hu; VII Erszébet körút 43-49; s €180-240, d €220-280, ste from €300; 🚊 4 or 6

The erstwhile Hotel Royal on the Big Ring Road has reopened as a *very* grand 414-room five-star hotel, and its lobby – a double atrium with a massive marble staircase – is among the most impressive in the capital.

HOTEL BAROSS Map pp218-19 Hotel

☎ 461 3010; www.barosshotel.hu; VII Baross tér 15; s/d/tr/q €78/90/102/114, apt for 4/6/8 people €120/145/160; Ⓜ M3 Keleti pályaudvar

The flagship hotel of the Mellow Moods group of hostels (p195), the Baross is a comfortable, 40-room caravanserai conveniently located directly opposite the Keleti train station. The bluer-than-blue inner courtyard is a delight, and reception, which is to be found on the 5th floor, is clean and bright with a dramatic central staircase.

HOTEL DOMINA FIESTA Map p224 Hotel

☎ 328 3000; www.dominahotels.it; VI Király utca 20; s/d/tr/q €120/140/190/220; Ⓜ M1/2/3 Deák Ferenc tér

This attractive boutique hotel, under the management of a small Italian hotel chain, has 112 tastefully furnished rooms and a vaulted wine-cellar restaurant just minutes from Pest's main square.

KING'S HOTEL Map p222 Hotel

☎ 352 7675; www.kosherhotel.hu; VII Nagy Diófa utca 25-27; s €40-50, d €50-60, tr €60-70; Ⓜ M2 Blaha Lujza tér

Budapest's only kosher hotel has 78 rooms and is within easy walking distance of both the orthodox and conservative synagogues. The hotel's restaurant is lemehadrin (or glatt) kosher and supervised by the chief rabbi of Budapest.

MERCURE HOTEL BUDAPEST MUSEUM Map p222 Hotel

☎ 485 1080; www.mercure.com; VIII Trefort utca 2; s & d/tr €110/140; Ⓜ M2 Astoria, 🚌 7 or 78

This hotel, though part of an expanding chain, is in a lovely building dating from

Guests in lobby of Corinthia Grand Hotel Royal (above), Erzsébetváros

1890 that is interesting enough to warrant consideration. The 54 guestrooms (some two-thirds of which are reserved for non-smokers) are nothing special, however.

STAR HOTEL Map pp218-19 Hotel

☎ 479 0400; www.starhotel.hu; VII István utca 14; s/d/tr/apt €64/80/90/120; trolleybus 74 or 79

A recent addition to the Mellow Mood hostel group's stable is this 48-room midrange hotel just a few minutes' walk north of the Keleti train station. The ground-floor lobby is quite spacious and most of the guestrooms are doubles spread over four floors.

Cheap Sleeps

10 BEDS Map p222 Hostel

☎ 06 20 933 5965; adrianzador@hotmail.com; VII Erzsébet körút 15, 3rd fl; dm 3000Ft; 🚊 4 or 6

OK, it's misnamed: the place has a dozen beds (in three rooms). But that's about the only thing wrong with this hostel. It's a laid-back place with a great kitchen, free use of a washing machine and an Australian owner who trusts his guests enough to give them their own set of keys. Beg, borrow and/or steal to stay here.

AQUARIUM YOUTH HOSTEL

Map pp218-19 Hostel

☎ 344 6143, 321 8444; www.budapesthostel.com; VII Alsóerdősor utca 12, 2nd fl; dm/d 3000/8000Ft; Ⓜ M2 Keleti pályaudvar

This sister hostel to the Museum Guest House is a mere 250m northwest of Keleti train station and has a total of 17 beds in four rooms. The kitchen is a good size, Internet access is free till 11pm and the natives are friendly, but this place should be a second choice after most of the other hostels in this section.

MARCO POLO HOSTEL Map p222 Hostel

☎ 413 2555; www.marcopolohostel.com; VII Nyár utca 6; dm €20, s €54, d/tr/q per person €38/28/26; Ⓜ M2 Blaha Lujza tér

The Mellow Mood group's flagship hostel, very central and open year-round is a swish, powder-blue, 47-room place, with telephones and TVs in all the rooms except the dorms and a lovely courtyard. Even the five spotless 12-bed dorm rooms (one reserved for women during the low season) are 'private', with beds separated by lockers and curtains.

MUSEUM GUEST HOUSE Map p222 Hostel

☎ 318 9508, 266 8879; www.budapesthostel.com; VIII Mikszáth Kálmán tér 4, 1st fl; dm 3200Ft; Ⓜ M3 Kálvin tér

The Museum is a pokey but creatively decorated and friendly place, with mostly eight beds in three rooms (though there is one room with four beds). Its free Internet access, location on a lovely square and proximity to the nightlife of VIII Krúdy utca and IX Ráday utca are all pluses.

JÓZSEFVÁROS & FERENCVÁROS

ATLAS HOTEL Map pp218-19 Hotel

☎ 299 0256; www.atlashotelbudapest.com; VIII Népszínház utca 39-41; dm €17, s/d/tr €60/75/80; 🚊 28 or 37

This enormous, 136-room place in less-than-salubrious district VIII has very basic dormitory rooms with between five and six beds on the first five floors and more-comfortable singles, doubles and triples on the next three. It is said that you'll always find a room at the Atlas, which may (or may not) be a recommendation.

CORVIN HOTEL Map pp228-9 Hotel

☎ 218 6566; corvin@mail.datanet.hu; IX Angyal utca 31; s/d/tr/ste €69/79/89/99 Apr-Oct; Ⓜ M3 Ferenc körút

Close to the Danube, this newly built hotel in up-and-coming Ferencváros has 47 very comfortable rooms with all the mod cons and secure parking in a covered garage.

GOLDEN PARK HOTEL

Map pp218-19 Hotel

☎ 477 4777; www.goldenparkhotel.com; VIII Baross tér 10; s/d/tr from €60/70/90; Ⓜ M3 Keleti pályaudvar

This old workhorse of a hotel has been completely de- and reconstructed, and today it is a shimmering four-star caravanserai number within spitting distance of the Keleti train station. We like the bright and airy lobby, the glass doors at either end of the corridors letting in light and some of the old features they managed to retain.

HOTEL SISSI Map pp228-9 Hotel

☎ 215 0082; www.hotelsissi.hu; IX Angyal utca 33; s/d €110/120, ste from €195; Ⓜ M3 Ferenc körút

Named in honour of Elizabeth, the Habsburg empress, Hungarian queen and consort of Franz Joseph who was much loved by Hungarians, the Sissi is decorated in a minimalist-cum-elegant sort of style, and the 44 guestrooms spread over six floors are of a good size.

HOTEL THOMAS Map pp228-9 Hotel

☎ 218 5505; www.hotels.hu/hotelthomas; IX Liliom utca 44; s €55-65, d €75-85; Ⓜ M3 Ferenc körút

A brightly coloured place in an odd spot, the Thomas has 45 rooms and is a real bargain for its location in up-and-coming Ferencváros. Some rooms – including No 14 – have balconies onto an inner courtyard.

IBIS CENTRUM HOTEL Map p224 Hotel

☎ 456 4100; www.ibishotel.com; IX Ráday utca 6; s & d €75-85; Ⓜ M3 Kálvin tér

It may not be the most atmospheric hotel in town, but Ibis Centrum is the right price for its location near the start of the Ráday utca pedestrianised nightlife area. It has 126 rooms over nine floors, an in-house garage and a leafy garden on the 1st floor.

MERCURE NEMZETI Map p222 Hotel

☎ 477 2000; www.mercure.com; VIII József körút 4; s & d €80-110; Ⓜ M2 Blaha Lujza tér

This powder-blue Art Nouveau beacon in a relatively grotty area of central Pest was originally built in 1896, and its public areas are awash in marble and gilt; the dining room's skylight of vintage stained glass is delightful. Among the 76 rooms those looking away from the ring road and onto a back courtyard are the most desirable.

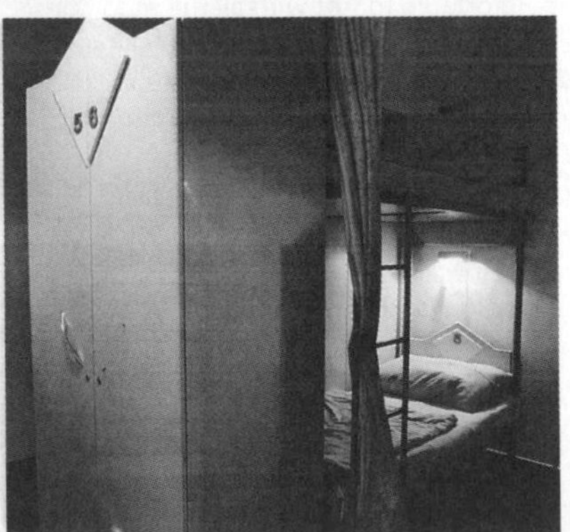

Dormitory, Marco Polo Hostel (p163), Józsefváros

Cheap Sleeps

FORTUNA HOTEL

Map pp228-9 Hotel & Hostel

☎ 215 0660; www.fortunahotel.hu; IX Gyáli út 3/b; dm 4500Ft, s 12,000-15,000Ft, d 14,000-17,000Ft; Ⓜ M3 Nagyvárad tér

With 29 rooms (including dorms with four or five beds) this place is not in the best part of Budapest but it's quiet, super clean and the huge Taiwan restaurant (p117) is just below. Reception (and all guestrooms, for that matter) are on the 2nd floor.

HOTEL RILA Map pp228-9 Hotel & Hostel

☎ 215 3278, 216 1621; www.hotelrila.com; IX Fehér Holló utca 2; dm 4400Ft, s/d 9000/12,000Ft, s/d/tr/q with bathroom 11,500/14,000/16,500/18,000Ft; Ⓜ M3 Nagyvárad tér, 🚊 24

The flagship property (and only hotel) in the Universum hostel group, the 31-room Rila is a former workers' hostel that has been spruced up into quite a nice little property. Open year-round, it has both hostel accommodation and hotel-style rooms.

HOSTEL KINIZSI Map pp228-9 Hostel

IX Kinizsi utca 2-6; dm 2400Ft, s/d/tr 5000/2700/2400Ft per person; 🕒 Jul & Aug; Ⓜ M3 Ferenc körút

Close to the Danube and the IX Ráday utca nightlife strip, the only summer hostel in Pest managed by the Mellow Mood group of hostels (p195) has basic rooms with one to five beds (total 210 beds) in a modern, six-storey student residence.

ANDRÁSSY ÚT

ANDRÁSSY HOTEL Map pp218-19 Hotel

☎ 462 2195; www.andrassyhotel.com; VI Andrássy út 111; standard s & d €134-240, ste from €161; Ⓜ M1 Hősök tere

This stunning five-star hotel along the main street has 70 tastefully decorated rooms (almost half of which have balconies) in a listed building. The use of etched glass and mirrors as well as wrought iron is inspired.

HOTEL BENCZÚR Map pp218-19 Hotel

☎ 479 5650; www.hotelbenczur.hu; VI Benczúr utca 35; s €49-79, d €69-99; Ⓜ M1 Bajza utca

This rather faded place done up in creams and oranges has 96 serviceable rooms (some of which look down on a leafy garden) spread over seven floors. It's just minutes away from Andrássy út, Hősök tere and City Park.

RADIO INN Map pp218-19 Pension

☎ 342 8347; www.radioinn.hu; VI Benczúr utca 19; s/d €52/75, 2-room apt €92; Ⓜ M1 Bajza utca

Just off leafy Andrássy út, this excellent guesthouse has 33 large one-bedroom apartments with bathroom and kitchen, 10 with two bedrooms and one with three, all spread over five floors. The lovely garden courtyard is a delight.

RESIDENCE IZABELLA Map p222 Serviced Apartment

☎ 475 5900; www.residenceizabella.com; VI Izabella utca 61; 1-bedroom apt €180-330, 2-bedroom €440-605; Ⓜ M1 Vörösmarty utca

This fabulous conversion of a 19th-century Eclectic building has 38 apartments measuring between 45 and 97 sq metres just off swanky Andrássy út. The units surround a delightful and very tranquil central courtyard garden and the décor mixes materials such as wood, terracotta and basketry to great effect.

CITY PARK

HOTEL DÉLIBÁB Map pp218-19 Hotel

☎ 342 9301; www.hoteldelibab.hu; VI Délibáb utca 35; s €52-68, d €62-79, tr €81-95; Ⓜ M1 Hősök tere

The 34-room 'Mirage' is housed in what was once a Jewish orphanage across from Hősök tere and City Park and is pretty basic as it awaits renovation by the Mellow Mood group. Ask for one of the nine rooms that face the quiet courtyard to the rear.

HOTEL LIGET Map pp218-19 Hotel

☎ 269 5300; www.liget.hu; VI Dózsa György út 106; s/d/tr €105/120/152; Ⓜ M1 Hősök tere

The 'Park' is an oddly shaped peach-coloured building facing verdant City Park, part of the zoo and a very busy road. But the 139 rooms are comfortable (try to get one of the four with a bow window); there are four nonallergenic rooms, four of seven floors are for nonsmokers, and the service here is excellent.

TOP FIVE HOSTELS & GUESTHOUSES

- KM Saga Guest Residence (p161)
- Back Pack Guesthouse (p157)
- Red Bus Hostel (p159)
- Green Bridge Hostel (p159)
- Station Guesthouse (p166)

Cheap Sleeps

DOMINIK PANZIÓ Map pp218-19 Pension

☎ 460 9428; dominikpanzio@axelero.hu; XIV Cházár András utca 3; s/d/€28/36, apt €75; 🚌 7

Close to Thököly út and beside a large church, this bare-bones *pension* is on a leafy street lined with 19th-century villas and just two stops northeast of Keleti train station by bus. The 36 rooms, which could use an upgrade, come with shared bathrooms and there is a five-person apartment available.

OUTER PEST DISTRICTS

HOTEL PLATÁNUS Map pp228-9 Hotel

☎ 333 6505, 210 2592; www.hunguesthotels.hu; VIII Könyves Kálmán körút 44; s/d/tr €90/110/120; Ⓜ M3 Népliget

Platánus, with 128 rooms on the noisy outer ring road, is moderately priced in the low season, but room prices jump in summer. It has a fitness centre with a well-equipped gym, sauna and aerobics room (8am to 10pm Monday to Friday, noon to 5pm Saturday and Sunday) and is a short distance from Népliget Park and the Népliget bus station.

ORIENTAL HOTEL Map pp226-7 Hotel

☎ 239 2399; hoteloriental@euroweb.hu; XIII Fáy utca 61; s/d/tr €56/66/97; 🚊 14, 🚌 4

This 95-room hotel is the place to stay should the untouristed Angyalföld district of northern Pest and the Chinese market (p150) attract. There are a few Asian restaurants in the vicinity.

Cheap Sleeps

HOTEL FLANDRIA Map pp226-7 Hotel

☎ 350 3181; hotelflandria@axelero.hu; XIII Szegedi út 27; s/d/tr/q with washbasin €5100/6300/7400/8600Ft, with shower 9500/9500/12,000/14,000Ft; 🚌 4

The Flandria is a classic example of a former workers' hostel that has been turned into a budget hotel. Don't expect anything within a couple of light years of luxury, but the 116 guestrooms, which have from one to four beds, a TV and refrigerator, are both clean and serviceable.

HOTEL GÓLIÁT Map pp218-19 Hotel

☎ 350 1456; www.gerandhotels.hu; XIII Kerekes utca 12-20; s/d/tr/q 6000/7100/7800/8900Ft; 🚌 4

This very basic but spotlessly clean hotel in Angyalföld northeast of the Inner Town and Lehel market has 135 basic rooms with between one and four beds. There are washbasins in the rooms, and showers and toilets on the corridor.

TOP FIVE HOTELS WITH A GARDEN

- Sydney Apartment Hotel (p161)
- Papillon Hotel (p157)
- Beatrix Panzió (p157)
- IBS Garden Hotel (p157)
- Radio Inn (p165)

STATION GUESTHOUSE

Map pp218-19 Hostel

☎ 221 8864; www.stationguesthouse.hu; XIV Mexikói út 36/b; dm 2300-2800Ft, d & t/q per person 3600/3800Ft; 🚌 red-numbered 7, 🚋 1 or 1A

This guesthouse in suburban Zugló is a real party place, with a 24-hour bar, pool table and occasional live entertainment. It has between 42 and 56 beds, depending on the season. For those intending to stay a while, rates drop by 100Ft a night from the second to the sixth nights.

Excursions

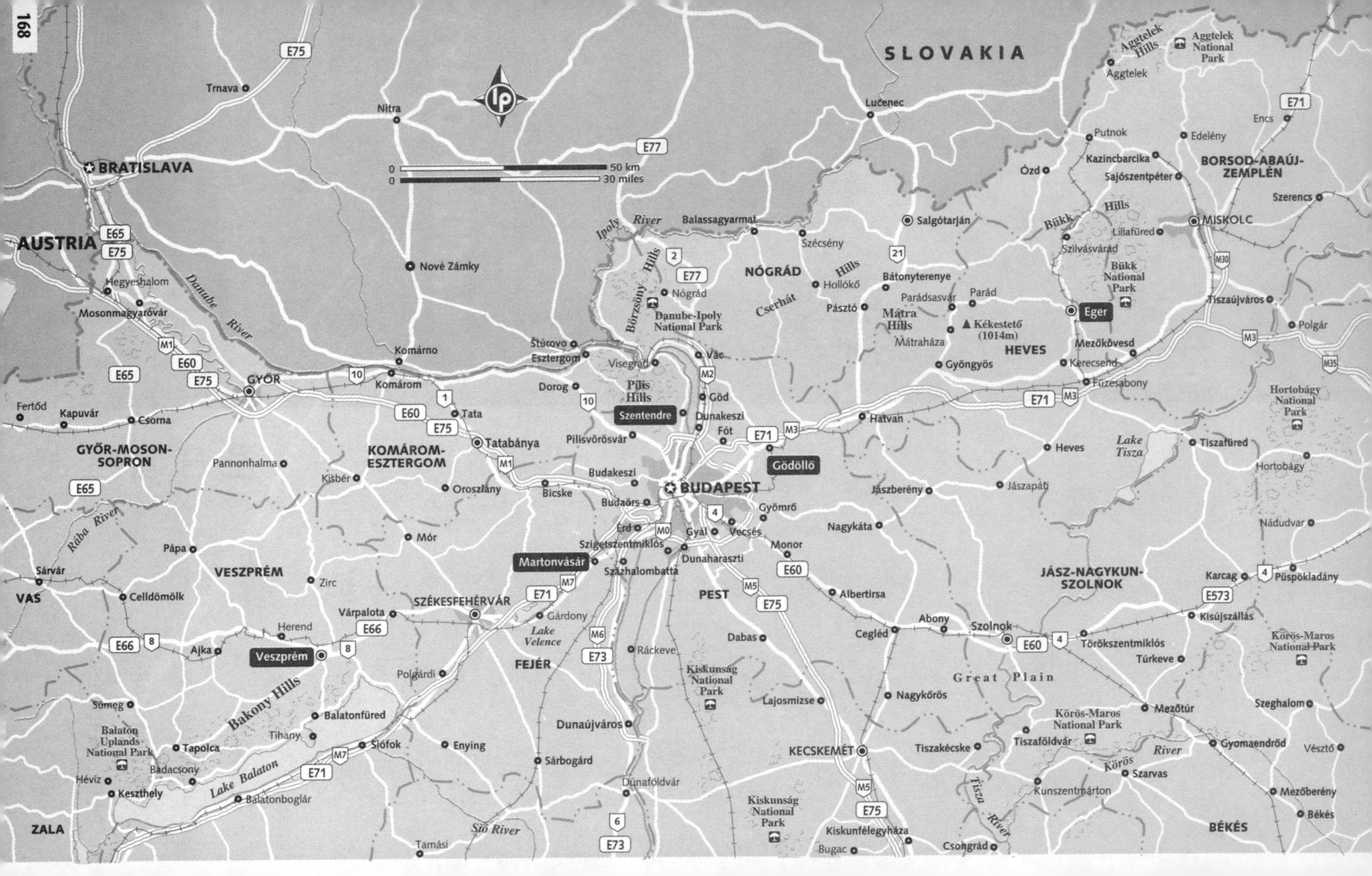

SLOVAKIA
AUSTRIA
BRATISLAVA
Trnava
Nitra
Nové Zámky
Lučenec
Komárno
Štúrovo
0 50 km
0 30 miles
E75
E77
E65
E71
Aggtelek
Aggtelek Hills
Aggtelek National Park
Putnok
Kazincbarcika
Sajószentpéter
Edelény
Encs
Szerencs
BORSOD-ABAÚJ-ZEMPLÉN
MISKOLC
M30
Lillafüred
Bükk Hills
Bükk National Park
Szilvásvárad
Eger
Ózd
Tiszaújváros
Polgár
M3
M35
Hortobágy National Park
Hortobágy
Tiszafüred
Lake Tisza
Mezőkövesd
Kerecsend
Füzesabony
HEVES
Kékestető (1014m)
Parád
Parádsasvár
Mátraháza
Mátra Hills
Gyöngyös
Heves
Salgótarján
Bátonyterenye
Pásztó
Hollókő
Szécsény
NÓGRÁD
Cserhát Hills
Balassagyarmat
Nógrád
Danube-Ipoly National Park
Börzsöny Hills
Ipoly River
Visegrád
Vác
Göd
Dunakeszi
Fót
Gödöllő
Hatvan
Jászapáti
Jászberény
Nagykáta
Gyömrő
Monor
Vecsés
BUDAPEST
Gyál
Dunaharaszti
Szentendre
Pilis Hills
Pilisvörösvár
Budakeszi
Budaörs
Érd
Szigetszentmiklós
Százhalombatta
Martonvásár
Esztergom
Dorog
Tatabánya
Tata
Bicske
Oroszlány
Komárom
KOMÁROM-ESZTERGOM
Mór
Kisbér
GYŐR
Danube River
Mosonmagyaróvár
Hegyeshalom
Csorna
Kapuvár
Fertőd
GYŐR-MOSON-SOPRON
Pannonhalma
Pápa
Zirc
VESZPRÉM
Várpalota
Veszprém
Herend
Ajka
Bakony Hills
Celldömölk
Rába River
Sárvár
VAS
Sümeg
Tapolca
Badacsony
Balaton Uplands National Park
Hévíz
Keszthely
ZALA
Tihany
Balatonfüred
Lake Balaton
Balatonboglár
Siófok
Polgárdi
Enying
Tamási
SZÉKESFEHÉRVÁR
Gárdony
Lake Velence
FEJÉR
Sárbogárd
Dunaújváros
Dunaföldvár
Sió River
Ráckeve
Kiskunság National Park
Dabas
PEST
Albertirsa
Cegléd
Lajosmizse
KECSKEMÉT
Kiskunfélegyháza
Bugac
Nagykőrös
Abony
Szolnok
Great Plain
Tiszakécske
Tisza River
Csongrád
Kunszentmárton
Tiszaföldvár
Körös-Maros National Park
Szarvas
Körös River
Mezőtúr
Túrkeve
Törökszentmiklós
JÁSZ-NAGYKUN-SZOLNOK
Kisújszállás
Karcag
Püspökladány
Nádudvar
Gyomaendrőd
Szeghalom
BÉKÉS
Mezőberény
Békés
Vésztő
E60
E66
E73
E573
M0
M1
M2
M5
M6
M7

Excursions

A lot in Hungary is within easy striking distance of Budapest, and many of the towns and cities in the Danube Bend (to the north of Budapest), Transdanubia (west), Northern Uplands (north and northeast) and even the Great Plain (east and southeast) could be visited on a day trip from the capital. You can get to Szentendre to the north in less than an hour by the HÉV commuter train, for example, and Eger, a lovely Mediterranean-like town lying between the Bükk and Mátra Hills to the northeast, is just two hours away by InterCity train.

This chapter assumes you'll be returning to Budapest after a day of sightseeing, though we've included a few accommodation options in each section in case you miss your train or bus, or simply decide you like the place so much you want to stay a night or two. For fuller treatment of these and other destinations, see Lonely Planet's *Hungary*.

CASTLES & MANOR HOUSES

Some of Hungary's most dramatic castles and opulent manor houses are near to Budapest. First and foremost, is the hilltop fortress at **Eger** (p175), a castle and a half if there ever was one and the stuff of legend (see the boxed text, p177). The **Royal Mansion** (p171) at Gödöllő is Hungary's largest baroque – and now best preserved – manor house. The **Brunswick Mansion** (p173) at Martonvásár may not be able to compete in size or opulence, but it will give any place a run for its money in terms of the company it has kept.

CATHEDRALS

If you haven't had your fill of grand churches in Budapest, travel the extra distance north to Szentendre, whose **Belgrade Cathedral** (p170) is the seat of the Serbian Orthodox primate in Hungary and contains an important collection of church plate and liturgical objects. Windy Veszprém, set high up on a plateau, has so many fine churches that the locals exclaim, 'Either the wind is blowing or the bells are ringing in Veszprém'. But first and foremost is the **Cathedral of St Michael** (p174) with an important Gothic crypt. The cathedral, is on the site of the first bishop's palace, and parts of it date from the beginning of the 11th century. The enormous **neoclassical cathedral** (p176) at Eger, however, is the most important architecturally and, despite its size and scale, is surprisingly light and airy inside.

WINE

Eger, the birthplace of the famed Bikavér (Bull's Blood wine; see p177), is inextricably linked with wine, and one of the best places in Hungary to sample the fruit of the vine is at the nearby **Valley of the Beautiful Women** (p176). If you're driving towards Eger from Budapest, you might consider leaving Rte 3 at **Gyöngyös** and following the

ORGANISED TOURS

If you're pressed for time or too lazy to do it yourself, a number of travel agencies (p195) and tour operators (p52) organise excursions to destinations outside Budapest. By way of example, a 4½-hour tour by boat and bus to Szentendre or to Gödöllő just by bus with Cityrama costs 11,000Ft (children under 12 free or half price), while an 8½-hour tour of the Danube Bend by coach and boat with stops at Visegrád and Esztergom costs 14,000Ft. Cityrama also offers day trips to Lake Balaton (Balatonfüred and Tihany) and Herend (16,000Ft, nine to 10 hours) as well as to Lajosmizse on the Southern Great Plain (18,000Ft, eight hours). Hungary Program Centrum operates similar tours at almost the same prices, as well as an eight-hour trip to Bugac in Kiskunság National Park (19,000Ft) and a nine-hour tour of the Eger wine region (22,000Ft). Vista has a six-day tour of the country including accommodation and half-board that takes in parts of the Northern Uplands, Great Plain, Southern Transdanubia and Lake Balaton region for €599/499 per person single/double (sharing).

circuitous Rte 24 through the **Mátra Hills** to Parádsasvár and then cutting eastward onto Eger. The region's whites – Rieslings, Leányka and Hárslevelű – are all worth trying. And from Veszprém the **Badacsony region** along the northwestern shore of Lake Balaton, famed for its crisp white Olaszrizling and unique Kéknyelű (Blue Stalk), is within easy driving distance.

SZENTENDRE

Szentendre (St Andrew; population 22,700) is the gateway to the Danube Bend, the S-shaped curve in Hungary's mightiest river that begins just below Esztergom and twists for 20km before reaching the capital. As an art colony turned lucrative tourist centre, Szentendre strikes many as a little too 'cutesy', and the town can be crowded and relatively expensive. Still, it's an easy destination from Budapest, and the many art museums, galleries and Serbian Orthodox churches make the trip well worthwhile. Just try to avoid it on summer weekends.

Right in the centre of **Fő tér**, the colourful heart of Szentendre surrounded by 18th- and 19th-century burghers' houses, stands the **Plague Cross** (Pestis-kereszt), an iron cross decorated with icons on a marble base, erected in 1763 as an ex-votive. Across the square to the northeast is the Serbian Orthodox **Blagoveštenska Church**, built in 1754. The church, with fine baroque and rococo elements, hardly looks 'eastern' from the outside (it was designed by András Mayerhoffer), but once you step inside, the ornate iconostasis and elaborate 18th-century furnishings give it away.

If you descend Görög utca and turn south (right) onto Vastagh György utca, you'll reach the entrance to the **Margit Kovács Ceramic Collection**, Szentendre's biggest draw and one of the few museums here open all year. Kovács (1902–77) was a ceramicist who combined Hungarian folk, religious and modern themes to create elongated, Gothic-like figures. Some of her works are overly sentimental, but many are very powerful, especially the later ones in which she became obsessed with mortality.

Castle Hill (Vár-domb), which can be reached via Váralja lépcső, the narrow set of steps between Fő tér 8 and 9, was the site of a fortress in the Middle Ages, but all that's left of it is the **Parish Church of St John**, from where you can enjoy views of the town. The red spire of **Belgrade Cathedral**, seat of the Serbian Orthodox bishop in Hungary and built in 1764, rises from within a walled courtyard to the north. One of the church outbuildings contains the

TRANSPORT

Distance from Budapest 19km

Direction North

Travel time 40 minutes by HÉV suburban train

Boat From May to August, one daily Mahart ferry plies the Danube to/from Vigadó tér (Map p224) in Pest and Batthyány tér (Map p220) in Buda, departing at 9am and arriving at Szentendre at 10.40am (one way/return 990/1485Ft). The return boat leaves at 5.45pm. The service dwindles to weekends only in April, late September and October. From June to mid-September two extra boats depart from Budapest at 10.30am and 2pm bound for Szentendre, returning at 12.20pm and 5pm (one way 1400Ft); in the last half of May and September only the 10.30am and 5pm services run.

Bus Buses from Pest's Árpád híd station (Map pp226–7), which is on the M3 metro line, run to Szentendre at least once an hour throughout the day (241Ft, 30 minutes).

Car Rte 11 from Buda

HÉV Trains depart from Batthyány tér (Map p224) in Buda (160Ft, 40 minutes) every 10 to 20 minutes throughout the day. Remember that a yellow city bus/metro ticket is good only as far as the Békásmegyer stop on the way; you'll have to pay extra to get to Szentendre. Also, many HÉV trains run only as far as Békásmegyer, where you must cross the platform to board the train for Szentendre. The last train leaves Szentendre for Budapest at 11.10pm.

Serbian Ecclesiastical Art Collection, a treasure-trove of icons, vestments and other sacred objects in precious metals.

The **Hungarian Open-Air Ethnographical Museum**, 3km northwest of the centre and accessible by bus from bay 7 at the station, is Hungary's most ambitious open-air museum. While plans ultimately call for some 300 farmhouses, churches, bell towers, mills and so on to be set up in 10 regional units, so far only five have been built.

Information

Tourinform (☎ 26-317 965; szentendre@tourinform.hu; Dumtsa Jenő utca 22; 🕑 9.30am-4.30pm Mon-Fri year-round, plus 10am-2pm Sat & Sun mid-Mar–Oct)

Sights

Belgrade Cathedral (Belgrád Székesegyház; Alkotmány utca; adult/child incl art collection 300/150Ft; 🕑 10am-6pm Tue-Sun Mar-Oct, 10am-4pm Fri-Sun Jan & Feb)

Blagoveštenska Church (☎ 26-310 554; admission 200Ft; 🕑 10am-5pm Tue-Sun)

Hungarian Open-Air Ethnographical Museum (Magyar Szabadtéri Néprajzi Múzeum; ☎ 26-502 500; Sztaravodai út 1; admission free Tue & Wed, adult/child Thu & Fri 600/400Ft, Sat & Sun 800/400Ft; 🕑 9am-5pm Tue-Sun Apr-Oct)

Margit Kovács Ceramic Collection (Kovács Margit Kerámiagyűjtemény; ☎ 26-310 224; Vastagh György utca 1; adult/child 600/300Ft; 🕑 9am-5pm Mar, 10am-6pm Apr-Oct)

Parish Church of St John (Szent János Plébánlatemplom; Templom tér; 🕑 10am-4pm Tue-Sun Apr-Oct)

Serbian Ecclesiastical Art Collection (Szerb Egyházművészeti Gyűjtemény; ☎ 26-312 399; Pátriárka utca 5; adult/child 400/200Ft; 🕑 10am-6pm Tue-Sun Mar-Oct, 10am-4pm Fri-Sun Jan & Feb)

Eating

Aranysárkány (Golden Dragon; ☎ 26-301 479; Alkotmány 1/a; mains from 2000Ft; 🕑 noon-10pm) This place may sound Chinese but it serves superb Hungarian and Austrian dishes at above-average prices.

Palapa (☎ 26-302 418; Batthyány utca 4; mains 1000-1500Ft; 🕑 5pm-midnight Mon-Fri, noon-midnight Sat & Sun) The food at this colourful Mexican restaurant makes it the perfect place for a change from heavy Hungarian fare.

Promenade (☎ 26-312 626; Futó utca 4; mains 1500-2500Ft; 🕑 noon-midnight) Vaulted ceilings, whitewashed walls and a wonderful terrace overlooking the Danube are all highlights here, one of Szentendre's best restaurants serving Hungarian and international dishes.

Sleeping

Bükkös (☎ 26-312 021; Bükkös part 16; s/d 8500/11,000Ft) This small hotel has a touch of style about it and its 16 rooms are cosy and warm; ask for one overlooking Bükkös Stream.

Centrum (☎ 26-302 500; www.hotelcentrum.hu; Bogdányi utca 15; s/d 9000/10,000Ft) A stone's throw from the Danube, this quaint *pension* occupies a well-renovated house. Its half-dozen rooms are large and bright and filled with antique furniture.

Ilona (☎ 26-313 599; Rákóczi Ferenc utca 11; s/d 5000/6600Ft) Ilona is a perfect little *pension* with plenty going for it – superb central location, locked parking, inner courtyard for breakfast and six small but tidy rooms.

GÖDÖLLŐ

Easily accessible on the HÉV suburban train, Gödöllő (population 32,400), which is roughly pronounced 'good-duh-ler', is an easy day trip from Budapest. The main attraction here is the Royal Mansion completed in the 1760s, which is Hungary's largest baroque manor house. But the town of Gödöllő itself, full of lovely baroque buildings and monuments and home to the seminal Gödöllő Artists' Colony (1901–20), is worth the trip.

The **Royal Mansion**, sometimes called the Grassalkovich Mansion after its commissioner, Count Antal Grassalkovich (1694–1771), confidante of Empress Maria Theresa, was designed by András Mayerhoffer in 1741. After the formation of the Dual Monarchy in 1867, the mansion (or palace) was enlarged as a summer retreat for Emperor Franz Joseph and soon became the favoured residence of his consort, the much beloved Habsburg empress and Hungarian queen, Elizabeth (1837–98), affectionately known as Sissi. Between the two world wars, the regent, Admiral Miklós Horthy, also used it as a summer residence, but after the communists came to power, part of the mansion was used as Soviet barracks, then subsequently as an old people's home and temporary housing. The rest was left to decay.

Partial renovation of the mansion began in 1994, and today there are some 26 rooms that open for public inspection as the Palace Museum on the ground and 1st floors. They have been restored (some would say too heavily) to the period when the imperial couple were in residence, and Franz Joseph's suites (done up in manly greys and golds) and Sissi's lavender-coloured private apartments are impressive. Check out the **Decorative Hall**, all gold tracery and chandeliers, where chamber-music concerts are held year-round but especially in late June and early July during the Palace Concerts Chamber Music Festival; the **Queen's Salon**, with a Romantic-style oil painting of Sissi patriotically repairing the coronation robe of King Stephen with needle and thread; and the **Study Annexe**, with a restored ceiling painting and an 18th-century tapestry of the huntress Diana.

Several other recently opened rooms and buildings can be visited on a guided tour only at extra cost, including the baroque **Palace Theatre** in the southern wing; the **Royal Hill Pavilion** in the park, built in the 1760s; and the **Royal Baths**.

TRANSPORT

Distance from Budapest 27km

Direction Northeast

Travel time 40 minutes by HÉV suburban train

Bus Buses from Stadionok bus station (Map pp218–19) in Pest serve Gödöllő (302Ft, 40 minutes) about every half-hour throughout the day. The last bus back is just after 7.15pm weekdays (shortly after 8pm on Saturday and Sunday).

Car Rte 3 from central Pest

HÉV Trains from Örs vezér tere at the terminus of the M2 metro link Budapest with Gödöllő (326Ft, 40 minutes, half-hourly) throughout the day. Make sure you get off at the Szabadság tér stop, which is the third to last. The last train leaves for Budapest from this stop just before 10.45pm.

Information

Tourinform (☎ 28-415 402; godollo@tourinform.hu; ⏲ 10am-6pm Tue-Sun Apr-Oct, 10am-5pm Tue-Sun Nov-Mar) Just inside the entrance to the Royal Mansion. Has sample menus from restaurants around town.

www.godollotourinform.hu Town website in English.

Sights

Royal Mansion (Királyi Kastély; ☎ 28-410 124; www.kiralyikastely.hu; Szabadság tér 1; adult/child/family 1400/700/2800Ft; ⏲ 10am-6pm Tue-Sun Apr-Oct, 10am-5pm Tue-Sun Nov-Mar) Cultural programmes take place here throughout the year.

The Decorative Hall of the Royal Mansion, Gödöllő

Eating

Kastélykert (☎ 28-527 020; Szabadság tér 4; starters 480-1990Ft, mains 1000-1840Ft; ⏲ noon-11pm) Situated in a lovely old baroque house opposite the mansion, the 'Castle Garden' is an upmarket choice for an evening meal.

Mei Shi Lin (☎ 28-412 658; Kossuth Lajos utca 33; rice & noodle dishes 450-1680Ft, mains 950-2150Ft; ⏲ 11am-10pm Sun-Thu, 11am-11pm Fri & Sat) This pleasant eatery serves surprisingly good Chinese food.

Pizza Palazzo (☎ 28-420 688; Szabadság tér 2; pizza & pasta 750-1250Ft, mains 950-1590Ft; ⏲ 11am-11pm) A popular pizzeria with some more-substantial main courses, conveniently attached to the Szabadság tér HÉV station.

Sleeping

Galéria (☎ /fax 28-418 691; Szabadság tér 8; s/d with shared bathroom 6500/8700Ft, with shower 8500/10,900Ft, with shower & toilet 9800/12,500Ft) This five-room *pension*, which is 300m northeast of the mansion, is in as central a position as you'll find if you are planning to spend the night in Gödöllő. There's a range of options to choose from.

GATE College (☎ 28- 410-200; gatekollegium@freemail.hu; Páter Károly utca 1; dm about 2000Ft) A short distance east of the HÉV terminus, this college at St Stephen University has dormitory accommodation from June to August.

MARTONVÁSÁR

Lying almost exactly halfway between Budapest and the Central Transdanubian city of Székesfehérvár and easily accessible by train, Martonvásár (population 5200) is the site of the former **Brunswick Mansion**, one of the loveliest summertime concert venues in Hungary. The mansion was built in 1775 for Count Antal Brunswick (Magyarised as Brunszvik), the patriarch of a family of liberal reformers and patrons of the arts; his daughter, Teréz, established Hungary's first nursery school in Pest in 1828.

Beethoven was a frequent visitor to the manse, and it is believed that Jozefin, Teréz's sister, was the inspiration for his *Appassionata* and *Moonlight* sonatas, which the great Ludwig composed here.

Brunswick Mansion was rebuilt in neo-Gothic style in 1875 and restored to its ivory and sky-blue glory a century later. It now houses the Agricultural Research Institute of the Hungarian Academy of Sciences, but you can see at least part of the mansion by visiting the small **Beethoven Memorial Museum** to the left of the main entrance.

A walk around the **park grounds** – one of Hungary's first 'English parks' to be laid out when these were all the rage in central Europe in the early 19th century – is a pleasant way to spend a warm summer afternoon. The highlight of the so-called **Martonvásár Days** (Martonvásár Napok) festival in July are the Beethoven Evenings (Beethoven estjei) on Saturday at 7pm, when concerts are held on the small island in the middle of the lake (reached by a wooden footbridge).

The baroque **Catholic church** (1775), attached to the mansion but accessible from outside the grounds, has frescoes by Johannes Cymbal. There's also delightful the **Nursery Museum** in the park, crammed with school-related materials as well as dolls and other toys.

Information

Agricultural Research Institute of the Hungarian Academy of Sciences (www.mgki.hu) Includes some information about the mansion and museums.

Martonvásár Days (www.filharmonikusok.hu)

Sights

Beethoven Memorial Museum (Beethoven Emlékmúzeum; ☎ 22-569 500; adult/child/family 200/100/400Ft; ⏲ 10am-noon & 2-4pm Tue-Fri, 10am-6pm Sat & Sun Apr-Oct, 10am-noon & 2-4pm Tue-Fri, 10am-4pm Sat & Sun Nov-Mar)

Brunswick Mansion (Brunszvik-kastély; Brunszvik út 2)

TRANSPORT

Distance from Budapest 33km

Direction Southwest

Travel time 40 minutes by train

Car Rte 7 from southern Buda

Train Dozens of trains between Déli train station (Map p220) and Kelenföld train station (Map pp228–9) in Buda and Székesfehérvár stop at Martonvásár (326Ft, 40 minutes, every 20 minutes) every day. If you attend a concert in summer, you can easily make your way back to Budapest on the last train, which departs just before 11.30pm.

Nursery Museum (Óvodamúzeum; ☎ 22-569 518; adult/child 250/120Ft; ⌚ 10am-2pm Tue-Fri, 11am-6pm Sat & Sun mid-Mar–mid-Oct, 10am-2pm Tue & Fri, 11am-3pm Sun mid-Oct–mid-Mar)

Park (adult/child/family 200/100/400Ft; ⌚ 8am-6pm May-Oct, 8am-4pm Nov-Apr)

Eating & Sleeping

Macska (☎ 22-460 127; Budai út 21; r per person 3200Ft) A *pension* with six rooms whose name means actually 'Cat' is crawling with felines and is definitely not the place for hyperallergenic travellers. Its on-site **restaurant** (soups 350-580Ft, mains 850-2050Ft; ⌚ noon-10pm Sun & Mon, noon-11pm Tue-Thu, noon-midnight Fri & Sat) serves the standard Hungarian *csárda* (inn) dishes.

Postakocsi (☎ 22-460 013; Fehérvári utca 1; soups & starters 280-880Ft, mains 930-2200Ft; ⌚ 10am-10pm) In the centre of town, this is a convenient place for lunch and has courtyard seating. Expect basic Hungarian fodder.

VESZPRÉM

Spreading over five hills between the northern and southern ranges of the Bakony Hills, Veszprém (population 62,900) has one of the most dramatic locations in Central Transdanubia. The walled castle district atop a plateau, once the favourite residence of Hungary's queens, is now a living museum of baroque art and architecture, and it's a delight to stroll through the Castle Hill district's single street, admiring the embarrassment of fine churches and civic buildings. What's more, Lake Balaton, the nation's playground, is only 13km to the south and Herend, home of Hungary's finest porcelain (p178) is the same distance to the northwest.

As you ascend Castle Hill (Vár-hegy) and its sole street, Vár utca, you'll pass under **Heroes' Gate** (Hősök-kapuja), an entrance built in 1936 from the stones of a 15th-century castle gate. On the left is the **Firewatch Tower**, an architectural hybrid of Gothic, baroque and neoclassical styles, which can be climbed.

The U-shaped **Bishop's Palace**, designed by Jakab Fellner of Tata in the mid-18th century, is where the queens' residence stood in the Middle Ages. It faces Szentháromság tér, named for the **Trinity Column** (1751) in the centre.

Next to the Bishop's Palace is the early Gothic **Gizella Chapel**, named after the wife of King Stephen, who was crowned near here early in the 11th century. Inside the chapel are some Byzantine-influenced 13th-century frescoes of the Apostles. The **Queen Gizella Museum** of religious art is opposite.

The **cathedral**, dedicated to St Michael, is on the site of the first bishop's palace. Parts of it date from the beginning of the 11th century, but the cathedral has been rebuilt many times since then. The early Gothic crypt is original, though. Beside the cathedral, the octagonal foundation of the 13th-century **Chapel of St George** sits under a glass dome.

From the rampart known as **World's End** at the end of Vár utca, you can gaze north to craggy Benedict Hill (Benedek-hegy) and the Séd Stream and west to the concrete viaduct (now St Stephen's Valley Bridge) over the Betekints Valley. Below you to the north, in Margit tér, are the ruins of the medieval **Dominican Convent of St Catherine** and to the west what little remains of the 11th-century **Veszprém Valley Convent**, whose erstwhile cloistered residents are said to have stitched Stephen's crimson silk coronation robe early in the 11th century. The **statues of King Stephen and Queen Gizella** at World's End were erected in 1938 to mark the 900th anniversary of Stephen's death.

TRANSPORT

Distance from Budapest 112km

Direction Southwest

Travel time Two hours by train

Bus Connections with Budapest (1450Ft, 2¼ hours) are excellent, with between half-hourly and hourly departures.

Car Rte M7 to Székesfehérvár and Rte 8 to Veszprém

Train Three lines meet at Veszprém. Some seven trains a day link Budapest with Veszprém (1212Ft, two hours) via Székesfehérvár.

Information

Tourinform (☎ 88-404 548; veszprem@tourinform.hu; Vár utca 4; ⌚ 9am-6pm Mon-Fri, 10am-4pm Sat, 10am-4pm Sun Jun-Aug, 9am-5pm Mon-Fri Sep-May)

www.veszprem.net Useful town website partly in English.

Sights

Bishop's Palace (Püspöki Palota; ☎ 88-426 088; Vár utca 16; adult/child 500/250Ft; 🕑 10am-6pm May-Aug, 10am-5pm Tue-Sun Sep–mid-Oct)

Cathedral (Székesegyház; ☎ 88-328 038; Vár utca 18-20; 🕑 10am-6pm May-Aug, 10am-5pm Sep–mid-Oct)

Chapel of St George (Szent György Kápolna; ☎ 88-426 088; adult/child 100/70Ft; 🕑 10am-6pm May-Aug, 10am-5pm Tue-Sun Sep–mid-Oct)

Firewatch Tower (tűztorony; ☎ 88-425 204; Vár utca 9; adult/child 300/200Ft; 🕑 10am-6pm May-Oct, 10am-5pm mid-Mar–Apr)

Gizella Chapel (Gizella kápolna; ☎ 88-426 088; Vár utca 18; adult/child 100/70Ft; 🕑 10am-6pm May-Aug, 10am-5pm Tue-Sun Sep–mid-Oct)

Queen Gizella Museum (Gizella Királyné Múzeum; ☎ 88-426 088; Vár utca 35; adult/child 300/150Ft; 🕑 10am-6pm May-Aug, 10am-5pm Sep–mid-Oct)

Eating

Café Piazza (☎ 88-444 445; Óváros tér 4; pizzas 800Ft; 🕑 8.30am-10pm) A simple Veszprém pizzeria with big pies as well as seating on the square to enjoy the summer weather.

Elefánt Bisztró (☎ 88-329 695; Óváros tér 6; mains from 1000Ft) From steaks to salads, Elefánt has a go at most Hungarian dishes and has outdoor seating.

Óváros (☎ 88-326 790; Szabadság tér 14; mains from 6500Ft; 8am-midnight Jun-Aug, 10am-10pm Sep-May) This restaurant attracts diners throughout the day with its baroque setting, an extensive menu including fish dishes, and reliable cuisine.

Sleeping

Oliva (☎ 88-403 875; www.oliva.hu; Buhim utca 14-16; s/d 13,800/15,400Ft) This exquisite 11-room *pension* has stylish and modern rooms with enough space to be comfortable and is only a short stroll to the Castle Hill district.

Péter Pál (☎ 88-567 790; info@peterpal.hu; Dózsa György utca 3; s/d 6600/8900Ft) Only a short walk to the centre of town, Péter Pál is another fine choice with 14 simple yet stylish rooms, a pleasant garden, above an average restaurant. The staff are very friendly and helpful to guests.

EGER

Everyone loves Eger (population 58,300), and it's immediately apparent why: the beautifully preserved baroque architecture gives the town a relaxed, almost Mediterranean, feel; it is the home of the celebrated Egri Bikavér (Eger Bull's Blood) wine, known the world over; and it is flanked by two of the Northern Uplands' most beautiful ranges of hills. Hungarians visit Eger for those reasons and more, for it was here that István Dobó and his troops fended off the Turks for the first time during the 170 years of occupation in 1552 (p177).

The best overview of the city can be had by climbing up the cobblestone lane from Dózsa György tér to **Eger Castle**, which was erected in the 13th century after the Mongol invasion. Much of the castle is of modern construction, but you can still see the foundations of 12th-century **St John's Cathedral**. Models and drawings in the **István Dobó Museum**, housed in the former Bishop's Palace (1470) in the castle grounds, show how it once looked. On the ground floor, a statue of Dobó takes pride of place in **Heroes' Hall**. The 19th-century building on the northwestern side of the courtyard houses the **Eger Art Gallery**, with several works by Mihály Munkácsy.

Beneath the castle are **casemates** hewn from solid rock, which you are able to tour with a Hungarian-speaking guide included in the admission fee (English-language guide 600Ft extra). Other exhibits, including the **Waxworks** and **Minting Exhibit** cost extra. You can still tour the castle grounds on Monday, when all the other exhibits are closed.

TRANSPORT

Distance from Budapest 128km

Direction Northeast

Travel time Two hours by direct train

Bus Buses link Eger with Budapest (1570Ft, 2¼ hours) hourly via the high-speed M3.

Car Rte 3 from central Pest to Kerecsend and then Rte 25 to Eger

Train Eger is on a minor line linking Putnok and Füzesabony; you usually have to change at the latter for Budapest (1624Ft). There are up to seven direct trains a day to and from Budapest's Keleti train station (Map pp218–19) that do not require a change (two hours).

Back in town, you can begin a walking tour of the city at **Eger Cathedral**, a neoclassical monolith designed in 1836 by József Hild. Despite the cathedral's size and ornate altars, the interior is surprisingly light and airy.

Directly opposite the cathedral is the sprawling Zopf-style **Lyceum** dating from 1765. The 20,000-volume **library** on the 1st floor of the south wing contains hundreds of priceless manuscripts and codices. The **ceiling fresco** (1778) here is a *trompe l'œil* masterpiece depicting the Counter-Reformation's Council of Trent (1545–63) and a lightning bolt setting heretical manuscripts ablaze. The **Astronomy Museum** on the 6th floor of the east wing contains 18th-century astronomical equipment and an **observatory**; climb three more floors up to the observation deck for a great view of the city and to try out the **camera obscura**, the 'eye of Eger', designed in 1776 to spy on the town and to entertain townspeople.

On the southern side of central Dobó István tér stands the **Minorite church**, built in 1771 and one of the most glorious baroque buildings in the world. The altarpiece of the Virgin Mary and St Anthony of Padua was completed by Johann Kracker, the Bohemian painter who also did the fire-and-brimstone ceiling fresco in the Lyceum library. Statues of István Dobó and his comrades-in-arms routing the Turks in 1552 fill the square in front of the church.

To the north of the square is the 40m-high **minaret** topped with a cross. Only non-claustrophobes will want to brave the 97 narrow spiral steps to the top. To the south of Dobó István tér is Kossuth Lajos utca, a tree-lined street with dozens of architectural gems. The former **Orthodox synagogue**, built in 1893, is now a furniture store backing onto a shopping mall. (A **neoclassical synagogue** dating from 1845 and now partly renovated is around the corner at Dr Hibay Károly utca 7.) You'll pass several baroque and Eclectic buildings, including the **county hall**, with a wrought-iron grid above the main door of Faith, Hope and Charity by Henrik Fazola, a Rhinelander who settled in Eger in the mid-18th century. Walk down the passageway, and you'll see more of his magnificent work – two baroque wrought-iron gates. The one on the right shows the seal of Heves County and has a comical figure on its handle. The more graceful gate on the left is decorated with grapes. The wrought-iron balcony and window grilles of the rococo **Provost's Palace** were also done by Fazola.

Don't miss visiting the wine cellars of the evocatively named **Valley of the Beautiful Women** (Szépasszony-völgy), which is southwest of the centre. From the western end of the cath-

Steps of neoclassical Eger Cathedral

edral, walk south along Trinitárius utca to Bartók Béla tér and then west down Király utca to Szépasszony-völgy utca. Veer to the left as you descend the hill, passing the large Talizmán restaurant, and head into the valley, where you'll find dozens of cellars. Alternatively take the **mini train** from Dobó István tér to the valley's entrance in season.

This is the place to sample Bull's Blood – one of very few reds produced in Eger – or any of the whites: Leányka, Olaszrizling and Hárslevelű from nearby Debrő. The choice of wine cellars can be a bit daunting and their characters can change, so walk around and have a look yourself. Nos 16, 17, 29 and 48 are always popular; for schmaltzy Gypsy music, try No 32 or 42. But if you're interested in good wine, visit cellars Nos 5, 18 and 31. Be careful though; those 100mL glasses (50Ft to 80Ft) go down easily. Hours are erratic, but a few cellars are sure to be open till the early evening. The taxi fare back to Eger centre is about 1000Ft.

THE SIEGE OF EGER

The story of the Turkish attempt to take Eger Castle is the stuff of legend. Under the command of István Dobó, a mixed bag of 2000 soldiers held out against more than 100,000 Turks for a month in 1552. As every Hungarian kid in short trousers can tell you, the women of Eger played a crucial role in the battle, pouring boiling oil and pitch on the invaders from the ramparts. A painting by Bertalan Székely called *The Women of Eger* in the castle's art gallery pays tribute to these brave ladies.

Also significant was Eger's wine. If we're to believe the tale, Dobó sustained his soldiers with the ruby-red vintage. When they fought on with increased vigour – and stained beards – rumours began to circulate among the Turks that the defenders were gaining strength by drinking the blood of bulls. Thus was born the name – and brand – Bikavér (Bull's Blood).

Géza Gárdonyi's *Eclipse of the Crescent Moon* (1901), which describes the siege and is required reading for many young Hungarians, can be found in English translation (Corvina) in the bookshops of Budapest.

Information

Tourinform (☎ 36-517 715; eger@tourinform.hu; Bajcsy-Zsilinszky utca 9; 🕑 9am-5pm Mon-Fri, 9am-1pm Sat & Sun mid-Jun–mid-Sep, 9am-5pm Mon-Fri, 9am-1pm Sat mid-Sep–mid-Jun) Ask for the useful *Insight to Eger* magazine available in a number of languages.

Sights

Astronomy Museum (adult/student 500/350Ft)

Casemates (🕑 9am-5pm)

County hall (megyeháza; Kossuth Lajos utca 9)

Eger Castle (Egri Vár; ☎ 36-312 744; www.div.iif.hu; Vár 1; adult/child castle & grounds 1000/500Ft, grounds only 400/200Ft, underground passageways 300Ft; 🕑 8am-8pm Tue-Sun Apr-Aug, 8am-7pm Tue-Sun Sep, 8am-6pm Tue-Sun Oct & Mar, 8am-5pm Tue-Sun Nov-Feb)

Eger Cathedral (Egri Főszékesegyház; Pyrker János tér 1; 🕑 9am-7pm Mon-Sat, 1-5pm Sun)

István Dobó Museum (🕑 9am-5pm Tue-Sun Apr-Oct, 9am-3pm Tue-Sun Nov-Mar)

Lyceum (Líceum; ☎ 36-520 400; Eszterházy tér 1; library adult/student 500/350Ft; 🕑 9.30am-3.30pm Tue-Sun Apr-Sep, 9.30am-1pm Sat & Sun Oct-Mar)

Minaret (🕑 36-410 233; Knézich Károly utca; admission 200Ft; 🕑 9am-6pm Apr-Oct)

Mini train (one way 450Ft; 🕑 10am-6pm Apr-Oct)

Minorite church (Minorita templom; ☎ 36-312 744; Dobó István tér 6; 🕑 9am-5pm Tue-Sun)

Minting Exhibit (adult/child 240/120Ft)

Orthodox synagogue (Ortodox zsinagóga; Kossuth Lajos utca 17)

Provost's Palace (Kispréposti palota; Kossuth Lajos utca 4)

Waxworks (adult/child 350/250Ft)

Eating

Elefanto (☎ 36-411 031; Katona István tér 2; mains 1000-2000Ft; 🕑 noon-midnight) Perched high above the market, this is a great place, with a nonsmoking interior and covered balcony for alfresco dining when the weather's right.

Palatscintavár (☎ 36-413 986; Dobó utca 9; mains around 1200Ft) This restaurant sports a contemporary art theme and a veg-heavy menu. *Palacsinta* (Hungarian-style pancakes) are served with an abundance of fresh vegetables and range in flavour from Asian to Italian and back again.

Szántófer (☎ 36-517 298; Bródy utca 3; mains around 1000Ft; 🕑 8am-10pm) With farming equipment and cooking utensils hanging from its walls and hearty peasant cuisine filling its menu, Szántófer oozes a rural-rustic atmosphere.

HEREND PORCELAIN

Herend porcelain is among the finest of all goods produced in Hungary and makes a wonderful gift or memento. The stuff also has a long and fascinating pedigree.

A terracotta factory was set up in Herend (population 3330) in 1826 and began producing porcelain 13 years later under Mór Farkasházi Fischer. Initially it specialised in copying and replacing the nobles' broken chinaware settings imported from Asia, and you'll see some pretty kooky 19th-century interpretations of Japanese art and Chinese faces on display at the **Porcelánium** (☎ 523 262; www.porcelanium.com; Kossuth Lajos utca 140; adult/child/family 1500/500/3100Ft; ⏲ 9am-5.30pm Apr-Oct daily, 9am-4.30pm Tue-Sat Nov-Mar), a museum that displays the most prized pieces of the rich Herend collection and a mini-factory where you can witness first-hand how ugly clumps of clay become delicate porcelain.

The factory soon began producing its own patterns; many, like the Rothschild bird and petites roses, were inspired by Meissen and Sèvres designs from Germany and France. The popular Victoria pattern of butterflies and wild flowers was designed for Queen Victoria after she admired a display of Herend pieces at the Great Exhibition in London in 1851.

To avoid bankruptcy in the 1870s, the Herend factory began mass production; tastes ran from kitschy pastoral and hunting scenes to the animal figurines with the distinctive scalelike triangle patterns still popular today. In 1993, 75% of the factory was purchased by its 1500 workers and became one of the first companies in Hungary privatised through an employee stock-ownership plan. The state owns the other 25%.

From Veszprém there is a bus to Herend at least every 30 minutes (203Ft, 20 minutes).

Sleeping

Minaret (☎ 36-410 233; Knézich Károly utca 4; s/d €35/45) In the shadow of the minaret is this family-run hotel, with 42 good-sized rooms, a fine restaurant and a central location.

Romantik (☎ 36-310 456; www.romantikhotel.hu; Csíky Sándor utca 26; s/d 12,000/15,500Ft) This very friendly and homey hotel with a dozen rooms and a pretty back garden is an easy walk to the centre of town but far enough away to escape any noise in summer.

Senator Ház (☎ 36-320 466; www.senatorhaz.hu; Dobó István tér 11; s/d €52/72) Arguably the finest small hotel in provincial Hungary, 'Senator House' has 11 warm and cosy rooms on the upper two floors of this delightful 18th-century inn on Eger's main square. Its ground floor is shared between a quality restaurant and a reception that could easily moonlight as a history museum.

Directory

Directory

TRANSPORT

AIR

Budapest can be reached directly from destinations around the world, including the USA, but its most important gateways are in Continental Europe, especially now that what Hungarians call the *fapados* (wooden bench) airlines – the super discount carriers such as **Air Berlin** (www.airberlin.com), **EasyJet** (www.easyjet.com), **SkyEurope** (www.skyeurope.com) and **Wizzair** (www.wizzair.com) – have arrived, bringing the cost of flying between Budapest and dozens of European cities to a level that fits most travellers' budget. Fares vary greatly depending on the destination, availability and the time of the flight.

Note that there are no scheduled flights within Hungary.

Airlines

National carrier, **Malév Hungarian Airlines** (MA; ☎ in Hungary 06-40 212 121, from abroad 36-1 235 3888; www.malev.hu), flies nonstop or to Budapest via Prague, Madrid or Amsterdam from North America, the Middle East and almost 60 cities in continental Europe and the UK. It also flies to/from Beijing, Shanghai and Guangzhou in China.

The main **Malév Customer Service Centre** (Map pp218–19; ☎ 235 3222; www.malev.hu; XIII Váci út 26; 🕒 8.30am-7pm Mon-Fri, 10am-6pm Sat & Sun; Ⓜ M3 Nyugati pályaudvar) is just northwest of Nyugati train station. Malév also has ticket-issuing desks at Ferihegy airport (right).

Other major carriers serving Budapest:

Aeroflot (SU; ☎ 318 5955; www.aeroflot.com; hub Moscow)

Air Canada (AC; ☎ 266 8435; www.aircanada.com; hub Toronto)

Air France (AF; ☎ 483 8800; www.airfrance.com; hub Paris)

Alitalia (AZ; ☎ 483 2170; www.alitalia.it; hub Rome)

Austrian Airlines (OS; ☎ 327 9080; www.aua.com; hub Vienna)

British Airways (BA; ☎ 411 5555; www.ba.com; hub London)

CSA Czech Airlines (OK; ☎ 318 3045; www.czech-airlines.com; hub Prague)

El Al (LY; ☎ 266 2970; www.elal.com; hub Tel Aviv)

EgyptAir (MS; ☎ 266 4300; www.egyptair.com.eg; hub Cairo)

Finnair (AY; ☎ 317 4022; www.finnair.com; hub Helsinki)

KLM Royal Dutch Airlines (KL; ☎ 373 7737; www.klm.com; hub Amsterdam)

LOT Polish Airlines (LO; ☎ 317 2444; www.lot.com; hub Warsaw)

Lufthansa (LH; ☎ 266 4511; www.lufthansa.com; hub Frankfurt)

SAS (SK; ☎ 266 2633; www.scandinavian.net; hub Copenhagen)

Tarom Romanian Airlines (RO; ☎ 235 0809; www.tarom.ro; hub Bucharest)

Turkish Airlines (TK; ☎ 266 4291; www.turkishairlines.com; hub Istanbul)

Airports

Budapest's **Ferihegy International Airport** (☎ 296 7000; www.bud.hu), 24km southeast of the city centre, has two modern terminals side by side and an older one about 5km to the west.

Malév flights and, for the most part, those of its 18 or so code-share partners arrive and depart from Terminal 2A. Most other

WARNING

The information in this section is particularly vulnerable to change: prices for international travel are volatile, routes are introduced and cancelled, schedules change, special deals come and go, and rules and visa requirements are amended. In addition, the travel industry is highly competitive and there are many lurks and perks.

Get opinions, quotes and advice from as many airlines and travel agents as possible before you part with your hard-earned cash, and double-check you understand how a fare (and any ticket you may buy) works. The details given in this chapter should be regarded as pointers and are not a substitute for your own careful, up-to-date research into the current situation.

international airlines use Terminal 2B, which is next door and within easy walking distance. Malév has a ticketing desk at **Terminal 2A** (☎ 296 7211; 🕑 5am-11pm) and another one at **Terminal 2B** (☎ 296 5767; 🕑 6am-8.30pm); at the latter you'll also find a **left-luggage office** (per item per 1/3/6hr 350/1050/1400Ft, per day/week 2200/6500Ft; 🕑 24hr). The super-discount European carriers, recent arrivals to Budapest, now use the refurbished Terminal 1.

The **Airport Minibus Service** (☎ 296 8555; minibus@bud.hu; one way/return 2300/3900Ft) ferries passengers in eight-seater vans from all three of the airport's terminals directly to their hotel, hostel or residence. Tickets are available at a clearly marked desk in the arrival halls. You need to book your journey to the airport 24 hours in advance but remember that, with up to seven pick-ups en route, this can be a nerve-wracking way to go if you're running late.

If you want to take a taxi, call one of the companies listed on p185 with a mobile or from a public phone at arrivals (dispatchers understand English) and expect to pay about 5000Ft. If you book in advance, **Tele 5** (☎ 355 5555) charges 3490Ft between the airport and Pest and 3990Ft for Buda. Its taxis are just down the road, awaiting your call.

The cheapest – but most time-consuming – way to get into town from Ferihegy is to take the airport bus (look for the stop marked 'BKV Plusz Reptér Busz' on the pavement between terminals 2A and 2B), which terminates at the Kőbánya-Kispest metro station. From there take the M3 metro into the centre. The total cost is 320Ft.

BICYCLE

More and more cyclists are seen on the streets and avenues of Budapest these days, taking advantage of the growing network of bike paths. The main roads in the city might be a bit too busy and nerve-wracking to make for enjoyable cycling but the side streets are fine, and there are some areas (City Park, Margaret Island etc) where cycling is positively ideal. See p138 for ideas on where to cycle, and information on where to rent bikes.

Cyclists may have problems crossing Hungarian border stations connected to main roads since bicycles are banned on motorways and national highways with single-digit route numbers. In general, border crossings

> **BOOKINGS ONLINE**
>
> Flights, tours and train tickets can be booked online at www.lonelyplanet.com/travel_services.

that allow pedestrian crossings also allow cyclists through.

BOAT

Local

Between May and mid-September passenger ferries run by **BKV** (☎ 369 1359; www.bkv.hu) depart from IX Boráros tér (Map pp228–9) beside Petőfi Bridge between six and eight times daily and head for III Rómaifürdő and Csillaghegy in Óbuda, a two-hour trip with 10 stops along the way. Tickets (adult/child 600/300Ft from end to end or between 500/250Ft and 200/150Ft for intermediate stops) are sold on board. The ferry stop closest to the Castle District is I Batthyány tér, and V Petőfi tér is not far from Vörösmarty tér. Transporting a bicycle costs 500Ft.

International

A hydrofoil service on the Danube between Budapest and Vienna (5½ to 6½ hours, 282km) operates daily from early April to October and allows passengers to disembark at Bratislava with advance notice. One-way/return adult fares for Vienna are €79/99 and for Bratislava €69/89. Students with ISIC cards pay €67/84 to Vienna and €59/76 to Bratislava and children under six go free. Taking along a bicycle costs €18 each way.

In Budapest, ferries arrive and depart from the **International Ferry Pier** (Nemzetközi hajóállomás; Map p224; V Belgrád rakpart), which is between Elizabeth and Independence Bridges on the Pest side. In Vienna, the boat docks at the Reichsbrücke pier near Mexikoplatz.

In April and from mid-September to October there is a daily sailing at 9am from both Budapest and Vienna. From May to mid-September the boats leave both of these cities at 8am.

For information, tickets and reservations contact **Mahart PassNave** (Map p224; ☎ 484 4013; www.mahartpassnave.hu; V Belgrád rakpart; 🕑 8am-6pm).

GETTING AROUND TOWN

Budapest has an ageing but safe, efficient and inexpensive public transport system that will never have you waiting more than five or 10 minutes for any conveyance. There are five types of vehicles in general use: metro trains on three city lines; green HÉV trains on four suburban lines; blue buses; yellow trams and red trolleybuses. All are run by **BKV** (Budapest Transport Company; ☎ 342 2335, 06-80 406 688; www.bkv.hu).

Anyone planning to travel extensively by public transport in Budapest should buy a copy of the invaluable *Budapesti Közlekedési Hálózata Térképe* (Budapest Transport Network Map; 380Ft) available at most metro ticket booths.

Daytime public transport in Budapest runs from about 4am to between 9pm and 11.30pm, depending on the line. From 11.30pm to 4am some 30 night buses (always with three digits and beginning with '9') operate every 10 to 60 minutes, again depending on the line.

Fares & Travel Passes

To ride the metro, trams, trolleybuses, buses and the HÉV (as far as the city limits, which is the Békásmegyer stop north of Óbuda) you must have a valid ticket, which you can buy at kiosks, newsstands or metro entrances. Children up to the age of six travel free when accompanied by an adult. Bicycles can only be transported on the HÉV, all Mahart boats and on the Cog and Children's Railways.

The basic fare for all forms of transport is 185Ft (1665/3145Ft for a block of 10/20 tickets), allowing you to travel as far as you like on the same metro, bus, trolleybus or tram line without changing. A ticket allowing unlimited stations with one change within 1½ hours costs 320Ft.

On the metro exclusively, the base fare drops to 130Ft if you are just going three stops within 30 minutes. For 200Ft you can travel five stops and transfer at Deák Ferenc tér to one of the other two metro lines within one hour. Unlimited stations travelled with one change within one hour costs 300Ft.

You must always travel in one continuous direction on any ticket; return trips are not allowed. Tickets have to be validated in machines at metro entrances and aboard other vehicles – inspectors will fine you for not validating your ticket.

Life will most likely be much simpler if you buy a travel pass. Passes are valid on all trams, buses, trolleybuses, HÉV (within the city limits) and metro lines, and you don't have to worry about validating your ticket each time you get on. The most central places to buy them are ticket offices at the Deák Ferenc tér metro station (Map p224), the Nyugati pályaudvar metro station (Map p222) and the Déli pályaudvar metro station (Map p220), all of which are open from 6am to 8pm daily.

A one-day pass is poor value at 1150Ft, but the three-day pass (*touristajegy,* or tourist ticket) for 2500Ft and seven-day pass (*hetijegy,* or one week) for 3400Ft are worthwhile for most people. You'll need a photo for the fortnightly/monthly passes (4500/6900Ft). All but the monthly travel passes are valid from midnight to midnight, so buy them in advance and specify the date(s) you want.

Travelling 'black' (ie without a valid ticket or pass) is risky; with increased surveillance (especially in the metro), there's an excellent chance you'll get caught. (NB: Tickets are *always* checked by a conductor on the HÉV.) The on-the-spot fine is 2500Ft, which rises to 7000Ft if you pay at the **BKV office** (Map p222; ☎ 461 6800; VII Akácfa utca 22; 6am-8pm Mon-Fri, 8am-1.45pm Sat; M2 Blaha Lujza tér) up to 30 days later and 14,000Ft after that.

BUS

Local

An extensive system of almost 200 buses serves greater Budapest. On certain bus lines the same number bus may have a black or a red number. In such cases, the red-numbered one is an express, which makes limited stops and is, of course, faster.

Some buses (always shown with a blue line on a Budapest map or atlas) that you might find useful include the following:

4 – Runs from northern Pest via VI Hősök tere to V Deák Ferenc tér (the red 4 follows the same route but crosses over Chain Bridge into central Buda).

7 – Cuts across a large swathe of central Pest from XIV Bosnyák tér and down VII Rákóczi út before crossing Elizabeth Bridge to Kelenföld train station in southern Buda (the red-numbered 7 follows the same route with limited stops).

86 – Runs the length of Buda from XI Kosztolányi Dezső tér to Óbuda.

105 – Goes from V Deák Ferenc tér to XII Apor Vilmos tér in central Buda.

Night bus 906 – Follows tram 6's route along the Big Ring Road.

Night bus 907 – Traces an enormously long route from the M2 Örs vezér tere metro stop in Pest to Kelenföld train station in Buda.

Long-Distance & International

All international buses and some domestic ones (especially to/from north and north-central Hungary) arrive at and depart from Pest's **Népliget bus station** (Map pp228–9; ☎ 219 8000; IX Üllői út 131; Ⓜ M3 Népliget). The **international ticket office** (⏰ 6am-6pm Mon-Fri Sep-May, 6pm-8pm Mon-Fri Jun-Aug, 6am-4pm Sat & Sun) is upstairs. **Eurolines** (☎ 219 8021; www.eurolines.com), an association of more than 30 European bus companies that link Budapest with points abroad as close as Bratislava and as far as London, is represented here as is its Hungarian associate, **Volánbusz** (☎ 382 0888; www.volanbusz.hu). There's a **left-luggage office** (per piece per day 190Ft; ⏰ 6am-9pm) downstairs.

Stadionok bus station (Map pp218–19; ☎ 251 0125; XIV Hungária körút 48-52; Ⓜ M3 Stadionok) serves cities and towns to the east of Budapest. The **ticket office** (⏰ 6am-6pm Mon-Fri, 6am-4pm Sat & Sun) as well as the **left-luggage office** (per piece 200Ft; ⏰ 6am-7pm) are on the ground floor. Buses to southwest Hungary use **Etele tér bus station** (Map pp228–9; ☎ 382 4900; XI Etele tér; ⏰ 6am-6pm; 🚌 red-numbered 7) in Buda.

The **Árpád Bridge bus station** (Map pp226–7; ☎ 329 1450; XIII Róbert Károly körút; ⏰ ticket office 6am-8pm; Ⓜ M3 Árpád híd), on the Pest side of Árpád Bridge, is the place to catch buses for the Danube Bend and parts of northern Hungary. The small **Széna tér bus station** (Map pp218–19; ☎ 201 3688; I Széna tér 1/a; ⏰ ticket office 6.30am-4.30pm; Ⓜ M3 Moszkva tér) in Buda handles some traffic to and from the Pilis Hills and towns northwest of the capital, with a half-dozen departures to Esztergom as an alternative to the Árpád Bridge bus station.

CAR & MOTORCYCLE

Driving in Budapest, especially during the daytime, can be a nightmare: ongoing road works reduce traffic to a snail's pace, there are more serious accidents than fender-benders, and parking spots are difficult to find. The public-transport system is good and cheap. Try to use it.

Foreign driving licences are valid for one year after entering Hungary but if you don't hold a European driving licence, obtain an International Driving Permit (IDP) from your local automobile association before you leave. It is usually inexpensive and valid for one year only. Remember that an IDP is not valid unless accompanied by your original driver's licence.

Third-party liability insurance is compulsory in Hungary. If your car is registered in the EU, it is assumed you have it. Other motorists must show a Green Card or they will have to buy insurance at the border.

Hire

In general, you must be at least 21 years old and have had your licence for at least a year to rent a car. Drivers under 25 sometimes have to pay a surcharge.

All the international car-rental firms have offices in Budapest but don't expect many bargains. An Opel Corsa from **Avis** (Map p224; ☎ 318 4158; www.avis.hu in Hungarian; V Szervita tér 8; ⏰ 9am-6pm Mon-Fri, 9am-3pm Sat; Ⓜ 1/2/3 Deák Ferenc tér), for example, costs €33/198 per day/week plus €0.33 per kilometre and €23 CDW and theft protection insurance. The same car with unlimited kilometres and insurance costs from €99 per day or €88 per weekend. The 25% ÁFA (value-added tax) doesn't apply to nonresidents paying with foreign currency or by credit card.

One of the cheapest, most reliable outfits for car hire is **Anselport** (☎ 362 6080, 06-20 945 0279; www.anselport.hu; XXII V utca 22; ⏰ 9am-6pm; 🚌 14 or 114) in south Buda. A Suzuki Swift is €19 to €43 per day, including unlimited kilometres and insurance, depending on the length of rental (one day to three weeks). Another good bet is **Fox Autorent** (☎ 382 9000; www.fox-autorent.com; XXII Nagytétényi út 48-50; ⏰ 8am-8pm; 🚌 3, 14 or 114), which charges from €46/230 per day/week for a Fiat Seicento, €55/320 for a Smart car and €59/349 for a Fiat Punto, kilometres and insurance included.

Parking

Parking on the street in Budapest currently costs between 120Ft and 400Ft between 8am and 6pm Monday to Friday and 8am and noon Saturday. There are 24-hour covered car parks charging up to 500/5000Ft per hour/day at V Váci utca 25 (below the Millennium shopping centre; Map p224); V Szervita tér 8 (Map p224); V Aranykéz utca 4-6 (Map p224) in the Inner Town; and at VII Nyár utca 20 (Map p222).

Illegally parked cars are not normally towed in Budapest these days but 'booted'. If you are trying to trace a vehicle you believe has been towed, ring ☎ 383 0700 or ☎ 383 0770. To have a boot removed, which is going to cost you 15,000Ft, ring the telephone number on the sticker placed on the windscreen or ☎ 313 0810.

Road Rules

You must drive on the right. Speed limits for cars and motorcycles are consistent across the country and strictly enforced: 50km/h in built-up areas (from the town sign as you enter to the same sign with a red line through it as you leave); 90km/h on secondary and tertiary roads; 110km/h on most highways/dual carriageways; and 130km/h on motorways. Exceeding the limit will earn a fine of between 5000Ft and 30,000Ft, to be paid by postal cheque or at post offices.

The use of seat belts in the front (and in the back – if fitted – outside built-up areas) is compulsory in Hungary, but this rule is often ignored. Motorcyclists must wear helmets, a law strictly enforced. Another law taken very seriously indeed is the one requiring all drivers to use their headlights throughout the day outside built-up areas. Motorcycles must illuminate headlights at all times everywhere. Using a mobile phone while driving is prohibited in Hungary but this law is universally ignored.

There is virtually a 100% ban on alcohol when driving – this is very strictly enforced. It's not much fun while on holiday, but you'll have to follow the lead of Hungarians and take turns with a companion in abstaining at meals and other times. If you are found to have even 0.001% of alcohol in the blood, you'll be fined up to 30,000Ft on the spot. If the level is high, you will be arrested and your licence almost certainly taken away. In the event of an accident, the drinking party is automatically regarded as guilty.

Assistance and/or advice for motorists is available from the **Hungarian Automobile Club** (Magyar Autóklub; Map pp218–19; ☎ 212 2821, 24hr helpline ☎ 345 1755; II Rómer Flóris utca 4/a; 🚊 4 or 6) off Margit körút near Margaret Bridge. Motorists anywhere in Hungary can call the automobile club on ☎ 188 for assistance.

For information on traffic and public road conditions in the capital ring **Főinform** (☎ 317 1173).

METRO & HÉV

Budapest has three underground metro lines that converge (only) at V Deák Ferenc tér: the little yellow (or Millennium) line designated M1 that runs from Vörösmarty tér to Mexikói út in Pest; the red M2 line from Déli train station in Buda to Örs vezér tere in Pest; and the blue M3 line from Újpest-Központ to Kőbánya-Kispest in Pest. A possible source of confusion on the M1 is that one station is called Vörösmarty tér and another, five stops later, is Vörösmarty utca.

The HÉV suburban train line, which runs on four lines (north from Batthyány tér in Buda via Óbuda and Aquincum to Szentendre, south to both Csepel and Ráckeve and east to Gödöllő), is almost like an additional above-ground metro line.

The metro is the fastest – but obviously the least scenic – way to go. All three lines run from 4.30am and begin their last journey at 11.10pm. See the boxed text on page p182 for fares and passes.

TAXI

Taxis in Budapest are not expensive compared to other European countries, but with such an excellent public transport network available, you don't really have to use them very often. We've heard from many readers who were grossly overcharged and even threatened by taxi drivers in Budapest, so taking a taxi in this city should be approached with a certain amount of caution. However, the reputable firms listed here have caught on to the concept of customer service, and they take complaints very seriously nowadays.

Avoid taxis with no name on the door and only a removable taxi light-box on the roof; these are just guys with cars and the ones most likely to rip you off. Never get into a cab that does not have a yellow licence plate and an identification badge displayed on the dashboard (as required by law), the logo of one of the reputable taxi firms listed here on the side doors, and a table of fares posted prominently.

Not all taxi meters are set at the same rates, and some are much more expensive than others, but there are price ceilings under which cab companies are free to manoeuvre. From 6am to 10pm the highest flag-fall fee that can be legally charged is

300Ft, the per-kilometre charge 240Ft and the waiting fee 60Ft. From 10pm to 6am the equivalent fees are 420/330/80Ft.

Budapest residents – local or foreign – rarely flag down taxis in the street. They almost always ring for them, and fares are actually cheaper if you book over the phone. Make sure you know the number of the landline phone you're calling from as that's how they establish your address (though you can, of course, call from a mobile phone, too).

The following are the telephone numbers of reliable taxi firms.

Buda	☎ 233 3333
City	☎ 211 1111
Fő	☎ 222 2222
Rádió	☎ 377 7777
Tele 5	☎ 355 5555

TRAIN

Magyar Államvasutak (Hungarian State Railways; www.mav.hu in Hungarian), or MÁV, links up with the European rail network in all directions, running trains as far as London (via Munich and Paris), Paris (via Munich), Stockholm (via Hamburg and Copenhagen), Moscow, Rome and Istanbul (via Belgrade).

Budapest has three main train stations. Most international trains arrive and depart from **Keleti train station** (Eastern train station; Map pp218–19; ☎ 313 6835; VIII Kerepesi út 2-6; Ⓜ M3 Keleti pályaudvar); trains to certain destinations in the east (eg Romania) leave from **Nyugati train station** (Western train station; Map p222; ☎ 349 0115; VI Teréz körút 55-57; Ⓜ M3 Nyugati pályaudvar), while **Déli train station** (Southern train station; Map p220; ☎ 375 6293, 355 8657; I Krisztina körút 37; Ⓜ M2 Déli pályaudvar) handles trains to some destinations in the south (eg Osijek in Croatia and Sarajevo in Bosnia). These are not hard-and-fast rules, so always make sure you check which station the train leaves from when you buy a ticket.

The handful of secondary train stations are of little importance to long-distance travellers. Occasionally, though, a through train will stop at **Kelenföld train station** (Map pp228–9; ☎ 203 1687; XI Etele tér 5-7; 🚊 19 or 49) in Buda. For 24-hour information on international train services call ☎ 461 5500 or ☎ 06-40 494 949.

Budapest's train stations are generally pretty dismal places, with some unsavoury-looking characters hanging about day and night, but all have some amenities. The **left-luggage offices** (normal/large piece per 6hr 150/300Ft, per day 300/600Ft) at **Keleti station** (🕑 24hr) is next to platform 6. At **Nyugati station** (🕑 4am-midnight) and at the **Déli station** (🕑 3.30am-11.30pm) they are beside the information and ticketing hall. You'll also find post offices and grocery stores that are open late or even round the clock in the stations.

The three main stations are on metro lines, and night buses serve them when the metro is closed. If you need to take a taxi, avoid the sharks hovering around the stations. At Déli, cross over to I Alkotás utca and hail one there. At Keleti station, get into one of the legal cabs at the rank on VIII Kerepesi út, just south of the terminal. Nyugati tér is a major intersection, so you'll have no problem finding a legitimate taxi there.

You can buy tickets at the three international train stations in Budapest, but the queues are often long, passengers are in a hurry, and sales staff at the stations are not the most patient in the city. It's easier at the **MÁV international information & ticket centre** (Map p222; ☎ 461 5500, 352 2800; VI Andrássy út 35; 🕑 9am-6pm Mon-Fri Apr-Sep, 9am-5pm Mon-Fri Oct-Mar; Ⓜ M1 Opera). For fares, check www.elvira.hu.

TRAM

Trams are often faster than buses in Budapest and usually more pleasant for sightseeing. The most important tram lines (always marked with red lines on a Budapest map or atlas) are the following:

2 & 2/a – Scenic trams that travel along the Pest side of the Danube as far as V Jászai Mari tér

4 & 6 – Extremely useful trams that start at XI Fehérvári út and XI Móricz Zsigmond körtér in south Buda respectively and follow the entire length of the Big Ring Road in Pest before terminating at II Moszkva tér in Buda

18 – Runs from southern Buda along XI Bartók Béla út through the Tabán to II Moszkva tér

19 – Covers part of the same route as 18, but then runs along the Buda side of the Danube to I Batthyány tér

47 & 49 – Link V Deák Ferenc tér in Pest with points in southern Buda via the Little Ring Road

61 – Connects XI Móricz Zsigmond körtér with Déli train station and II Moszkva tér in Buda

TROLLEYBUS

Trolleybuses go along cross streets in central Pest and, in general, are of little use to most visitors, with the sole exception of the ones to and around City Park (70, 72 and 74) and Népliget Park (75 and 77). A broken red line on a map or atlas signifies a trolleybus.

PRACTICALITIES

ACCOMMODATION

The accommodation options in this guide are listed alphabetically by area for midrange and top-end hotels, followed by a separate 'cheap sleeps' section. When budgeting for your trip, remember that hotel rates rise in April and stay at that level till at least September. There are often some bargains to be had during the late autumn and winter months.

Useful accommodation-booking websites include www.hotelshungary.com, www.holidayhungary.com and www.szallasinfo.hu for hotels, and www.youthhostels.hu for hostel accommodation. Both www.ingatlan.com and www.alfaapartments.com are useful for short-term flat rentals.

For details on accommodation costs and types in Budapest see p152.

BUSINESS HOURS

With rare exceptions, the opening hours *(nyitvatartás)* of any concern are posted on the front door. *Nyitva* means 'open' while *zárva* is 'closed'.

Very generally speaking, retail shops (including grocery stores) and department stores are open from 10am to 6pm Monday to Friday and 10am to 1pm on Saturday. In summer, some private retail shops close early on Friday and at least part of August.

Most neighbourhoods have a 'nonstop' – a convenience store open round-the-clock (or very late/early) that sells basic food items, bottled drinks and cigarettes. Many of the hyper-supermarkets around Budapest open on Sunday.

Banking hours change from institution to location but are usually 7.45am to 5pm or 6pm Monday, 7.45am to 4pm or 5pm Tuesday to Thursday and 7.45am to 4pm on Friday. The main post office in any Budapest district is open 8am to 7pm or 8pm weekdays and till noon or even 2pm on Saturday. Branch offices close much earlier – usually at 4pm – and are never open at the weekend.

For restaurant opening hours see p92.

CHILDREN

Successful travel with young children requires planning and effort. Don't try to overdo things; packing too much into the time available can cause problems. Make sure the activities include the kids as well – balance that morning at the Museum of Fine Arts with an afternoon at the nearby Municipal Great Circus or a ride on the Budapest Eye (p73). If children are allowed to help work out where you will be going, they'll be much more interested when they get there. Lonely Planet's *Travel with Children* is a good resource.

Most car-rental firms in Budapest have children's safety seats for hire at a nominal cost, but it is essential that you book them in advance. The same goes for highchairs and cots (cribs); they're standard in many restaurants and hotels but numbers are limited.

CLIMATE

Budapest has a temperate, transitional climate – somewhere between the mild, rainy weather of Transdanubia protected by the Alps to the west and the harsh, variable climate of the flat and open Great Plain to the east.

Spring arrives in early April in Budapest and is usually quite wet. Summer can be very hot and humid. It rains for most of November and doesn't usually get cold until mid-December. Winter is relatively short, often cloudy and damp but sometimes brilliantly sunny. What little snow the city gets usually disappears after a few days.

January is the coldest month (with the temperature averaging -4°C) and July and

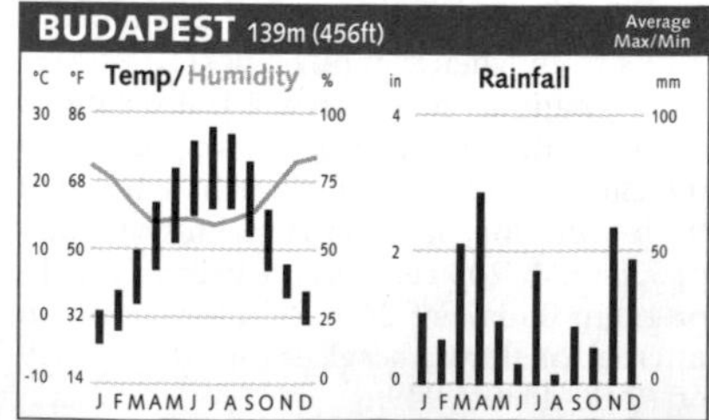

August the hottest (average temperature 26°C during each). The number of hours of sunshine a year averages between 1900 and 2500 – among the highest in Europe. From late April to the end of September, you can expect the sun to shine for about 10 hours a day. The mean annual precipitation in the capital is 650mm.

The climate chart on this page shows you what to expect and when to expect it. For information on specific weather conditions in Budapest, contact the **national weather forecast service** (☎ 346 4600, 06-90 504 001; www.met.hu in Hungarian only).

COURSES

Language

Schools teaching Hungarian to foreigners have proliferated in Budapest recently, but they vary greatly in quality, approach and success rates. You should establish whether your teacher has a degree in the Hungarian language and whether they have ever taught foreigners. You should be following a text or at least a comprehensive series of photocopies produced by your teacher. Remember also that you'll never get anywhere by simply sitting in class and not studying at home or practising with native speakers. Expect to pay 850Ft to 1000Ft per hour in a classroom with six to 12 students and 3500Ft to 4200Ft for a private lesson.

The granddaddy of all Hungarian language schools is the **Debrecen Summer University** (Debreceni Nyári Egyetem; ☎ 52-532 594; www.nyariegyetem.hu; Egyetem tér 1) in Debrecen, eastern Hungary. It organises intensive two- and four-week courses in July and August and 80-hour, two-week intensive courses in January and a superintensive two-week course in May/June. The emphasis is not just on language but the whole Magyar picture: art, history, culture, literature. The two-/four-week (60-/120-hour) summer courses cost €390/760; board and lodging in a triple room cost €90/180 (singles and doubles available at extra cost). The **Budapest branch** (Map p222; ☎ 320 5751; Jászai Mari tér 6, 2nd fl) has intensive courses lasting three weeks (60 hours) for €282 and regular evening classes of 72/96 hours for €236/322.

Some other recommended Hungarian-language schools:

Hungarian Language School (Map p224; ☎ 266 2617; www.hls.hu; VIII Brody Sándor utca 4, 1st fl)

InterClub Hungarian Language School (Map pp228–9; ☎ 279 0831; www.interclub.hu; XI Bertalan Lajos utca 17)

International House Language School (Map pp218–19; ☎ 212 4010; www.ih.hu; II Bimbó út 7)

CUSTOMS

Duty-free shopping within the EU was abolished in 1999 and Hungary, as an EU member since 2004, now adheres to the rules.

The usual allowances apply to duty-free goods purchased at airports or on ferries originating outside the EU: 200 cigarettes, 50 cigars or 250g of loose tobacco; 2L of still wine and 1L of spirits; 100mL of perfume; 250cc of eau de toilette. You must declare the import/export of any amount of cash, cheques, securities etc exceeding the sum of 1,000,000Ft.

When leaving the country, you are not supposed to take out valuable antiques without a special permit, which should be available from the place of purchase. For details see p146.

DISABLED TRAVELLERS

Budapest has made great strides in recent years in making public areas and facilities more accessible to the disabled. Wheelchair ramps, toilets fitted for the disabled and inward opening doors, though not as common as they are in Western Europe, do exist and audible traffic signals for the blind are becoming commonplace in the cities.

For more information, contact the **Hungarian Federation of Disabled Persons' Associations** (MEOSZ; Map pp226–7; ☎ 250 9013, 388 2387; www.meoszinfo.hu; III San Marco utca 76). Its website includes a list of hotels with rooms adapted for the disabled as well as accessible restaurants and tourist sights.

DISCOUNT CARDS

A hostel card is not particularly useful in Budapest as no hostel here requires you to be a Hostelling International (or associated) member. Having said that, a hostel card will sometimes get you a 10% discount on quoted rates. The **Hungarian Youth Hostel Association** (MISZSZ; Map p224; ☎ 411 2392; www.youthhostels.hu; V Molnár utca 3) and the **Express travel agency** (p195) issue HYHA cards valid for a year to Hungarian citizens and residents for 2300Ft, which includes a 300Ft NeoPhone phonecard.

Many attractions offer reduced-price admission for retired people (currently 58 and 62 for women and men respectively, but being increased), but this is usually just for Hungarian *nyugdíjasok* (pensioners) holding national ID cards. Of course, it never hurts to try.

Useful discount cards:

Budapest Card (☎ 266 0479; www.budapestinfo.hu; 48/72hr 5200/6500Ft) The Budapest Card offers free or reduced admission to 60 museums and other sights, unlimited travel on all forms of public transport and discounts on organised tours, car rental, at thermal baths and at selected shops and restaurants. It is sold at Tourinform offices, travel agencies, hotels and main metro stations.

Hungary Card (☎ 266 3741, 267-0896; www.hungary card.hu; 1yr 5520Ft) The national equivalent of the Budapest Card, this gives free admission to many museums nationwide, 50% discounts on a half-dozen return train fares and some bus and boat travel as well as other museums and attractions, up to 20% off selected accommodation and 50% off the price of the Budapest Card. It is available at the tourist offices.

International Student Identity Card (ISIC; www.isic .org; 1 yr 1300Ft) This plastic ID-style card with a photo, provides bona fide students with discounts on some forms of transport and cheap admission to museums and other sights. If you're aged under 26 but not a student, you can apply for ISIC's **International Youth Travel Card** (IYTC; 1 yr 1300Ft) or the **Euro<26 card** (valid for summer break 1600Ft, 1 yr 2200Ft) issued by the European Youth Card Association (EYCA), both of which offer the same discounts as the student card. Teachers can apply for the **International Teacher Identity Card** (ITIC; 1 yr 1300Ft).

ELECTRICITY

The electric current in Budapest is 220V, 50Hz AC. Plugs are the European type with two round pins.

EMBASSIES

Selected countries with representation in Budapest are listed here. The opening hours indicate when consular or chancellery services are available.

Australia (Map pp218–19; ☎ 457 9777; XII Királyhágó tér 8-9, 4th fl; 🕑 9-11am Mon-Fri)

Austria (Map pp218–19; ☎ 413 0240; VI Benczúr utca 16; 🕑 8-10am Mon-Fri)

Canada (Map pp218–19; ☎ 392 3360; II Ganz utca 12-14; 🕑 8.30-11am & 2-3.30pm Mon-Thu)

Croatia (Map pp218–19; ☎ 269 5657; VI Munkácsy Mihály utca 15; 🕑 1-3pm Mon, Tue, Thu & Fri)

France (Map pp218–19; ☎ 374 1100; VI Lendvay utca 27; 🕑 9am-noon Mon-Fri)

Germany (Map p220; ☎ 488 3505; I Úri utca 64-66; 🕑 9am-noon Mon-Fri)

Ireland (Map p222; ☎ 301 4960; Bank Center, Granite Tower, 7th fl, V Szabadság tér 7; 🕑 9.30am-12.30pm & 2.30-4.30pm Mon-Fri)

Netherlands (Map pp218–19; ☎ 336-6300; II Füge utca 5-7; 🕑 10am-noon Mon-Fri)

Romania (Map pp218–19; ☎ 384 0271; XIV Thököly út 72, enter from Izsó utca; 🕑 8.30am-noon Mon, Tue, Thu & Fri)

Serbia & Montenegro (Map pp218–19; ☎ 322 1436; VI Dózsa György út 92/b; 🕑 10am-1pm Mon-Fri)

Slovakia (Map p216; ☎ 273 3500; XIV Gervay utca 44; 🕑 8.30am-noon Mon-Fri)

Slovenia (Map p216; ☎ 438 5600; II Csatárka köz 9; 🕑 9am-noon Mon-Fri)

South Africa (Map p216; ☎ 392 0999; II Gárdonyi Géza út 17; 🕑 9am-12.30pm Mon-Fri)

UK (Map p224; ☎ 266 2888; V Harmincad utca 6; 🕑 9.30am-12.30pm & 2.30-4.30pm Mon-Fri)

Ukraine (Map pp218–19; ☎ 422 2122; XIV Stefánia út 77; 🕑 9am-noon Mon-Wed & Fri by appointment only)

USA (Map p222; ☎ 475 4164; V Szabadság tér 12; 🕑 1-4.30pm Mon-Thu, 9am-noon & 1-4pm Fri)

EMERGENCY

Any crime must be reported at the police station of the district you're in. In central Pest that would be the Belváros-Lipótváros Police Station (Map p222; ☎ 373 1000; V Szalay utca 11-13; 🚌 15). If possible, bring along a Hungarian speaker.

Ambulance	☎ 104
Central emergency number (English spoken)	☎ 112
English-language crime hotline	
(8am-8pm)	☎ 438-8080
(8pm-8am)	☎ 06-80 660 044
Fire	☎ 105, 321 6216
Police	☎ 107
24-hour car assistance	☎ 188, 345 1755

GAY & LESBIAN TRAVELLERS

For up-to-date information on venues, events, parties etc, pick up the freebie pamphlet *Na Végre!* (At Last!; navegre@hotmail.com) at gay venues or contact them directly. Useful websites include www.budapestgayvisitor.hu and http://budapest.gayguide.net. A lesbian website is www.labrisz.hu but it's in Hungarian only. In 2004, the age of consent for gays and lesbians was lowered to 14 to come into line with that of heterosexual couples.

In this book gay and lesbian bars, clubs and other entertainment venues are listed in the boxed text, p130, and under gay-owned and gay-friendly accommodation, p161.

The **Háttér Gay & Lesbian Association** (☎ 329 3380, 06-40 200 358; www.hatter.hu; 🕒 6pm-11pm) has an advice and help line operating daily. **Budapest Gayguide.net** (☎ 06 30 932 3334; http://budapestgayguide.net; 🕒 4pm-8pm Mon-Fri Apr-Oct) can offer advice and/or provide information via email or, seasonally, by telephone.

Two AIDS lines to contact are the **Anonymous AIDS Association** (☎ 466-9283; 🕒 5-8pm Mon, Wed & Thu, 9am-noon Tue & Fri) and the **AIDS Help Line** (☎ 338 2419, 266 0465; 🕒 8am-3pm Mon-Thur, 8am-1pm Fri).

HOLIDAYS

Hungary currently celebrates 10 public holidays *(ünnep)* every year.

New Year's Day 1 January

1848 Revolution/National Day 15 March

Easter Monday March/April

International Labour Day 1 May

Whit Monday May/June

St Stephen's/Constitution Day 20 August

1956 Remembrance/Republic Day 23 October

All Saints' Day 1 November

Christmas holidays 25-26 December

INTERNET ACCESS

The Internet has arrived in a big way in Hungary, and the blue signs announcing 'eMagyarország Pont' are telling you that you can log on somewhere in the vicinity – be it via a free-access terminal, at a commercial Internet café or at a wi-fi hotspot. Many libraries have free terminals; at hotels, you usually have to pay to use the service. It's hit-or-miss with hostels, but most now have at least one terminal available to guests either for free or for a nominal sum.

Internet Service Providers

Well-trafficked ISPs in Budapest include **T-Online Magyarország** (☎ 371 3400; www.t-online.hu in Hungarian), **GTS-Datanet** (☎ 814 4444; www.datanet.hu in Hungarian) and **Inter.net** (☎ 465 7800; www.hu.inter.net).

Internet Cafés

Budapest has dozens of Internet cafés, but the smaller ones can get crowded in the early evening. Many of the year-round hostels and almost all hotels in Budapest now offer Internet access. If the place you're staying at doesn't have it or you just feel like checking your mail on the trot, the following 10 are among the more central Internet cafés.

Ami Internet Coffee (Map p224; ☎ 267 1644; www.amicoffee.hu in Hungarian; V Váci utca 40; per 15/30/60min 200/400/700Ft, 5/10hr 3250/6400Ft; 🕒 9am-2am; Ⓜ M3 Ferenciek tere) This Internet café in the university area of Pest has 40 terminals.

CEU NetPoint (Map p224; ☎ 328 3506; www.ceunet.ceu.hu; V Október 6 utca 14; per 30/60min 250/400Ft; 🕒 11am-10pm; 🚌 15) Just up from the Central European University.

Chatman Internet (Map p222; ☎ 266 0856; http://chatman.us.to/; VII Kazinczy utca 3; per 1/3hr 200/500Ft; 🕒 8am-midnight Mon-Fri, 10am-midnight Sat & Sun; trolleybus 74) This small and very friendly café in Pest offers a free hour online after your first.

Cybercafé Zone (Map pp218–19; ☎ 315 2259, 34 2057; II Lövőház utca 12; per 30/60min 175/350Ft, 10hr 3130Ft; 🕒 8am-3am Mon-Sat, 10am-midnight Sun; Ⓜ M2 Moszkva tér) A very flash place behind the gigantic Mammut shopping mall in Buda.

Electric Café (Map p222; ☎ 413 1803; www.electriccafé.hu; VII Dohány utca 37; per 30/60min 100/200Ft; 🕒 9am-midnight; Ⓜ M2 Blaha Lujza tér) Popular with travellers.

Mystery Bar (Map p222; ☎ 312 1436; www.mysterybar.hu; V Nagysándor József utca 3; per 30/60min 300/500Ft; 🕒 4pm-4am Mon-Fri, 6pm-4am Sat & Sun; Ⓜ M3 Arany János) This Internet café is also a neighbourhood gay bar (p124).

Nagyi Palacsintázója (Granny's Palacsinta Place; Map p224; ☎ 418 0721; V Petőfi Sándor tér 17-19; per 30/60min 300/600Ft; 🕒 24hr; Ⓜ M1/2/3 Deák Ferenc tér) This popular *palacsinta* eating spot (p98) also offers Internet access round the clock.

Narancs (Map p222; ☎ 413 6071; VII Akácfa utca 5; per 30/60min 100/200Ft; 🕒 10am-midnight; Ⓜ M2 Blaha Lujza tér) Small but charming French-run 'neighbourhood' Internet café.

Parknet (Map p224; ☎ 270 2249; V Váci utca 23; per 15/30/60min 170/270/500Ft, 5/10hr 1800/3000Ft; 🕒 9am-8pm Mon-Sat, 10am-8pm Sun; Ⓜ M3 Ferenciek tere) About as central as you'll find in Pest.

Private Link (Map pp218–19; ☎ 334 2057; www.private-link.hu; VIII József körút 52; per 1/5/10hr 690/2000/3500Ft; 🕑 24hr; Ⓜ M3 Ferenc körút) Budapest's largest and most comfortable Internet café, and the only one open round the clock.

LAUNDRY

Most hostels have some sort of laundry facilities; expect to pay from 1000Ft to 1500Ft per load. *Patyolat* (commercial laundries) are fairly common in Budapest. You can elect to have your laundry done in six hours or one, two or three days – and pay accordingly. About the only self-service laundrettes in town are **Irisz Szalon** (Map p224; ☎ 317 2092; V Városház utca 3-5; 7kg wash/dry 1700/1500Ft; 🕑 7am-7pm Mon-Fri; Ⓜ M3 Ferenciek tere) and **Liliom Szalon** (Map pp228–9; ☎ 215 6782; IX Liliom utca 7-9; 8kg wash 1590Ft; 🕑 8am-6pm Mon-Fri, 8am-noon Sat; Ⓜ M3 Ferenc körút).

The **Top Clean** (☎ 227 1500, pickup ☎ 227 5648) chain does a reliable and affordable job on both laundry and dry cleaning and has some 30 locations around Budapest, usually combined with Mister Minit key cutters, including a **Northern Inner Town branch** (Map p222; V Arany János utca 34; 🕑 7am-5.30pm Mon-Fri, 8am-1pm Sat; Ⓜ 3 Arany János utca) and a **Terézváros branch** (Map p222; Skála Metro department store, VI Nyugati tér 1-2; 🕑 7am-7pm Mon-Fri, 9am-2pm Sat; Ⓜ Nyugati pályaudvar).

LIBRARIES

Libraries in Budapest with foreign-language books and periodicals include the following:

Ervin Szabó Central Library (Fővárosi Szabó Ervin Könyvtár; Map p222; ☎ 411 5000; www.fszek.hu in Hungarian; VIII Reviczky utca 3; 🕑 10am-8pm Mon-Fri, 10am-4pm Sat; Ⓜ M3 Kálvin tér) This stunning place, completed in 1894, is the main repository of Budapest's central library system with access to 800,000 books, 1000 periodicals and 40,000 audiovisual and digital items. You'll need an ID with a Hungarian address and pay a subscription of 2800Ft a year if you want to take items away.

National Foreign Language Library (Országos Idegennyelvű Könyvtár; Map p224; ☎ 318 3688; www.oik.hu in Hungarian; V Molnár utca 11; 🕑 10am-8pm Mon, Tue, Thu & Fri, noon-8pm Wed; Ⓜ M3 Ferenciek tere) You can join this library for adult/student 2000/1000Ft a year, but you'll need to be introduced by a Hungarian citizen.

National Széchenyi Library (Országos Széchenyi Könyvtár; Map p220; ☎ 224 3700; www.oszk.hu; Royal Palace, Wing F; 🕑 9am-9pm Tue-Fri, 10am-8pm Sat) This library allows members (annual adult/student 6000/3000Ft, daily 500/300Ft) to do research, peruse the general stacks and read the large collection of foreign newspapers and magazines.

MAPS

Lonely Planet's *Budapest City Map* covers the more popular parts of town in detail.

The best folding maps of the city are Cartographia's 1:22,000 (690Ft) and 1:28,000 (570Ft) ones. If you plan to explore the city thoroughly, the *Budapest Atlas*, also from Cartographia, is a must. It comes in two sizes of the same scale (1:20,000): a smaller format (1950Ft) and a larger one (2600Ft). There is also a 1:25,000 pocket atlas of just the Inner Town available for 1210Ft.

Many bookshops, including **Libri Könyvpalota** (p149), stock a wide variety of maps. **Cartographia** (Map p222; ☎ 312 6001; www.cartographia.hu; VI Bajcsy-Zsilinszky út 37; 🕑 10am-6pm Mon-Fri; Ⓜ M3 Arany János utca) has its own outlet in Budapest, but it's not self-service, which can be annoying. A better bet is the nearby **Térképkirály** (Map King; Map p222; ☎ 472 0505; VI Bajcsy-Zsilinszky út 23; 🕑 10am-6pm Mon-Fri; Ⓜ M3 Arany János utca) or even the tiny **Párisi Udvar Könyvesbolt** (Párisi Udvar Bookshop; Map p224; ☎ 235 0379; V Petőfi Sándor utca 2; 🕑 9am-7pm Mon-Fri, 10am-2pm Sat; Ⓜ M3 Ferenciek tere) in the Párisi Udvar.

MEDICAL SERVICES

Medical care in Budapest is generally adequate and good for routine problems but not complicated conditions. Foreigners are entitled to first-aid and ambulance services only when they have suffered an accident and require immediate medical attention; follow-up treatment and medicine must be paid for.

Treatment at a public outpatient clinic *(rendelő intézet)* costs little, but doctors working privately will charge much more. Very roughly, a consultation in a Hungarian doctor's surgery *(orvosi rendelő)* costs from 5000Ft while a home visit is from 10,000Ft.

If you do need health insurance while travelling, consider a policy that covers you for the worst possible scenario, such as an accident requiring an emergency flight home.

Clinics

Consultations and treatment are much more expensive in Western-style clinics. Dental work is usually of a high standard and cheap by Western European standards.

FirstMed Centers (Map pp218–19; ☎ 224 9090; www.firstmedcenters.com; I Hattyú utca 14, 5th fl; ⏰ appointments 8am-7pm Mon-Thu, 8am-6pm Fri, 24hr emergency care; Ⓜ M2 Moszkva tér) This is a modern private medical clinic with round-the-clock emergency services, but it's hardly cheap: a basic consultation costs 12,600/25,200Ft for up to 10/20 minutes.

SOS Dental Services (Map p224; ☎ 267 9602, 269 6010; VI Király utca 14; ⏰ 24hr; Ⓜ M1/2/3 Deák Ferenc tér) This dental surgery charges 2000Ft for a consultation, 5000Ft to 6000Ft for extractions and 6000Ft to 10,000Ft for fillings.

MONEY

Hungary's currency is the forint (Ft). There are coins of 1Ft, 2Ft, 5Ft, 10Ft, 20Ft, 50Ft and 100Ft. Notes come in seven denominations: 200Ft, 500Ft, 1000Ft, 2000Ft, 5000Ft, 10,000Ft and 20,000Ft.

There are automated teller machines (ATMs) everywhere in Budapest, including in the train and bus stations, and quite a few foreign-currency exchange machines. If you need to change cash or travellers cheques, avoid moneychangers (especially those on V Váci utca) in favour of the banks. Among those offering the best rates and service are **OTP** (National Savings Bank; Map p224; V Deák Ferenc utca 7-9; ⏰ 7.45am-6pm Mon, 7.45am-5pm Tue-Fri; Ⓜ M1/2/3 Deák Ferenc tér) and **K&H** (Map p224; V Váci utca 40; ⏰ 8am-5pm Mon, 8am-4pm Tue-Thu, 8am-3pm Fri; Ⓜ M3 Ferenciek tere). Be sure to arrive about an hour before closing to ensure the *bureau de change* counter is still open, though.

Credit cards, especially Visa, MasterCard and American Express, are widely accepted here and you'll be able to use them at many restaurants, shops, hotels, car-rental firms, travel agencies and petrol stations. They are not usually accepted at museums, supermarkets or train and bus stations.

A HEALTHY MIX OF MONIES

Though Hungary is now part of the EU, it will retain its own currency until at least 2010. Prices in shops and restaurants in Budapest are uniformly quoted in forint, but many hotels and guesthouses and even MÁV, the national rail company, quote their prices in euros. In such cases, we have followed suit and you can usually pay in either euros or forint.

NEWSPAPERS & MAGAZINES

There are two English-language, general-interest weekly newspapers available in the city: the long-established tabloid *Budapest Sun* (www.budapestsun.com; 399Ft), which appears on Thursday, with a useful classified section and the Style arts and entertainment supplement; and the *Budapest Times* (www.budapesttimes.hu; 420Ft; Mondays), a new kid on the block with good reviews and opinion pieces, including 'The Weekly Stink' by local gadfly Erik D'Amato. The erudite *Hungarian Quarterly* (www.hungarianquarterly.com; 1500Ft), which looks at issues in great depth, is a valuable source of current Hungarian thinking in translation. For Hungarian-language press, see p13.

The best place in Budapest for foreign-language newspapers and magazines is **Világsajtó Háza** (World Press House; Map p224; ☎ 317 1311; V Városház utca 3-5; ⏰ 7am-7pm Mon-Fri, 7am-2pm Sat, 8am-noon Sun; Ⓜ M3 Ferenciek tere). Almost as good is **Immedio** (Map p224; ☎ 318 5604; V Váci utca 10; ⏰ 8am-8pm).

PHARMACIES

Each of Budapest's 23 districts has a rotating all-night pharmacy; a sign on the door of any pharmacy will help you locate the closest 24-hour one. Pharmacies with extended hours:

Csillag Gyógyszertár (Map p222; ☎ 314 3695; VIII Rákóczi út 39; ⏰ 7.30am-9pm Mon-Fri, 7.30am-2pm Sat; Ⓜ M2 Blaha Lujza tér)

Déli Gyógyszertár (Map pp218–19; ☎ 355 4691; XII Alkotás utca 1/b; ⏰ 8am-8pm Mon-Fri, 8am-2pm Sat; Ⓜ M2 Déli pályaudvar)

Teréz Patika (Map p222; ☎ 311 4439; VI Teréz körút 41; ⏰ 8am-8pm Mon-Fri, 8am-2pm Sat; Ⓜ M3 Nyugati pályaudvar)

PHOTOGRAPHY & VIDEO

Major brands of film are readily available and one-hour processing places are common in Budapest and larger Hungarian cities and towns.

Film prices vary but generally 24 exposures of 100 ISO Kodacolor II, Agfa or Fujifilm cost 999Ft, and 36 exposures are 1290Ft. Ektachrome 100 costs 1790Ft for 36 exposures. Developing print film is 1099Ft a roll; for the prints themselves, you choose the size and pay accordingly (eg 10cm x 15cm prints cost 89Ft each). Developing a 40-exposure roll of Kodak 200/400 APS film costs from 1999/2800Ft; slide film costs only 1099Ft to process. Video tape such as TDK EHG 30/45 minutes costs 990/1310Ft.

POST

The Hungarian Postal Service (Magyar Posta; www.posta.hu) has improved greatly in recent years; perhaps its jaunty logo of a stylised St Stephen's Crown has helped kick-start it into the 21st century. But post offices in Budapest are usually still crowded, service is slow and staff generally speak Hungarian only.

Postal Rates

Sending letters within Hungary costs 52Ft (90Ft for priority mail), while for the rest of Europe it's 170Ft (190Ft priority). Airmail *(légiposta)* letters of up to 20/50g are 185/270Ft within Europe and 210/350Ft for the rest of the world. Postcards cost 52Ft to send within Hungary, 120Ft within the rest of Europe and 140Ft to the rest of the world.

Sending & Receiving Mail

To beat the crowds at the post office, ask at kiosks, newsagents or stationery shops if they sell stamps *(bélyeg)*. If you must deal with the post office, you'll be relieved to learn that most people are there to pay electric, gas and telephone bills or parking fines. To get in and out with a minimum of fuss, look for the window marked with the symbol of an envelope. Make sure the destination of your letter is written clearly, and simply hand it over to the clerk, who will apply the stamps for you, postmark it and send it on its way.

To send a parcel, look for the sign 'Csomagfeladás' or 'Csomagfelvétel'. Standard packages sent domestically cost 690Ft for up to 20kg. Packages going abroad must not weigh more than 2kg or else you'll face a Kafkaesque nightmare of permits and queues; try to send smaller ones. You can send up to 2kg in one box for 3470Ft to Europe and 4390Ft to the rest of the world. Airmail rates are much higher and depend on which of five zones the destination is located.

Hungarian addresses start with the name of the recipient, followed on the next line by the postal code and city or town and then the street name and number. The Hungarian postal code consists of four digits. The first indicates the city or town ('1' is Budapest), the second and third the *kerület* (district) and the last the neighbourhood.

The **main post office** (Map p224; V Petőfi Sándor utca 13-15; 8am-8pm Mon-Fri, 8am-2pm Sat; M 1/2/3 Deák Ferenc tér) is a few minutes' walk from Deák Ferenc tér and the Tourinform office. This is where you buy stamps, mail letters, send packages and faxes and pick up poste restante. For the last, go around the corner to the **main post office annexe** (Map p224; V Városház utca 18), which keeps the same hours. Since the family name always comes first in Hungarian usage, have the sender underline your last name, as letters are often misfiled under foreigners' first names.

Two other convenient post offices with extended hours are the **Nyugati train station post office** (Map p222; VI Teréz körút 51-53; 7am-9pm Mon-Sat, 10am-5pm Sun; M M3 Nyugati pályaudvar) and the **Keleti train station post office** (Map pp218–19; VIII Kerepesi út 2-6; 7am-9pm Mon-Fri, 8am-2pm Sat; M M2 Keleti pályaudvar).

SAFETY

No parts of Budapest are 'off-limits' to visitors, although some locals now avoid Margaret Island after dark off-season, and both residents and visitors give the dodgier parts of the 8th and 9th districts (areas of prostitution) a wide berth.

As elsewhere while travelling, you are most vulnerable to car thieves, pickpockets, taxi louts and scammers. To avoid having your car ripped off, follow the usual security procedures: don't park it in a darkened street, make sure the burglar alarm is armed, have a steering-wheel lock in place and leave nothing of value inside.

Pickpocketing is most common in markets, the Castle District, Váci utca and

Hősök tere, near major hotels and on certain popular buses (eg 7) and trams (2, 2/a, 4, 6, 47 and 49).

Taking a taxi in Budapest can be an expensive and even unpleasant experience. Never hail a cab on the street; instead, call one from a phone – private, mobile or public – and give the number (almost always posted somewhere in the phone box) to the dispatcher. For more information see p184.

Scams that involve attractive young women, gullible guys, expensive drinks in nightclubs and a frog-marching to the nearest ATM by gorillas-in-residence have been all the rage in Budapest for a decade now, and we get letters from male readers complaining they've been ripped off. Guys, please, do us ALL a favour. If it seems too good to be true, it is. Trust us and the mirror; such vanity has cost some would-be Lotharios hundreds and even thousands of dollars.

If you've left something on any form of public transport in Budapest contact the **BKV lost & found office** (Map p222; ☎ 267 5299; VII Akácfa utca 18; 8am-5pm Mon, Tue, Thu & Fri, 8am-6pm Wed; Ⓜ M2 Blaha Lujza tér).

TAXES & REFUNDS

ÁFA, a value-added tax of between 5% and 20% (down from 25% in January 2006), covers the purchase of all new goods in Hungary. It's usually included in the quoted price but not always, so it pays to check. Visitors are not exempt, but non-EU residents can claim refunds for total purchases of at least 50,000Ft on one receipt as long as they take the goods out of the country (and the EU) within 90 days. The ÁFA receipts (available from the shops where you make the purchases) should be stamped by customs at the border, and the claim has to be made within 183 days of exporting the goods. You can then collect your refund – minus commission – from the **Global Refund** (www.globalrefund.com) desk in the departures halls of Terminal 2A and 2B at Ferihegy airport in Budapest or at branches of the Ibusz chain of travel agencies at some 16 border crossings. You can also have it sent by bank cheque or deposited into your credit-card account.

Like municipalities throughout the land, Budapest levies a tourist tax on most forms of accommodation (p153).

TELEPHONE

You can make domestic and international calls from public telephones, which are usually in good working order. They work with both coins and phonecards, though the latter are now far more common. Telephone boxes with a black and white arrow and red target on the door and the word 'Visszahívható' display a telephone number, so you can be phoned back.

Local & International Calls

All localities in Hungary have a two-digit telephone area code, except for Budapest, which has just a '1'. To make a local call, pick up the receiver and listen for the neutral and continuous dial tone, then dial the phone number (seven digits in Budapest, six elsewhere). For an intercity landline call within Hungary and whenever you are calling a mobile telephone, dial ☎ 06 and wait for the second, more melodious, tone. Then dial the area code and phone number. Cheaper or toll-free blue and green numbers start with the digits ☎ 06-40 and ☎ 06-80 respectively.

The procedure for making an international call is the same as for a local call except that you dial ☎ 00, wait for the second dial tone, then dial the country code, the area code and then the number. The country code for Hungary is ☎ 36.

Phonecards

Phonecards, which are available from post offices, newsagents, hotels and petrol stations, come in message units of 50/120 and

USEFUL TELEPHONE NUMBERS

The following are useful numbers to know when using the phone in Budapest. For emergency numbers, see p188 and inside the front cover.

Information Plus (any inquiry; English spoken) ☎ 197

Domestic operator/inquiries (English spoken) ☎ 198

International inquiries/operator (English spoken) ☎ 199

Time/speaking clock (in Hungarian) ☎ 180

Wake-up service (in Hungarian) ☎ 193

cost 800/1800Ft. But these are by far the most expensive way to go. As everywhere else these days, there is a plethora of phonecards on offer. Among the most widely available are T-Com's **Barangoló** (☎ 06-80 501 255; www.magyartelekom.hu), which comes in denominations of 400Ft, 1000Ft, 2000Ft and 5000Ft, and **NeoPhone** (☎ 06-80 188 202; www.neophone.hu), with cards valued at 300Ft, 1000Ft, 2000Ft and 5000Ft. Sample per-minute costs with these cards are 25Ft to most European countries and the USA, 29Ft to Australia and New Zealand, and 50Ft to South Africa.

Mobile Phones

In Hungary you must always dial ☎ 06 when ringing mobile telephones, which have specific area codes depending on the telecom company: Pannon GSM (☎ 06-20; www.pgsm.hu/index_en.php), T-Mobile (☎ 06 30; www.magyartelekom.hu) and Vodafone (☎ 06 70; www.vodafone.hu).

If you're going to spend more than just a few days here and expect to use your phone quite a bit, consider buying a rechargeable SIM chip, which will reduce the cost of making local calls (between 19Ft and 27Ft a minute) to a fraction of what you'd pay on your own foreign mobile. For example, **Vodafone** (Map p222; ☎ 238 7281, 238 7588; Shop 46, 4th fl, West End City Centre, VI Váci út 3; 🕑 10am-9pm Mon-Sat, 10am-6pm Sun; Ⓜ Nyugati pályaudvar) has prepaid vouchers available for 1000/2500Ft with 500/1500Ft worth of credit. Top-up cards cost 3000/7000/12,000Ft and are valid for three/six/12 months.

TIME

Budapest lies in the Central European time zone. Winter time is GMT plus one hour and in summer it's GMT plus two hours. Clocks are advanced at 2am on the last Sunday in March and set back at the same time on the last Sunday in October.

Without taking daylight-saving times into account, when it's noon in Budapest, it's: 11pm in Auckland, 1pm in Bucharest, 11am in London, 2pm in Moscow, 6am in New York, noon in Paris, 3am in San Francisco, 9pm in Sydney and 8pm in Tokyo. For information about other time zones and their relation to Hungary, see the World Times Zones map (p214).

Like some other European languages, Magyar tells the time by making reference to the next hour – not the one before as we do in English. Thus 7.30 is 'half eight' (*fél nyolc óra*) and the 24-hour system is often used in giving the bus and train departures as well as the times of movies, concerts and so on. So a film at 7.30pm could appear on a listing as 'f8', 'f20', '1/28' or '1/220'. A quarter to the hour has a 3/4 in front (thus '3/48' means 7.45) while quarter past is 1/4 of the next hour (eg '1/49' means 8.15). Got it?

TIPPING

Hungary is a very tip-conscious society and nearly everyone in Budapest will routinely tip waiters, hairdressers and taxi drivers. Doctors and dentists accept 'gratitude money', and even petrol-station and thermal-spa attendants expect something. If you aren't impressed with the service at a restaurant, the joyride in a taxi or the way someone cut your hair, leave little or nothing at all. He or she will get the message loud and clear.

To learn more about the unusual way to tip a waiter see p92.

TOURIST INFORMATION

Tourist Offices

Many of the travel agencies listed in the next section also provide information, brochures and maps.

Budapest Tourist Office (BTO; ☎ 266 0479; www.budapestinfo.hu) Budapest Tourist has three equally convenient and far less frantic outlets than Tourinform for information and advice, including a **Castle Hill branch** (Map p220; ☎ 488 0475; I Szentháromság tér; 🕑 9am-8pm May-Sept, 10am-7pm Oct-Apr; 🚌 16 or Várbusz); an **Oktogon branch** (Map p222; ☎ 322 4098; VI Liszt Ferenc tér 11; 🕑 9am-7pm Apr-Oct, 10am-6pm Nov-Mar; Ⓜ M1 Oktogon); and a **Nyugati train station branch** (Map p222; ☎ 302 8580; Nyugati pályaudvar, platform 10; 🕑 9am-7pm Apr-Oct,9am-6pm Nov-Mar; Ⓜ M3 Nyugati pályaudvar). It also maintains offices at Ferihegy airport's Terminals 1, 2A (arrivals) and 2B (departures).

Tourinform (Map p224; ☎ 438 8080, ☎ 24hr information hotline 06-80 630 800; www.tourinform.hu; V Sütő utca 2; 🕑 8am-8pm; Ⓜ M1/2/3 Deák Ferenc tér). This is usually the single best source of information about Budapest but it can get hopelessly crowded in summer, and the staff are no longer very patient or even helpful.

Visitors' Guide Budapest (www.visitorsguide.hu) This is the *Budapest Sun*'s site.

Travel Agencies

If your query is about private accommodation, flights or international train travel or you need to change money, you could turn to a commercial travel agency, such as Ibusz, arguably the best for private accommodation (p153), or Express, which issues student, youth, teacher and hostel cards (p187) and sells discounted Billet International de Jeunesse (BIJ) train and cheap air tickets.

Express (Map p224; ☎ 327 7290, 266 3277; www.express-travel.hu; V Semmelweis utca 4; 🕑 8.30am-5pm Mon-Fri, 9am-1pm Sat; Ⓜ M2 Astoria) The main office of this youth- and student-orientated agency can book accommodation, particularly hostels and colleges, and sell transport tickets.

Ibusz (Map p224; ☎ 485 2700; www.ibusz.hu; V Ferenciek tere 10; 🕑 9am-6pm Mon-Fri, 9am-1pm Sat; Ⓜ M3 Ferenciek tere) The main office of this travel agency giant supplies travel brochures, changes money, books all types of accommodation and accepts credit-card payments.

Mellow Mood (Map p224; ☎ 411 2390; www.youthhostels.hu, www.mellowmood.hu; V Molnár utca 3; 🕑 9am-6pm Mon-Fri; Ⓜ M3 Ferenciek tere) This new kid on the block run by the hostel group of the same name can organise accommodation in private rooms and hostels, book tours, sell you discounted air tickets etc.

Vista (Map p224; ☎ 429 9751; www.vista.hu; VI Paulay Ede utca 2; 🕑 9am-6.30pm Mon-Fri, 9am-2.30pm Sat; Ⓜ M1/2/3 Deák Ferenc tér) Vista is an excellent one-stop shop for all your travel needs, both outbound (air tickets, package tours etc) and incoming (room bookings, organised tours, study and ecological tours in Hungary etc).

Wasteels (☎ 343 3492; VIII Kerepesi út 2-6; 🕑 8am-8pm Mon-Fri, 8am-6pm Sat; Ⓜ M2 Keleti pályaudvar) This agency at the top of platform 9 at Keleti train station (Map pp218–19) sells BIJ tickets but you must have a student or youth card (p188) to get the discounted fares.

VISAS

Citizens of virtually all European countries as well as Australia, Canada, Israel, Japan, New Zealand and the USA do not require visas to visit Hungary for stays of up to 90 days. Nationals of South Africa (among others) still require visas. Check current visa requirements at a Hungarian consulate, any HNTO or Malév Hungarian Airlines office or on the website of the **Hungarian Foreign Ministry** (www.mfa.gov.hu.) as requirements often change without notice.

Visas are issued at Hungarian consulates or missions, most international highway border crossings, Ferihegy airport and the International Ferry Pier in Budapest. They are rarely issued on international buses and never on trains. Be sure to retain the separate entry and exit forms issued with the visa that is stamped in your passport.

Single-entry tourist visas are issued at Hungarian consulates or missions in applicants' country of residence upon receipt of S$40 (or equivalent) and three photos (US$65 at a mission outside the country of residence or at the border). A double-entry tourist visa costs US$75/100, and you must have five photos. A multiple-entry visa is US$180/200. Single and double-entry visas are valid for six months prior to use. Multiple-entry ones are good for a year.

Be sure to get a tourist rather than a transit visa; the latter – available for single (US$38/50), double (US$65/90) and multiple (US$150/180) entries – is only good for a stay of 48 hours, you must enter and leave through different border crossings and already hold a visa (if required) for the next country you visit.

Tourist visas are only extended in emergencies (such as medical; 3000Ft) and this must be done at the main police station *(rendőrkapitányság)* of the *kerület* in which you are staying five days before the original one expires.

You are supposed to register with the police if staying in one place for more than 30 days, and your hotel, hostel or private room booked through an agency will do this for you. In other situations – if you're staying with friends or relatives, for example – you or the head of household has to take care of this yourself within 72 hours of moving in. Address registration forms for foreigners *(lakcímbejelentő lap külföldiek részére)* are usually available at post offices.

WOMEN TRAVELLERS

Hungarian men can be sexist in their thinking, but women in Budapest do not suffer any particular form of harassment (though domestic violence and rape get relatively little media coverage here). Most men – even drunks – are effusively polite with women. Women may not be made to feel especially welcome when eating or drinking alone, but it's really no different from most other countries in Europe.

If you do need assistance and/or information ring the **Women's Line** (Nővonal; ☎ 06-80 505 101; 🕑 6-10pm Thu-Tue) or **Women for**

Women against Violence (NANE; ☎ 267 4900; info@nane.hu).

WORK

Travellers on tourist visas in Budapest are not supposed to accept employment, but many end up teaching, doing a little writing for the English-language press or even working for foreign firms without permits. Check the English-language telephone book or advertisements for English-language schools in the *Budapest Sun*, which also has job listings, though pay is generally pretty low. You can do much better teaching privately (up to 4000Ft per 45-minute 'hour', depending on your experience).

For the most part, EU nationals can come and work freely in Hungary, though they do require a residency permit, which can only be obtained in Budapest (1500Ft). For non-EU nationals, however, obtaining a work permit *(munkavállalási engedély)* involves a considerable paper chase. You'll need a letter of support from your prospective employer, copies of your birth certificate, your academic record and results of a recent medical examination (including a test for exposure to HIV) costing about 20,000Ft. The employer then submits these to the local labour centre *(munkaügyi központ)*, and you must return to your country of residence and apply for the work permit (US$50 or equivalent) at the Hungarian embassy or consulate there.

When you return to Hungary, you have 15 days to gather all the documents required to apply for a one-year renewable residence permit (*tartózkodási engedély*; 5000Ft) through the Residency Department of the Ministry of Internal Affairs' Immigration office at XI Budafoki út 60 in Budapest or through the main police station *(főkapitányság)* in your district or city.

Doing Business

The main source of information in English for businesspeople in Budapest is the *Budapest Business Journal* (BBJ; www.bbj.hu; 575Ft), which is an almost archival publication of financial news and business stories that has been around for nearly 15 years and appears on Monday. Another useful publication for businesspeople is the feature-oriented *Business Hungary* (900Ft), compiled monthly by the American Chamber of Commerce.

Following are some important addresses and/or useful sources of information:

American Chamber of Commerce in Hungary (Map p224; ☎ 266 9880; www.amcham.hu; V Deák Ferenc utca 10, 5th fl; Ⓜ M1 Vörösmarty tér)

British Chamber of Commerce in Hungary (Map p222; ☎ 302 5200, www.bcch.com; V Bank utca 6, 2nd fl; Ⓜ M3 Arany János utca)

Budapest Chamber of Commerce & Industry (Budapesti Kereskedelmi és Iparkamra; Map p220; ☎ 214 1826; www.bkik.hu in Hungarian; I Krisztina körút 99; 🚊 18)

Economy & Transport Ministry (Gazdasági és Közlekedési Minisztérium; Map p222; ☎ 374 2700; www.gkm.hu; V Honvéd utca 13-15; Ⓜ M2 Kossuth Lajos tér)

Finance Ministry (Pénzügy Minisztérium; Map p224; ☎ 318 2066; www.meh.hu in Hungarian; V József nádor tér 2-4; Ⓜ M1 Vörösmarty tér)

Hungarian Chamber of Commerce & Industry (Magyar Kereskedelmi és Iparkamra; Map p222; ☎ 474 5100; www.mkik.hu in Hungarian; V Kossuth Lajos tér 6-8, 5th fl; Ⓜ M2 Kossuth Lajos tér)

For photocopying, digital printing and computer services like scanning, visit any of the eight outlets of **Copy General** (www.copygeneral.hu in Hungarian), including its **district V branch** (Map p222; ☎ 302 3206; V Kálmán Imre utca 22; 🕑 24hr; Ⓜ M3 Nyugati pályaudvar). A similar – and aptly named – place nearby is **CopyCat** (Map p222; ☎ 312 7636; www.copycat.hu; V Alkotmány utca 18; 🕑 7am-10pm Mon-Fri, 10am-8pm Sat & Sun; Ⓜ M3 Nyugati pályaudvar).

All the major courier companies are represented here, including **DHL** (☎ 06-40 454 545; www.dhl.hu), **FedEx Hungary** (☎ 06-40 980 980; www.fedex.com), **TNT Express** (☎ 431 3131; www.tnt.hu) and **UPS** (☎ 06-40 262 000; www.ups.com).

Language

Language

It's true – anyone can speak another language. Don't worry if you haven't studied languages before or that you studied a language at school for years and can't remember any of it. It doesn't even matter if you failed English grammar. After all, that's never affected your ability to speak English! And this is the key to picking up a language in another country. You just need to start speaking.

Learn a few key phrases before you go. Write them on pieces of paper and stick them on the fridge, by the bed or even on the computer – anywhere that you'll see them often.

You'll find that locals appreciate travellers trying their language, no matter how muddled you may think you sound. So don't just stand there, say something! If you want to learn more Hungarian than we've included here, pick up a copy of Lonely Planet's user-friendly *Hungarian Phrasebook*.

PRONUNCIATION

The letters ö and ő, and ü and ű, are listed as separate pairs of letters in dictionaries (following o, ó and u, ú respectively). The consonant combinations cs, dz, dzs, gy, ly, ny, sz, ty and zs also have separate entries.

Vowels

a	as in 'hot'
á	as in 'father'
e	as in 'bet'
é	as in 'air"
i	as in 'hit'
í	as in 'meet'
o	as in 'law' but short
ó	as in 'awl'
ö	as in 'curt' but short (with no 'r' sound)
ő	as in 'her' (with no 'r' sound)
u	as in 'pull'
ú	as in 'rule'
ü	like i but with rounded lips (like 'u' in French *tu*)
ű	as in 'strewn'

Consonants

c	as the 'ts' in 'rats'
cs	as the 'ch' in 'cheese'
dz	as in 'adze'
dzs	as the 'j' in 'joke'
gy	as the 'du' in 'dune' (British)
j/ly	as in 'yes'
ny	as the 'ny' in 'canyon'
r	as in 'run' (but rolled)
s	as the 'sh' in 'ship'
sz	as the 's' in 'sit'
ty	as the 'tu' in 'tube' (British)
zs	as the 's' in 'pleasure'

SOCIAL

Meeting People

In the following phrases, the polite form of 'you' (*Ön* and *Önök*) is given except for situations where you might wish to establish a more personal relationship.

Note that when you want to say 'Hello', 'Hi', or 'Bye', the word will change depending on whether you are speaking to one person or more than one. Look for the symbols 'sg' (singular) or 'pl' (plural) to determine which word to use.

Hello.	Szervusz. (sg) Szervusztok. (pl)
Hi.	Szia/Sziasztok. (sg/pl)
Good ...	Jó ... kívánok.
morning	reggelt
afternoon/day	napot
evening	estét
Goodbye.	Viszlát. (pol) Szia. (inf sg) Sziasztok. (inf sg/pl)
Good night.	Jó éjszakát.
Yes.	Igen.
No.	Nem.
Please.	Kérem. (pol) Kérlek (inf)
Thank you (very much).	(Nagyon) Köszönöm.

You're welcome.	Szívesen.
Excuse me. (to get attention)	Elnézést kérek.
Excuse me. (to get past)	Bocsánat.
Sorry.	Sajnálom.
How are you?	Hogy van? (pol) Hogy vagy? (inf)
Fine. And you?	Jól. És Ön/te?
What's your name?	Mi a neve? (pol) Mi a neved? (inf)
My name is ...	A nevem ...
I'm pleased to meet you.	Örvendek.
Where are you from?	Ön honnan jön?
I'm from ...	Én ... jövök.
Do you speak English?	Beszél angolul?
I (don't) understand.	(Nem) Értem.
What does ... mean?	Mit jelent az, hogy ...?
Could you please write it down?	Leírná, kérem.

Going Out

What's on ...?
Mi a program ...?

locally	helyben
this weekend	ezen a hétvégén
today	ma
tonight	ma este

Where can I find ...?
Hol találok ...?

clubs	klubokat
gay venues	meleg szórakozóhelyeket
places to eat	egy helyet, ahol enni lehet
pubs	pubokat

Is there a local entertainment guide?
Van itt helyi programkalauz?

PRACTICAL

Directions

Where's (the market)?
Hol van (a piac)?
What's the address?
Mi a cím?
How do I get there?
Hogyan jutok oda?
How far is it?
Milyen messze van?
Can you show me (on the map)?
Meg tudja mutatni nekem (a térképen)?
It's straight ahead.
Egyenesen előttünk van.

Turn ...
Forduljon ...

at the corner	a saroknál
at the traffic lights	a közlekedési lámpánál
left/right	balra/jobbra

Signs

Bejárat	Entrance
Kijárat	Exit
Nyitva	Open
Zárva	Closed
Foglalt	Reserved/Occupied
Belépni Tilos	No Entry
Tilos	Prohibited
Tilos a Dohányzás	No Smoking
Toalett/WC	Toilets
Férfiak	Men
Nők	Women

Question Words

How many?	Hány?
How much?	Mennyi?
What?	Mi?
What kind?	Milyen?
Where?	Hol?
When?	Mikor?
Which?	Melyik?
Who?	Ki?
Why?	Miért?

Numbers & Amounts

The word kettő is used when expressing the number two on its own, while két is used when it is followed by the counted noun.

0	nulla
1	egy
2	kettő/két
3	három
4	négy
5	öt
6	hat
7	hét
8	nyolc
9	kilenc
10	tíz
11	tizenegy

12	tizenkettő
13	tizenhárom
14	tizennégy
15	tizenöt
16	tizenhat
17	tizenhét
18	tizennyolc
19	tizenkilenc
20	húsz
21	huszonegy
22	huszonkettő
30	harminc
31	harmincegy
32	harminckettő
40	negyven
41	negyvenegy
42	negyvenkettő
50	ötven
60	hatvan
70	hetven
80	nyolcvan
90	kilencven
100	száz
200	kétszáz
1000	ezer

Days

Monday	hétfő
Tuesday	kedd
Wednesday	szerda
Thursday	csütörtök
Friday	péntek
Saturday	szombat
Sunday	vasárnap

Banking

I'd like to ...
Szeretnék ...

change a travellers cheque	beváltani egy utazási csekket
change money	pénzt váltani

Do you accept ...?
Elfogadnak ...?

credit cards	hitelkártyát
travellers cheques	utazási csekket

Where is ...?
Hol van ...?

an ATM	egy bankautomata
a foreign exchange office	egy valutaváltó ügynökség

Post

Where's the post office?
Hol van a postahivatal?

I want to send a ...
... szeretnék küldeni.

letter	Levelet
parcel	Csomagot
postcard	Képeslapot

I want to buy a/an...
... szeretnék venni.

airmail envelope	Légipostai borítékot
ordinary envelope	Sima borítékot
stamp	Bélyeget

Phones & Mobiles

Where's the nearest public phone?
Hol a legközelebbi nyilvános telefon?
I want to make a collect/reverse-charge call.
'R' beszélgetést szeretnék kérni.

I want to ...
Szeretnék ...
buy a phonecard
telefonkártyát venni
call (Singapore)
(Szingapúr)ba telefonálni
make a (local) call
(helyi) telefonbeszélgetést folytatni

I'd like a ...
Szeretnék egy ...
charger for my phone
töltőt a telefonomhoz
mobile phone/cellphone for hire
mobiltelefont bérelni
(prepaid) SIM card
(előre kifizetett) SIM-kártyát

Internet

Where's the local Internet café?
Hol van a legközelebbi internet kávézó?

I'd like to ...
Szeretném ...
check my email
megnézni az e-mailjeimet
get Internet access
rámenni az internetre

Transport

Which ... goes to (the Parliament)?
Melyik ... megy (a Parlamenthez)?

bus	busz
train	vonat
tram	villamos
trolleybus	trolibusz
metro line	metró

When's the ...?
Mikor megy ...?

first	az első
last	az utolsó
next	a következő

Is this taxi available?
Szabad ez a taxi?
Please put the meter on.
Kérem, kapcsolja be az órát.
How much is it to ...?
Mennyibe kerül ... ba?
Please take me to (this address).
Kérem, vigyen el (erre a címre).
What time does it leave?
Mikor indul?

FOOD

breakfast	reggeli
lunch	ebéd
dinner	vacsora
snack	snack

Can you recommend a ... ?
Tud/Tudsz ajánlani egy ...? pol/inf

bar/pub	bárt/pubot
beer bar	sörözőt
restaurant	éttermet
self-service restaurant	önkiszolgálót

Is service included in the bill?
A kiszolgálás díja benne van a számlában?

For more detailed information on food and dining out, see p25 and p91.

EMERGENCIES

Help!	Segítség!
Could you please help?	Tudna segíteni?
Call the police!	Hívja a rendőrséget!
Call a doctor!	Hívjon orvost!
Where's the police station?	Hol a rendőrség?
Go away!	Menjen el!

HEALTH

Where's the nearest ...?
Hol a legközelebbi ...?

dentist	fogorvos
doctor	orvos
hospital	kórház
medical centre	orvosi rendelő
(night) pharmacist	(éjszaka nyitvatartó) gyógyszertár

I'm allergic to ...
Allergiás vagyok ...

antibiotics	az antibiotikumokra
penicillin	a penicillinre

Symptoms

I have a headache.	Fáj a fejem.
I have a sore throat.	Fáj a torkom.

I have (a) ...
... van.

asthma	Asztmám
diarrhoea	Hasmenésem
fever	Lázam
nausea	Hányingerem

GLOSSARY

ÁFA – value-added tax (VAT)
ÁVO – Rákosi's hated secret police in the early years of communism; later renamed ÁVH
BKV – Budapest Közlekedési Vallálat (Budapest Transport Company)
bolhapiac – flea market
borozó – wine bar; any place serving wine
Bp – commonly used abbreviation for Budapest
búcsú – farewell; also a church patronal festival
büfé – snack bar

centrum – town or city centre
cukrászda – cake shop or patisserie

Eclectic – an art and architectural style that was popular in Hungary in the Romantic period, drawing from sources both indigenous and foreign
eszpresszó – coffee shop, often also selling alcoholic drinks and snacks; strong, black coffee; same as *presszó*
étkezde – canteen that serves simple dishes
étterem – restaurant

fasor – boulevard, avenue
forint (Ft) – Hungary's monetary unit
főkapitányság – main police station

gyógyfürdő – bath or spa
gyógyszertár – pharmacy

hajó – boat
hajóallomás – ferry pier or landing
ház – house
hegy – hill, mountain
HÉV – Helyiérdekű Vasút (suburban commuter train in Budapest)
híd – bridge

HNTO – Hungarian National Tourism Office

ifjúsági szálló – youth hostel

kastély – manor house or mansion (see *vár*)
kerület – city district
kincstár – treasury
Kiskörút – 'Little Ring Road' in Budapest
könyvesbolt – bookshop
könyvtár – library
kórház – hospital
körút – ring road
korzó – embankment or promenade
köz – alley, mews, lane
központ – centre
krt – abbreviation for *körút* (ring road)

lekvár – fruit jam
lépcső – stairs, steps
liget – park

Mahart – Hungarian passenger ferry company
Malév – Hungary's national airline
MÁV – Magyar Államvasutak (Hungarian State Railways)
megye – county

Nagykörút – 'Big Ring Road' in Budapest
nyitva – open

önkiszolgáló – self-service

pálinka – fruit brandy
palota – palace
pályaudvar – train or railway station
panzió – *pension*, guesthouse
patika – pharmacy
pénztár – cashier
piac – market
pince – wine cellar
porta – type of farmhouse in Transdanubia
presszó – same as *eszpresszó* (coffee shop; strong, black coffee)
pu – abbreviation for *pályaudvar* (train station)
puttony – the number of 'butts' of sweet *aszú* essence added to other base wines in making Tokaj wine

rakpart – quay, embankment
rendőrkapitányság – police station

Secessionism – art and architectural style similar to Art Nouveau
sedile (pl **sedilia**) – medieval stone niche with seats
sétány – walkway, promenade
söröző – beer bar or pub
strand – grassy 'beach' near a river or lake
szálló or **szálloda** – hotel
székesegyház – cathedral
személyvonat – passenger trains that stop at every city, town, village and hamlet along the way
sziget – island

táncház – folk music and dance workshop
templom – church
tér – town or market square
tere – genitive form of *tér* as in Hősök tere (Square of the Heroes)
tó – lake
turul – eagle-like totem of the ancient Magyars and now a national symbol

u – abbreviation for *utca* (street)
udvar – court
úszoda – swimming pool
út – road
utca – street
utcája – genitive form of *utca* as in Ferencesek utcája (Street of the Franciscans)
útja – genitive form of *út* as in Mártíroká útja (Street of the Martyrs)

vágány – platform
vár – castle
város – city
városház or **városháza** – town hall
vendéglő – a type of restaurant
Volán – Hungarian bus company

zárva – closed

Behind the Scenes

THE LONELY PLANET STORY

The story begins with a classic travel adventure: Tony and Maureen Wheeler's 1972 journey across Europe and Asia to Australia. There was no useful information about the overland trail then, so Tony and Maureen published the first Lonely Planet guidebook to meet a growing need.

From a kitchen table, Lonely Planet has grown to become the largest independent travel publisher in the world, with offices in Melbourne (Australia), Oakland (USA) and London (UK). Today Lonely Planet guidebooks cover the globe. There is an ever-growing list of books and information in a variety of media. Some things haven't changed. The main aim is still to make it possible for adventurous travellers to get out there – to explore and better understand the world.

At Lonely Planet we believe travellers can make a positive contribution to the countries they visit – if they respect their host communities and spend their money wisely. Every year 5% of company profit is donated to charities around the world.

THIS BOOK

This 3rd edition of *Budapest* was written and updated by Steve Fallon, as were the first two editions. This guidebook was commissioned in Lonely Planet's London office and produced by the following:

Commissioning Editors Fiona Buchan, Janine Eberle

Coordinating Editor Yvonne Byron

Coordinating Cartographer Amanda Sierp

Coordinating Layout Designer Christine Wieser

Managing Cartographer Mark Griffiths

Assisting Editors Lutie Clark

Cover Designer Annika Roojun

Project Manager Rachel Imeson

Language Content Coordinator Quentin Frayne

Thanks to Sally Darmody, Bruce Evans, Wibowo Rusli

Cover photographs Main rotunda, Parliament building, David Greedy/Lonely Planet Images (top); Enjoying the Széchenyi Baths, Matias Costa/Panos Pictures (bottom); Souvenir bags of paprika with spoons, Jonathan Smith/Lonely Planet Images (back)

Internal photographs by Lonely Planet Images and Richard Nebesky, except for the following: p105 (#5) Christer Fredriksson; p39 Kim Grant; p102 (#3) David Greedy; p86, p90, p104, p105 (#2), p105 (#3), p105 (#4), p108, p109 (#2), p109 (#4), p109 (#5), p172, p176 Martin Moos; p101 (#4), p109 (#3) Jonathan Smith; p2 (#2) Roberto Soncin Gerometta; p78 Christopher Wood.

THANKS

STEVE FALLON

Special thanks to my good friend Bea Szirti for all her helpful suggestions and to Erzsébet Tiszai, who assisted with the research and has the patience of Job. Dr Zsuzsa Medgyes of M&G Marketing came forward with all those wonderful little details during a particularly difficult time; I am very grateful. Brandon Krueger and Anna Reich of the Central European University, László Józsa of TV2 and Eric D'Amato of Pestiside.hu added insights into what's on in Budapest after dark. Ildikó Nagy Moran was as welcoming and helpful as always.

As always, *Budapest* is dedicated to my – now official – partner Michael Rothschild, with love and gratitude and memory.

OUR READERS

Many thanks to the travellers who used the last edition and wrote to us with helpful hints, useful advice and interesting anecdotes:

Ian Allred, Leonardo Aversa, JB Barnard, Rosemary Black, Eleanor Butler, Richard Butler, Marice Caplan, Sarah Capper, Marie Corn, Vanessa Creedon, Jac Crowle, Jill Davies, Jez & Julie Davis, Pascal de Meyer, Bruce Denner, Barbara Dorrell, Jill Drury, Heather Ebbott, Rogier Etman, Roland Evans, Daniel Fiott, Geer Furtjes, Patrick Gallagher, Peter

SEND US YOUR FEEDBACK

We love to hear from travellers – your comments keep us on our toes and help make our books better. Our well-travelled team reads every word on what you loved or loathed about this book. Although we cannot reply individually to postal submissions, we always guarantee that your feedback goes straight to the appropriate authors, in time for the next edition. Each person who sends us information is thanked in the next edition – and the most useful submissions are rewarded with a free book.

To send us your updates – and find out about Lonely Planet events, newsletters and travel news – visit our award-winning website: www.lonelyplanet.com/feedback.

Note: We may edit, reproduce and incorporate your comments in Lonely Planet products such as guidebooks, websites and digital products, so let us know if you don't want your comments reproduced or your name acknowledged. For a copy of our privacy policy visit www.lonelyplanet.com/privacy.

Gebauer, Anders Grahn, Tom Grevatte, Gabi Gulyas, Frederik Helbo, Derek & Judy Henchliffe, Michele Hendricks, Howard Hodges, Phyllis Kirik, Cees Krommenhoek, Viktoria Ladanyi, Mark Ladd, Andrew Laidler, Charles Marcotte, Anna Morris, Anna Moss-Gibbons, Alvaro Ruiz Navajas, Axel Nelms, Vincent O'Callaghan, James Oehlcke, Marina Pantazidou, Laura Paris, Erin Propas, Carsten Püttgen, Eric Reber, Gail Resnick, Jayne Rimmer, Andrew Ruttkay, Korino Sango, Amanda Sharp, Alan Smith, Alice Smith, Simon, Judy & Matthew Smith, Damian Spellman, Cath Stobbart, Yael Straver-Lerys, Edel Tobin, Ildiko Varga, Judith Vasey, Helen Vincent, Arnie Wickens, Chad Williams, Anne Zielisch

Notes

Index

See also separate indexes for Eating (p211), Entertainment (p212), Shopping (p213) and Sleeping (p213).

000 map pages
000 photographs

000 map pages
000 photographs

Index

000 map pages
000 photographs

EATING

ENTERTAINMENT

000 map pages
000 photographs

SHOPPING

SLEEPING

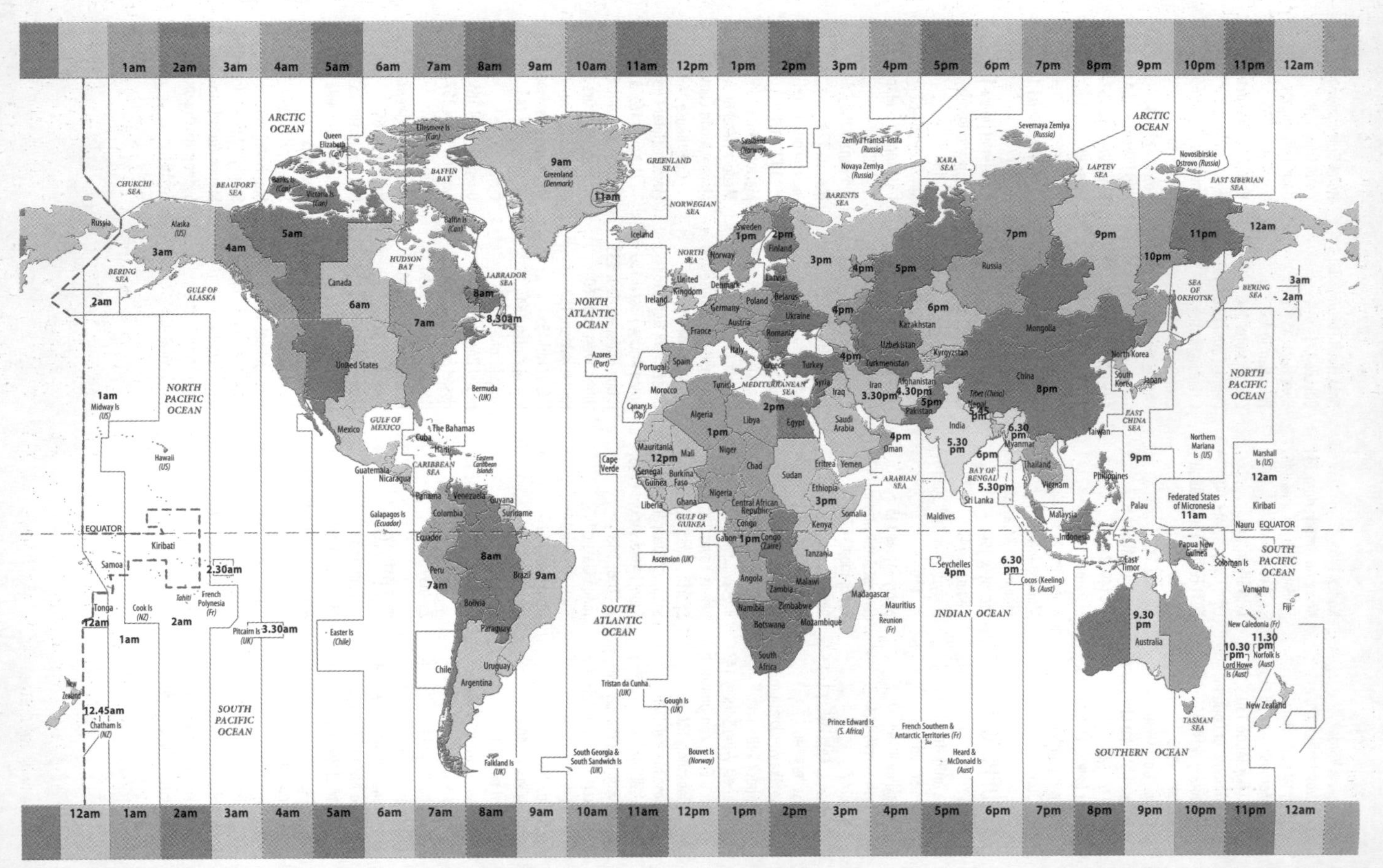

1am
2am
3am
4am
5am
6am
7am
8am
9am
10am
11am
12pm
1pm
2pm
3pm
4pm
5pm
6pm
7pm
8pm
9pm
10pm
11pm
12am
ARCTIC OCEAN
CHUKCHI SEA
BEAUFORT SEA
BERING SEA
GULF OF ALASKA
Russia
Alaska (US)
3am
4am
5am
Queen Elizabeth Is (Can)
Banks Is (Can)
Victoria Is (Can)
Ellesmere Is (Can)
BAFFIN BAY
Baffin Is (Can)
HUDSON BAY
LABRADOR SEA
Canada
6am
7am
8am
8.30am
9am
Greenland (Denmark)
11am
GREENLAND SEA
NORWEGIAN SEA
Iceland
NORTH SEA
United Kingdom
Ireland
Svalbard (Norway)
Zemlya Frantsa-Iosifa (Russia)
Novaya Zemlya (Russia)
BARENTS SEA
KARA SEA
Severnaya Zemlya (Russia)
LAPTEV SEA
Novosibirskie Ostrovo (Russia)
EAST SIBERIAN SEA
ARCTIC OCEAN
Sweden
1pm
Norway
2pm
Finland
Denmark
Latvia
Belarus
Poland
Germany
France
Austria
Ukraine
Romania
Italy
Spain
Portugal
Greece
Turkey
3pm
4pm
4pm
5pm
Russia
6pm
7pm
9pm
10pm
11pm
12am
SEA OF OKHOTSK
BERING SEA
3am
2am
2am
United States
Mexico
GULF OF MEXICO
The Bahamas
Cuba
Haiti
CARIBBEAN SEA
Eastern Caribbean Islands
Guatemala
Nicaragua
Bermuda (UK)
NORTH ATLANTIC OCEAN
Azores (Port)
Canary Is (Sp)
Cape Verde
1am
Midway Is (US)
NORTH PACIFIC OCEAN
Hawaii (US)
EQUATOR
Kiribati
Samoa
2.30am
Tonga
12am
Cook Is (NZ)
Tahiti
French Polynesia (Fr)
2am
1am
Pitcairn Is (UK)
3.30am
Easter Is (Chile)
New Zealand
12.45am
Chatham Is (NZ)
SOUTH PACIFIC OCEAN
Panama
Venezuela
Guyana
Suriname
Colombia
Ecuador
Galapagos Is (Ecuador)
Peru
7am
8am
Brazil
9am
Bolivia
Paraguay
Chile
Uruguay
Argentina
Falkland Is (UK)
South Georgia & South Sandwich Is (UK)
SOUTH ATLANTIC OCEAN
Tristan da Cunha (UK)
Gough Is (UK)
Bouvet Is (Norway)
Ascension (UK)
Morocco
Algeria
Tunisia
MEDITERRANEAN SEA
Libya
Egypt
2pm
1pm
Mauritania
12pm
Mali
Niger
Chad
Sudan
Senegal
Guinea
Burkina Faso
Liberia
Ghana
Nigeria
Central African Republic
GULF OF GUINEA
Gabon
Congo
1pm
Congo (Zaire)
Eritrea
Yemen
Ethiopia
3pm
Somalia
Kenya
Tanzania
Angola
Zambia
Malawi
Namibia
Zimbabwe
Botswana
Mozambique
South Africa
Madagascar
Mauritius
Reunion (Fr)
Prince Edward Is (S. Africa)
French Southern & Antarctic Territories (Fr)
Heard & McDonald Is (Aust)
Syria
Iraq
Iran
3.30pm
Saudi Arabia
Oman
4pm
ARABIAN SEA
Kazakhstan
Uzbekistan
Turkmenistan
Kyrgyzstan
Afghanistan
4.30pm
Pakistan
5pm
India
5.30 pm
Nepal
5.45 pm
Tibet (China)
6pm
6.30 pm
Myanmar
BAY OF BENGAL
5.30pm
Sri Lanka
Maldives
Seychelles
4pm
INDIAN OCEAN
6.30 pm
Cocos (Keeling) Is (Aust)
Mongolia
China
8pm
North Korea
South Korea
Japan
EAST CHINA SEA
Taiwan
Thailand
Vietnam
Philippines
Malaysia
Indonesia
9pm
Palau
East Timor
Papua New Guinea
Northern Mariana Is (US)
Federated States of Micronesia
11am
NORTH PACIFIC OCEAN
Marshall Is (US)
12am
Kiribati
Nauru
EQUATOR
Solomon Is
SOUTH PACIFIC OCEAN
Vanuatu
Fiji
New Caledonia (Fr)
9.30 pm
Australia
10.30 pm
Lord Howe Is (Aust)
11.30 pm
Norfolk Is (Aust)
New Zealand
TASMAN SEA
SOUTHERN OCEAN
12am
1am
2am
3am
4am
5am
6am
7am
8am
9am
10am
11am
12pm
1pm
2pm
3pm
4pm
5pm
6pm
7pm
8pm
9pm
10pm
11pm
12am

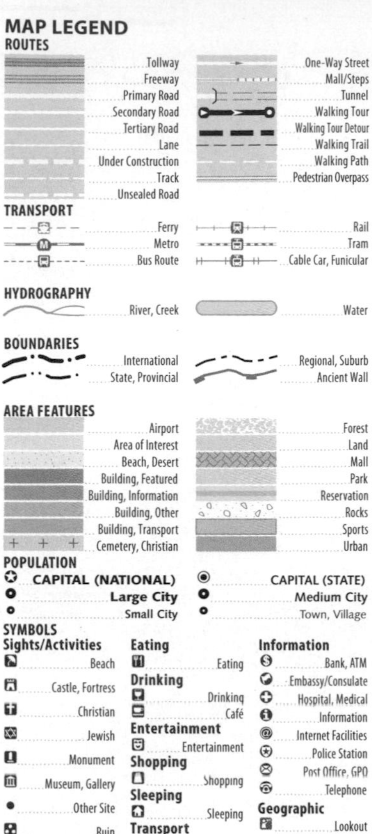
MAP LEGEND
ROUTES
Tollway
Freeway
Primary Road
Secondary Road
Tertiary Road
Lane
Under Construction
Track
Unsealed Road
One-Way Street
Mall/Steps
Tunnel
Walking Tour
Walking Tour Detour
Walking Trail
Walking Path
Pedestrian Overpass
TRANSPORT
Ferry
Metro
Bus Route
Rail
Tram
Cable Car, Funicular
HYDROGRAPHY
River, Creek
Water
BOUNDARIES
International
State, Provincial
Regional, Suburb
Ancient Wall
AREA FEATURES
Airport
Area of Interest
Beach, Desert
Building, Featured
Building, Information
Building, Other
Building, Transport
Cemetery, Christian
Forest
Land
Mall
Park
Reservation
Rocks
Sports
Urban
POPULATION
CAPITAL (NATIONAL)
Large City
Small City
CAPITAL (STATE)
Medium City
Town, Village
SYMBOLS
Sights/Activities
Beach
Castle, Fortress
Christian
Jewish
Monument
Museum, Gallery
Other Site
Ruin
Swimming Pool
Zoo, Bird Sanctuary
Eating
Eating
Drinking
Drinking
Café
Entertainment
Entertainment
Shopping
Shopping
Sleeping
Sleeping
Transport
Bus Station
General Transport
Parking Area
Information
Bank, ATM
Embassy/Consulate
Hospital, Medical
Information
Internet Facilities
Police Station
Post Office, GPO
Telephone
Geographic
Lookout
Mountain, Volcano
National Park
River Flow

Maps

BUDAPEST & ENVIRONS

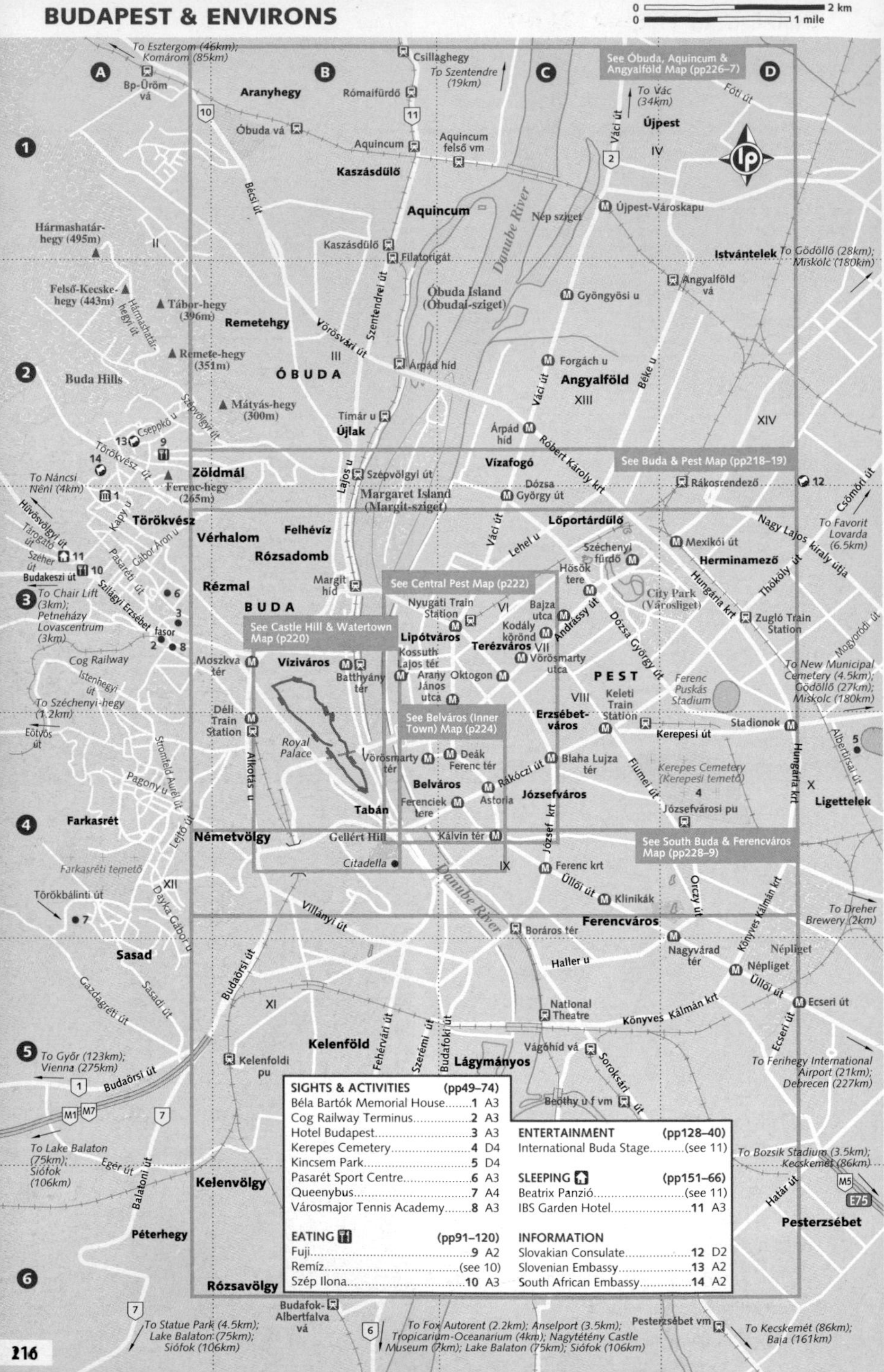

BUDA & PEST (pp218–19)

SIGHTS & ACTIVITIES (pp49–74)

Alfréd Hajós National Sports Pool **1** C2
Anonymous Statue **2** F2
Applied Arts Museum **3** E6
Aviation Museum (see 95)
Béla Komjádi Swimming Pool **4** C2
BVSC **5** G1
Calvinist Church (City Park) **6** F3
Centennial Monument **7** C2
City Park Ice-Skating Rink (Winter Only) **8** F2
City Zoo & Botanical Garden **9** F2
Egger Villa **10** F3
Ferenc Hopp Museum of East Asian Art **11** F3
Former Communist Party Headquarters **12** F4
Former Telephone Exchange Building **13** F5
Foundry Museum **14** B3
Franciscan Church & Monastery Ruins **15** C1
Funfair Park **16** F2
Geology Institute **17** G3
George Washington Statue **18** F2
Gül Baba's Tomb **19** B2
György Ráth Museum **20** F3
Hélia Thermal Spa & Pools **21** D1
Hungarian Agricultural Museum **22** F2
International House Language School **23** B2
Ják Chapel **24** F2
Király Baths **25** C3
Lukács Baths **26** C2
Miksa Róth Memorial House **27** F4
Military Court of Justice & Fő utca Prison **28** C3
Millenary Monument **29** F2
Millennium Exhibition Hall **30** A3
Millennium Park **31** B3
Municipal Great Circus **32** F2
Museum of Fine Arts **33** F2
Műcsarnok (Palace of Art) **34** F2
National Institute for the Blind **35** G2
Palace of Miracles **36** E2
Raoul Wallenberg Memorial **37** D2
St Florian Chapel **38** C3
Sétacikli Bike Rental **39** C2
Sonnenberg Mansion **40** E2
Széchenyi Baths **41** F2
Top Squash (see 101)
Transport Museum **42** G2
Újlak Synagogue **43** C1
Vajdahunyad Castle (see 22)
Vidor Villa **44** F3

EATING (pp91–120)

Arcade **45** A5
Bagolyvár **46** F2
Csülök Csárda **47** F4
Déli Kinai Gyorsétterem **48** A4
Durcin Branch **49** A3
Fény utca Market **50** B3
Firkász **51** D2
Gasztró Hús-Hentesáru **52** C2
Han Kuk Guan **53** G3
Il Treno **54** A4
Íz-É Faloda **55** A3
Kacsa **56** C3
Keleti Sarok **57** F4
Lanzhou **58** F4
Lehel Csarnok **59** D2
Malomtó **60** B2
Maros Söröző **61** A4
Marxim **62** B3
Mongolian Barbecue **63** A5
Móri Kisvendéglő **64** D2
Nagyi Palacsintázója **65** B3
Napfényes Ízek **66** E3
Nefrit **67** A5
Pink Cadillac **68** E6
Pozsonyi Kisvendéglő **69** D2
Premier **70** E3
Rákóczi tér Market **71** E5
Robinson **72** F2
Shiraz **73** E6
Stex Alfred **74** E5
Szent Jupát (see 113)
Toldi Étkezde **75** B3
Troféa Grill **76** D2
Új Lanzhou **77** C3
Vogue **78** D1

DRINKING (pp123–8)

Auguszt **79** A3
Café Csiga **80** E5
Demmer's Teahouse **81** A3
Hauer Cukrászda **82** E4
Kultiplex **83** F6
Oscar American Bar **84** B3
Paris, Texas **85** E6
Poco Loco Pub **86** C1

ENTERTAINMENT (pp128–40)

Almássy tér Recreation Centre **87** E4
Budapest Congress Centre **88** A5
Central Europe Dance Theatre **89** F3
Cha Cha Cha Terasz **90** C2
Corvin Film Palace **91** E6
Erkel Theatre **92** F4
Kaméleon (see 102)
Közgáz Pince Klub **93** D6
Marczibányi tér Cultural Centre **94** A2
Petőfi Csarnok **95** G2
West Balkan Club Bar **96** E6

SHOPPING (pp141–50)

BÁV Branch **97** C2
Budapest Wine Society Shop **98** B3
Ciánkáli **99** F4
City Park Flea Market (see 95)
Herend Village Pottery **100** C3
Mammut I Shopping Mall **101** B3
Mammut II Shopping Mall **102** B3
MOM Park Shopping Mall **103** A5
Monarchia Borászati **104** E6
Mountex **105** E2
Museum of Fine Arts Office **106** E2
Pendragon **107** D2
Sporthorgász **108** B3

SLEEPING (pp151–66)

Andrássy Hotel **109** F3
Aquarium Youth Hostel **110** F4
Atlas Hotel **111** F5
Boat Hotel Fortuna **112** D2
Büro Panzió **113** A3
Dominik Panzió **114** G3
Golden Park Hotel **115** F4
Hostel Bakfark **116** B3
Hotel Baross **117** F4
Hotel Benczúr **118** F3
Hotel Császár **119** B2
Hotel Délibáb **120** F2
Hotel Góliát **121** F1
Hotel Liget **122** F2
Hotel Margitsziget **123** C1
KM Saga Guest Residence **124** D6
Papillon Hotel **125** B2
Peter's Apartments **126** D2
Radio Inn **127** F3
Red Bus 2 **128** F4
Star Hotel **129** F3
Station Guesthouse **130** H3
Sydney Apartment Hotel **131** D2

TRANSPORT (pp180–6)

Hungarian Automobile Club **132** D2
Malév Customer Service Centre **133** D2
Stadionok Bus Station **134** H4
Széna tér Bus Station **135** B3

INFORMATION

Australian Embassy **136** A5
Austrian Consulate **137** E3
Canadian Embassy **138** B3
Croatian Consulate **139** E2
Cybercafé Zone (see 102)
Déli Gyógyszertár **140** A4
Dutch Embassy **141** B2
FirstMed Centers **142** B3
French Consulate **143** F2
Post Office **144** F4
Private Link **145** E5
Romanian Consulate **146** G3
Serbia & Montenegro Consulate **147** F2
Ukrainian Consulate **148** G3
Wasteels **149** F4

BUDA & PEST

See Óbuda, Aquincum & Angyalföld Map (p226–7)
See Belváros (Inner Town) Map (p224)
See Castle Hill & Watertown Map (p220)
Margaret Island (Margit-sziget)
Danube River
Zöldmál
Vérhalom
Rózsadomb
Rézmal
Városmajor
Felhévíz
BUDA
Víziváros (Watertown)
Vérmező
Royal Palace
Tabán
Németvölgy
Gellért Hill
Citadella
Jubilee Park
Lipótváros
Újlipótváros
Terézváros
Erzsébetváros
Belváros
Vízafogó
Palatinus strand
Margaret Bridge (Margit híd)
Széchenyi Chain Bridge (Széchenyi lánchíd)
Elizabeth Bridge (Erzsébet híd)
Independence Bridge (Szabadság híd)
Déli Train Station
Nyugati Train Station
Sas-hegy (266m)

0 500 m
0 0.3 miles
E
F
G
H
1
2
3
4
5
6
Véső u
Apály u
Klapka u
Csángó u
Huba u
Dózsa György út
Botond u
Visegrádi u
Gidófalvy Lajos u
Tüzér u
Csata u
Üteg u
Kartács u
Gömb u
Béke u
Jász u
Kerekes u
Kis Gömb u
Mór u
Reitter Ferenc u
Szent László u
Ambrus u
Szegedi út
Tatai u
Rákosrendező
Ungvár u
Dorozsmai u
Teleki Blanka u
Lőcsei u
Czobor u
Ilosvai Selymes u
Fűrész u
Gervay u
Nagy Lajos király útja
Róbert Károly krt
Mohács u
Déványi út
Páloc u
Hajcsár u
BVSC
5
Lehel u
Hun u
Lőportárdűlő
Szabolcs u
Váci út
Taksony u
Kassák Lajos u
Aba u
Dózsa György út
36
105
Dévai u
Bulcsú u
Lőportár u
Vágány u
Varannó u
16
32
9
Állatkerti krt
41
Mexikói út
Szőnyi út
Mexikói út
Erzsébet királyné út
46
Széchenyi fürdő
72
Állatkerti út
Kós Károly sétány
Hermina út
Pálma u
Herminamező
See Central Pest Map (p222)
Városligeti krt
Liezen-Mayer sétány
33
Colonnades & Statues
122
24
2
Hősök tere
29
Hősök tere
Városligeti tó
22
95
Hungária krt
Gyarmat u
Thököly út
Podmaniczky u
40
106
143
8
34
City Park (Városliget)
42
35
Andrássy út
139
147
18
Olof Palme sétány
Zichy Mihály út
Kmetty György u
109
120
Dózsa György út
Zugló Train Station
Bajza utca
11
Benczúr u
70
127
118
Városligeti fasor
Dvorák sétány
Ajtósi Dürer sor
Zichy Géza u
Szugló u
130
Kodály körönd
137
10
44
Mexikói út
Bajza u
20
Damjanich u
Abonyi u
Izsó u
148
53
Andrássy út
Lövölde tér
6
Peterdy u
Dembinszky u
146
Thököly út
Egressy út
Vörösmarty utca
Hunyadi tér
Erzsébetváros
Csázár András u
114
Oktogon
66
Marek József u
17
PEST
Oktogon
Király u
Izabella u
Rózsa u
Rottenbiller u
Rethlen Gábor u
Nefelejcs u
129
89
Murányi u
Hernád u
Cserhát u
Sajó u
Dózsa
Reiner F Park
Kisstadion
To Tesco (500m)
Liszt Ferenc tér
Jósika u
Dob u
Hevesi Sándor tér
Bethlen Gábor tér
27
Péterfy Sándor u
Garay tér
István u
Szinva u
Istvánmezei út
Ferenc Puskás Stadium
Stefánia út
Mogyoródi út
Csengery u
Rózsák tere
Garay u
Thököly út
Százház u
Jobbágy u
Györgyi út
Budapest Sportaréna
Erzsébet krt
99
Verseny u
144
Verseny u
134
Erzsébetváros
Wesselényi u
Almássy tér
87
Szövetség u
Munkás u
Keleti Train Station
Stadionok
Klauzál tér
Barcsay u
Dohány u
Alsóerdősor u
117
Keleti pu
149
Kerepesi út
Hungária krt
110
57
115
Fiumei út
Mosonyi u
Osvát u
Nyár u
Dohány u
Rákóczi út
128
47
Trotting Race Track
12
58
Blaha Lujza tér
82
Luther u
Bezerédj u
92
Gázláng u
Rákóczi út
Köztársaság tér
Dologház u
Népszínház u
Kun u
Alföldi u
Vay A u
Kerepes Cemetery (Kerepesi temető)
Asztalos Sándor u
Rákóczi út
Bacsó u
Tolnai Lajos u
Bérkocsis u
111
Teleki László tér
ELTE
Józsefváros
80
Aurora u
Nagy Fuvaros u
Kis Fuvaros u
Gutenberg tér
Vásár u
71
Déri Miksa u
Erdélyi u
Hungária Stadium
József krt
Német u
Mátyás tér
Szerdahelyi u
Karácsony Sándor u
Dobozi u
Lőrinc Pap tér
József u
Őr u
Tavaszmező u
Dankó u
Lujza u
Salgótarjáni u
Mikszáth Kálmán tér
Rigó u
13
Horváth Mihály tér
Magdolna u
Józsefvárosi pu
Salgótarjáni u
Kálvin tér
Baross u
74
Kis Stáció u
Baross u
Kálvária tér
Baross u
See South Buda & Ferencváros Map (pp228–9)
Üllői út
Mária u
145
Józsefváros
Csobánc u
Kőbányai út
Erkel u
Nap u
Visi Imre u
85
104
Köztelek u
Korvin köz
Práter u
Losonci tér
Kőris u
Sárkány u
68
83
3
Ferenc krt
91
96
Molnár F tér
Práter u
Illés u
Kálvária u
Markusovszky tér
Hőgyes E u
Jázmin u
Tömő u
Illés köz
73
Tűzoltó u
Futó u
Nagy Templom u
Leonardo da Vinci u
János u
Szigony u
Balassa u
Fűvészkert u
Dugonics u
Diószeghy Sámuel u
Orczy út
Kinizsi u
Knézich K u
Üllői út
Vajda Péter u
Könyves Kálmán körút
Lónyay u
Ráday u
Bakáts tér
Ferenc krt
Angyal u
Liliom u
Páva u
Apáthy István u
Korányi Sándor u
Klinikák
Tompa u
Berzenczey u
Bokréta u
Clinics
Bakáts u
Mester u
Ferencváros
Viola u
Thaly Kálmán u
Ludovika tér
Orczy-kert
Közraktár u
Balázs

CASTLE HILL & WATERTOWN

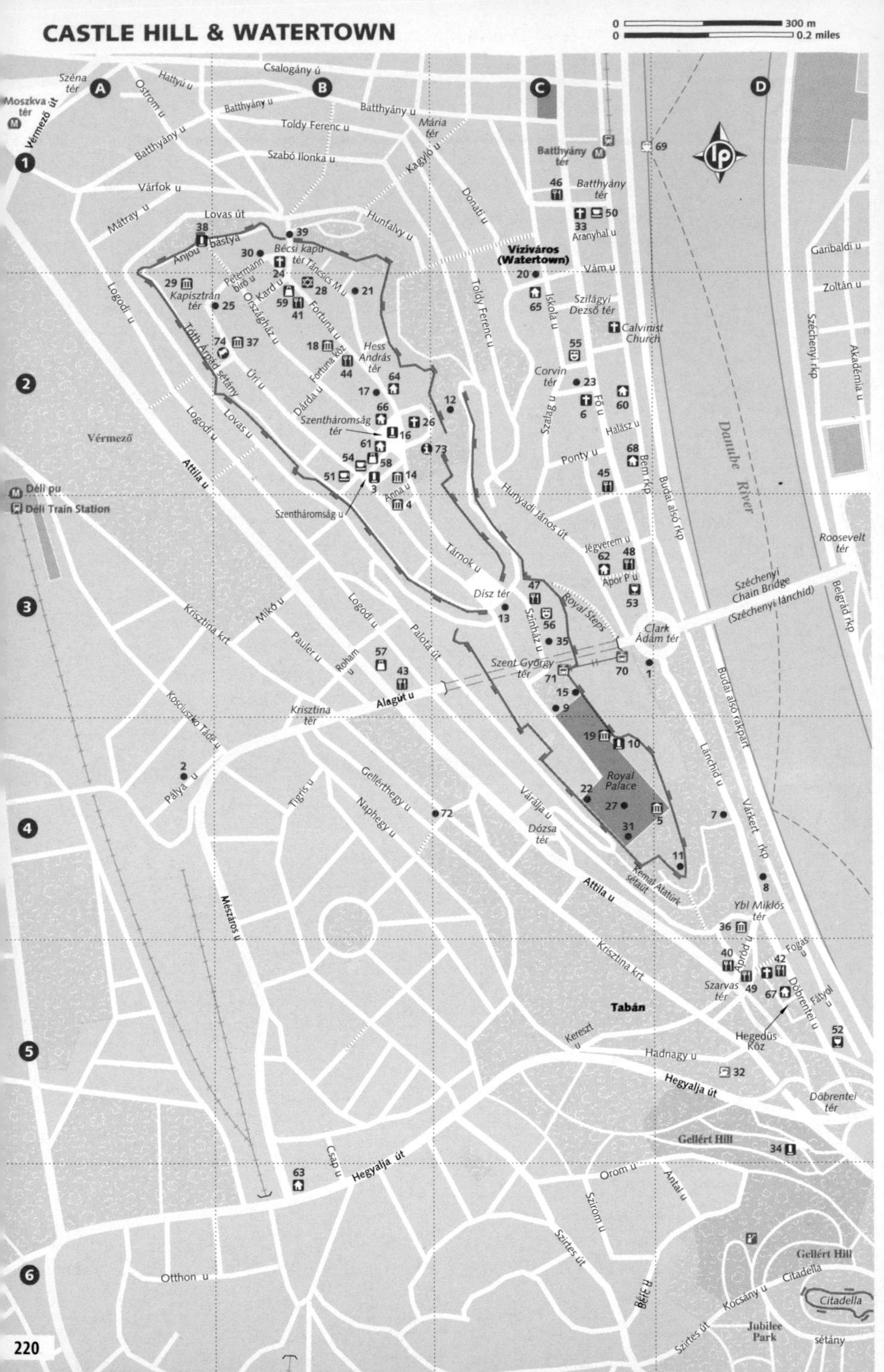

CASTLE HILL & WATERTOWN

SIGHTS & ACTIVITIES (pp49–74)

0km Stone ... **1** C3
A&TSA Fitness Club ... **2** A4
András Hadik Statue ... **3** B2
Buda Castle Labyrinth ... **4** B3
Budapest History Museum ... **5** D4
Capuchin Church ... **6** C2
Castle Bazaar ... **7** D4
Castle Garden Kiosk (Casino) ... **8** D4
Corvinus Gate ... **9** C3
Eugene of Savoy Statue ... **10** C4
Ferdinand Gate ... **11** D4
Fishermen's Bastion ... **12** C2
Former Ministry of Defence ... **13** C3
Golden Eagle Pharmacy Museum ... **14** B2
Habsburg Steps ... **15** C3
Holy Trinity Statue ... **16** B2
House of Hungarian Wines ... **17** B2
Hungarian Museum of Commerce & Catering ... **18** B2
Hungarian National Gallery ... **19** C4
Iron Stump ... **20** C2
Kossuth Jail ... **21** B2
Lift to Dózsa tér ... **22** C4
Louis Fountain ... **23** C2
Lutheran Church ... **24** B1
Mace Tower ... (see 11)
Mary Magdalene Tower ... **25** B2
Matthias Church & Collection of Ecclesiastical Art ... **26** B2
Matthias Fountain ... **27** C4
Medieval Jewish Prayer House ... **28** B2
Military History Museum ... **29** A2
National Archives ... **30** B1
National Széchenyi Library ... **31** C4
Rác Baths (Renovating) ... **32** D5
St Anne's Church ... **33** C1
St Gellért Monument ... **34** D5
Sándor Palace ... **35** C3
Semmelweis Museum of Medical History ... **36** D4
Telephony Museum ... **37** B2
Tomb of Abdurrahman ... **38** A1
Turul Statue ... (see 15)
Vienna Gate ... **39** B1

EATING (pp91–120)

Aranyszarvas ... **40** D5
Café Pierrot ... **41** B2
Éden ... **42** D5
Ezred Nonstop ... **43** B3
Fortuna Önkiszolgáló ... **44** B2
Le Jardin de Paris ... **45** C2
Nagyi Palacsintázója Branch ... **46** C1
Rivalda ... **47** C3
Seoul House ... **48** C3
Tabáni Terasz ... **49** D5

DRINKING (pp123–8)

Angelika ... **50** C1
Café Miró ... **51** B2
Erzsébethíd Eszpresszó ... **52** D5
Lánchíd Söröző ... **53** C3
Ruszwurm ... **54** B2

ENTERTAINMENT (pp128–40)

Buda Concert Hall ... **55** C2
National Dance Theatre ... **56** C3

SHOPPING (pp141–50)

Almárium ... **57** B3
Herend ... **58** B2
Hungaricum ... **59** B2

SLEEPING (pp151–66)

Art'otel Budapest ... **60** C2
Burg Hotel ... **61** B2
Carlton Hotel ... **62** C3
Charles Hotel & Apartment ... **63** B6
Hilton Budapest ... **64** B2
Hotel Astra ... **65** C2
Hotel Kulturinnov ... **66** B2
Hotel Orion ... **67** D5
Hotel Victoria ... **68** C2

TRANSPORT (pp180–6)

Batthyány tér Pier ... **69** C1
Sikló (Lower Station) ... **70** C3
Sikló (Upper Station) ... **71** C3

INFORMATION

Budapest Chamber of Commerce and Industry ... **72** C4
Budapest Tourist Office Branch ... **73** B2
German Embassy ... **74** B2

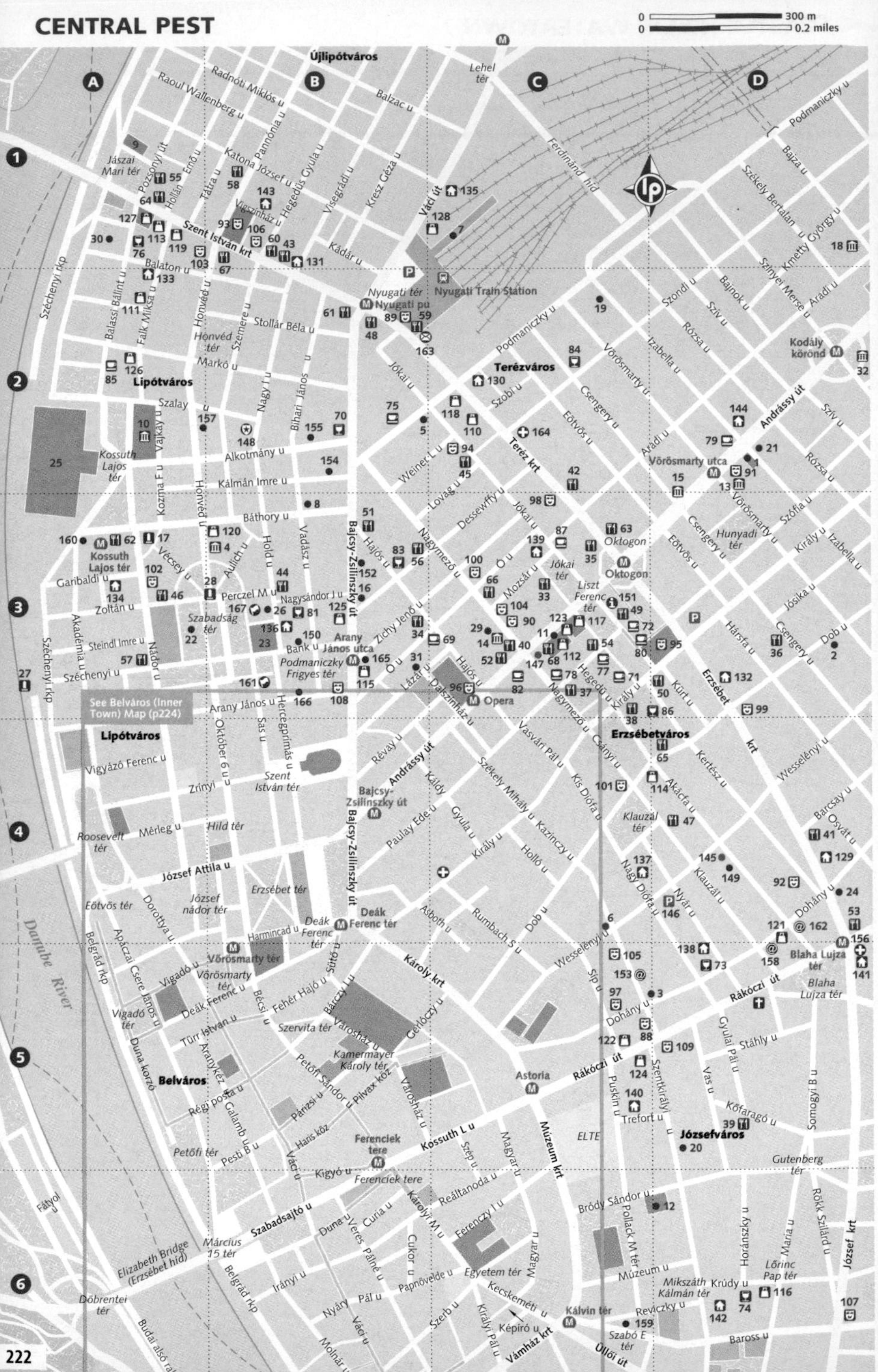
CENTRAL PEST
0 300 m
0 0.2 miles
Újlipótváros
Lehel tér
Raoul Wallenberg u
Radnóti Miklós u
Pannónia u
Balzac u
Katona József u
Hegedűs Gyula u
Visegrádi u
Kresz Géza u
Váci út
Ferdinánd híd
Podmaniczky u
Jászai Mari tér
Pozsonyi út
Hollán Ernő u
Tátra u
Vígszínház u
Szent István krt
Kádár u
Balaton u
Bajza u
Székely Bertalan u
Kmetty György u
Szinyei Merse u
Aradi u
Szondi u
Bajnok u
Szív u
Rózsa u
Izabella u
Nyugati tér
Nyugati pu
Nyugati Train Station
Széchenyi rkp
Balassi Bálint u
Falk Miksa u
Honvéd u
Szemere u
Stollár Béla u
Honvéd tér
Markó u
Lipótváros
Kodály körönd
Terézváros
Vörösmarty u
Csengery u
Eötvös u
Jókai u
Bihari János u
Nagy I u
Szalay u
Vajkay u
Kossuth Lajos tér
Alkotmány u
Kálmán Imre u
Kozma F u
Báthory u
Vadász u
Hold u
Szobi u
Weiner L u
Lovag u
Dessewffy u
Teréz krt
Andrássy út
Vörösmarty utca
Hunyadi tér
Király u
Szófia u
Oktogon
Jókai tér
Liszt Ferenc tér
Vécsey u
Aulich u
Garibaldi u
Zoltán u
Perczel M u
Nagysándor J u
Hajós u
Bajcsy-Zsilinszky út
Nagymező u
Ó u
Mozsár u
Jósika u
Dob u
Hársfa u
Akadémia u
Steindl Imre u
Nádor u
Szabadság tér
Bank u
Arany János utca
Zichy Jenő u
Podmaniczky Frigyes tér
Lázár u
Dalszínház u
Opera
Hegedű u
Király u
Kürt u
Erzsébet krt
Széchenyi u
See Belváros (Inner Town) Map (p224)
Arany János u
Október 6 u
Sas u
Hercegprímás u
Révay u
Vasvári Pál u
Csányi u
Erzsébetváros
Vigyázó Ferenc u
Zrínyi u
Szent István tér
Bajcsy-Zsilinszky út
Káldy Gyula u
Székely Mihály u
Kis Diófa u
Akácfa u
Kertész u
Wesselényi u
Roosevelt tér
Mérleg u
Hild tér
Paulay Ede u
Kazinczy u
Klauzál tér
Barcsay u
Osvát u
József Attila u
Holló u
Nagy Diófa u
Klauzál u
Nyár u
Eötvös tér
Dorottya u
József nádor tér
Erzsébet tér
Deák Ferenc tér
Ásbóth u
Rumbach S u
Dohány u
Danube River
Apáczai Csere János u
Harmincad u
Vörösmarty tér
Sütő u
Károly krt
Sip u
Blaha Lujza tér
Belgrád rkp
Vigadó u
Deák Ferenc u
Fehér Hajó u
Bárczy I u
Gerlóczy u
Rákóczi út
Vigadó tér
Türr István u
Bécsi u
Szervita tér
Városház u
Gyulai Pál u
Stáhly u
Duna korzó
Aranykéz u
Petőfi Sándor u
Kamermayer Károly tér
Pilvax köz
Astoria
Somogyi B u
Belváros
Régi posta u
Galamb u
Párizsi u
Városház u
Múzeum krt
Puskin u
Szentkirályi u
Vas u
Kőfaragó u
Haris köz
ELTE
Trefort u
Józsefváros
Petőfi tér
Pesti B u
Váci u
Ferenciek tere
Kossuth L u
Szép u
Magyar u
Gutenberg tér
Kígyó u
Reáltanoda u
Bródy Sándor u
Fátyol u
Szabadsajtó u
Duna u
Curia u
Károlyi M u
Ferenczy I u
Pollack M tér
Horánszky u
Mária u
Rökk Szilárd u
József krt
Elizabeth Bridge (Erzsébet híd)
Március 15 tér
Veres Pálné u
Cukor u
Lőrinc Pap tér
Belgrád rkp
Irányi u
Papnövelde u
Egyetem tér
Múzeum u
Mikszáth Kálmán tér
Krúdy u
Döbrentei tér
Nyáry Pál u
Kecskeméti u
Kálvin tér
Reviczky u
Szerb u
Képíró u
Szabó E tér
Budai alsó rakpart
Molnár u
Királyi Pál u
Vámház krt
Üllői út
Baross u

CENTRAL PEST

SIGHTS & ACTIVITIES (pp49–74)

Academy of Fine Arts ... 1 D2
Art Nouveau Primary School ... 2 D3
Astoria Fitness Centre ... 3 C5
Bedő House ... 4 B3
Bike Base ... 5 B2
Budapest Bike ... 6 C4
Budapest Eye ... 7 C1
Cityrama ... 8 B3
Debrecen Summer University ... 9 A1
Ethnography Museum ... 10 A2
Fashion House ... 11 C3
Former Hungarian Radio Headquarters ... 12 D6
Franz Liszt Memorial Museum ... 13 D2
House of Hungarian Photographers ... 14 C3
House of Terror ... 15 D3
Hungarian Bicycle Touring Association ... 16 B3
Imre Nagy Statue ... 17 A3
Lédere Mansion ... 18 D1
Lindenbaum Apartment Houses ... 19 C2
Makovec Office Building ... 20 D5
MÁV Headquarters ... 21 D2
MTV Headquarters ... 22 A3
National Bank of Hungary ... 23 B3
New York Palace ... 24 D4
Palatinus House ... (see 9)
Parliament ... 25 A2
Royal Postal Savings Bank ... 26 B3
Shoes on the Danube Memorial ... 27 A3
Soviet Army Memorial ... 28 B3
Thália Theatre ... 29 C3
White House ... 30 A1
Yellow Zebra Bikes ... 31 B3
Zoltán Kodály Memorial Museum ... 32 D2

EATING (pp91–120)

Alhambra ... 33 C3
Articsóka ... 34 B3
Biopont ... (see 74)
Butterfly ... 35 C3
City Maharaja ... 36 D3
Falafel Faloda ... 37 C3
Frici Papa Kifőzdéje ... 38 C3
Fülemüle ... 39 D5
Főzelék Faló ... 40 C3
Három Testvér ... 41 D4
Három Testvér Branch ... 42 C2
Három Testvér Branch ... 43 B1
Hold utca Market ... 44 B3
Holly ... 45 C2
Iguana ... 46 A3
Kádár ... 47 D4
Kaiser's Szupermarket ... 48 B2
Leroy Café ... 49 C3
Magdalena Merlo ... 50 D3
Marquis de Salade ... 51 B3
Match Supermarket ... 52 C3
Match Supermarket ... 53 D4
Menza ... 54 C3
Mézes Kuckó ... 55 A1
Mini Coop ... 56 B3
Momotaro Ramen ... 57 A3
Mosselen ... 58 B1
Nyugati ABC ... 59 B2
Okay Italia ... 60 B1
Okay Italia ... 61 B2
Pick Ház ... 62 A3
Rothschild Supermarket ... 63 C3
Rothschild Supermarket ... 64 A1
Shalimar ... 65 D4
Soho Palacsintabár ... 66 C3
Szeráj ... 67 B1
Vörös és Fehér ... 68 C3

DRINKING (pp123–8)

Ballet Cipő ... 69 C3
Becketts ... 70 B2
Birdland ... 71 C3
Café Vian ... 72 C3
CoXx Pub ... 73 D5
Darshan Udvar ... 74 D6
Demmer's Teahouse ... 75 B2
Fehér Gyűrű ... 76 A1
Incognito Café ... 77 C3
Két Szerecsen ... 78 C3
Lukács ... 79 D2
Miró Grande ... 80 C3
Mystery Bar & Internet Café ... 81 B3
Művész ... 82 C3
Picasso Point ... 83 B3
Pótkulcs ... 84 C2
Szalai ... 85 A2
Szimpla ... 86 D3
Teaház a Vörös Oroszlánhoz ... 87 C3

ENTERTAINMENT (pp128–40)

Angel ... 88 C5
Bank Dance Hall ... 89 B2
Budapest Operetta ... 90 C3
Budapest Puppet Theatre ... 91 D2
Club Vittula ... 92 D4
Comedy Theatre ... 93 B1
Cotton Club ... 94 C2
Ferenc Liszt Music Academy ... 95 D3
Hungarian State Opera House ... 96 C3
M4 Music Club ... 97 C5
Művész Cinema ... 98 C3
Old Music Academy ... (see 13)
Örökmozgó Film Museum ... 99 D3
Piaf ... 100 C3
Sark Café ... 101 C4
Satchmo ... 102 A3
Süss Fél Nap ... 103 A1
Symphony Ticket Office ... 104 C3
Szimpla Kert ... 105 C5
Szindbád Cinema ... 106 B1
Ticket Express ... 107 D6
Upside Down ... 108 B3
Uránia National Cinema ... 109 D5

SHOPPING (pp141–50)

Ajka Kristály ... 110 C2
Anna Antikvitás ... 111 A2
BÁV Branch ... 112 C3
BÁV Shop ... 113 A1
Billerbeck ... 114 D4
Dárius ... (see 133)
Haas & Czjzek ... 115 B3
Iguana ... 116 D6
Írok Boltja ... 117 C3
Játékszerek Anno ... 118 C2
Kieselbach Galéria ... 119 A1
Kódex ... 120 B3
Lekvárium ... 121 D4
Libri Könyvpalota ... 122 C5
Liszt Ferenc Zebneműbolt ... 123 C3
Magyar Pálinka Ház ... 124 C5
Nyugat Antikvárium ... 125 B3
Pintér Antik ... 126 A2
Szőnyi Antikváriuma ... 127 A1
West End City Centre Shopping Mall ... 128 C1

SLEEPING (pp151–66)

10 Beds ... 129 D4
Best Hostel ... 130 C2
Caterina Hostel ... (see 98)
City Hotel Ring ... 131 B1
Corinthia Grand Hotel Royal ... 132 D3
Eastside Hostel ... 133 A2
Garibaldi Guesthouse ... 134 A3
Hilton West End ... 135 C1
Hotel Hold ... 136 B3
King's Hotel ... 137 C4
Marco Polo Hostel ... 138 D5
Medosz Hotel ... 139 C3
Mercure Hotel Budapest Museum ... 140 C5
Mercure Nemzeti ... 141 D5
Museum Guest House ... 142 D6
NH Budapest ... 143 B1
Residence Izabella ... 144 D2

TRANSPORT (pp180–6)

BKV Office ... 145 D4
Covered Car Park ... 146 D4
MÁV Central Ticket Office ... 147 C3

INFORMATION

Belváros-Lipótváros Police Station ... 148 B2
BKV Lost & Found Office ... 149 D4
British Chamber of Commerce ... 150 B3
Budapest Tourist Office Oktogon Branch ... 151 C3
Cartographia ... 152 B3
Chatman Internet ... 153 C5
Copy General ... 154 B2
CopyCat ... 155 B2
Csillag Gyógyszertár ... 156 D5
Economy & Transport Ministry ... 157 A2
Electric Café ... 158 D5
Ervin Szabó Library ... 159 C6
Hungarian Chamber of Commerce and Industry ... 160 A3
Irish Embassy ... 161 B3
Narancs ... 162 D4
Post Office ... 163 B2
Teréz Patika ... 164 C2
Térképkirály ... 165 B3
Top Clean Laundry Branch ... 166 B3
Top Clean Laundry Branch ... (see 48)
US Embassy ... 167 B3
Vodaphone ... (see 128)

BELVÁROS (INNER TOWN)

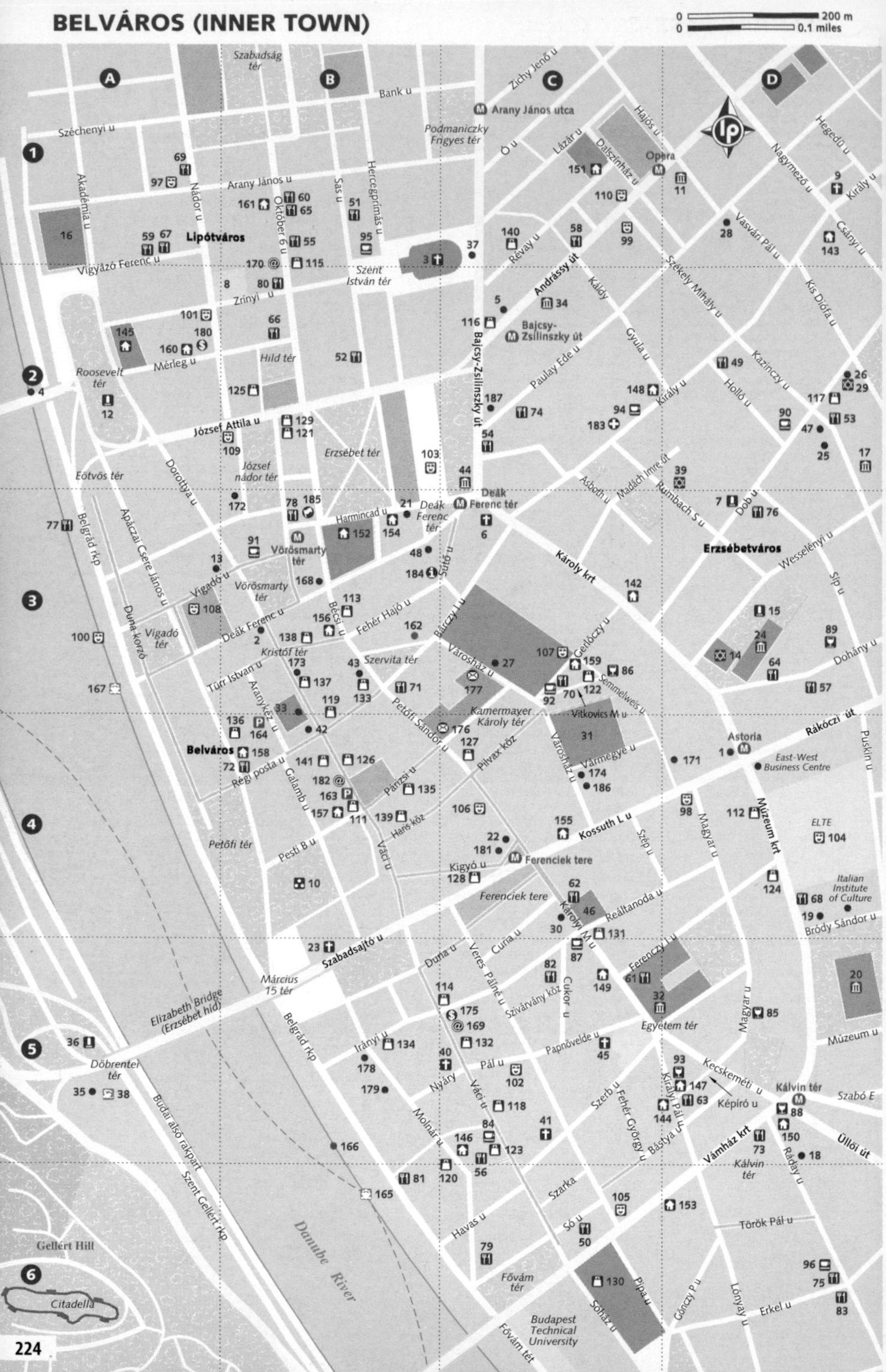

BELVÁROS (INNER TOWN)

SIGHTS & ACTIVITIES (pp49–74)
Absolute Walking Tours (see 48)
Astoria Fitness Branch 1 D4
Bank Palace 2 B3
Basilica of St Stephen 3 B1
Budapest Bike Kiosk (Summer) 4 A2
Budatours 5 C2
Calvinist Church (Deák Ferenc tér) 6 C3
Carl Lutz Monument 7 D3
Central European University 8 B2
Church of St Teresa 9 D1
Contra Aquincum Ruins 10 B4
Drechsler House 11 D1
Ferenc Deák Statue 12 A2
Government Building with 'Pater Noster' 13 A3
Great Synagogue 14 D3
Gresham Palace (see 145)
Holocaust Memorial 15 D3
Hungarian Academy of Sciences 16 A1
Hungarian Electrotechnology Museum 17 D2
Hungarian Equestrian Tourism Association 18 D5
Hungarian Language School 19 D4
Hungarian National Museum 20 D5
Hungary Program Centrum 21 B3
Ibusz (Main Office) 22 C4
Inner Town Parish Church 23 B5
Jewish Museum 24 D3
Kosher Bakery 25 D2
Kővári Butchers 26 D2
Legenda (see 167)
Municipal Council Office 27 C3
New Theatre 28 D1
Orthodox Synagogue 29 D2
Pegazus Tours 30 C4
Pest County Hall 31 C4
Petőfi Literary Museum 32 C5
Philanthia Flower Shop 33 B3
Postal Museum 34 C2
Pump Room 35 A5
Queen Elizabeth Statue 36 A5
Queenybus Departures 37 C1
Rudas Baths & Pools 38 A5
Rumbach Sebestyén utca Synagogue 39 D2
St Michael's Church 40 C5
Serbian Orthodox Church 41 C5
Thonet House 42 B4
Török Bank House 43 B3
Underground Railway Museum 44 C2
University Church 45 C5
University Library 46 C4
Wigmaker 47 D2
Yellow Zebra Bikes 48 B3

EATING (pp91–120)
Al-Amir 49 D2
Bangkok House 50 C6
Café Kör 51 B1
Café Mokka 52 B2
Carmel Pince 53 D2
Central European University Cafeteria (see 8)
Durcin 54 C2
Durcin Branch 55 B1
Fatál 56 C5
Fausto 57 D3
Goa 58 C1
Govinda 59 A1
Gresham Kvéház (see 145)
Hanna (see 29)
Kama Sutra 60 B1
Károlyi Étterem 61 C5
Kárpátia 62 C4
Képíró 63 D5
Kinor David 64 D3
Kisharang 65 B1
La Fontaine 66 B2
Lou Lou 67 A1
Múzeum 68 D4
Nagy Fal 69 A1
Nagy Tamás 70 C3
Nagycsarnok Food Market (see 130)
Nagyi Palacsintázója Branch 71 B3
Oceán Bár & Grill & Delicatessen 72 B4
Pata Negra 73 D5
Pesti Vendéglő 74 C2
Soul Café 75 D6
Spinoza Café 76 D3
Spoon 77 A3
Sushi An 78 B3
Taverna Pireus Rembetiko 79 C6
Tom-George 80 B2
Trattoria Toscana 81 B6
Vegetarium 82 C5
Vörös Postakocsi 83 D6

DRINKING (pp123–8)
1000 Tea 84 C5
Action Bar 85 D5
Café Eklektika 86 C3
Centrál Kávéház 87 C5
Cha Cha Cha 88 D5
Champs Sports Bar 89 D3
Fröhlich 90 D2
Gerbeaud 91 B3
Gerlóczy Kávéház 92 C3
Janis Pub 93 D5
Mozaik Teahouse 94 C2
Negro 95 B1
Teaház a Vörös Oroszlánhoz 96 D6

ENTERTAINMENT (pp128–40)
Aranytíz Cultural Centre 97 A1
Candy 98 D4
Central Ticket Office 99 C1
Columbus Jazzklub 100 A3
Duna Palota 101 A2
Fat Mo's Music Club 102 C5
Gödör Klub 103 B2
Holdudvar 104 D4
Jazz Garden 105 C6
József Katona Theatre 106 C4
Merlin Theatre 107 C3
Pesti Vigadó 108 A3
Szoda Udvar 109 B2
Ticket Express 110 C1

SHOPPING (pp141–50)
Arten Stúdió 111 B4
Babaklinika 112 D4
Balogh Kesztyű (see 139)
BÁV Branch 113 B3
Belvárosi Aukciósház 114 C5
Bestsellers 115 B1
Bibliotéka Antikvárium 116 C2
Budapest Wine Society Branch (see 96)
Central European University Bookshop (see 8)
Concerto Hanglemezbolt 117 D2
Folkart Centrum 118 C5
Folkart Kézművészház 119 B3
Hephaistos 120 C6
Herend 121 B2
Holló Atelier 122 C3
Intuita 123 C5
Központi Antikvárium 124 D4
La Boutique des Vins 125 B2
Libri Studium 126 B4
Magma 127 C4
Monarchia 128 C4
Nádortex 129 B2
Nagycsarnok 130 C6
Náray Tamás 131 C4
Porcelánház 132 C5
Red Bus Secondhand Bookstore (see 159)
Rózsavölgyi és Társa 133 B3
Selene Lovas Bolt 134 B5
Számos Marcipán 135 B4
Tangó Classic 136 B4
Tangó Classic 137 B3
Thomas Sabo 138 B3
Vass 139 B4
Wave Music 140 C1
Zsolnay 141 B4

SLEEPING (pp151–66)
Carmen Mini Hotel 142 C3
Connection Guest House 143 D1
Downtown Hostel 144 D5
Four Seasons Gresham Palace Hotel 145 A2
Green Bridge Hostel 146 C5
Hotel Art 147 D5
Hotel Domina Fiesta 148 C2
Hotel Erzsébet 149 C5
Ibis Centrum Hotel 150 D5
K+K Hotel Opera 151 C1
Kempinski Hotel Corvinus 152 B3
KM Saga II 153 D6
Le Meridien Budapest 154 B3
Leó Panzió 155 C4
Mellow Mood Central Guest House 156 B3
Millennium Court 157 B4
Non-Stop Hotel Service 158 B4
Red Bus Hostel 159 C3
Starlight Suiten Hotel 160 A2
To-Ma 161 B1

TRANSPORT (pp180–6)
Avis 162 B3
Covered Car Park 163 B4
Covered Car Park 164 B4
Covered Car Park (see 162)
International Ferry Pier 165 B6
Mahart PassNave Ticket Office 166 B5
Vigadó tér Pier 167 A3

INFORMATION
American Chamber of Commerce 168 B3
Ami Internet Coffee 169 C5
CEU NetPoint 170 B1
Express Travel Agency 171 D4
Finance Ministry 172 B3
Hungarian Youth Hostel Association (see 178)
Immedio 173 B3
Irisz Szalon 174 C4
K&H Bank 175 C5
Main Post Office 176 C4
Main Post Office Annexe 177 C3
Mellow Mood Travel Agency 178 B5
National Foreign Language Library 179 B5
OTP Bank 180 A2
Párisi Udvar Könyvesbolt 181 C4
Parknet 182 B4
SOS Dental Service 183 C2
Tourinform (Main Office) 184 B3
UK Embassy 185 B3
Világsajtó Háza 186 C4
Vista 187 C2

ÓBUDA, AQUINCUM & ANGYALFÖLD

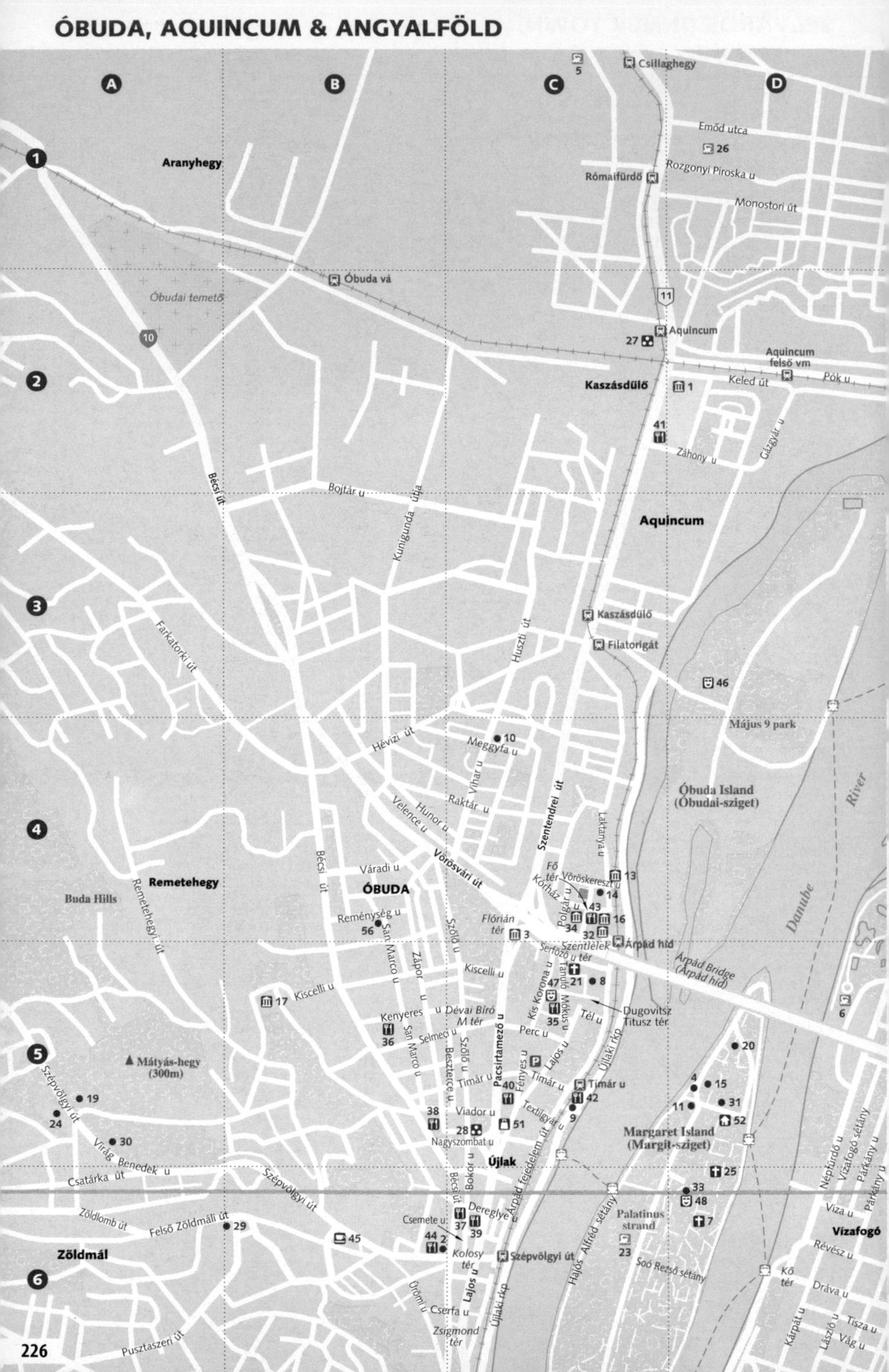

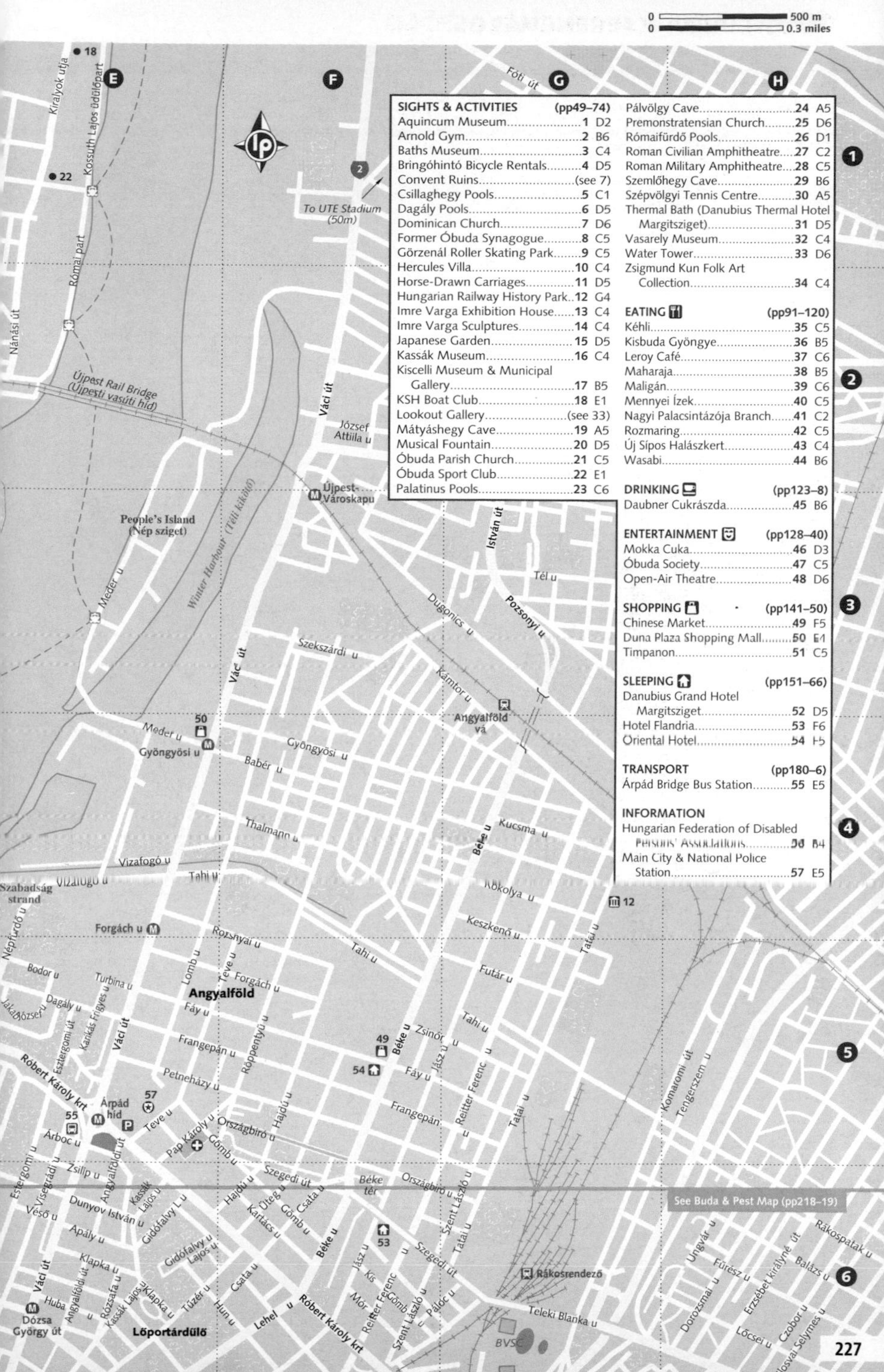

0 500 m
0 0.3 miles
E
F
G
H
1
2
3
4
5
6
SIGHTS & ACTIVITIES (pp49–74)
Aquincum Museum....1 D2
Arnold Gym....2 B6
Baths Museum....3 C4
Bringóhintó Bicycle Rentals....4 D5
Convent Ruins....(see 7)
Csillaghegy Pools....5 C1
Dagály Pools....6 D5
Dominican Church....7 D6
Former Óbuda Synagogue....8 C5
Görzenál Roller Skating Park....9 C5
Hercules Villa....10 C4
Horse-Drawn Carriages....11 D5
Hungarian Railway History Park..12 G4
Imre Varga Exhibition House....13 C4
Imre Varga Sculptures....14 C4
Japanese Garden....15 D5
Kassák Museum....16 C4
Kiscelli Museum & Municipal Gallery....17 B5
KSH Boat Club....18 E1
Lookout Gallery....(see 33)
Mátyáshegy Cave....19 A5
Musical Fountain....20 D5
Óbuda Parish Church....21 C5
Óbuda Sport Club....22 E1
Palatinus Pools....23 C6
Pálvölgy Cave....24 A5
Premonstratensian Church....25 D6
Rómaifürdő Pools....26 D1
Roman Civilian Amphitheatre....27 C2
Roman Military Amphitheatre....28 C5
Szemlőhegy Cave....29 B6
Szépvölgyi Tennis Centre....30 A5
Thermal Bath (Danubius Thermal Hotel Margitsziget)....31 D5
Vasarely Museum....32 C4
Water Tower....33 D6
Zsigmund Kun Folk Art Collection....34 C4
EATING (pp91–120)
Kéhli....35 C5
Kisbuda Gyöngye....36 B5
Leroy Café....37 C6
Maharaja....38 B5
Maligán....39 C6
Mennyei Ízek....40 C5
Nagyi Palacsintázója Branch....41 C2
Rozmaring....42 C5
Új Sípos Halászkert....43 C4
Wasabi....44 B6
DRINKING (pp123–8)
Daubner Cukrászda....45 B6
ENTERTAINMENT (pp128–40)
Mokka Cuka....46 D3
Óbuda Society....47 C5
Open-Air Theatre....48 D6
SHOPPING (pp141–50)
Chinese Market....49 F5
Duna Plaza Shopping Mall....50 E4
Timpanon....51 C5
SLEEPING (pp151–66)
Danubius Grand Hotel Margitsziget....52 D5
Hotel Flandria....53 F6
Oriental Hotel....54 F5
TRANSPORT (pp180–6)
Árpád Bridge Bus Station....55 E5
INFORMATION
Hungarian Federation of Disabled Persons' Associations....56 E4
Main City & National Police Station....57 E5
To UTE Stadium (50m)
Újpest Rail Bridge (Újpesti vasúti híd)
People's Island (Nép sziget)
Winter Harbour (Téli kikötő)
Újpest-Városkapu
Angyalföld vá
Gyöngyösi u
Forgách u
Szabadság strand
Angyalföld
Árpád híd
Rákosrendező
Dózsa György út
Lőportárdűlő
BVSC
Váci út
Róbert Károly krt
Teleki Blanka u
See Buda & Pest Map (pp218–19)

SOUTH BUDA & FERENCVÁROS

See Buda & Pest Map (pp218–19)

0 500 m
0 0.3 miles
E
F
G
H
1
2
3
4
5
6
Szabó E tér
Baross u
Horváth Mihály tér
Kis Stáció u
Józsefváros
Kálvária tér
Csobánc u
Visi Imre u
Kőbányai út
Ráday u
Mária u
Nap u
Futó u
Vinci köz
Beniczky L u
Köztelek u
Ferenc krt
Corvin köz
Práter u
Losonci tér
Molnár F tér
Kőris u
Sárkány u
Markusovszky tér
Hőgyes E u
Kisfaludy u
Vajdahunyad u
Nagy Templom u
Leonardo da Vinci u
János u
Szigony u
Jázmin u
Tömő u
Illés u
Illés köz
Kálvária u
Dugonics u
Diószeghy Sámuel u
Orczy út
Vajda Péter u
Könyves Kálmán körút
Kinizsi u
Knezich K u
Tűzoltó u
Üllői út
Lónyay u
Bakáts tér
Apáthy István u
Klinikák
Clinics
Korányi Sándor u
Ráday u
Bakáts u
Angyal u
Tompa u
Páva u
Berzenczey u
Bokréta u
Viola u
Thaly Kálmán u
Ludovika tér
Orczy-kert
Ferenc tér
Balázs Béla u
Vendel u
Lenhossék u
Benyovszky Móric u
Elnök u
Boráros tér
Ferencváros
Lilliom u
Mester u
Márton u
Sobieski János u
Telepi u
Nagyvárad tér
Petőfi Bridge (Petőfi híd)
Dandár u
Népliget Park
Könyves Kálmán krt
Haller u
Gyáli út
FTC Stadium
Népliget
Fehér Holló u
Soroksári út
Szent László Hospital
Vágóhíd u
Bajor Gizi Park
Lurdy Ház Shopping Mall
Ecseri út
National Theatre
Komor Marcell u
Thék Endre u
To Europark Market (2km)
Lágymányos Bridge (Lágymányosi híd)
Vágóhíd vá
Gubacsi út
Kopaszi gát
Kvassay J út
Ecseri út
Epreserdő út
Gyáli út
Szigetcsúcs
To Ecseri Piac (2km)
Illatos út
Szabadkikötő út
Mártírok útja
Határ út
Csepel Island (Csepel sziget)
Pesterzsébet
Jókai Mór u
Szabadkikötő vm
Ófalu
Török Flóris u
5
SIGHTS & ACTIVITIES (pp49–74)
Budapest Technical and Economic Sciences University....1 D2
Cave Chapel....2 D1
Citadella....3 C1
Former Swedish Embassy....4 C1
Gellért Baths & Swimming Pools....5 D1
Holocaust Memorial Center....6 E1
Hungarian Natural History Museum....7 F1
Independence Monument....(see 3)
InterClub Hungarian Language School....8 D2
Ludwig Museum of Contemporary Art....9 E3
Palace of Arts....(see 9)
Planetarium....10 H2
Vantage Point....11 C1
Zwack Unicum Museum....12 E2
'Ziggurat' Building....13 E3
National Theatre....26 E3
Trafó Bar Tango....(see 27)
Trafó House of Contemporary Arts....27 E1
Tűzraktár....28 F2
Wigwam Rock & Blues Club....29 B6
Zöld Pardon....30 D2
EATING (pp91–120)
Kaiser's Szupermarket....14 D2
Marcello....15 D2
Taiwan....(see 36)
DRINKING (pp123–8)
Café Ponyvaragény....16 D2
Castro Bisztró....17 E1
Kisrabló....18 D2
ENTERTAINMENT (pp128–40)
A38 Hajó....19 E2
Café del Rio....20 D2
Club Bohemian Alibi....21 E1
Fonó Buda Music House....22 C4
Jailhouse....23 E1
Laser Theatre....(see 10)
MU Színház....24 C2
Municipal Cultural House (Folklór Centrum)....25 C3
SHOPPING (pp141–50)
Iguana Branch....31 E1
SLEEPING (pp151–66)
Back Pack Guesthouse....32 B2
Citadella Hotel & Hostel....(see 3)
Congress Park Hotel Flamenco....33 C2
Corvin Hotel....34 E1
Danubius Gellért Hotel....35 D1
Fortuna Hotel....36 G2
Hostel Hill....37 C2
Hostel Kinizsi....38 D1
Hostel Landler....39 D2
Hostel Rózsa....40 D2
Hostel Schönherz....41 D2
Hostel Universitas....42 D2
Hostel Vásárhelyi....43 D2
Hotel Griff Junior....44 B3
Hotel Platánus....45 H2
Hotel Rila....46 F2
Hotel Sissi....47 E1
Hotel Thomas....48 E1
Hotel Ventura....49 C5
Martos Hostel....50 D2
TRANSPORT (pp180–6)
BKV Passenger Ferries (Petőfi Bridge)....51 E2
Etele tér Bus Station....52 A3
Népliget Bus Station....53 H2
INFORMATION
Liliom Szalon....54 E2

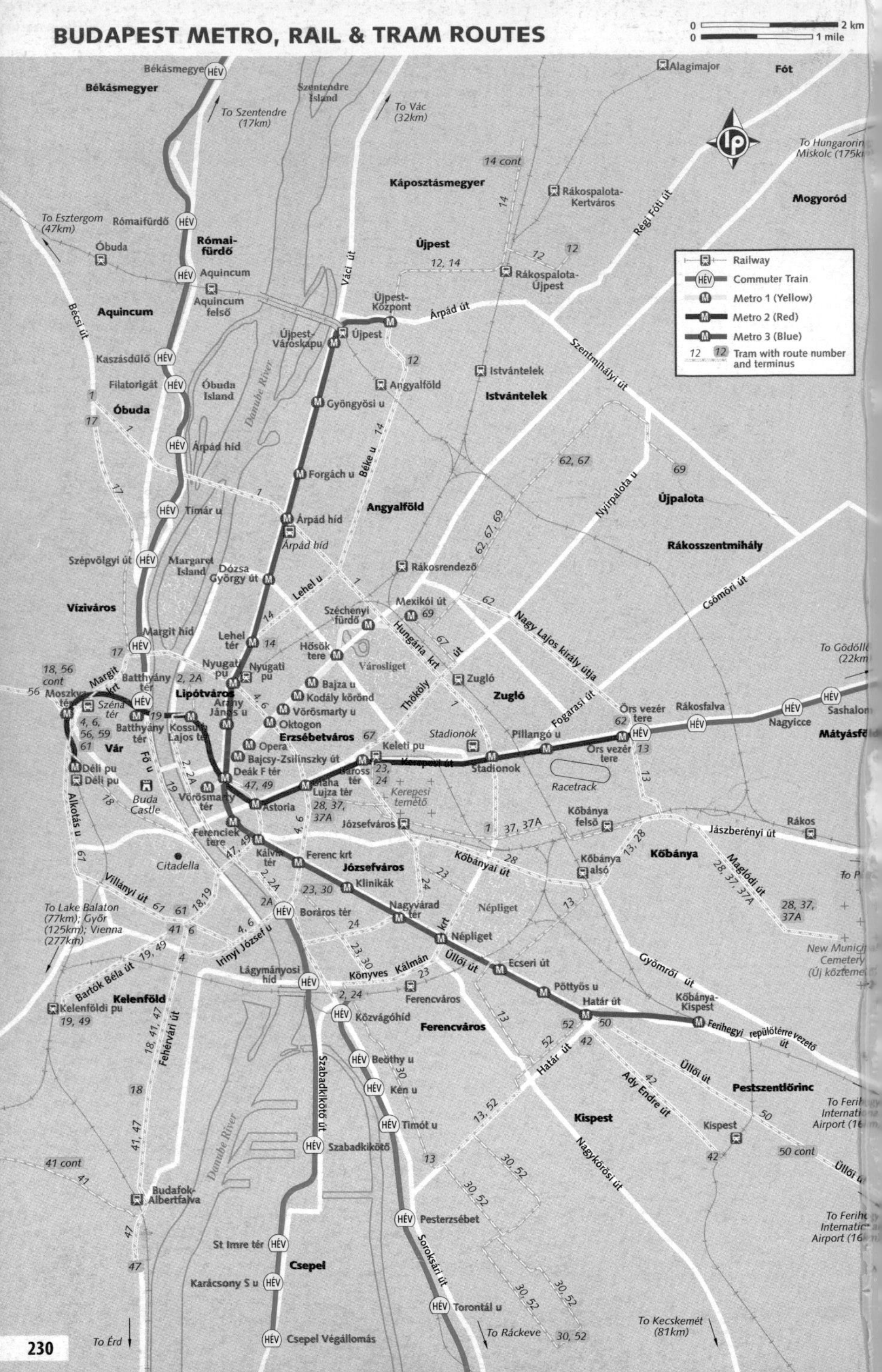

BUDAPEST METRO, RAIL & TRAM ROUTES
0 2 km
0 1 mile
Railway
Commuter Train
Metro 1 (Yellow)
Metro 2 (Red)
Metro 3 (Blue)
Tram with route number and terminus
Békásmegyer
To Szentendre (17km)
Szentendre Island
To Vác (32km)
Alagimajor
Fót
To Hungaroring; Miskolc (175km)
Mogyoród
Káposztásmegyer
14 cont
Rákospalota-Kertváros
Régi Fóti út
To Esztergom (47km)
Rómaifürdő
Óbuda
Római-fürdő
Újpest
12, 14
Rákospalota-Újpest
Aquincum
Aquincum felső
Váci út
Újpest-Központ
Árpád út
Bécsi út
Újpest-Városkapu
Kaszásdűlő
Filatorigát
Óbuda Island
Danube River
Angyalföld
Gyöngyösi u
Istvántelek
Szentmihályi út
Árpád híd
Forgách u
Béke u
62, 67
69
Újpalota
Nyírpalota u
Tímár u
Rákosszentmihály
Szépvölgyi út
Margaret Island
Dózsa György út
Rákosrendező
Lehel u
Mexikói út
Csömöri út
Víziváros
Margit híd
Széchenyi fürdő
Hungária krt
Nagy Lajos király útja
Lehel tér
Hősök tere
Városliget
To Gödöllő (22km)
Nyugati pu
Margit krt
Moszkva tér
Batthyány tér
Lipótváros
Arany János u
Bajza u
Kodály körönd
Vörösmarty u
Oktogon
Thököly út
Zugló
Fogarasi út
Széna tér
Vár
Erzsébetváros
Stadionok
Pillangó u
Örs vezér tere
Rákosfalva
Sashalom
Nagyicce
Mátyásföld
Kossuth Lajos tér
Opera
Bajcsy-Zsilinszky út
Keleti pu
Kerepesi út
Déli pu
Fő u
Deák F tér
Blaha Lujza tér
Baross tér
Kerepesi temető
Racetrack
Buda Castle
Vörösmarty tér
Astoria
Józsefváros
Kőbánya felső
Jászberényi út
Rákos
Alkotás u
Citadella
Ferenciek tere
Kálvin tér
Ferenc krt
Józsefváros
Kőbányai út
Kőbánya alsó
Kőbánya
Maglódi út
Villányi út
Klinikák
To Lake Balaton (77km); Győr (125km); Vienna (277km)
Boráros tér
Nagyvárad tér
Népliget
New Municipal Cemetery (Új köztemető)
Irinyi József u
Gyömrői út
Bartók Béla út
Lágymányosi híd
Könyves Kálmán krt
Üllői út
Ecseri út
Pöttyös u
Kelenföld
Kelenföldi pu
Ferencváros
Közvágóhíd
Határ út
Kőbánya-Kispest
Ferihegyi repülőtérre vezető út
Fehérvári út
Beöthy u
Szabadkikötő út
Pestszentlőrinc
Kén u
Ady Endre út
Kispest
To Ferihegy International Airport
Timót u
Szabadkikötő
Nagykőrösi út
Budafok-Albertfalva
Pesterzsébet
St Imre tér
Csepel
Soroksári út
Karácsony S u
Torontál u
To Kecskemét (81km)
To Érd
To Ráckeve
Csepel Végállomás